Me & Rumi

Me & Rumi

The Autobiography of Shams-i Tabrizi

Translated, Introduced, and Annotated by
William C. Chittick

FONS VITAE

In Memory of Annemarie Schimmel

This edition printed and distributed by
Fons Vitae, Louisville, Kentucky

Printed in South Korea

Library of Congress Control Number: 2003110356

ISBN-1-887752-52-8

This edition published by
Fons Vitae
49 Mockingbird Valley Dr.
Louisville,KY 40207-1366
fonsvitaeky@aol.com
www.fonsfitae.com
Book design by *Folio*.

With thanks to Justin Majzub for the use
of the Koranic *Shamsiyyahs*.

Contents

Foreword

Now that Rumi has become one of the best-selling poets in North America, interest in his life and times has increased dramatically. Practically every collection of his poetry provides a thumbnail biography, highlighting his encounter with Shams-i Tabrizi, the wandering mystic who became Rumi's beloved companion. Rumi had been a sober scholar, teaching law and theology to a small circle of students, but the coming of Shams turned him into a devotee of music, dance, and poetry. Three years after Shams's appearance out of nowhere, he abruptly vanished, never to be seen again. It was Rumi's longing for the lost Shams that transformed him into one of the world's greatest poets. Rumi immortalized Shams's name by constantly celebrating him in his poetry as the embodiment of the divine beloved.

Very little is known about the historical Shams—indeed, some have even doubted that he was a real person. Everyone interested in Rumi's poetry has been curious about him, and beginning with Rumi's own son and other hagiographers, a great deal of legend was built up. Over the centuries Shams became a trope of Persian, Turkish, and Urdu literatures. Modern scholarship has made little headway in explaining who Shams was or how he was able to play such a decisive role in Rumi's life, though a good number of theories have been advanced.

Me and Rumi represents a true milestone in the study of this enigmatic figure. It makes available for the first time in any European language first-hand accounts of Shams that have never been studied by Western scholars. When Rumi and Shams sat and talked, one or more members of the circle took notes. These were never put into final form, but they were preserved and sometimes copied by later generations, ending up in various libraries scattered around Turkey. Fifteen years ago an Iranian scholar completed the long process of collating and editing the manuscripts. The book that he published, called *Maqalat-i Shams-i Tabrizi*, "The Discourses of Shams-i Tabrizi", provides us with an extraordinary picture of an awe-inspiring personality.

In *Me and Rumi* William C. Chittick has translated about two-thirds of the *Discourses* into English and arranged them in a manner that clarifies their meaning and context. He provides notes and a glossary, which will go a long way toward helping readers decipher the more obscure passages. The net result is an exciting and readable book that brings Shams to life. For the first time in Western sources we are given access to him without the intermediary of Rumi and the myth-makers. Shams appears as raucous and sober, outspoken and subtle, harsh and gentle, learned and irreverent, and above all as an embodiment of the living presence of God. The book destroys the stereotypes that have been set up by the secondary literature, and it gives access to a far more fascinating and vivid personality than we have any right to expect from what hagiographers and scholars have written.

—Annemarie Schimmel

Translator's Introduction

Rumi has now become so famous in the West that it hardly seems necessary to introduce him. And anyone familiar with Rumi will have at least heard the name of his companion Shams ad-Din of Tabriz. The relationship between the two is so well known that no less an authority than Huston Smith, in his recent *Why Religion Matters*, can cite Rumi's love for Shams along with Dante's love for Beatrice in the same sentence.

The name of Shams comes up constantly in Rumi's poetry, and anecdotes about him abound in the later literature. The exact nature of their relationship, however, has puzzled almost everyone from the outset. How do we explain why a great and successful scholar, conventional in every respect, should suddenly throw away community approval—a very precious thing in traditional societies—and begin associating almost exclusively with someone who appeared to be one of the riffraff? What sort of person was Shams that he could have exercised such a profound effect on this outstanding cleric, poet, and spiritual teacher? Practically all those who have written about Rumi, beginning with his son and his disciples, have attempted to explain what happened. What we have not heard is Shams's own version of the story. This book fills that gap.

It was Rumi who gave Shams his mythic aura. Remember that Rumi's longest work is not his famous *Mathnawi*, which is a spiritual epic in six books and 25,000 couplets, but rather his 40,000-verse collection of short love poems known as *Diwan-i Shams-i Tabrizi*, "The collected poems of Shams-i Tabrizi." Despite the fact that this great hymnal to love bears Shams's name, no one has ever thought that he was its author. The collection was named after him because Rumi effaces himself in Shams's person and makes him the explicit and implicit object of devotion. Of course, the *Diwan-i Shams* is all about love for God, but in Rumi's retelling of love's trials and joys, Shams is not simply a human being, nor even a guide in the manner of the prophets. Rather, he is the actual, living embodiment of the true beloved, who is God himself.

The *Diwan* is also called after Shams because Rumi signs almost one-third of the 3,200 ghazals with his name, leaving most of the rest unsigned (a few are signed with other names, such as those of his disciples Salah ad-Din and Husam ad-Din). In the Persian ghazal, the poet customarily refers to himself by a pen-name in the last couplet. Most poets—such as Sa'di and Hafiz—are known precisely by their pen-names, not their personal names. A quick glance at the text of the *Diwan* might lead someone to think that Shams himself was the author, because his name occurs so often in the last lines.

By far the best analysis in English of the role that Shams played in Rumi's life and poetry is provided by Franklin Lewis in a long chapter of his excellent study, *Rumi: Past and Present, East and West.* There is no need for me to repeat the details of Lewis's account. His work can be consulted for historical, literary, and religious background and for information on both the primary and secondary literature on Rumi and Shams. The purpose of this book is not to repeat what can easily be found in other sources, but rather to offer the words of Shams himself. Let me then turn to a brief review of the legend of Shams, and then to a description of the *Maqalat* or "*Discourses*", the Persian text of Shams's sayings, which I am calling his "autobiography."

Jalal ad-Din Rumi was born in Balkh in present-day Afghanistan in 1207. His father, Baha Walad, was a great preacher and shaykh. The Arabic word shaykh means "elder" (as does its Persian synonym *pir*), and it is employed as a term of respect for teachers in many fields of learning. In the context of the spiritual discipline known as Sufism, it is a standard title for the *murshid*, the spiritual guide. Baha Walad was a shaykh in both the outward sciences, such as Koran, Hadith (sayings of the Prophet), jurisprudence (the Shariah or revealed law), and theology; and the inward sciences, such as the symbolic discourse and spiritual psychology associated with Sufism.

When the Mongol invasion was slowly approaching Balkh from the east, Baha Walad took his family west, eventually settling down in Anatolia, where he came to be revered as a teacher. His son Jalal ad-Din studied both the outward and the inward sciences under his guidance. By the time of Baha Walad's death in 1231, Rumi was teaching and preaching in Konya. His erudition and eloquence attracted many to his circle, and before long he was one of the best known shaykhs in the city, despite the fact that he was still in his twenties. As a scholar of the religious sciences, he was addressed by the standard title Mawlana, "our master." Eventually this title, used without any accompanying name, came to refer to Rumi himself. Thus the Sufi order that traces itself back to him is called "Mawlawi" (Mevlevi in Turkish), which means "ascribed to [our] master."

On October 11, 1244, Shams ad-Din of Tabriz arrived in Konya. The fact that the exact date has been preserved suggests something of the significance that was accorded to this event in the Mevlevi sources. The accounts tell us that he was sixty years of age. Rumi would have been thirty-seven. Encountering Rumi in the market, Shams asked him about the spiritual station of the great Sufi Abu Yazid Bastami, who famously declared, "Glory be to me! There is none in my cloak but God!" How is it, said Shams, that the Prophet Muhammad simply referred to himself as God's "servant"? Having heard the question, Rumi went into a "state" (hal). In other words, he was overcome by an influx of knowledge and awareness from the spiritual world.

For Mawlana it was love at first sight. He devoted himself totally to Shams. He shirked his teaching duties and began to occupy himself with sama, that is, listening to music and poetry and dancing along with it. Many of his disciples were shocked at this behavior, which was unbecoming of a respected scholar, and many of them complained, but Rumi paid them no heed. After two years, apparently because of the jealousy and hostility of Rumi's disciples, Shams left Konya. Rumi was distraught. He sent his son Sultan Walad after him to Damascus, and eventually Sultan Walad found him in Aleppo. Sultan Walad persuaded Shams to return, and for a few months he and Rumi were again together. Then, in 1247, Shams vanished. Rumi was devastated, and it was not until several years later that he gave up hope of seeing him again. He took refuge in sama, and it was during this period that he was transformed into one of the greatest poets of the Persian language.

This brief account raises many questions, and the numerous anecdotes about Shams that have been preserved raise many more. Hagiographers and scholars have devoted a good deal of effort to answering these questions. For example, what happened to Shams? No one really knows. A rather late report says that he was murdered by jealous disciples with the collusion of Rumi's son Ala' ad-Din, from whom Rumi seems to have been estranged (at least after the departure of Shams). Those who follow this theory locate his tomb in Konya, not far from the tomb of Rumi himself. Others claim that he died in 1273, and that for centuries his tomb was known in Khuy in Iran. There are also tombs attributed to him in other parts of the Islamic world, thus reinforcing his mythic stature. Lewis has argued convincingly that nowhere near enough evidence exists to suggest that Shams was in fact murdered.

If he was not murdered, why would he have left so suddenly and not returned? Here his own testimony can be of some help in discerning a motive. It is clear that he considered separation from the object of love as one of the best means to bring about spiritual maturity. On more than one occasion he implies that it would be best for him to leave, because Rumi was not yet mature enough to take full benefit from him. He says, for example, that he went to Aleppo because Rumi needed to be cooked by separation (3.220). When he did return, the fruit of separation was clear, because Rumi took much more benefit from him: "One day of this companionship is equal to a year of that [earlier] companionship" (3.223).

Rumi may be alluding to the role of Shams in a famous line that is often attributed to him by scholars of Persian:

> The fruit of my life is no more than three words—
> I was raw, I was cooked, I was burned.

Perhaps Shams left because Rumi was now cooked and needed to be burned. Certainly it was not simply a coincidence that Rumi was now forty, the traditional age of spiritual maturity. We will see

Shams mention several times that the Prophet Muhammad only began to speak at forty—in contrast to Jesus, who spoke in the cradle. Shams considers this a mark of the Prophet's perfection. Given the manner in which Shams sees cosmic significance in all events, and given the fact that he says that his only purpose in coming to Konya was to bring about Rumi's perfection, we cannot rule out the possibility that he left simply because his job was done.

Moreover, Shams tells us repeatedly that the greatest of God's saints always remain hidden, and he recounts some of his own efforts to keep his spiritual rank concealed from other people. Upon leaving Konya the second time, he presumably went back to keeping an extremely low profile. He even expresses his surprise that he and Rumi should appear so openly: "We've turned out to be two marvelous people. It's been a long time since two people like us have fallen together. We are extremely open and obvious. The saints didn't use to be obvious" (3.93).

Why did Shams meet so much hostility from Rumi's circle? The usual accounts tell us that the disciples were jealous. Before the coming of Shams, Rumi would spend all his time with them, but now he spent most of his time with Shams. Shams may indeed have spent a great deal of time alone with Rumi, but the very existence of the *Discourses* shows that at least one other person was present in many cases. Moreover, the texts provide evidence that Shams spent much of his time not only with Rumi's circle, but also with other Sufis and scholars.

The hostility of Rumi's own companions may have had something to do with jealousy, but the texts suggest that it had much more to do with Shams's no-holds-barred approach to teaching. He did not have much patience with the usual sort of courteous behavior employed to avoid friction among members of a group. He told people what he thought of them. His judgments were harsh and probably on the mark. Not many people like to be told that they are fools, especially in the direct and biting language that Shams employed. Moreover, he tells the circle that he is holding himself back from saying what he really thinks about them. If he were to speak his mind, they would drive him out of Konya. In one passage he says, "If I were to speak the truth, all of you in this madrasah would aim for my life, but you would not be able to do anything. The harm of it would turn back on you. If you want, try" (3.70).

The stories and anecdotes told in the later literature often make Shams out to be a spiritual genius, contemptuous of book learning and ignorant of the Islamic sciences. The *Discourses* show that there is little basis for this view. In fact, Shams knew the Koran by heart and used to make his living as a teacher. He had studied jurisprudence (*fiqh*)—the science of the Shariah, the religious law—and even in Konya he spent time in the company of jurists. He used to attend the sessions of scholars to learn what they had to say about the various disciplines. He seems to have had a particular fondness for philosophy, despite the scorn he heaped upon many of its practitioners. He certainly looked with contempt on superficial learning and the pretensions of the ulama, that is, the scholars who taught in the mosques and madrasahs. In his view, they were traitors to their calling because they employed religious learning to make a living rather than to find God.

According to both Shams and Rumi, the only purpose of gaining knowledge is to find the path to God, who is the absolute Truth, the Real (*haqq*). Students and seekers should be striving to achieve "realization" (*tahqiq*), which is to know the reality of God for oneself and to see all things as they actually and truly are. Shams frequently criticizes those who have simply memorized the words of others without discovering the truth in their own hearts. Even though such "imitation" (*taqlid*) is a necessary first step on the path to God, it must be overcome. Until people know for themselves—or rather, until they see God face-to-face—learning is a crutch. They must reach the point where they can throw the crutch away, not by negating the truth of the knowledge that they have learned by imitation, but by finding the truth within themselves. As long as they need the crutch, they do not know things as they should. They have not received the answer to the prophetic supplication, "O God, show us things as they are!"

Why does Rumi raise Shams practically to a divine stature? What did he see in Shams? One common explanation has been in terms of the story of the famous lovers Layla and Majnun. Only Majnun had the eyes to see Layla's beauty. Only Rumi had the eyes to see Shams's spiritual substance. The *Discourses*, however, make clear that Rumi was not alone in perceiving Shams's divine aura—Shams himself repeatedly tells us about his own exalted stature, and he does so in ways that let us sense that there is something compelling behind his words, even if they would have scandalized most people who heard them. We should also keep in mind that it would not have been easy to fool a companion as sharp and discerning as Rumi.

In short, numerous passages of the *Discourses* throw light on questions that have been asked about Rumi and Shams for centuries. It would be far beyond the scope of this introduction, however, to offer a thorough analysis. One hopes that the work in progress by Omid Safi will take us a long step toward accomplishing that. I offer these texts not to provide any definitive answers, but simply to give relatively direct access to a personality whose greatness was the trigger for Rumi's own unfolding. Readers can judge for themselves whether or not Shams deserves his mythic stature. What is certain is that his words do not disappoint.

There is one historical issue about which I should say something, given my familiarity with the writings of a famous contemporary of Shams, Muhyi ad-Din ibn Arabi, who died in Damascus in 1240. In the *Discourses*, Shams mentions two of his acquaintances more often than any others (excluding Mawlana). One is Shihab Hariwa, whom he also calls Shihab Nishaburi. This is most likely Shihab ad-Din Nishaburi, one of the outstanding students of the theologian and philosopher Fakhr ad-Din Razi (d. 1209), whom Shams also mentions on occasion.[1] Hariwa means "from Herat," and Fakhr-i Razi spent the last few years of his life teaching in that city. Nishapur is a city about two hundred miles to the northwest of Herat, and Shihab presumably grew up there, because Shams mentions that he would speak in the dialect of the city.

[1] The thirteenth century philosopher Shahrazuri writes about Razi, "His session had majesty and grandeur. He used to act grandly even toward kings. When he sat, Kashi, Misri, Shihab Nishaburi, and other great students sat near him. The rest of the people sat around him in keeping with their ranks. He would speak to the great ones, and they would discuss with the others" (*Nuzhat al-arwah*, vol. 2, p. 144). I thank my friend Christopher Alario for his help in tracking down information on Shihab.

Shams used to attend the sessions of Shihab in Damascus. He describes him with great affection. He considers him a "philosopher" and criticizes many of his teachings. He says that all the great scholars came to see him, but he gave no credit even to the most famous philosophers of the age. One anecdote suggests that he was a Shi'ite. Another tells us that his friend Shaykh Muhammad dreamed of him and interpreted the dream to mean that he had died. In the morning he went to his home and found him slumped over his books.

Shaykh Muhammad is the second figure whom Shams often mentions. One passage identifies him as "Ibn Arabi in Damascus." It is reasonable to expect that if Shams visited scholars in that city, he would have sought out Ibn Arabi, who appears with hindsight as one of the most famous Sufis and scholars of the time. On two occasions Shams calls Shaykh Muhammad "a mountain," which—given Ibn Arabi's later title of "The Greatest Master"—would support the idea that this is in fact the famous Ibn Arabi. We should remember, however, that he was not so famous in his own times, and he went unnoticed by many important contemporaries, as Alexander Knysh has shown. The editor of the Persian text, Mohammad-Ali Movahhed, is almost sure that Shaykh Muhammad and Ibn Arabi are the same person, and Omid Safi has written an article supporting Movahhed's view. Franklin Lewis is a bit more hesitant, saying that he would "like to believe" that Movahhed is correct.

For my part, I do not see enough evidence to judge one way or the other. We should keep in mind that Movahhed very much wants Shaykh Muhammad to be Ibn Arabi, not least because this would add to the importance of these texts. It would also confirm the general distaste for Ibn Arabi that seems to be characteristic of the early Mevlevis. Thus, for example, Shams tells us that although Shaykh Muhammad was a mountain, next to Mawlana he was a pebble next to a pearl (1.53). Many devotees of Mawlana would be happy to hear from Rumi's own teacher that this insignificant pebble was the "great" Ibn Arabi.

Shams recounts a number of conversations with Shaykh Muhammad, and many of the statements he quotes could easily have been said by Ibn Arabi, but they could also have been said by many others. Other passages sound much less like the Ibn Arabi whom we know from his writings. The evidence provided by Shams's accounts is simply not sufficient for us to make a conclusive judgment one way or the other.

One might say, "Who else could this Shaykh Muhammad be? What 'mountain' was there in Damascus other than Ibn Arabi?" On the basis of the *Discourses*, one could answer that Shams considered Shihab Hariwa nearly as important a figure as Shaykh Muhammad. Yet, who was Shihab Hariwa? He has left little historical trace, even though he was, in Shams's view, one of the greatest thinkers of the time. Moreover, how many Shaykh Muhammads were there in Damascus in the 1230s? Given that Muhammad has been the most common first name in the world, surely there were more than a few. The fact that we, at this distance, think immediately of Ibn Arabi does not mean that he was the only Shaykh Muhammad who could have appeared to Shams as a mountain.

What were the criteria of greatness in the eyes of Shams? He tells us repeatedly that the greatest of the saints remain hidden, and he marvels that it is Rumi's role to appear openly. In one passage, he remarks that there were people in his home town of Tabriz who made him appear like nothing: "There were people there of whom I am the least. They threw my ocean out just like flotsam that falls to the shore of the sea. I'm like this—what were they like!" (3.155).

The Text and Translation

The scholarly literature on Rumi has long acknowledged the existence of the *Discourses*. Although several manuscripts exist in Turkey, they were largely inaccessible for most of the twentieth century, and they are especially difficult to decipher. An inadequate edition was published in Tehran in 1970, and it was not until 1977 that a good edition began to appear in the same city due to the extraordinary efforts of Mohammad-Ali Movahhed (published in two volumes, the second appearing in 1990). The final text, excluding apparatus, fills about 550 pages.

Among Western scholars, only Lewis has looked closely at the *Discourses*. In his chapter on Shams, he discusses the important figures mentioned in the text and the light that the work throws on the relationship between Shams and Rumi, translating a few short passages. A great deal of study and analysis remains to be done, however, not least because *Discourses* is no ordinary book. The Persian text poses difficulties of a sort rarely encountered in printed texts.

The first thing we need to remember about the *Discourses* is that it was not *written* by Shams. Rather, one or more individuals in Rumi's intimate circle took notes while Shams was speaking, often, but not always, when Rumi was present. Manuscripts recording these conversations were preserved, but they were never edited into final form, so they remained collections of random notes.

Rumi's *Fihi ma fihi*, translated by A. J. Arberry as the *Discourses of Rumi*, provides a somewhat similar text. It is a collection of talks recorded by one or more of Rumi's listeners. The talks, however, were then edited and written out in clean copy. Most likely the text was shown to Rumi, who would have approved of its dissemination. As for the *Discourses* of Shams, what is certain is that he never saw a final version—or, if he did, it has not survived. He may, however, have seen the beginnings of a clean copy. Movahhed tells us that the six oldest manuscripts provide two versions. Three offer a longer version, largely a collection of unedited notes. Three provide a much shorter, partially edited version. The oldest copy of the short version is almost certainly in the hand of Rumi's son, Sultan Walad, who tells us in his books about his conversations with Shams. Movahhed thinks that Shams may have seen and approved parts of the short version, though it was never completed. He also thinks that some of the most smoothly written passages may have been dictated by Shams, not simply written down by someone listening to a conversation.

Movahhed put many years into poring over the six ancient manuscripts, several newer manuscripts, and various other sources that quote Shams, but the *Discourses* is still a disjointed collection of stories, anecdotes, and bits of advice ranging in length from one sentence to four or five pages. Movahhed acknowledges that he has arranged the passages in an order that is largely arbitrary. Many if not most of the passages have textual problems, and many are in any case difficult to decipher. The difficulty has much to do with the fact that Shams's words are surprisingly colloquial, even if he employs a good deal of technical language drawn from the Koran, the Hadith, jurisprudence (*fiqh*), Sufism, philosophy, and theology. In contrast to formal writing, the grammar may not be clear, or it may be plain wrong. Even more importantly, many of the passages have little or no context. Often we do not know what question or issue Shams is discussing, and the colloquial and sometimes jocular language makes it difficult to grasp what he is trying to say. He loves speaking in allusions and parables. There are both obvious and unobvious ellipses, and we do not know which of these stem from the fact that Shams was jumping around, and which from the fact that the note-taker was not able to keep up with the conversation. In any one passage, for example, there may have been many minutes of discussion between two recorded sentences, or perhaps even hours and days.

The editor has subdivided the passages by using punctuation and paragraphs, devices unknown in pre-modern Persian. I usually follow his lead, but often I do not, especially in paragraph structure. It seems to me that the sentences frequently need to be read more as headings of an outline than as the exact words of a discussion. Short paragraphs help to highlight the fact that these are abbreviated thoughts.

One of the most difficult questions to answer in many of the passages is who exactly is talking to whom. With few exceptions, I follow the use of pronouns as given in the text, not attempting to replace them with the appropriate name. Sometimes a passage will have "he said," sometimes "I said." Usually, it seems that Shams is speaking, but even the first person pronoun can refer to someone else. In some passages there are two speakers called "he," one of whom seems to be Shams's addressee, but it is not always clear which is which. Frequently the passages address "you," and this may or may not be Rumi. In some passages (for example, the very last in this book), Shams explicitly addresses individuals other than Rumi. We cannot be sure that Rumi is the addressee even when the passage mentions his name. We also need to keep in mind that, as the editor tells us, the manuscripts commonly have initials rather than actual names. This increases the possibility that the editor has misread or misinterpreted any given passage.

Despite all the textual difficulties of the *Discourses*, readers will agree that Movahhed's edition has done a great service to students of Rumi. For the first time we hear the voice of Shams. The texts radiate not only authenticity, but also the fire of love that inspires Rumi's poetry. No one but the Shams of legend could have said many of these things—some of them are simply too outlandish. In any case, my purpose is not to argue for their authenticity. That, I think, is proven by the words themselves, not simply by the provenance of the manuscripts. I present these texts not so much because we finally have Shams-i Tabrizi speaking for himself, but because the Shams who does speak is an astonishing character. He deserves to be read by everyone who appreciates Rumi or has a taste for Sufism. Indeed, I would have been happy to translate the *Discourses* if someone else had been the author. The texts do not need Rumi's stamp of approval.

I undertook the translation in September 2001, initially with no clear idea of what I would do with the finished product. For a while, I thought I might write an article or two, or put together a short book on his teachings. At first it did not seem to me that there was enough coherent material to produce a substantial book. Eventually I became more familiar with the style and the idiosyncrasies of the text. I went through the two volumes and translated every passage that struck my fancy—which was most of them. Some passages I did not attempt because I could not understand what was going on. Others I began and then abandoned half-way through, having hit a stone wall. For the most part I kept the passages in the units arranged by the editor. In a small number of cases I have included only part of a passage or I have split a passage into two or three pieces, placing them in different parts of the book. The final result gives us about two-thirds of the *Discourses*. Much of what is left out is full of serious textual problems, and I was not willing to spend months or years trying to solve them.

I have arranged the texts in three sections: first Shams's life before the encounter with Rumi, second his teachings, and third his time in Konya. I put the section on teachings before the section on Konya because much of what Shams says in the passages that are explicitly addressed to Mawlana or his circle is clarified by what he says elsewhere about the path to God. If I had put the more personal material before the more doctrinal material, I would have needed to add a great deal of additional explanation and cross-referencing.

The translation is as literal as I could manage without doing damage to plain English. If the style departs from that of other material that I have translated, particularly in its use of colloquial expressions, this is because of the oral nature of the original, not because my philosophy of translation has changed. The Persian is down to earth, sentences are usually simple and sometimes incomplete, repetition is not unusual, and incoherencies are common.

I often translate colloquial idioms literally rather than with some English parallel, especially when—as often happens—it is not completely clear what the idiom means. Dictionaries may or may not offer explanations, and there are plenty of expressions and words that are not necessarily used in the usual meanings (Movahhed provides a thirty-page glossary of "unusual words and expressions"). When textual problems are relatively minor, I have simply translated as accurately as I could, not worrying whether or not the result is completely coherent. Hopefully, readers will not suppose that obscurities are simply my fault, even though, in many cases, they may be.

A few of the passages in the *Discourses* are in Arabic, and some are found in both Arabic and Persian versions. The editor thinks that in the latter case, the conversations were recorded in Arabic, and then were translated into Persian, presumably by the person responsible for the semi-edited version of the text. In any case, the style of the translated passages is the same as that of the texts that do not have Arabic versions—and the Arabic itself has a colloquial ring to it.

I italicize all Arabic sentences. When a passage is from the Koran, I indicate chapter and verse in brackets. Sources for other quotes are indicated in the notes on the section or in the Index of Hadiths and Sayings. Proper names and important technical terms are explained in the Glossary.

The reader will notice occasional lines of poetry. It is unlikely that Shams is the author of any of them. Some are well-known Arabic verses that played the role of proverbs. Many are Persian quatrains, typical of the "floating quatrains" well-known to scholars—poems of unknown authorship that appear in slightly different versions in the divans of various poets. Although many of them are found among Rumi's quatrains in the *Diwan-i Shams*, this does not suggest that either Rumi or Shams was the author. Certainly, it suggests that Rumi was not—that he had heard the verses from Shams, that he had then quoted them on occasion, and that one of his disciples wrote them down as coming from his mouth. Most of the poems whose authors are known are by Sana'i of Ghazna (d. 1131), about whom Shams has a good deal to say.

My first awareness of the existence of the *Discourses* dates back to about 1968, when I was a graduate student in Persian literature at Tehran University. I took a course on Rumi's *Mathnawi* with Badi'uzzaman Foruzanfar (d. 1970), the editor of his *Diwan* and *Fihi ma fihi* and probably the greatest modern authority on his historical and literary context. One day I asked him a question in class about the correct reading of a verse. Remarking on my American accent, he asked if I would be willing to give him English lessons, and I accepted with delight. For a few months I would go once every week or two to his home and we would do basic drills, often interspersed with long conversations. One day he told me about Shams's *Discourses*, of which he had a manuscript copy. I said that it sounded like a wonderful topic for a PhD dissertation. He kindly told me that it was not the work of a graduate student. It needed a major scholar of Sufism and a master of Persian and Arabic literature. Even he had not been willing to put in all the years it would have taken to sort out the manuscripts and make sense of them.

When the first volume of Movahhed's edition appeared in 1977, I was still in Tehran and immediately bought a copy. Back in the United States, I made use of it in an article I wrote on Rumi that was finally published in 1990. But in the past few years, I had no intention of working on the book, nor had I bothered to acquire the second volume of Movahhed's edition.

I owe my decision to undertake this translation to Camille and Kabir Helminski, and I am exceedingly grateful to them. In August 2001, they invited me and my wife as resource people to a "Sufi retreat" in a lovely monastery in San Juan Bautista, California. During our one-week stay, Camille showed me a few pages from an English translation of the *Discourses* done by Dr. Refik Algan and herself on the basis of a Turkish translation of the book. I could see that this was a valuable interpretation of the text based on the living Mevlevi tradition. When she then asked me to translate a few passages for the group directly from the Persian, I was delighted to oblige. Having done so, I was captivated. Without that propitious moment when Camille handed me the text of Dr. Algan's translation, I would certainly not have produced the book at this date.

While in the process of finalizing this book, I received the sad news of the passing of Annemarie Schimmel. During my last conversation with her, on Christmas Day 2002, we spoke a good deal about Shams, since she had just read through the manuscript of this book. Professor Schimmel was a great devotee of Mawlana, and her outstanding study of his life and work is known to everyone with a serious interest in Rumi. The reference in the title of her book, *The Triumphal Sun*, is of course to Shams, the literal meaning of whose name is "sun." The triumph of this sun became clear in the person of Rumi, and its reverberations have sounded down through the centuries. Professor Schimmel's life is the most obvious among its recent manifestations.

William C. Chittick
Mt. Sinai, NY
February 2, 2003

What is the utmost end of need?
Finding what has no needs.

What is the utmost end of seeking?
Finding what is sought.

What is the utmost end of the sought?
Finding the seeker.

My Years
Without Mawlana

CHILDHOOD

I.

Some of the sages say that the spirit is eternal. Some say that it is "newly arrived"—that is, at first it was not, then it came to be. Nonetheless, it's quite some time since there was the togetherness of the spirits. *The spirits are ranked troops.* However, this togetherness is of different sorts. The tavern-goers have a togetherness, as do the workers of corruption. But here I am speaking of the togetherness that is with the spirit. God's knowledge encompasses all.

But, this togetherness is with God. *Surely God is with those who are godfearing* [16:128]. He also says, *Surely God is with us* [9:40]. So, if at the beginning of his created nature the spirit of the Tatar had been familiar with us in that togetherness, right now he would be familiar with us, and with Imad as well.

God addressed that togetherness: "I am going to bring into existence the vicegerent of water and clay, and I am going to make you his progeny in the world of water and clay."

They said, "Our God, we are at ease with You in this world of togetherness. We fear that we will become scattered and remain far from this."

He said, "I know that you do not speak these words by way of protest and discourtesy. So, seek refuge in Me, and fear lest your togetherness be scattered. You should know that I am perfect in power. My power has no defect. In your very clothing and veil, I will gather you together and I will give you familiarity and togetherness with each other." (703-4)

2.

Beyond the world of water and clay, after the mountain of the Unseen, we were mixed together like Gog and Magog. All of a sudden, we rose up from there and came down at the call *Fall down!* [2:36]. From far away we saw the outline of the province of existence. From afar, the outskirts of the city and the trees were not apparent. In the same way, during infancy we saw nothing of this world. Little by little that came about. The harm of the bait and the trap gradually came forth to us. The flavor of the bait overcame the suffering of the trap. Otherwise, existence would have been impossible. (742)

3.

I came into this world to look around. I heard words without w, o, r, d, and s, and there was speech without s, p, e, e, c, h. I was hearing words from this side. I said to speech without letters, "If you are speech, what are these?"

It said, "For me, they're toys."

I said, "Then you sent me to toys?"

It said, "No, you wanted it. You wanted to have a house in water and clay, while I not know and not see."

Then I heard all the words, and I was looking upon the level of all speech. (702)

4.

In the time of my childhood, a marvelous apparition had come down upon me. No one was aware of my state. My father was unaware of my state. He was saying, "First of all, you are not mad. I don't know what's going on with you. It's also not the rearing and discipline, and it's not such and such."

I said, "Listen to one word from me: With me you're like duck eggs put under a hen.* The hen nurtured them, and baby ducks appeared. When the baby ducks became a bit larger, they went with the mother to the edge of the stream and entered the water. Their mother was a hen. She ran along the edge of the stream, with no possibility of going into the water. Now, father, I see that the ocean has become my mount, and this is my homeland and state. If you are of me or I am of you, come into the ocean. If not, go back to the hens. That's where you're hung up."

He said, "If you are like this with friends, how do you act with enemies?" (77)

5.

I never let my father see the outward form of my acts of obedience. How could I have wanted to make manifest my inwardness and my inward states? He was a good man, and he had a nobility. If you said a few words, the tears would roll down his beard. But, he was not a lover. A good man is one thing, a lover something else. (119)

6.

The fault is that of my father and mother, for they brought me up with so much kindness. When the cat would make a mess and break the bowl, my father would not strike it in front of me or say anything. Laughing, he would say, "What did you do this time? It's good. That was destiny, and it passed in this way. Otherwise, it might have fallen on you, or on me, or on mother.*The Lord took us to harm, but He brought it to pass in kindness."

From the reed they make candy with cajolery,
from the worm they make silk with the passing of days.
Make slowness your trade, show patience,
from grapes they make halva with time.*(625-26)

7.

There was a mad man who used to speak of unseen things. Whenever they tried to put him into a house, they would find him outside. One day my father had turned away from me and was talking to some people. The man came in anger toward him, his fist pulled back. He said, "Were it not for this child," pointing at me, "I would take you and throw you in the river." That was a river that would have taken away an elephant, flowing into the salt desert. Then he turned to me and said, "May you be happy!" He saluted and went away.

I never lost at dice—not out of trying, but by nature.

My hands wouldn't stay busy with anything. Wherever there was preaching, I would go there. (196)

8.

Inside me, there's good news.

I wonder at these people who are happy without that good news. If they were to be given golden crowns, that should still not satisfy them: "What should we do with these? We want opening on the inside. Let them take away everything we have and give us what belongs to us in reality."

When I was a child, they used to say to me, "Why are you sad?

Do you need clothes? Money?"

I used to say, "I wish they would take away even the clothes that I have, and then give me over to me." (236)

9.

When I was still growing up, not having reached puberty, for thirty or forty days love took away my desire for food. If they spoke of food, I would go like this with my hands and pull back my head. Yes, what a time that was. They would give me a mouthful of food. I would accept it and be polite, but conceal it my sleeve.

With such a love, the Companion with His hot state seized me in the *sama*. He was turning me around like a little bird. Like a husky young man who hasn't eaten for three days and finds bread—he grabs it, breaks it quickly and hastily. I was like that in His hand. My two eyes were like two plates full of blood. I was hearing a voice — "He's still raw. Leave him in a corner somewhere so he can burn in himself!" Now, God forbid, if you had brought a prostitute from the tavern—I was dancing a hundred times more quickly and skillfully. When a sincere man begins to dance, the seven heavens, the earth, and all creatures begin to dance. If a Muhammadan believer is dancing in the east* and there is a Muhammadan in the west, he also will be dancing and joyful. (677-78)

10.

The discussion was that when I was small, I had lost my appetite. Three or four days would pass and I would eat nothing—not because of the words of people, but because of the words of the howless and whyless God. My father was saying, "Oh my poor boy!" My mother was saying, "He won't eat anything."

I said, "After all, I'm not becoming weak. My strength is such that if you want, I'll fly like a bird out the window." Every four days, a little lethargy would overcome me, just a moment, and then it would go. Not a bite would go down.

"What has happened to you?"

"Nothing has happened. Do I appear mad? Have I torn anyone's clothes? Have I jumped at you? Have I torn your clothes?"

"But you don't eat anything."

"Today I'm not eating."

"Tomorrow, the day after, the next day?"

What is a "fellow townsman"? My father knew nothing of me. I was a stranger in my own town. My father was a foreigner to me, my heart was afraid of him. I fancied that he was going to jump at me. He spoke gentle words to me, and I fancied he was going to beat me and throw me out of the house.

I used to say, "If my meaning was born of his meaning, then this should be the result of that. It should become familiar with him and be perfected. A duck's egg under a chicken!" Tears would run from his eyes. (740-41)

11.

I saw that the house and the whole town were circling around him, and inside its borders there was a light that cannot be described by the tongue. I looked upwards and did not see the roof of the house. In that state, my father said to me, "Ah, my son." Like two streams, water flowed from his eyes, mixed with blood. In this state he wanted to say something else. But he couldn't talk and the fever increased. And then he went. (268)

My Teaching Career

12.

I had a group of students. Out of kindness and good advice, I spoke cruelly to them. They used to say, "When we were children with him, he never called us by these bad names. Maybe he's become melancholic."

I used to smash all that kindness. (615)

13.

There was a child who listened to my words. He was still young. He stayed away from his father and mother and was transfixed by me the whole day. He would say, "Let my service be that I cling to you." His father and mother were weeping and trembling. And he was fearful that I should become aware and shun him.

The situation got even worse. All day long he would sit with his head on his knees. He had struck out at his father and mother such that they did not dare to make any objections.

At times I would listen at the door to hear what He had to say. I heard this verse:

> In your lane, the lovers come and go,
> > liver's blood flows from their eyes and they go.
> I dwell at your door always, like dirt—
> > others come and go like the wind.*

I said, "Repeat that. What did You say?"
He said, "No."
He died at the age of eighteen. (209-10)

14.

Yes, how well I taught children! When a child came to me, I would say to his father, "Why did you bring him? Out of anguish at his memorizing and weariness at watching over him?"

If he said, "Yes, he plays in the streets, and it would be better for him to sit with the children," then I would seize the child's feet, beat him in front of his father, and expel them both from the school.

If he said, "I've brought him so that you may teach him," I would say, "It will be necessary for me to beat him. If he comes to you with a cracked head or broken foot, will you say to him, 'Why did he beat you?'"

If he said, "Yes," I would say, "Go away. God be with you—and take the boy." And if he said, "The command is yours, strike and kill as you want," and the boy heard that and saw that he had no escape and no place of refuge other than obeying the teacher, that he would not be sitting with the poor or eating hashish, nor doing anything else—then, if he were a boy of eight or nine years, whose eyes had not yet been opened, and who knew no way of escape, and who had no thought of flight or travel or discord, he would learn whatever I said to him. I taught a child the whole of the Koran in three months in Erzerum.

I said, "I shall teach him in three months," and I said that he should give me two hundred dirhems.

He said, "I will buy you a turban at two hundred."

I said, "No, I want you to give me two hundred dirhems." (343)

15.

I taught that child the Koran in the three months as I had said I would. "Before the end of the three months, ask nothing about what he has learned. If you ask, it will be your fault." He did that. He was a child who had gone to school for two years, and he had learned only the last one-thirtieth part of the Koran, and he still did not have it right.

In that gathering, he began reciting the Koran. His father was astonished. He was saying, "Are you my son?"

He said, "Yes."

He said, "Let me look at you carefully."

He said, "Look carefully."

On that side his mother cried out and fainted. She had been a servant girl, and now she had ten servant girls standing before her.

Instead of two hundred, he gave me five hundred dirhems.

As much as he was saying, "You sleep here in our house," I said, "The neighborhood will make accusations—a beautiful wife, a beautiful boy." I of course said that I did not want them making accusations.

He said, "What accusations? Who are these people?" (340)

16.

I was teaching. They brought me a cheerful child, his two eyes red, as if they were blood in motion. He entered in: "Peace be upon you, teacher! Should I give the call to prayer? I have a sweet voice. Should I be your assistant? Yes?" Then he sat down.

I laid down the condition to his father and mother that they not become upset if he came to them with a broken hand. They said, "Out of tenderness for our child, our hearts do not let us strike him with our own hands. But, if you do so, there is no blame on you whatsoever. We'll put it in writing. This boy has brought us to the top of the gallows."

All the children in my school put their heads down. Like someone preoccupied, he was looking around, seeking someone with whom to joke or play. He didn't see anyone who would give him an opportunity. He was saying to himself, "What kind of people are these?" He secretly pulled the hair of one of them, and secretly tormented another. They sat further away from him, but they did not dare to extend the disturbance.

I pretended that I was completely unaware. I said, "What is it? Why are you moving around?"

He said, "Nothing, teacher. There was someone motioning at him from outside."

I shouted, and he became frightened.

Before the afternoon prayer he got up. "I'll go now, teacher, a bit early. I'm still new."

He came the second day. I said, "What have you read?"

"Up to [Surah] Talaq."

I said, "Good for you. Come, read!"

He opened the Koran before me, and because of his hurry a page was torn. I said to him, "How do you lift up the Book?!" I slapped him, a blow that knocked him on the ground. Another, and then I tore his hair, and I was pulling it up, and scratching his hands such that blood began to flow. "Let me take him to the stocks!"

I secretly called the headmaster, with whom I had special signals. He came to intercede. He greeted me but I paid him no attention. The child was looking—"Oh! He treats the headmaster like this!"

I said, "Why did you come?"

He said, "I wished to see you, so I came." He was talking along, and the child was choking in secret. I gestured to him, meaning "Intercede!" He bit his lip, meaning "As soon as I find the opportunity."

Then he said, "I'm here. Don't be afraid now. Wait awhile." Then he said, "Give me permission to release him." I remained silent. A porter came and took him home. For a week he didn't come out of his house.

Early the next day, I was praying. His father and mother came. They fell at my feet and said, "How can we thank you? We've come to life."

I said, "Maybe he won't come again."

In short, after a week he came. He closed the door, and furtively sat from afar, trembling in fear. I called him forward: "Sit in your own place." This time he picked up the Koran with courtesy, he took the lesson, and he read with more courtesy than anyone else.

Several days later he had forgotten. Someone said that he was outside playing dice. Would that the informer had not informed! I went, and the boy who had informed followed me. I picked up a stick to frighten him, not to beat him.

They had swept the place and were playing. His back was towards me, and I was saying, "I wish he would see me and run away." All the children were strangers. They didn't know what his situation was in relation to me, or else they would have told him to run. The life of the boy behind me had gone out of him, and he was turning a thousand colors. He was hoping that the boy would turn toward him so he could tell him to run. His back was toward us, and he was immersed. I came in front of him and said, "Peace be upon you." He fell on the ground. His hands were shaking and his color went. He froze. I said, "Hey, get up, let's go."

We came, and I took him to the school. Then I put the stick in water. It was already soft, and it became something you don't want to ask about. They took him to the stocks. Someone who had beaten twelve children said, "Hello teacher." He put the weak child in the stocks and made him twist.

I said to the assistant, "You beat him, because my hand hurts from beating." The assistant beat him for a while. Then I said to the assistant, "You hold him. Is this how it's done?" He watched. I lifted up the stick and beat him myself. With the fourth strike, the skin came off his feet. He was raining something out from his heart, and it was falling. He screamed at the first and the second. Then he no longer shouted.

In short, they took him home. He didn't come out for a month. When he did come out, his mother asked him, "Where are you going?"

He said, "To the teacher."

She said, "How so?"

He said, "He is my God—what place is this for 'teacher'! I will not separate myself from him until death. God knows what I would have become, on which gallows they would have dried me out. He's brought me to worthiness."

He prayed for his father and mother because they had taken him to me. The father and mother were also praying for me, and the neighbors lifted up their hands in supplication: "He was a scoundrel, and he left neither young nor old alone. If the city king had spoken to him, he would have cursed him and thrown stones. He was as bold as if he had killed a hundred people, and he didn't care."

Anyway, he came, more courteous and intelligent than anyone else. If anyone would motion to him, he would put his hand to his mouth, meaning "Quiet!" In short, in a brief period I imparted the whole Koran to him, and he would make the call to prayer with a beautiful voice. Nothing was required other than those two times, and he became my assistant. (291-94)

17.

You're one of God's servants. Why should I conceal this and play the hypocrite? I'm good, and I was unblemished. I was in control of my soul, trustworthy, and I had no inclination toward these things. So, for a time I was in Erzerum. Ascetics who've been on the path for a hundred years go there and lose their way. I was so innocent that the child whom I taught—who was like a hundred thousand pictures—was driven to distraction by my innocence. Once intentionally he threw himself on me and clung to my neck in a way that cannot be described. I slapped him hard. Appetite was so dead in me that the organ had dried out—appetite had left the tool totally.

I kept on like that until once I saw a dream. He was saying to me, "*Surely your soul has a right against you*, give it its right!"*

There is a gate in that city known as "Beautiful Faces." I was passing by there, thinking about these things, when a beauty with Qipchaq* eyes clasped on to me. She brought me to a chamber. I gave her a few dirhems and stayed with her the night. This was at God's instruction and pleading. I was free and far away from that sort of thing. (776)

MY TRAVELS

18.

A group of Sufis became my traveling companions on the way to Erzincan. They made me the leader: "Without your command, we will not stop at a way station, without your command we will not spread the cloth for meals, and without your command we will not bring any disturbance, even if we are troubled by each other."

Several days passed, and they didn't find anything with which to fill their stomachs. It was the season for melons. Someone in a cucumber patch shouted from afar and indicated to us with his hands—"Dervishes, come over here! Help yourselves!"

They wanted to go, but I said, "Don't hurry." They said, "But we're hungry. Don't take the hungry to task! *Generosity should not be rejected.*"

I said, "That's not going anyplace. That's in our hands. Like the Sufi who turned to his loaf of bread: 'If I find better than you, you're delivered. Otherwise, you're in my hand.'"*

We made our ears heavy: "We don't understand what you're saying." We moved our hands: "What are you saying?" He came closer and showed himself to be serious. I said, "On condition that you give to the dervishes what you yourself eat."

He fell at my feet and was overcome by the moment, for that was his actual situation. He had gathered parings for dervishes. I said, "That's not fitting—that you eat the best parts, and you give the worst parts for the sake of God." He shouted and fell down. He kept the dervishes as guests for three days. He killed some sheep. I said, "This is the limit. You've kept the dear ones for three days, now it's time for yourself."

We went to Erzincan, and I separated from the companions. As long as they had not recognized me, it was pleasant. I was playing, and we would wrestle. When I was recognized, they came: "Indeed, it's all you."

For three days I went to be a laborer, but no one would take me, because I was weak. They took everyone and left me standing there. A gentleman saw me standing in the road and sent his servant to ask why I was standing.

I said, "Have you taken legal title to the road? If you've taken title to the city and the road, tell me." In short, he came forward in humility and took me to his house, putting me in a fine place. He brought food, and sat politely on his knees at a distance. When I had eaten he said, "As long as you're in this city, you'll come here every day and eat." These words of his prevented me from going.

One day he saw me and said, "Come now, release me from this difficulty. Friendship is never one-sided. *From heart to heart there is a window.* My heart feels for you and I know yours feels for me. But you keep me in a veil. Won't you tell me why this is so?"

I said, "My rule is that whenever I like someone, from the beginning I show him only severity so that I may belong to him completely—skin and flesh, severity and gentleness."

This is because the characteristic of gentleness is that, if you show it to a five-year-old child, he then belongs to you.* But a man is something else: When he sees how patient the leader is being with him and what affliction is reaching him, and that behind that affliction good fortune is showing its face, and [when he sees] where he is taking him, and that he is making him the possessor of the secret—he becomes bold and does not fear that he may perish, for he will not perish. Rather—subsistence upon subsistence, or rather, upon a thousand subsistences. (278-79)

19.*

He said, "There are villains in the road, and the Franks are there. I'll fear for you if you go."

What then do you know of me? I went into that thicket where lions wouldn't dare to go. The wind was noisily blowing through the trees. A coarse youth was coming and saying to me, "Woe on you!" I paid no attention to him and did not look at him. He shouted several times, and finally awesomeness settled into me. He had a battle-axe that would have crushed a boulder. After that, when he said once more "Woe on you!", I turned my face toward him.

I had not reached for any weapon, but he fell down on his backside. He motioned with his hand: "I've got no business with you—go!" (222)

20.

I was staying in the corner of that caravanserai. Someone said, "Aren't you coming to the khanaqah?"

I said, "I don't consider myself deserving of the khanaqah. They built the khanaqah for that group so that they wouldn't have to worry about cooking and earning. Their days are precious, so they don't have time for that. I'm not one of them."

He said, "Aren't you coming to the madrasah?"

I said, "I'm not one who can debate. If I understand literally, then there's nothing to debate about. And if I debate in my own language, they'll laugh at me, call me an unbeliever, and ascribe what I say to unbelief. I'm a stranger. The caravanserai is appropriate for a stranger."

Do you want a key to open the door? The key should be given to a thief. You're trustworthy. Companionship with thieves is pleasant. The trustworthy one will give the house to the wind. The thief is manly and clever. He'll watch over the house. Companionship with disbelievers is pleasant, for they consider me a disbeliever. (140-41)

21.

Someone was saying about me, "He's a logician!" He laughed. He became angry. He became hot. Sweating, he shook his head. He was laughing, "What does he say? Logician! Shmogician!"

I was saying, "I still suppose that I'm not."

He said, "The whole war is over this: Why shouldn't you be?" He begged me to go along with him, "because the children are accustomed to you and familiar with you."

"Of course, yes"—he did not make me fortunate. Because of frailty and ill-nature, places like this would appear for me—wealth, comfort. Again I fled from this frailty, and I threw it all away.

I made do with that cubicle, where they used to defecate by the door. I would come out in the morning, and sweep away the defilement of those inebriates and drunkards from in front of the door, not saying a word.

They suddenly heard something, and they bowed their heads in apology. I would say, "No, no! If I were any good, would I be living here?"

At night I would go to the lamb's-head seller and would eat bread and soup. He caught a scent and instructed them to give me the good part. I no longer bought from there. I went. I would speak sour, sour words. You would have said, "He's mad."

Throughout Ramadan a hundred people kept on inviting me and requesting that one night I break the fast with them. Some I rejected. I instructed the keeper of the caravanserai that if anyone came at an appointed time, he should say, "Someone else has taken him." (626-27)

22.

Look at this world. It makes a state that has lasted one year cold for them. Jesus used to flee from this world like a mouse from a cat. A man should be a seven-headed lion—he should lose it all, not worry, and sacrifice everything.

In that caravanserai there was one of those merchants—seventy bales of silk, several servants and slave girls. He did not know who had created him. All the others were doing the sacrifice. They didn't have enough daily bread for me to eat a mouthful with them. I led them in the prayers for the whole of Ramadan. Once I said to him, "For whom did you do the sacrifice? I, who am the imam, saw nothing of it."

He said, "By God, it was in my mind to call you so that we could eat together, but others called me, and I was busy."

Why shouldn't they have ambushed him on the road to Homs, and why shouldn't the bodyguard have fled? He had placed all his possessions in front, before the caravan, and they ambushed him first.

The great scholars are far away. Completely dead, totally asleep, they talk in their dreams.

I said, "I'll pluck a rose without thorns,
> or become the companion of one who has no companions."
(744)

23.

He was complaining, "They've plundered my property!"

I said, "It's the story of the Indian slave. His master the grocer would take from everyone's pot a finger of oil or honey, after having weighed it. The Indian slave disavowed this in his heart, but he didn't dare say anything. One day a large leather bag broke open and the honey went out. The Indian slave found his opportunity. He said, 'Yes, you take it finger by finger, and it goes bag by bag. *He who digs a well for his brother will fall in.*'

"Don't do bad lest you fall badly. Don't dig wells lest you fall in." (283)

24.

Everyone was talking about the history of chivalry: When it reached Adam, it was such and such, and when it reached Abraham it was such and such, and when it reached Ali, the Commander of the Faithful, it was such and such. Each spoke in turn according to his own measure. When it was my turn, as much as they insisted, I wouldn't say anything. I said, "I won't talk."

There was a dervish there, his head hung down, and he had not said a thing. The inclination to talk came to me. I said, "The child of Adam must slip once in his life*—if he is to slip—and the rest of his life he should be asking forgiveness for that, in the tradition of his father. *He who is similar to his father has done no wrong.*" Then I began discoursing on Adam's slip and his repentance. (166-67)

TEACHERS AND SHAYKHS I HAVE MET

25.

Despite the degree in which Judge Shams ad-Din Khunji* believed in me, I told him that I was going to go and work, since he would not give me lessons. He said, "But this is the way I have trained you."

I said, "No, I will find some work."

He said, "My son, how can you work with this immersion and this delicate state?" He would show me to the jurists in wonder: "Look at him. With this station and sultanate he works."

I said to myself, "You've taken me to loss, you've made me warm in the work." A new morning had come near, but it went back— not the morning that the beggars all talk about. (241)

26.

The reason I separated from Judge Shams ad-Din was that he

would not teach me. He said, "I do not want to be ashamed before God. You are just as God created you—the dust and the man—and He has created you beautifully. I cannot make God's creatures ugly. I see a very noble pearl. I cannot put an engraving on this pearl." (221)

27.

I would say, "Don't drink when I'm around."

The others would say, "We're jurists in the madrasahs and mosques. We're not afraid. You work with the labor of your own hands. What fear would there be if you drank in the middle of the bazaar?"

I did not flee at these words of theirs. If I were to go into the vat and sit down, my clothing would not be defiled for prayer. How could that harm me? However, I had none of that from the time I was little. I fled from it. When I saw drunkenness from afar, I abhorred it, fearing it would fall upon me.

That scholar also used to drink. Judge Khunji used to revere him immensely. He used to say, "He has a greater birth than mine, he's well-born." As much as he was told that he did such and such, he paid no attention. One day he said, "I know that I'm helpless with him, but it would be a bit more respectable."

He said to me, "The Judge said such-and-such to me, and I was ashamed." He was laughing. "From childhood we were the sons of a nobleman. We used to drink. Now it's an old habit. If I don't drink for two or three days, a shaking appears in my limbs, something like a paralysis and an illness."

Since the judgment of the Law is that [wine is permissible] in the time of necessity, and since, if he abstains, he will be destroyed, Muslims have no right to his blood.

In our city, it was like that. There was an ascetic who became ill. They told him that he should drink medicine. He did not drink it because of his asceticism, and he died. Someone saw him in a dream. His face was turned away from the kiblah. He said, "In the dream, I was so surprised that I went and dug up his grave with my fingers. I looked inside, and a bit of smoke rose up. I fled. The man said to me, 'Do you flee from this small amount that you see?' I went back and looked. I saw that he had become all black. I looked carefully. His face was turned away from the kiblah."

The sultan compels someone to commit fornication. If he doesn't do it, he will kill him. If he does do it, he dies as a Muslim. This is like that, because illness is a forceful sultan. Indeed, this is part of the Law.

In reality, for Sayyid, drinking made no difference for him, and it was permissible for him, especially since he had difficult illnesses. This is especially so since his existence was necessary for the people. It was incumbent upon him to build up his brain, especially during illness.

However, if Rashid had done that, he would have been an infidel and an unbeliever. It would have been necessary to bury him in the Jewish graveyard.

I was not disavowing that in him, except that he was not saying his prayers. Mawlana, do you know what the difference is between me and him? Speak a bit. By God the Great, I am joyful and happy on the day that I say my prayers. I take it that He Himself says, "Upon him be peace." After all, a dervish set something down:* *Poverty is my pride.* Doesn't it make one happy to conform to that dervish?

And then he didn't confine himself to that. He would talk against prayer and those who say their prayers, he would make fun of them. The reason that Rashid was sent away was exactly this. The reason that I kept myself away from him and pulled out my hair was this.

I used to say, "Sayyid, you've been speaking a long time. Does this praying become a veil for you?"

I would say, "Do you sometimes have intercourse with that slave girl?"

He would say, "Yes, yes. That doesn't become a veil."

If I should sleep on my side just like this until the day of resurrection, it would not harm me at all. Rather, every day would be greater and better. Nonetheless, on the day that I miss the prayer, I suffer, and I am unhappy until night. On the day when I perform it, I am happy-hearted and joyful.

Within the Kaaba, it's fitting that there be no kiblah—
    outside the Kaaba, there's no escape from the kiblah.
    (753-55)

28.

That judge of Damascus, Shams ad-Din Khu'i—if I had given myself to him, his work would have turned good at the end of his life. But, I acted with deception, and he used to swallow that deception. Woe on the day that I begin to act with deception! What is my work other than deception? God's work is this—deceiving.*

If you buy a horse so that I may go, what would it matter? You say, "I don't want you to go. It's not like this. I'll buy a horse, but you stay—don't go." You say this, and this also is deception. That's not my work. (831)

29.

Someone objected to Shams ad-Din Khu'i. His purpose was to criticize a jurist: "So-and-so has memorized so much in every field, and his stipend is so much. But the other one, who has memorized nothing, receives that much stipend!"

He said, "Although he hasn't done the memorization, he isn't bookish. He has control over his words, and he has experience. Don't you see how he debates when the time for debate arrives? As for so-and-so, although he has the memory, he doesn't have the experience. Don't you see that he can't explain himself at the time of debate?" (608)

30.

It is incumbent upon the believer to render thanks that he is not an unbeliever, and it is incumbent upon the unbeliever to render thanks that at least he's not a hypocrite.

Among the hadiths that are unusual and not well known, one tells us that when hell is empty of the folk of hell, and its nether reaches are empty, a people will come to look around. When they come near to the nether reaches, they will see that the doors are banging together, opening and shutting, and that it is empty like a ruined house. They will hear the lamenting of the folk of hypocrisy. "Are you still here?"

They will say, "We were the tribe of hypocritical folk, who have no possibility of deliverance, nor the possibility of becoming settled."

Shams ad-Din Khu'i narrated this hadith in the public lesson, but it has not become well known. However, those who are aware of the meaning will take the meaning from it.

Now, hypocrisy is open and secret. Open hypocrisy is far from us and far from our companions. But, one must strive against the hidden hypocrisy so that it will leave the human make-up.

The believer is the mirror of the believer. This means either that God is the mirror of the servant, or that the servant is the mirror of God.* The words of the perfect are full like this. (607–8)

31.

Someone was weeping: "The Tatars killed my brother. He was a man of knowledge."

I said, "If you have knowledge, you know that with the strike of that sword the Tatar gave him endless life. But what do the dead, or dead preachers, know about that life? They come up to the pulpit, and they begin a lamentation. I mean, the Prophet said, *This world is the prison of the believer.* Someone escapes from prison. Then you weep for him? 'What a pity that he escaped from this prison!' The Tatars, or some other cause, made a hole in the prison. He escaped. He was *transferred from one abode to another abode.* Then you weep. 'What a pity that they struck the wall of the prison with that arrow! Why did they strike that stone? Didn't they regret that fine marble?'

"Or, there were stocks on his legs. They cut them off, and he escaped. You shout out and strike your head and weep: 'What a pity that they cut off the stocks!' Or, they broke a cage, and you weep in anguish—'Why did they break the cage! Why did they let the bird go!' Or, they lance a boil, and the filth and pus come out. You begin lamenting, 'What a pity that the pus left!'"

Shams-i Khujandi* was weeping for the Household [of the Prophet]. I was weeping for him: "Why do you weep for the Household? Someone joins with God, you weep for him, and you don't weep for yourself! If you were aware of your own state, you would weep for yourself. Rather, you would gather all your people together, all your relatives, and you would lament in anguish for yourself!"

There is no change in God. The change is in you. Sometimes you like bread and you seek for it, and sometimes you turn away.

Sometimes you become warm towards a friend and he appears as your beloved. You say, "I love him." Then you change your color and you say, "I hate him." If you were to stay constant in that state, he would always be sought and loved. (204-5)

32.

Khujandi says, "I'm observing the tragedy of the Household." He's forgotten his own tragedy!

Shihab Hariwa* in Damascus, who was the elder of the Household, used to say, "For me death is like this: The officers unjustly place a heavy sack on the back of a weak man. He goes into the mire, or up a high mountain, knocking himself out a thousand times over. Someone comes and undoes the rope that had bound the sack to his neck, so the sack falls off his back. How light he becomes! He is delivered and his soul is renewed."

Now, the state of someone like him—who was the servant of the Household—was like this. What will be the state of the Household?

If he had faith, he would look upon death like this. Instead he mourns for the Household, and he looks upon the candles of that Household, who are God's servants, with contempt and envy!

Why don't you plead to God? Wake up in the middle of the night, get up, and prostrate yourself twice. Need, need, need! Put your face on the ground, and rain down tears: "Lord, if You do not want the prophets and saints to remain like a knocker on the door, now that You have shown me the great man so-and-so, open up my eyes through him!"

Happy is he who sees me, and happy is he who sees him who has seen me! (286-87)

33.

Shihab Hariwa, a theologian in Damascus, was accepted by all the logicians. Naturally, he considered busying oneself with women and the appetites a weakness, and he used to say that this is the fatwa of intellect.

Muhammad Guyani said to him, "Does the intellect ever make mistakes in its fatwas?"

He replied, "No, intellect makes no mistake. It's that other thing that makes mistakes." (82)

34.

This Hariwa was from Khorasan. They called him Shihab. He wouldn't give credit to anyone. He used to say [about me], "This man is congenial." I was at ease when sitting with him. I found ease. (641)

35.

Concerning God, Shihab Hariwa would say, "He is necessary by His Essence; He is not freely-choosing. If all the prophets had said that He is so, I would not accept it."

I would say, "I don't want that God. I want a God who acts by free choice. I seek that God. *The fire, without shame.*" I would tell him to destroy that God of whom he spoke. I would say, "Even if He did not act by free choice, in any case you act by free choice. Destroy that one. The least of the servants upon whom He has cast His ray acts by free choice; he is not made helpless by himself.

"Every moment, He destroys a thousand worlds. Who is more helpless than someone who does something and is made helpless by that act, not being able to change it? And then that thing itself says that He has no free choice, he calls Him without free choice. Pharaoh has turned your stomach sour."

If the whole world were to accept that from Shihab, I wouldn't accept it. (635-36)

36.

Shihab in Damascus used to say, "For me it is a plain intellectual truth that He is necessary by the Essence. He is not *Doer of what He desires* [11:107]. Khwarazmshah used to give rich food, robes of honor, and golden boots to Fakhr-i Razi so that he would say, '*Doer of what He desires.*'"

He said, "For me, life is as if someone has been heavily loaded down with a back-pack on the neck. His feet are in the mud, and he is old and weak. Suddenly someone comes and cuts the rope. That heavy load falls off his neck and he is released."

They would come to this Shihab and hear a thousand intellectual truths. They would take benefit and prostrate themselves before him. They would come out and say, "He's a philosopher. The philosopher is the knower of everything."

I erased that from the book. I said, "It is God who is the knower of everything." Instead I wrote, "The philosopher is the knower of many things."

He denied the resurrection. He said, "Otherwise, the spheres would be held back in their journeying."

I said, "How does the world remain established?"

He used to say about the prophets that they were sages, but they said the sorts of things that they did for the sake of people's best interests.

He denied the splitting of the moon.*

There is a saying of Ali: "If it's what you say, then we're all delivered."* There is incapacity and a fleeing from debate. One must cut short the debate.

All this *Upon the day the earth shall be changed into other than the earth* [14:48] and suchlike he saw in himself.* Within himself he achieved [*Upon the day when*] *We shall roll up heaven* [21:104].

After all, why is it that the earth and the heaven will be rolled up and the resurrection take place? To make them understand their own account. In itself, it's not required. (657–58)

37.

The resurrection will be of the bodies. The philosopher says there will be a resurrection of the spirits. He's a fool. He's reading his own page*—he's not reading the page of the Companion. He's saying that whatever he does not know will not be. If he knew everything there is to know, Abu Yazid would be carrying his saddle-cloth. (697)

38.

It has been said that there are "seventy-two veils of light,"* but this is to speak deceptively. The veils of light are infinite. Hence His words: *Say: "Were the sea ink for the words of my Lord,* [*the sea would run out before the Words of my Lord run out, though We brought replenishment the like of it* (18:109)]. Unless the seeker reaches these veils, the path will not be opened up to him. One must pass beyond these infinite veils to reach the meaning. How can words be compared with meaning? I'm a disbeliever if you know what I'm talking about!

"The generation lacks a large tree." For example, there's a large tree with much fruit, throwing shade over a world, in the midst of a desert. The sun is warm, and beneath the tree are a hundred springs with all their attributes. Doesn't anyone ask which tree gave forth this shoot? What was the tree from which this branch was cut, giving such results?

When I was in Aleppo, I was busy supplicating for Mawlana. I was making a hundred supplications and bringing into my mind things that stir up kindness. I didn't bring to mind anything that would cool the kindness. However, I had no intention of coming.

If Shihab, the sage of Herat, were to hear what I am saying about the weeping of inanimate things and the laughter of inanimate things,* he would have said, in the dialect of Nishapur, "What's this?" The intellect of the philosopher does not reach it.

Do you have any idea where in your body or your heart is the locus of wrath, ease, hardship, and other such things?* Now, you are that locus, invisible and undesignated. Tongue, letters, organs, and other parts are your tools. When a man reaches someplace—from there he makes it known that for a time he was a man here. How is this connected with *A man is concealed by holding his tongue*? (118-19)

39.

For example, there's a whirlpool in an ocean. A whirlpool is dreadful—especially in an ocean. Everyone flees from it. But this man doesn't avoid it. He says, "Certainly I'll pass by."

I talk of the speaking of inanimate things and their acts. The sages deny it. So what should I do with my own eyes? And there's the hadith of the Moaning Pillar.*

Now, where is *A man is concealed by holding his tongue*? Also his *words*: "If a man speaks, at that very moment I know him, and if he doesn't speak, I'll know him in three days."*

But that probably was not his state. He spoke in the measure of and in keeping with the understanding of the listeners. For, it is he himself—I mean Ali—who said, "*Were the covering removed, my certainty would not increase.*" If the state did belong to him, then this second saying is not his state. (110-11)

40.

Shihab Hariwa in Damascus, who had been thoroughly melted by ascetic discipline, used to look on all the prophets with a wink. He would say, "It was because of the angels' jealousy* that they were made to turn their faces toward the people, so they busied themselves with creatures."

Shihab never let anyone sit with him in seclusion. He used to say that Gabriel was a bother to him, and he used to say that his own existence was a bother.

Despite all this weariness, he would say to me, "You, come, because with you my heart is at ease."

One day I said, "Since he's talking about me, let me ask him a question." I said, "These words bring duality for me."

He put his hand down for a time. Then he began: "What place is this for duality? A hundred thousand enter inside, are distributed, become obliterated, and fixed." In discoursing on this and explaining it he spoke, and he spoke, and he spoke. In the end he said, "And there are some people like this, to whom He turns His face, but they are rare."

I said to myself, "After all, I'm asking you about the rare ones. Begin from there. You've wandered around the world in the direction where the goal is not to be found. You should have answered the question." Concerning that direction, he had nothing to say. (271-72)

41.

A group of the philosophers preferred the angels over the prophets. They find Muhammad and the prophets defective because they busied themselves with people. They say that the angels were jealous of the prophets and made them turn their faces toward this world. They deceived them so they would give advice to the people: "That's not to go far from God or to become veiled."

As for the miracles of the prophets, they say, "We accept the truths of intellect, but we do not accept what is not a truth of intellect. Intellect is God's proof, and *God's proofs do not contradict each other.*"

I say that the "miracle" is exactly that thing whose qualities cannot be perceived by your intellect. *The miracle is that which disables the intellect from perceiving it.** Intellect is God's proof, but when you don't employ it correctly, it comes up with contradictions. This is why there are "seventy-two" creeds.* The intellects disagree and contradict each other.

For example, you ask two people, "How much is two times two?" Both will give the same answer, without disagreement, because thinking that out is easy. When you ask, "How much is seven times seven?" or "seventeen times seventeen," then two intelligent people will disagree, because thinking that out is harder.

When someone is lazy and does not use the intellect, it is like holding a mirror crookedly. Otherwise, if you hold a hundred thousand mirrors straight, they will say one thing, *confirming what was before it . . . and guarding over it* [5:48]. Lights are all friends of each other.

For example, a hundred people are standing in the sun, with clear eyes, and a lone person comes toward them from afar, playing a drum and dancing. They won't disagree. But if it's a dark and cloudy night, with the sound of the drum coming, a hundred disagreements will appear among them. One will say that it is an army, another that it is a circumcision party, and so on.

In short, the philosophers consider the prophets defective because they busied themselves with people, and they were ambushed in the road by love for position and prophethood. However, they have not fully lost the way, and the road of the celestial realm has not fully been closed to them. Nonetheless, they have been held back from the degrees of disengagement and seclusion. They also say that the fact that the prophets wanted wives was a defect and a taint. (192-93)

42.

The silly philosopher says, "The intellects are ten,* and they have encompassed all possible things." I used to listen to the greatest among them—who considered Athir and others to be nothing— to see what he had to say. For him Athir and the others and a hundred like them were nothing. He would gaze in the direction of the prophets with a wink. He had become sheer light. He ate nothing. All his life he looked at neither permitted nor forbidden.* He gave no credit to Avicenna. The great ones used to come forward, humble themselves, and take benefit. I would ask him questions right to the end. He would become upset, obliterated, and destroyed. He used to say, "I wish Tabrizi would sleep over one night."

His little student would say, "Haven't you become bored even with the Prophet?"

He would say, "Silence, he's a fine fellow." (339)

43.

Shihab was a lovely unbeliever. In the dialect of Nishapur he used to say, "Do something so that you don't become weary, for you're detached from both boys and women."

As for our Shaykh Muhammad, he was a great man. "Necessary in existence by His Essence"*—he sat back and said "Allah." He laughed: "What kind of name have they given Him!"

Not a tip of [Shihab's] hair remained that I did not see plainly, naked—his belief, his happiness, what it was that kept him back from food. He did not come to know a single tip of my hair—he remained searching.

That student of his who sold his trivial things paid no attention to anyone. When he saw me, he offered his salutations. I said, "Everything's fine."

He said, "What do you do to make these people believe in you? I mean my master, who says, 'If Muhammad, the Messenger of God, should come to me at night, I would be bored.'"

He said, "Silence, he's a sweet man." (697)

44.

Those dogs used to call Shihab an unbeliever openly. I said, "Beware! How could Shihab be an unbeliever? He's luminous. True, before the sun, Shihab is an unbeliever. When he appears in the service of the sun, he becomes the full moon and becomes perfect." (275)

45.

Because of the boiling of the ocean of the Real's speech, an *alif* was drawn on the Tablet. The command came, "O spiritual Gabriel, read out that glorious letter from the Lordly Tablet." I hadn't finished talking and Shihab fled. He said, "I can't tolerate looking at your face." He fled.

I said, "I mean, what is it?"

He was fleeing and saying, "A marvelous thing, a marvelous thing!"

Although Shihab spoke words of unbelief, he was limpid and spiritual. He had become sheer spirit. He no longer ate food.

One day I was speaking in symbols and offering unveilings. I didn't want the meaning not to be unveiled for him.

You say, "He does not know the particulars, He knows the universals."*

What do you mean by these universals? When I say "the whole," I know of no part that is outside of it. Yes, and if they say "part," the whole is not inside it. You can never say that there is a garden such that trees are not included, but you can indeed say the opposite. If there are no trees, that isn't a garden, it's an enclosure.

Shihab said, "I don't say that it's a defect that He doesn't know the particulars. For example, there's a worm in my stomach, lying in the impurity. I don't know that worm. What defect is there in not knowing it or in knowing it?"

Right now I don't know the Hindi language, not because of incapacity. But what about Arabic itself? If that Indian should hear it, he will say that it's better. And what about the Persian language with this subtlety and beauty? Those meanings and subtleties that come out in Persian don't come out in Arabic. (225-26)

46.

Shaykh Muhammad used to laugh at the state of Sayyid and others: "What sort of words are these—'God has taken up my whole body'?" And I used to laugh. He fancied that I was agreeing with him, but I was in fact laughing at his state: "Don't you see it in yourself?"

He had a dream of Shihab Nishaburi, for they were intimates. And this Shihab was much more excellent than Shaykh Shihab ad-Din. He saw him in a dream, running to the top of a mountain, and a woman was running after him. He reached the mountain top and ran down the other side. The woman put her finger in her mouth—"You've saved yourself!" Early the next morning he came to the madrasah and knocked on the door: "Shihab ad-Din has passed away!" They became upset, and Shaykh Muhammad disappeared. They said, "That was the devil."

Day arrived, and he entered in among the books. He had put his head on his hands and given up his soul, smiling. Shaykh Muhammad kissed

his eyes and his face, bid farewell, and went. The people there were saying, "No, that was Khizr who went, or it was an angel." (697-98)

47.

The philosopher becomes a denier. His intellect tells him that
whatever he does not know does not exist, that he has the universal
intellect. Let's take it that he does have the universal intellect—how
can the universal intellect encompass its Creator, of whom it is the
effusion? How can he put God's spacious world in a box? He's reading his own page.* He has not read a larger page or his own Creator.

He was saying, "Let's make peace."

He said, "Whatever you do makes it worse. Rather, let it all go
gradually. Through working together, clemency, and cajolery it will
leave him, just as through working together, it has left the assembly
of disciples. Those people destroy the souls of seekers.* Being their
companion kills the seeker on the path of God. Yes, true companionship also kills,* but that killing results in a thousand lives."

One day Shaykh Muhammad was saying that studied knowledge*
is better, because the knowledge gained without study is like a
child who spontaneously says something of which an adult is incapable. How can that have any worth?

I said, "*He struck the target without aiming.* When you ask the child,
he doesn't know heads or tails of those words. It's you who know
because you're an adult. That's different from someone who gives
birth to words, and when you call him to account, he speaks a hundred thousand demonstrations and proofs in support of those words."

He looked at the floor—meaning that he had accused many of
the great ones, like Fakhr-i Razi and Shihab Maqtul,* and pointed
out their mistakes. He said, "Recite *No, I swear* [surah 90]!"

I recited, and he was weeping loudly. I was laughing, but in
secret, so that he would not become cold.

Right now, you also preach, but you have no realization. My
meaning is born from you without your intention. It passes
through you and you are unaware. (338)

48.

Shaykh Muhammad would often say that so-and-so was mistaken, and so-and-so was mistaken. But then I saw that he was making mistakes. Sometimes I would point that out to him. He would throw down his head. He would say, "Child, you strike a hard whip."

He was a mountain, a mountain! I have no purpose here, but every time he spun the wheel, a hundred thousand like these would fall flat and be shucked off.

For example, he was in a state, and he would tell about his state. I would show him how he stood in that station.

For example, one day we had fallen into the talk that whenever a hadith has its equal in the Koran, the hadith is sound. He recounted a hadith and said, "Where is the equal of this in the Koran?"

I saw that in that instant, he had a state. I wanted to bring him from that dispersion to togetherness through words that would be appropriate to his question. I said, "There is a disagreement as to whether the hadith that you mention is a hadith or not. But, where is the equal of the hadith *The knowers are like one soul* in the Koran?"

He fancied that I was asking him. He quickly answered, "*The believers indeed are brothers* [49:10]. *Your creation and your uprising are as but one soul* [31:28]." Then he went into himself. He understood that my purpose had not been the question, my purpose was something else. He said, "Child, you strike a hard whip." At first he would say "child," and in the end he would say "child." Then he would laugh, meaning, "What place is this for 'child'?!" (239–40)

49.

Shaykh Muhammad said, "The plain of speech is very spacious. Whoever wants says whatever he wants."

I said, "The plain of speech is very narrow—the plain of meaning is spacious. Come forth from speech so as to see spaciousness and the plain. The plain of meaning is spacious. Look and see if you are the far who is near, or the near who is far."

He said, "You know better."

He said: However that may be, you are what you are. But, come forth from form, for *Congregation is a mercy*. If words are not spoken to you, don't be afraid and don't flee. The secrets of the Path are not spoken to me from beyond form when there is a gathering of others, whether outside or inside your own existence—only when there is seclusion.

Although you have good character traits in your existence, and you are pure of the attributes of spitefulness, treachery, and theft, there are hidden treacheries and thieveries in this existence. Thus, in the time of David,* the chain of justice fled to heaven because of hidden thievery, and no one was aware of that thievery. However, when they looked upon the fleeing of the chain, they all knew that there was some reason for that.

Now, the chain of justice is bright-heartedness, limpidness, and tasting. When it is pulled back from the seeker of the secret, it is not without reason, for *God does not change His blessing on a people unless they change what is in themselves* [8:53]. If you don't busy yourself with gazing upon your own purity and goodness, and if you set out to clean away those hidden treacheries, then the purity and goodness that you have will increase. (96-7)

50.

The reality of these words did not reach them. However, a meaning reached them and their color changed. When man changes, there's a cause.

Indeed, I repeated the words to make them understand. They criticized me: "He's repeating his words because he lacks substance."

I said, "You're the ones who lack substance. My words are beautiful and well-formed. If I should say them a hundred times, each time another meaning would be understood from them, and that root meaning would stay virgin."

When he was saying that the plain of speech is very spacious, I wanted to answer, "No, the plain of meaning is very spacious, the plain of speech is very narrow." However, I played the hypocrite with him. Although he was a mountain, he also knew hypocrisy. I said to him, "Listen to these words with the other ear. Don't listen with the ear with which you've heard the words of the shaykhs. In the place where there are these words, how should there be Abu Yazid and *Glory be to me?*" (168)

51.

Shaykh Muhammad used to say, "If I were to say that something should have been like this, or it should have been like that, that for me would be unbelief."

I was patient until one day he was giving advice to someone. I said to him, "So, with this advice, you are saying, 'You should be like this,' but for you that is unbelief."

If he were to say, "That is one state, and this another state," that would be variegation. If in the words, "*I have a moment with God*," the moment is not continuous—and the literal meaning demands that it not be continuous—then the words of A'isha would be correct: "*Whoever thinks that Muhammad saw God with his eyes has uttered a great falsehood*." For, when someone sees God, no variegation remains, and this state is continuous for him. It is not cut off. So also are His words, "*Whoever hopes for the encounter with his Lord, let him do worthy deeds and not associate with the worship of his Lord any one*" [18:110]. This "one" is he himself. (777)

52.

In the same way, Shaykh Muhammad ibn Arabi in Damascus used to say, "Muhammad keeps my curtain."

I would say, "Why don't you see in Muhammad what you see in yourself? Everyone keeps his own curtain."

He said, "There where the reality of gnosis is, where are claims? Where are 'Do!' and 'Don't do!'?"

I said, "After all, he had this meaning, and he had this other virtue in excess. This denial of him that is in you, this taking charge—is it not a claim? Calling me brother and child, is that not a claim? So you make claims and you say that one must not make claims."

He was a good sympathizer, a good familiar. He was a magnificent man, Shaykh Muhammad. But he was not in following.

Someone said, "He was nothing but following itself."*

I said, "No, he did not follow." (299)

53.

Many times Shaykh Muhammad would bow and prostrate himself and say, "I am the servant of the Folk of the Law." But, he did not have following. I took much benefit from him, but not as much as from you. What is from you is not like what is from him. *How different a pearl from a pebble!*

However, the children* have not grasped you at all, and that is strange. It may be that in the end they will grasp you. You have not bound yourself to showing yourself to the children or other than the children.

One person makes a thousand efforts to show something from himself, and another hides himself with a hundred tricks. The more I make myself apparent, the more trouble I have. The privy and the not-privy gather around, and I cannot live as I should. (304–5)

53 bis.

A breast like this, which is greater than I in all the sciences—it prostrates itself a hundred times. I will not consider it the same—if I go up on the pulpit and speak one word, everyone will laugh at me.

I talk about these a lot, but when will you accept it? A hundred thousand mercies on that face! God make me worthy to kiss that face! God make me deserving of that!

Shaykh Muhammad, who was seeking the Real, hoped that this would happen between him and me, but it was not granted. And I hoped that what he hoped for between him and me would happen between you and me. So, what is your level? (144)

54.

God has servants whom He brings into the veil and to whom He talks of the secrets.

Shaykh Awhad took me to *sama* and showed reverence toward me. One day he said, "Why don't we be together?"

I said, "On condition that you sit in the open and drink in front of the disciples and I don't drink."

He said, "Why won't you drink?"

I said, "So that you may be ungodly and fortunate, and I may be ungodly and unfortunate."*

He said, "I can't."

After that I said a word, and he struck his forehand with his hand three times. (294)

55.

Wishing for this world, though it may be necessary, fills my liver with grief. That's not because of any shortcoming of yours. But wishing for that world—there's no grief there. I want someone who will come in through the door a hundred thousand times, one after another. I seek refuge in God lest it be the opposite!

For some people everything pertaining to this world is quickly facilitated. Others wish for this world with a thousand laments, entreaties, weepings, and praises—every once in a while a drop arrives after a thousand tricks. Right now, that's the least of things for me—whoever turns toward me for the sake of God must be disgusted with it. This is the first step.

Awhad ad-Din said to me, "Why don't you come over to me so that we can be together?"

I said, "Let's take goblets, one for me, one for you, and pass them around where they gather for the *sama*."

He said, "I can't."

I said, "Then being my companion is not your work. You must sell your disciples and the whole world for a goblet." (217-18)

I wonder what these people think
friendship with God is.
That God who created the heavens,
who created the earth,
who made the universe appear—
is His friendship gained so easily
that you come in and sit before Him,
you talk and you listen?
Do you fancy this is a soup kitchen?
You come in and you drink it down?
Then you just leave?

My Path to God

The Profit and Loss of Study

1.

This world is a treasure, and it is a serpent. Some people play with the treasure, some with the serpent. Those who play with the serpent must give their hearts over to being bitten by it. It bites the tail, and the head. If it bites the tail and you don't wake up, it will bite the head.

Those who turn away from the serpent and have not been deluded by its jewels and kindness put the shaykh that is intellect in front—because the shaykh of intellect is the emerald [that blinds] the serpent's gaze. When the dragon-like serpent sees that the shaykh of intellect is the leader of the caravan, it becomes low, lowly, and frail. In that water it used to be like a shark, but under the foot of intellect it becomes a bridge. Its poison becomes sugar, its thorns roses. It used to be a highwayman, but it becomes the escort. It used to be the stuff of fear, but it becomes the stuff of security. (313)

2.

Intellect takes you to the threshold,* but it doesn't take you into the house. There intellect is a veil,* the heart a veil, the secret heart* a veil. (180)

3.

Intellect is a master archer. It can pull the bowstring to the ear. However, the this-worldly intellect is laid low by nature. It can pull the string, but not to the ear. With a thousand tricks it makes it reach the mouth. If you let go of the bowstring from the mouth, what work can it do? Only if you let it go from the ear will it make a wound.

So, words that come from the mouth are nothing—only if they come from action and practice. *I am the least of the least and the lowest of the low. God knows my soul better than I, and I know my soul better than you.*

The words of the this-worldly intellect come from the mouth. The words of the that-worldly intellect are an arrow shot from the depth of the soul. Therefore, *If only a Koran, whereby the mountains were set in motion, or the earth were cleft* [13:31].

Words that don't spring up from thought
    aren't suited for speaking or writing.

One should look both before and behind so that love for this world does not become a barrier, for *your love for a thing makes you blind and deaf.* When love for this world dominates over love of religion, *it makes you blind and deaf.* The result is *We have put before them a barrier, and behind them a barrier* [36:9]. It may be that they will repent and wakefulness will arrive. Then that love will decrease, and the barrier will become thinner. For the most part, this is achieved through companionship with good companions. Good companions last with someone who is sweet-tempered and long-suffering. (313-14)

4.

A king had two sons, one well-mannered and high in aspiration, the other unworthy, stupid, timid, and effeminate. Out of zeal, the king sought out a man-colored, courageous, self-sacrificing, Rostam-like man and made him the comrade and friend of this boy.

Night and day he told him about the attributes of men and showed him. He taught him how to handle weapons and move like a man. For two months, night and day, this stalwart recounted the stories and the conduct of men, but it had no effect. The boy would make toys and dolls and play with them like a girl.

After two months, the king asked him to bring the child so that he could see him. The child had put a veil over his head and held his toys. The teacher was so flustered that he made his turban into a mask and sat down next to him.

The king came down. "Where's the teacher?" Looking left and right he kept asking, "Where's the teacher."

The teacher removed his veil and offered his salutations. With an effeminate voice he said, "Hi there, I'm the teacher."

The king said, "What's this?"

He said, "O king of the world! During these two months, no matter how much I beat him and pushed him to make him the same color as myself, I was completely unable to do so. So now, I've become the same color as he."

But he was a man. How could making himself similar in that respect harm him? (310-11)

5.

At first I didn't sit with jurists, I sat with dervishes. I used to say, "They're strangers to being dervishes." Then I came to know what it is to be a dervish and where they are, and now I would rather sit with jurists than with these dervishes. At least the jurists have taken trouble. The others simply brag about being dervishes. I mean, where is a dervish?

All the great prophets burned in love for being a dervish. Even Moses cried out, "*Make me one of the community of Muhammad!*" The Muhammadans are those to whom this has been given.

Every story has a kernel. The great ones brought the story for the sake of the kernel, not to fend off boredom. They brought it in the form of a story so as to show the purpose within it. Nonetheless, *He who remains silent will be saved* in the service of the great ones, especially since,

> Whatever the youngster sees in a mirror
> the old man sees in a baked brick. (249)

6.

After all, I was a jurist. I read *Tanbih** and others many times. Right now, none of it comes to mind. There's nothing. Unless we should be going along like this, and it lifts up its head before my face—then it falls right in front of me. Otherwise, I've got no head for fairy-tales. Oh, go! You, come! *Sweeter than the age of youth and mixing with men of intelligence!* (676)

7.

Someone said to someone, "Sir, are you a Jew?"
He said, "No, I'm a jurist."
He said, "Oh, too bad you're not a Jew."
He said, "Why?"
He said, "I need some sulfur."
In that place it was the custom for the Jews not to come out in

the morning, out of fear of torment by the Muslims, who considered tormenting them a good deed. It was they who sold sulfur
and such things.

He said, "Is that why you want me to be a Jew?"

He said, "Yes."

He said, "Sir, I'll bring some sulfur for you. Don't wish
Jewishness on me. I'll do what you want." (134)

8.

Intellect's legs are weak. Nothing comes from it. However, it's
not left without share. It's a newly arrived thing, and the newly
arrived thing takes to the door of the house. But it doesn't have
the pluck to go into the harem.

An *alif* was recorded on the Tablet. Sometimes we say that it was
written on the Tablet, sometimes on the earth, sometimes on the
heart. Its light has filled the high and the low. Where is a speaker?
Where indeed is an eye? Where is vision so that you may see? (307)

9.

Then, they say, all is the Real, there is no creation. If there were
no creation, there would be speech without letters and sound.
Where the Real is, there are no letters and no sounds. (648)

10.

When everything becomes known from the *alif*, there's no need
for anything else. When it doesn't become known for someone,
one must explain it to him. Perhaps he doesn't understand *ba* or *ta*,
and so on down the alphabet. Someone else didn't understand, and
for him the Koran came as explanation.

That *alif* is disengaged. It's sitting in the forefront of the Divinity.
Ba has love for it in its heart and has thrown its head down at its
feet. (659)

11.

First tell me what *alif* is, then I'll tell you about *ba*. That would be
long. Now, however, long and short are the same for me, so let me be
long or short. Short and long are attributes of the body, and its attrib-

utes are newly arrived. First and last rise up from that. Without it, there's neither first nor last, neither manifest nor nonmanifest. (188)

12.

Of all the secrets, no more than an *alif* fell out. Everything else they said was to explain the *alif.* And of course the *alif* was not understood.

O you who died trying to undo knots!
    Born in union, you died in separation.
You went to sleep thirsty on the lip of the ocean!
    You died in poverty on top of the treasure!* (241)

13.
O you who died trying to undo knots!

Man was created for a purpose—so that he should know where he came from and whence he will return. He was given the outward and inward senses so that they would be the equipment for his seeking. When he employs them for something else, he gains no security for himself such that his life would be happy and delightful, nor does he come to be aware of his beginning and his end. Occupying himself with the sciences—which are the best occupation of the folk of this world—he passes his days and is kept back from his purpose.

At the end of his life, the best of the investigators in this domain says, "*from this world we've obtained torment and bane.*" This is advice for the whole world. That wasn't the time to stand on ceremony, it wasn't the time to offer interpretations of words.

Our spirits are in dread of our bodies—
    *from this world we've obtained torment and bane.** (678)

14.
Let the days be blessed from you.* The blessed are you! The days come so that they may become blessed through you.

He has prepared the Night of Qadr* in the not-Qadr. It is in it.

The knower of speech* is one thing, the speaking knower something else.

He said a thousand words. He said, "The rest?" He was sitting idle. Moses was the knower of speech—"God's speaking-companion."* *You will not see Me* [7:143] charged like horses on the double. It came forward, and he was prevented. "Hey, some other time!— *The days are there between us."*

The sea would run out [18:109], but the meaning of *alif* would not be finished.

It jumped out from the Divine Court. For what wisdom did it jump out? He knows the secret of His wisdom.

It said, "Intellect makes no mistakes," but it was mistaken while saying "It makes no mistakes."

Ba fell into the footsteps of *alif*. It said, "Why did you come?"

It replied, "I will be your explanation. I have one dot, and that's the love for you that I have in my soul. I'm the meaning of *alif*. I speak the secret of disengagement."

Ta came: "I have two dots on my head so that I may overthrow this world and the afterworld."

Tha also fits itself in. It was further, just as the Torah was earlier and gave the meaning of the Koran.

Jim has two sections more than *alif*, but it has fastened the belt of service around its waist. *Dal* also has two *alifs*. (636)

15.

There is the story of Sa'id Musayyib, who had the post of professor in Baghdad. He had a daughter, the description of whose gentleness and beauty had reached the caliph. He tried every sort of stratagem and entreaty short of oppression and wrongdoing to make the girl his wife. Of course, he was not successful.

There was a jurist in his class who was more destitute than anyone else and sat back by the shoes. His mother was poor. The gaze of that great man fell upon him. When the class was finished, he called him forward. He greeted him and said, "I will give you my daughter, and you will be my deputy."

He recounted this story to his mother. His mother feared that he had gone mad because of constant memorization at night, study in the day, thinking, and indigence: "O child, have you dreamed all this? Are you imagining it? I have no wealth with which to cure you."

He said, "O mother, this is neither a dream, nor imagination, nor the result of exhaustion. What I saw yesterday was real."

The mother became worse. She consulted with the women of the neighborhood: "This boy is driving me out of my mind." They said that she should frighten him so that he would speak no more of these imaginings. If people were to hear him, they would give witness that he has gone mad.

When he went to class the next day, again he called him and insisted much more than before. This learned man, seeking knowledge, was rubbing his eyes. He was saying, "I wonder! Perhaps this is imagination or a dream. My mother and all the women agree: 'Because of all this thinking and gloom, you've lost your intellect. You've been overcome by melancholia.'" Again, he looked at the madrasah, himself, and the professor. He was saying, "No, by God, I'm not imagining things. There's no melancholia, no dreaming, no madness."

Again he went home and told the story. They said, "The gloom has become firmly fixed. He will drive himself and us out of our minds!" In short, the more he insisted, the more they denied. Even when the time of the nuptials came close, and he put on the robes and came into the house, giving her gold and silver, his mother fell into doubt and kept on doubting.

At night they brought the girl. The neighborhood women and the mother looked on in wonder. A group of women who knew the girl went forward. They expressed the absurdity of the situation. The girl shouted at them, "What's absurd about it? He's one of the folk of knowledge, the folk of learning, and we also are among the folk of knowledge and learning. Rather, he is superior to us, because we are folk of this world, and he has nothing of this world. So he is nobler and better than us. We need to abandon this world and be like him." (669-70)

16.

Know that studying is also a great veil. Man goes into it, as if he has gone into a well or a moat. Then at the end he regrets it, because he comes to know that he was kept busy with licking the pot so that he would be held back from the subsistent, endless food. After all, words and sounds are the pot. (202)

17.

At the time of death, Sana'i was saying something under his tongue. When they put their ears next to his mouth, they heard,

I've turned away from all I've said—
    there's no meaning in speech, no speech in meaning.* (668)

18.

O servant of the body! How long will you run in its service?

They say that the poem is by Abu'l-Ala Ma'arri.* His words aren't much. It's not like they say, that he was strong. Look at what the Sage* says:

My knowledge reached the point
    that I came to know I'm ignorant.

From this one word you catch the scent of something. They showed him something: "I came to know that what I said from beginning to end was nothing." (227)

19.

Whoever is more learned is further from the goal. The more abstruse is his thinking, the further he is. This is the work of the heart, not the forehead.

That's the story of the one who found directions to a treasure: "Go out to such-and-such a gate. There's a dome. Put your back to the dome, your face toward the kiblah, and let an arrow go. Wherever the arrow falls, there is the treasure."

He went and let fly. No matter how much he tried, he didn't find it. Then the news reached the king. The master archers let fly, and of course no trace appeared.

When he referred back to God, he received an inspiration: "We did not say that you should pull the bow." He came, placed the arrow in the bow, and it fell in front of him. When solicitude comes, *Two strides and he arrived.*

So, what does this have to do with practice? What does it have to do with ascetic discipline? Whoever threw the arrow further was more deprived. This is because you need a "stride" to reach the treasure. And what sort of stride! Which is that stride? *He who* *knows his soul knows his Lord.* The one they named "commanding to evil"* is itself "at peace." (75-76)

20.

Although these meanings, when expressed, are like water in a pot, I don't find any water without a pot. I want to grasp those meanings that are in Arabic writings, in Arabic clothing. There is no other reason to learn Arabic.

My goal in Kaaba and idol-temple is You.

My goal in the idol-temple is the image and beauty of Your face. If I want the idol of words for the sake of those meanings, it will not happen without the Companion. The Companion must be there. (676)

21.

I should have spoken of those sciences and Arabisms with them, because it's a pity to speak of my own knowledge with them. How can you turn away from this knowledge and busy yourself with that? They should keep themselves busy with just that, because they're not up to this.

They're all seeking the benefit of knowledge. You should seek for good deeds, so that you may obtain good from the Companion. This is the kernel, that's the husk. (185)

22.

The preacher preaches to show the goal and to show the road and the traveler. When the imperfect shaykh and the poet recite poetry for explicating and showing, they become even more disgraced in the eyes of the knower.

Someone was speaking of fish. Somebody said to him, "Quiet. What do you know about fish? Why do you explain something that you don't know?"

He said, "I don't know what a fish is?"

He said, "That's right. If you do, tell me the mark of a fish."

He said, "The mark of a fish is that it is has two horns, just like a camel."

He said, "Well! I already knew that you don't know what a fish is. Now that you've given the mark, I've come to know something else: You can't tell the difference between a cow and a camel."

If the tulip didn't laugh so foolishly,
        who would see the blackness of its heart?
Even if it's rolling in its own blood,
        its face is worthy of the black-hearted.

Yes, but there is also this: "*Speak to people in the measure of their intellects.*" That "measure of intellect" is their blight.

*Intellect is the fetter of men,
        love undoes the fetters.
Intellect says, "Don't overdo it,"
        love says, "I don't care."* (76–77)

23.

I said to him, "Don't buy the mill, and don't make it into an endowment. Give me the two thousand, and I'll turn for you. When I turn, I'll produce a flour that can't be described."

Do you see what an ill man does? If he undertook a hundred acts of discipline—he wouldn't do that by choice.

He said, "With this much humility, what will reach him?"

He said, "I won't talk of humility. Rather: an unbeliever was taking a pot of water with him on the road. Someone needed it, so he gave the water to him. He did not look upon him with the glance of kindness, but his insides were put at ease by the water. On the day of resurrection that unbeliever will take the hand of a hundred thousand Muslims. God's work has no causes.* There may be someone who spends two hundred dirhems for the dervishes, and it does not have the effect of the five dirhems of someone else."

If it were fitting to perceive these meanings by study and debate, then it would be necessary for Abu Yazid and Junayd to rub their heads in the dirt out of regret before Fakhr-i Razi. They would need to become his student for a hundred years.

They say that Fakhr-i Razi composed a thousand folios in the exegesis of the Koran. Some say five hundred folios. A hundred thousand Fakhr-i Razis couldn't reach the dust of the road of Abu Yazid. He's like the knocker on the door—not the private door inside the house, rather the outside door. That private room is something else. It's where the sultan is alone with his elect—not the knocker on that door, the knocker on the outside gate.

This striving in debate is exactly what you want to make known through knowledge. But for this, you must go and strive. For example, if you had debated about the road to Damascus and Aleppo* with Mawlana for a hundred years, would I ever have come here from Aleppo? Not until he brought out four hundred dirhems, and you undertook dangers for yourself and your wealth. You say, "Even if there were villains?" Go ahead, say it. Let it be danger, or recklessness. In the end, the work will get done.

He asked: "First, one must debate about the knowledge of the road. Then it's possible to take the road."

He answered: "I told the story of the road and going to Aksaray.* I explained that you haven't gone, yet you ask about the other side. I say, 'Go that far, and I will be with you. After that, all right, look to see which side is safer from thieves, wolves, villains, and so on—is it the road to Malatya, or to Iblistan*?'" (127-28)

24.

There were seven Sufis who sat together for a few days. They required food, but because of the joy of encountering each other, they didn't want to scatter in search of food. A nobleman became aware of their state. He came and from afar put his head on the ground. He said, "What do your minds desire?"

One of them said, "Go, prepare adequate food, and lots of it, without delay. Empty the house of young and old, and of yourself as well—such that no one will knock on the door."

He did that. He said, "These are seven people. I will prepare food for twenty men just in case. I'll send all the family to the houses of relatives, and I'll instruct them, 'Beware of coming around the house today.'" He filled up the bowls and placed the loaves of bread on the table. He brought them in and sat them down. He said, "I have served you, and you are free of me. I won't show myself until tonight."

He slammed the door and shut it fast. He pretended to leave, but he went upstairs and looked from a hidden hole to see how they would eat. They put the bowls one by one in front of themselves and ate. One would become empty, and they'd take another. All of a sudden, one of them became bloated and fell down. He joined with *the sitting place of truthfulness* [54:55], for *everyone returns to his root*, and he had heard the call, "*Return to thy Lord*" [89:28]. He was in fact in *the sitting place of truthfulness*, both here and there. A thin curtain remained so that, because of that curtain, he could be seen here.

The other six stood there eating. After a time, another became bloated and fell. This kept on happening, until only the seventh remained with the food.

The master of the house lost his patience. He came down and opened the door, pretending to be coming from outside. He entered and said, "Shaykh, how was it? Was there enough food as you had charged, or no?"

He said, "No."

He said, "How so?"

He said, "If it had been adequate, would I still be alive? Since I still have breath, it wasn't adequate."

A satiating, adequate answer is one that leaves your insides with none of the agitation of question and answer. As long as there is seeking for questions and answers, it was not adequate. As long as someone is happy with more talk and more answers, that's proof that his insides still have doubt and he requires answers. (190-91)

25.

Speech is for the sake of practice. Practice is not for the sake of speech. It's so that you will know that ease is with the dervishes. (131)

26.

Three particles are used in taking oaths: wa, bi, *and* ta. *Thus we have* wa'llah, bi'llah, *and* ta'llah.

The reason these people study in the madrasahs is, they think, "We'll become tutors, we'll run madrasahs." They say, "*Good deeds*—one must act beautifully!" They talk of such things in these assemblies so that they can get positions.

Why do you study knowledge for the sake of worldly mouthfuls? This rope is for people to come out of the well, not for them to go from this well into that well.

You must bind yourself to knowing this: "Who am I? What substance am I? Why have I come? Where am I going? Whence is my root? At this time what am I doing? Toward what have I turned my face?" (178)

27.

This differentiation and level pertain to the outward knowledge of the sensory things and to the intellectual truths that belong to the intellect of this world and the senses of this world. How then are the levels of the intellect of that world!

But this also is deception. I say to you, "Pull the cotton out of your ears so that you will not be the prisoner of the speech of the tongue. Then you will not be the prisoner of the outward flatterer and you will not fall for every display. Open your eyes and ears so that you may be informed of the inner practice, for no one becomes informed of it save God, or *a messenger such as He is well pleased with* [72:27]." (608)

28.

A Jew, a Christian, and a Muslim were friends.* They found some money and prepared halva. It was late: "We'll eat it tomorrow. But this isn't much. Whoever has a fine dream will eat it." Their purpose was not to give any to the Muslim.

The Muslim woke up in the middle of the night: "What is sleep? A deprived lover, then sleep?" He got up and ate the halva.

The Christian said, "Jesus came down and pulled me up."

The Jew said, "Moses took me to gaze upon paradise. Your Jesus was in the fourth heaven.* What are its wonders compared to the wonders of paradise?"

The Muslim said, "Muhammad came. He said, 'Helpless fellow! Jesus has taken one of them to the fourth heaven, and Moses took the other to paradise. You're deprived and helpless. At least get up and eat the halva.' So I got up and ate the halva."

They said, "The dream you saw—that was the dream! Ours was all imagination and illusion."

Be careful with this story! Watch what you imagine from it. Don't think in the end: "You went out to the garden, I secretly ate the honey and the medicine." (652)

29.

Blessing is with your great ones. There's disagreement as to what is meant by these *great ones.* Are they the great ones through the form of age? The great ones through meanings that are subordinate to form, tied down, and not everlasting? Or the great ones through subsistent meaning?

Some say that what is meant is the great ones through age, that is, through the passage of time, and that is form and things subordinate to form. Some say that what is meant is the great ones through meaning. Everybody moves from where he is—*The pot leaks what is in it.* But, one does not ask questions from that "elder."

You say, "They shake the tree so the fruit will fall." Sometimes, you shake it and the fruit stays back and doesn't come. All of it is not such that it will come. There's no help for it save silence and submission. Not every tree is found in [the realm of] form. Here, there is no path save silence and submission. *When the Koran is recited, listen to it and remain silent* [7:204].

For example, a theologian begins talking—a topic of which he speaks from beginning to end. There are no objections while he recounts the topic completely to the end. After you have understood it and memorized it, such that you can reiterate all of it from beginning to end, you take exception to it in your heart. Perhaps you speak of it not as it is, but such that you repeat half the topic and not the other half.

You say, "That's not the custom."

I say, "The custom is crooked. It's not right."

You say, "But this is not perfection. Perfection is that even if he were to voice thousands, you make no omissions."

I say, "That perfection is in another form. Perfection is that you take the defect upon yourself. 'I have not completely understood it or memorized it.' In this question, points may have been voiced. But the first words are gone. Thus he said, *'When it was said to the fakir, "Why did the blessing leave the assembly"?'* In other words, the blessing of the first words, which were the beginning—that left."

> The fire of love has roasted my heart,
>> the blood of my liver has stained my face,
> the balm of the Beloved's lips has become my wine—
>> what use to me are the *Dhakhira* and the *Lubab*?*

The profit lies in eating the morsel. You wait for a while until the morsel gives its profit, then you eat another morsel. The wisdom is found in this, and this is the way in listening and wisdom. But, if someone has such a burning and suffering that he eats very quickly, that's something else. He himself knows. But he should not try that with my food.

If I had begun in these outward sciences, as long as I had not mastered one lesson, I would not have begun another; like someone who reads something many times such that no exception can be voiced, or anything added. This is because these lessons have not been digested.* Thus, until I was able to reiterate all the points and the exceptions to them that Mawlana has deigned to voice, tomorrow I would never start another lesson. I would review that same lesson. If someone digests a problem as is due to it, that is better than reading a thousand problems that stay raw. (136–38)

30.

The *interpretation of narratives** [12:101] is a great work. It's a great rank to know the intention of the speaker from the words. Joseph the Sincere was a great prophet. He was proud of the science of the interpretation of narratives, and he gave thanks. (684)

31.

I asked two questions in order to take benefit. The shaykh didn't answer. I wonder if he saw that I was not the confidant of the answer or I was not prepared for it, or if he didn't have the provisions? He said that it was not his habit to begin answering just like that. Only when words began to come out from tasting would he speak.

He said, "Did you see? Were you a spectator? All this is transmission and imitation, or Hadith, or tales, or the poetry of a poet."*

He did not begin discoursing on any discussion. I say: "Where's your own? Come on, answer!"

Through the tongue of his state he was speaking just like this wall speaks: "Why do you want an answer from me? Does anyone want answers and questions from this wall?"

He said, "This meaning is obvious." So why didn't you say this obvious meaning in the room? I'll block my ears. I don't want to hear. If he's alive, I didn't hear it from him.

What use to me are the *Dhakhira* and the *Lubab*?* (744-45)

32.

Although they have some knowledge, they keep on changing from state to state. Thereby you know that these sciences have no connection with the inside, for it's the inside strength that requires one to say, "No, I will see for myself." One does not accept the talk of anybody. The words "gnosis" and "dervishhood" have now come to be used by anyone, but the only thing they know is what they've heard. (687)

33.

Muhammad Guyani is a man of faith. He's full of his own faith. He is not empty of self like me. If these words were to stay with him, it would be enough for his whole life—and the resurrection, and the Narrow Path, all the way to union with God. And if they do not stay with him, he will go back to his root, and these words will also go back to their own place.

Once the night-watch caught a fellow. He said, "Oh, if they beat me, I won't be able to bear it. And if they take anything from me, that would be worse." If they take one dirhem from a beggar, it's as if they've killed him.

He said, "I will lead you to a gathering in which are sitting fifty of those you're looking for"—that is, suspects.

They said, "He's right. What can we get from this beggar? Come on, show us where they are."

Up until now, he had been their prisoner. At this moment, they became his prisoner. They became companions and friends. He brought them to a door. Then he said, "You sit here, and I will go and see them. But don't say anything."

They became suspicious: "If there must be no talking, why is he talking?"

In short, he shut the door and went up on the roof and sat down. He saw that they weren't going. He said, "I didn't find them."

They said, "Scoundrel, you did what you did, and we'll do what we do."

He said, "Bang your heads against the wall, I'm home free. If you want, go this way, if you want, that way."

When the receiver of words does not grasp the words, he goes back home. He looks down from the roof, and that is what he says.

If he receives the words, how is it that he is helpless in answering the words of others?

He said, "He's not helpless."

He said, "By 'helpless,' I mean that he gives no answer."

People don't like to hear talk of salvation. They like to hear talk of the denizens of hell. Words in which salvation is found are true. So, I too will make hell so hot that they will die of fright.

Fatima—God be pleased with her—was not a gnostic, she was an ascetic. That is why she kept asking the Prophet to talk about hell. (141-42)

34.

Someone was beating on the door.

"Who is it?'

He said, "God's nephew."

The master of the house came out to be of service: "Give me your hand, I have business with you." He took him to the mosque. "Here's your uncle's house, you know. Go on in, you won't have to come back out."

"Come on now," he should have said, "he's voicing a riddle. He doesn't mean that."

With your disputation, you would make Fakhr-i Razi helpless. What a wonder that you are not made helpless by all these answers! (349)

35.

All right, those are the attributes of the Pure, the Possessor of Majesty, and that is His blessed Speech. Who are you? Which is yours? These hadiths are true and full of wisdom. And those are the allusions of the great ones. Yes, they are. You bring something. Which one is yours?

I speak words from my own state. I make no connection with those. You also, speak to me, if you have words, discourse upon them! If sometimes one mentions some exact words for the sake of calling to witness—as Mawlana says, they seal it with the Koran and the hadiths so that it will be explained—that is permissible. (72)

36.

Indeed, if you become heated with your own words and your own poetry, and the words of others come in keeping with that, then the heat will increase. That's good.

However, you were saying that sometimes a cloak will speak.* After all, your state should be better than the state of a cloak. You aren't able to talk except by quoting others and citing poetry. How can a cloak have speech? Speech is impossible for it. Among inanimate things, speech came from the Samaritan's calf.* It has not been the custom since then. However, how could someone who took the calf as a god accept the prophethood of Moses? He considered the state of Moses like that of a tramp.

After all, the disciple of someone was saying that he sees God face-to-face seventy times a day. His shaykh said, "If you were to see Abu Yazid once, that would be better than seeing God seventy times." Abu Yazid* was coming out of the woods. He came and saw him, fell down, and died. For he was a lover and a seeker. He died. In other words, some of the soul had remained with him, but now it did not remain. With his own incapable vision, his own inadequate insight, he had seen Him in the form of his own conception. He did not see God with the strength of Abu Yazid.

Now, a hundred thousand Abu Yazids will not arrive at the dust of Moses' sandals.* You also say, by way of imitation, that thousands of saints do not reach the dust of the prophets. So, how do you consider it allowable that a tramp should see Him a thousand times a day, and that Moses, God's speaking-companion, did not see Him?

And if someone should interpret the speech of God just as it is, you say one must give a fatwa. The discussion is with the interpretation. Even if they call him to account, he is correct in the interpretation.

This is not like *I am the Real*—disgraced and naked, incapable of interpretation. Hence his head had to go. (761-62)

37.

Every corruption that has appeared in the world appeared because someone believed in someone else on the basis of imitation, or he denied on the basis of imitation.

That exalted person felt pain. They did not know that he was exalted except on the basis of imitation. Imitation is always changing—an hour hot, an hour cold. Is it permitted to consider an imitator a Muslim?

When he suffered, and, when in actual fact he is the exalted of the Exalted, this became the cause of ruination in the world. *They disobeyed the messenger of their Lord, so He seized them* [69:10].

He said, "This indeed is good. But, there is also this: If at first he believed in someone through imitation, he fell under the curtain of supposition, and in the end the curtain was lifted. Or, it appeared that the curtain was lifted, but in fact the curtain increased. Then he turned back on that belief. However, he does not let it appear that he has turned back. Then people's opinion of him won't go bad and they won't lose confidence in his being pleasing [to God]."

He said, "However, if he doesn't let it appear, he has thrown the people into misguidance."

He said, "How should he let it appear that he has lost confidence in himself?"

The final word is this: If he lets it appear that he has turned back, this has an interpretation, and if he doesn't let it appear, that also has an interpretation. So said a dervish, and Mawlana knows that this dervish is not one to speak idly. This is finished.

When you begin talking in the presence of such a knower of speech, you see that the worthiness is in your outwardness, not your inwardness. Otherwise, you would hang down your head in this station, for the words are about conforming to a man whose religion is the best of religions. If you ask a Jew, "Who's better, a Christian or a Muslim?", he'll say, "The Muslim." And if you ask a Christian, he'll say the same. Seeing this necessitates that the man of good fortune will increase his belief in the true religion. *All the people came to know their drinking places* [2:60].

> In seeking the Friend, I'm rushing.
>   My life has reached its end, but I'm sleeping.
> I grasp that I'll find union with the Friend,
>   but how will I grasp the life that's gone by?* (161-62)

38.
If you must cover yourself with dust
*   then take dust from the greatest of dunes.*

If you must be an imitator, then imitate the Koran. This is like that well-known sage. He said: There was a sage who had no equal in the science of medicine and experimentation in the inhabited quarter. He had servants a hair of whose heads was worth a hundred like him. He had an ugly appearance and a tremendously repulsive form, such that few cities had anyone more repulsive in visage. His head and face were so twisted over that nothing appeared—not mouth, not eyes.

He came down with an illness that in fact had no cure except eating human filth, and then putting him into a rug and rolling him around. Many physicians were sitting around him, and they were looking at each other, but they couldn't speak. He understood, and he knew, because he was the master of all of them. He said, "I know, I know. I have to eat such-and-such. Well, since I must eat it, let it be that of Qimaz," whom he liked very much. (207-8)

39.
They say that the Antichrist will kill goats and sheep. He will kill birds, pulling off their feathers and wings, then he will rub them with his hands and they will be put aright and come to life. He will place hands on a dry goat, and it will give birth. He will cut a goat

in half, rub it with his hands, and it will be put aright. The servants of the Real and the followers of Muhammad will not be deceived by that, though he brings what is similar to a miracle.

This fellow is an imitator. However, he is imitating a belief that is the solicitude of his Guardian. When on occasion the trace of that solicitude reaches his soul in a concealed and hidden way, his imitation becomes so strong that he wouldn't give away that report if he saw with his own eyes a thousand things like this from the Antichrist.

Now, when someone has that state continually, it is never cut off from him—not at the time of eating, nor the time of sleeping, nor in the toilet. He is seated in the toilet and that state is established. What is his state like? After all, he's mounted on the toilet.

Of course, his beard is the right size for a beard. Say that you will show him sincere disciples in the measure of his beard. Since they don't have the inward, let them at least do the outward. (213-14)

40.

They are imitators. He who is more of a verifier is more of an imitator. One group imitate the heart, others imitate limpidness, others imitate Muhammad, and others imitate God. They narrate from God. There is another group who do not imitate God, who do not narrate from God, but who speak from themselves. *Say: Were the sea ink for the words of my Lord . . .* [18:109]. He says *"for the words of my Lord."*

Now, "He says" is of two sorts: One is "He," the other is "the reality of the He." Another says "He." He Himself says, "Who is this 'He' that you say?"

He says, "Like this, it has more flavor." (674-75)

41.

A deaf man was coming from the mill*. He saw someone coming to the mill. He reasoned to himself that the man will ask him where he's coming from, but he forgot about the greeting. When he made a mistake at the beginning, from beginning to end he was mistaken.

He reasoned, "He will say, 'From where are you coming?', and I will say, 'From the mill.' He will say, 'How much flour did you prepare?', and I will say, 'One and a half measures.' He will say, 'Was the water good?', and I will say, 'It was right up to the middle.'"

The man came and said, "Peace be upon you."

He said, "From the mill."

The man said, "Dirt on your head!"

He said, "A measure and a half."

He said, "Up your wife's behind!"

He pointed and said, "Right up to the middle."

The man had seen that he was deaf, so after that he said anything that came to his mind. But, if he had given him the correct answer, he would have said, "I shouldn't speak idle words with him. One can't do just anything." (666-67)

42.

Someone went to a sermon in Hamadan, where they all declare God's similarity. The city preacher came out and sat on his seat. The Koran-reciters purposefully began to recite before him verses that are connected to declaring similarity,* such as *The All-merciful sat upon the Throne* [20:5]; His words *Are you secure that He who is in heaven will not make the earth swallow you?* [67:16]; and *Your Lord and the angels will come, row upon row* [89:22]; and *They fear their Lord above them* [16:50]. Since the preacher was one of those who declare similarity, he spoke of the meaning of the verses in terms of the declaration of similarity. He also quoted hadiths: *You shall see your Lord as you see the moon when it is full; God created Adam in His form; I saw my Lord in a red robe.* He offered fine expositions in the manner of declaring similarity. He said, "Alas for anyone who does not declare God similar in these attributes, who does not know God in this form! His outcome will be hell, even if he performs the worship, for he will have denied the form of God. How can his obedience be acceptable?"

Questioners were standing up and interpolating verses and hadiths connected to God's howlessness and placelessness, such as *He is with you wherever you are* [57:4] and *Nothing is as His likeness* [42:11]. He interpreted them all in the way of declaring similarity. He got the whole gathering warmed up to the declaration of similarity, and he made them all fear the declaration of incomparability. They went home and told their children and wives. They advised them all, "You must know that God is on the Throne, in a beautiful form, His two feet hanging down and placed on the Footstool, with the angels all around the Throne! The city preacher said, 'If anyone negates these forms, his faith is negated. Woe upon his death! Woe upon his grave! Woe upon his outcome!'"

Next week, a preacher arrived who was a Sunni and a stranger. The Koran-reciters read out verses that declare God's incomparability: His words, *Nothing is as His likeness* [42:11]; *He was not born and does not give birth* [112:3]; *the heavens are rolled up in His right hand* [39:67]. He began skinning alive those who declare God similar: "Anyone who declares God similar becomes an unbeliever. Anyone who says He has a form will never be released from hell. Anyone who says He has a location—woe upon his religion! Woe upon his grave!"

He interpreted away all the verses that seem to declare God's similarity. He kept speaking of threats and talking of hell: "If anyone speaks of form, his obedience is not obedience, his faith is not faith. He says God requires a location! Woe upon him who hears these words!" The people became extremely frightened, and they returned to their houses weeping and fearful.

One man returned to his house and did not eat dinner. He went to a corner of the house and put his head on his knees. As was their custom, the children gathered around him. He drove them away and shouted at them. All of them gathered around their mother in fear. His wife came and sat before him. She said, "Is the master well? The food has become cold. Won't you eat? You've struck the children and driven them away. They're all weeping."

He said, "Go away, I have nothing to say. A fire has fallen on me."

She said, "By the God in whom you hope, won't you tell me what state has overcome you? You're a patient man. Many difficult events have happened to you, and you were patient and took them lightly. You trusted in God. God took you past them and made you happy. In gratitude for all that, turn this suffering over to God too. Take it lightly, and mercy will come down."

The man felt sorry for her and said, "What should I do? They've confused me, they've brought me to the edge. Last week that scholar said, 'You must hold that God is upon the Throne. Anyone who does not hold that God is upon the Throne is an unbeliever and will die as an unbeliever.' This week another scholar sat on the

seat: 'If anyone says that God is upon the Throne, or thinks intentionally that He is upon the Throne or in heaven, his works will
not be accepted. His faith will not be accepted. God is incomparable with location.' So now, which one should I follow? In which
belief should I live? In which should I die? I'm confused!"

The woman said, "Husband, don't be confused. Don't think
about perplexity. Whether He is on the Throne or has no Throne,
whether He is in a place or has no place, wherever He may be,
long may He live! May His good fortune last!"

You must occupy yourself with being a dervish and think about
being a dervish. (176-78)

PHILOSOPHY

43.

The easiest of the sciences is the science of purification rituals
and the branches of jurisprudence. More difficult than that is the
principles of jurisprudence. Still more difficult is the principles of
theology, and even more difficult is the science of philosophy and
metaphysics. Those who speak of it trade punches with the
prophets: "Were it not for fear of the sword, we would establish
our own way," and they talk rubbish. What Plato and his followers
say—"If everyone were like us, prophets would not be
required"—is rubbish.

Suppose Plato were to hear that someone turns dirt into gold
without any treatment: "If you do the like of that, you'll be his
brother. Now, since you can't do it, and you see that he is superior
to you, why don't you consider it necessary to follow him?"

Nowadays, the clever and the philosophers are all "sages," but the
master of the charismatic act is more of a philosopher than they,
for these people lose themselves in that and begin to deny, and
they don't perceive it. And miracles are stronger than charismatic
acts, for the prophet can display a miracle any time he wants, in
contrast to the master of the charismatic act. Why shouldn't a servant whom the prophets themselves wish to see—*Make me one of
the community of Muhammad!*—be more clever and more of a
philosopher than any of those?

So, he has become the companion of someone like this,* who takes no account of these clever sayings that make your intellects unfortunate.

Your knowledge is such that you have no regret about your acts, and you never say, "Would that I hadn't done that!" How then can you gain a share of his companionship? You have gained nothing from what is less than his companionship, so how can you want what is more? Tell the group that the situation here is *first put up the house, then paint.* (711-12)

44.

The school of the Sunnis is closer to the work than the school of the Mu'tazilites*. The latter is near to philosophy. *He who digs a well for his brother falls in.* (739-40)

45.

Of what sort are *the possessors of the kernels** [2:179]? God doesn't mean the intellect that everyone has. The philosopher says, "I speak of intellectual truths," but he hasn't caught a whiff of the lordly intellect. (646-47)

46.

Indeed, God's work is like this. He makes impossibilities and absurdities possible. He makes a congenitally deaf man listen, He makes him hear. When the eye turns completely white,* the philosophers will certainly deny that sight is possible. But this finds room in the intellect of the prophets. If the philosopher gives it its due, he says, "This is not my work. I don't have that power." But, if he were to say that, then indeed he would be a Muslim. (753)

47.

It is not strange that no one sees a pearl placed in a heavy box, wrapped in a black cloth, hidden under ten layers, and pulled into the sleeve or a sheepskin. Thus, the scent of the spirit and the sweetness of the spirit had reached Sayyid—not that he had seen the spirit itself. It is a great distance from the level of reaching the spirit to seeing the spirit. Once the spirit is seen, one must go forward on the path of God from there, so that one may plainly see God in this life. I don't say "already in this world."

Although that pearl is within those curtains, the pearl has a radiance that strikes out. The person with perfect gaze knows it without its being brought out. It's not strange that someone doesn't know it when it hasn't been brought out. What is strange is that it should be brought out for someone, held before him, and he should see nothing. Otherwise, who would talk of Socrates, Hippocrates, the Ikhwan as-Safa, and the Greeks in the presence of Muhammad, the household of Muhammad, and the children of Muhammad's spirit and heart?—not the children of water and clay. And when God is present too!

Umar—God be well pleased with him—was studying a part of the Torah. Muhammad snatched it from his hand: "If that person upon whom the Torah was sent down were alive, he would follow me."* (83–84)

48.

Avicenna was half a philosopher. The perfect philosopher was Plato.

He lays claim to love. After all, give justice to the situation. You are accepted, you're a lover. Are these the words of the accepted? Fire should come down over your head and face. (231)

49.

Muhammad Ghazali—God's mercy be upon him—read the *Isharat* of Avicenna with Umar Khayyam.* He was learned. That is why they criticize his *Ihya*—because he made deductions from [the *Isharat*].

He read it twice. Khayyam said, "You still haven't understood it." He read it a third time. Then Khayyam secretly called out the minstrels and drummers so that, when Ghazali went out from him, they should play. Then he would become famous because he had read with him, and that would benefit him.

That fellow who kept on bragging, *I am the Real*—
    enough that he hung himself on this rope. (649)

50.

Shihab Suhrawardi, called Maqtul, was very much accepted and held dear by the king of Aleppo. People became envious. They said, "Let's all write a letter to the king so that we may put him in the catapult." When he read the letter, he took away his turban and had his head cut off. At once he regretted this. The deception of the enemies became manifest [*zahir*] to him. After all, they called him by the title "King Zahir." He commanded that they should lick up his blood like dogs. He killed two or three of them—"You stirred this up."

He brought out that learned man and gave him to auction. They bought him secretly for forty dinars, and a fine Koran for five dirhems, because they did not understand the Koran.

This Shihab ad-Din wanted to do away with dirhems and dinars, because they are the cause of disturbances and the cutting off of hands and heads. The people's transactions should be with something else.

He abandoned following [the Prophet]. Muhammad killed him. If you ask me if he himself had following—no, Shihab ad-Din did not.

One day King Zahir was describing the army to him. He said to him, "How do you know what an army is?" The king looked up and down. He saw standing soldiers, their swords drawn. The doors, roof, hall, and corridors were full of awesome individuals. He jumped up and went to the treasury. It was because of the effect of this in his heart that he aimed for his life before investigating.

Shihab ad-Din's knowledge dominated over his intellect. The intellect must dominate over knowledge. It should rule over it. The brain, which is the place of intellect, had become weak.

His words swallowed down the words of Shihab Suhrawardi.* Then that theologian Asad cursed him. How unjust of him! (296–97)

51.

Fakhr-i Razi was one of the philosophers, or something like that. It happened that Khwarazmshah met him. He began, "It was thus that I went into the fine points of the roots and the branches. I went through all the books of the ancients and the moderns from the time of Plato until now. I designated, clarified, and memorized the level of every reputable composition. I went through the notebooks of all the ancients and came to know the measure of each. I stripped the folk of these times completely, and I saw what each had acquired. I learned this discipline, and that discipline"—and he listed them—"and took them to a place that cannot be imagined."

A favorite commander said so as to criticize him, "And that other knowledge, too—I know, and you know."

He said, "Indeed, I saw people afraid and fleeing. I went forward, and they tried to frighten me and they warned me: 'Beware, a dragon has appeared that makes a mouthful of a world.' I had no fear. I went further forward. I saw an iron door, so wide and tall that it cannot be described. A five-hundred-maund lock had been placed on it. They told me that a seven-headed dragon was inside. 'Beware, don't circle around this door.' I struck and broke the lock. I entered and saw a worm. I stepped on it, put it under my feet, ground it under my feet, and killed it." *And God knows best.*

Now, how is it that all of his words are about that worm, and all the books and compositions are full of that worm? (658-59)

52.

What gall Fakhr-i Razi had! He said, "Muhammad Tazi [the Arab]* says this, and Muhammad Razi says that." Isn't he the apostate of the time?! Isn't he an unqualified unbeliever? Unless he repents.

Why do they give themselves trouble? Why do they strike themselves against a sharp sword? And then, what a sword! God's servant has pity on them, but they show no pity on themselves. (288)

53.

Who is Sayf Zangani that he should speak ill of Fakhr-i Razi? If Fakhr were to break wind, a hundred like Sayf would come into existence and disappear. I defile his grave and his mouth. My fellow townsman? What kind of fellow townsman! Dirt on his head! (641)

54.

Those who pretend to philosophy* make an exegesis of the "chastisement of the grave after death." They offer expositions by the path of intellectual truths. They say this: The spirit has come here in order to perfect itself. It takes the goods of its own perfection from this world. Then, when it leaves this world, it will have no regrets. Right now a person should come out of form [and enter] into meaning and make the body accustomed to the spirit. If he occupies himself with form and makes the spirit accustomed to the body, that upper door will close, and no expansiveness and spaciousness will remain for the spirit.

For example, he sees possessions, women, and honor on this side. He acquires familiars, comrades, and various sorts of pleasures on this side. Therefore he inclines to this side. Then, if someone mentions the name "death" to him, he suffers a thousand deaths.

If he were to see his desires as coming from that world, he would yearn to go there. Hence, that death is not death. It is life. Thus the Prophet said, "*The believers do not die. Rather, they are transferred.*" Hence we see that "transferal" is one thing, and "death" something else.

For example, if you are in a dark and narrow room, you cannot enjoy luminosity there, nor can you stretch out your legs. You are then "transferred" from that room to a large room and a great house, within which there are gardens and flowing streams. That is not called "death."

So, these words are like a bright mirror.* If you have any luminosity and taste, then you will yearn for death. *God bless you!* May it be blessed for you! And don't forget me in your supplications.

If you do not have such a light and such a taste, then set out to grasp it. Seek and struggle, for the Koran tells us that if you seek such a state, you will find it. So, seek! *Wish for death, if you are sincere* believers [2:94]. Just as among men there are sincere ones and believing ones who seek death, so also among women, there are sincere ones and believing ones.

This is a bright mirror within which is found the explanation of your own state. Whenever there is a state or a work in which you like death, that is a good work. So whenever you hesitate between any two works, look into this mirror. Which of these two works is more appropriate for death? You must sit like a limpid light, prepared and waiting for death. Or, sit like a struggler and struggle to achieve this state.

Do you imagine that the person who takes full pleasure will have fewer regrets? In truth, his regrets will be more, because he has made himself more accustomed to this world.

What they have said concerning the chastisement of the grave in terms of form and image, I have clarified for you in terms of meaning. (86-87)

55.

A single one of God's servants can empty Plato of all those sciences. He can do it in a moment. However, he will show consideration toward him and enter in little by little. Thus he will say that this man was clever and a philosopher, for he was a philosopher and knowing. After all, trading punches with these prophets is no idle task. They did find an enjoyment, they found a happiness, and they did it with this strength.

Sulayman Tirmidi used to say, "Well, at least speak the words of the folk of religion. Those who in our times speak from the pulpits and sit upon the prayer-carpets are the highwaymen of the religion of Muhammad. On the prayer-carpet of Abu Yazid! On the pulpit of Shaqiq Balkhi!" (716)

Following Muhammad

56.

If a tailor does blacksmithing, his beard will burn.* He should do his own work. Or, he should come to the blacksmith and say, "O blacksmith, teach me blacksmithing," so that he may teach him blacksmithing. Then his beard will not burn, just as the smith's beard does not burn.

If you spend a hundred dirhems on food, but you don't add two cents-worth of salt, it will be nothing. It won't go down the throat. If you do add two cents-worth of salt, whatever you pick up will be salty.

Someone may say "salt," but its meaning and state won't be there. Until it is, ascetic discipline will have no result. Rather, it will produce darkness, since the substance is not there.

The Prophet by no means came to give news to him who doesn't have it. Rather, to the one who has it, he said, "You also have it." *A good-news giver and a warner* [17:105]—it will become apparent who has it and who doesn't. (640)

57.

Whenever someone has substance, the messenger and the prophet get that substance moving and put it on the road. When there's no substance, what can they put on the road? (268)

58.

The prophets all make each other known. Jesus says, "O Jew, you did not know Moses well. Come and see me so that you may know Moses." Muhammad says, "O Christian, O Jew, you did not know Moses and Jesus well. Come and see me so that you may know them." The prophets all make each other known. The words of the prophets explain and clarify each other.

After that, the Companions said, "O Messenger of God! Every prophet makes known him who came before him. Now, you are the Seal of the Prophets. Who will make you known?"

He said, *He who knows his soul knows his Lord.* In other words, *He who knows my soul knows my Lord.* (75)

59.

God indeed has a sensory aroma. It reaches the nose like musk and ambergris. But, how could it be similar to musk and ambergris! When His self-disclosure is coming, that aroma comes as a precursor, and man becomes totally drunk.

Also, those words weren't finished: Muhammad says, "You did not know Jesus, O Christian! Know me, and you will have known him—and me as well."

Now, when Muhammad is made known, he is the Seal of the Prophets. They said, "What should we do?"

He was ashamed to say, *He who knows my soul knows my Lord,* so he said, *He who knows his soul knows his Lord.*

Here, everyone has made an interpretation out of ignorance. Then, the intelligent said to themselves, "When we know this filthy, dark, patched-up little soul, will we gain knowledge of God?" The possessors of the secret understood what he had said.

I said, "How is it my place to eat and sleep? As long as that God who created me this way does not speak to me without intermediary, and until I ask things of Him and He answers, how should I sleep and eat? Have I come to eat in blindness? Since it is like this and I speak to Him and listen face-to-face and orally, only then do I eat and sleep. I know how I have come and where I am going, what my refuge is and what my outcome will be. I live free."

Now, from childhood I have turned my face to the roots.

It's as if a mother has one boy in the world, and that boy is good and beautiful. He puts his hand in burning fire. How that mother would leap and pull him back! For me, God's aroma has been like that. (734–35)

60.

The food of one is sufficient for two. It depends on who the *one* is. If he's Muhammad, his food is sufficient for both worlds. (642)

61.

What the other prophets gained in a thousand years, Muhammad passed through in a brief period, because [*You receive the Koran*] *from One Wise, Knowing* [27:6], for he had been brought out for that work. This is like Jesus. Although Jesus gave that one talk at the beginning of his infancy, that was not by his own choice. *He struck the target without aiming.* It's as if a child all at once draws an *alif* and does it well.

Although Muhammad spoke late and after forty, his words were more perfect. I mean, the words of both of them hit the mark.

"He is the leader of the first and the latter folk."* *They recognize him as they recognize their own sons* [2:146]. (196–97)

62.

A king holds back nothing of gold, kingdom, and possessions, but he does hold back two things: First, he does not give his inner sanctum to anybody. And second, the unique pearl—he does not put it somewhere where it might be seen, even by the keeper of the treasury. On occasion, a ray of it may strike the closest of his friends, but jealousy makes him hold it back. However, no ray of his inner sanctum strikes anyone.

If a ray of Muhammad should strike, you would be burnt up, and so would the person in whom you believe.

The pearl gives light. You can leap up, or jump down. Who are you? A little worm. If someone shows something, then pulls it back, you shouldn't deny. Take the side of possibility. This is a good reminder—a reminder.

I do not revere the Koran because God spoke it. I revere it because it came out of Muhammad's mouth. (691)

63.

A poor man entered into the assembly of the Prophet. A rich man spread the tail of his garment over that of the poor man in pride and arrogance. God's Messenger became angry, and he looked at him with the gaze of an angry man. The rich man said, "I will give him half of my possessions if you absolve me of that." He absolved him.

I would not trade the least report from Muhammad for a hundred thousand treatises by Qushayri, Qurayshi, and the others.* They have no flavor, no taste. They have not found the tasting of that.

They don't give one gulp to the self-worshipers.* (209)

64.

Poverty is my pride. A master who does not fit into the whole world—what kind of poverty is it of which he should be proud? He's poor, he's indigent, he's helpless before the light of God, his breast is burning in God's light, he says, "I wish I had a hundred breasts. Every day they would burn in this light. They'd fall apart and rot, and He would make another one grow up."

He knows from whence he has comfort and in what he has taste. *Had We sent this Koran down on a mountain, [you would see it humbled, split apart in fear of God]* [59:21]. That which He places on a mountain and cannot be borne by it—that light shines upon him. (280-81)

65.

It is God who is God. Whatever is created is not God—whether it's Muhammad or other than Muhammad. (303)

66.

There's a fakir who is a dervish for food, and a fakir who is a dervish for God. What does being a dervish have to do with a tattered cloak? Every year nine hundred thousand dinars were the expense of that dervish's rooms—every day ten sheep, and indeed the expense of the fowl was beyond calculation. He would say, "*I have a moment with God,*" and it would reach him.

I ask these shaykhs about *I have a moment with God.* Is this moment continuous? These stupid shaykhs say, "No, it is not continuous."

I said, "A dervish from the community of Muhammad was supplicating and saying to God that he should give all of you togetherness."

He said, "Hey, hey—don't let him supplicate that for me. Supplicate for me, 'O Lord, take this togetherness away from him! O God, give him dispersion!' For I've become helpless, I've become wasted in togetherness." (281)

67.

There are Awhadian* imaginings—before knowledge, they take to misguidance. After that, there's knowledge. After knowledge, there are imaginings that are correct and very good. After that, the eyes open.

The sincere imitator is better than the clever man who wants to carve out his own method and path. For we've seen a blind man who puts his hand on the back of a seeing man and goes to Aksaray.* Another blind man takes his hand off the seeing man's back, but he doesn't see. He takes the road without guide and goes toward nonexistence. He lives his life in nonexistence, and he gives up his soul in nonexistence. Either he dies of hunger and thirst, or a wild animal falls on him and eats him.

The common people who do the five prayers are delivered from chastisement. Woe on those who let go of following Muhammad!

A nomad said, "O Messenger of God! What is obligatory?"

He said, "Five prayers."

He said, "I will not add a single cycle. Fasting?"

He said, "Thirty days."

"Alms?"

"Such and such."

He said, "Is there anything else I must do?"

He said, "No."

He said, "I will add nothing to these," and he went.

When he had left, the Messenger said, "If he sticks to this, he will find deliverance."

They said, "Well! Should we content ourselves with this amount?" They washed their hands of following, and they didn't see. (217)

68.

The lover alone knows the states of the lover—especially these sorts of lovers who go forward in following. If I were to display my following, even the great ones would despair.

"Following" is that one does not complain about commandments. And if he does complain, he must not abandon following.

Thus, the Messenger said, *The surah Hud has whitened my hair.** If you say, *The surah Hud has whitened my hair,* I'll put you next to the Prophet.

There would be no reason to say *it has whitened my hair* if the commandment were not heavy. Look how the truthful Messenger began to cry out when *Go thou straight as thou hast been commanded* [11:112] was sent down in the surah of Jonah. We may debate about the meaning of that cry.

There are many sorts of debate, and many sorts of non-debate. You will not debate when there is just the gist, or when you consider me stronger in debate. Or, you may be bored, or you do not feel like debating. Which of these is it?

Shaykh Muhammad also submitted. He wouldn't debate. If he had debated, there would have been more benefit, because for me it was necessary that he debate.

I said, "*Meaning is God.*"*

He said, "Indeed."

If the Companions had debated with the Messenger, they would have taken more benefit from him. The benefit of meaning arrives itself. However, when something is obtained through debate—if there is debating—then you will obtain benefits.

I think this way about you, but you act with me like that. If you are bored, you must be renewed. If you're old, you must become young. You must open your head, ears, and awareness so that you may take a share—so that you may hear about meaning, and also eat [of it].* You say, "At this time, I'm busy with another job. How can anyone do two jobs at once?" You must do two jobs at once.

God has let me do seven or eight diverse and incumbent jobs all at once. God predominates over everything. Some of the saints show sharpness so they appear to you as predominating, but they are not so predominating. Other saints appear as soft and gentle, but they are extremely active and predominating—what happens is what they want.

It will be a long time before Sharaf Lahawari comes to be empty of making claims. The mark of it is that he has no gnosis. He's not able to speak of gnosis. When someone makes up words from our words, like Sharaf Lahawari, that is like sinking down into dark water. That is why he saw in a dream that he was sinking down into a great, dark water. He was moving two fingers to catch my attention: "O Mawlana Shams ad-Din, take my hand, take my hand!" He didn't learn anything from that. Again, in my presence, he began distinguishing between the miracles of the prophets and the charismatic acts of the saints. He was explaining that the prophets display miracles whenever they want.

What does talk of the saints have to do with you?

He began saying that for some there is continuous effusion, and for some the effusion is discontinuous. Some have effusion by choice, some without choice. He conceived of the saint and his states in his own imagination. When I turned away from his words for the sake of his own best interest, he said, "He is envious of me and being spiteful."

It is my disposition to supplicate for Jews. I say, "God guide them!" When someone curses me, I say in supplication, "O God, give him something better and more pleasant to do than to curse people!" In place of that, perhaps he will pronounce glorifications and recite the Shahadah, busying himself with the world of the Real.

How could he fall upon me—"Is he a saint, or is he not a saint?" What's it to you if I'm a saint or not?

They said to Juhi, "Look over there, they're taking the trays."

Juhi said, "What's it to me?"

They said, "They're taking them to your house."

He said, "What's it to you?"

So, now, what's it to you? This is why I avoid people. (119-21)

69.

He said, "Do you see how the commandment is heavy? There were men who pulled mountains up by their roots. They did that, yet they were stopped short by the command. Look at Muhammad, who complained about the commandment: *Hud has whitened my hair.* After all, this was a complaint. As for Ayaz, the commandment was not heavy, it was light."

I said, "Well, it was Ayaz's aspiration that made the commandment light."

He said, "Ayaz was kind and loving to dogs, not to speak of the light of his eyes. Why wouldn't he be?"

Now, if our words go back to derision, will anyone ever reap any fruit from this work?

Mahmud did not accept a person who was discourteous and had not bathed: "He's come to me with the smell of sweat and filth." So how could "Muhammad," which is an intensive form of "Mahmud"— accept that? After all, the spirit of the great ones is present. It gazes, and it provides help. How could anyone act discourteously and speak words about the Prophet that are not appropriate for his station?

This is absurd, because you read your own page, but you do not read the page of the Prophet. In other words, you judge on the basis of your own state, and you do not judge on the basis of his state. What he said—"My outward self was created of what the inward self of others was created"—by these others he means the saints and the prophets. In other words, "What they knew in their hearts and inmost minds I know outwardly just like that." He saw it outwardly!

That person speaks with himself. He has come outside of himself and speaks with himself for the sake of calling others to remember. He's the inspector who's come outside his own house.

O Turner of hearts and eyes, fix my heart upon my religion! This is a supplication for others. If they are tried by such events, they should plead to God like this. Otherwise, is it your opinion of the sent prophet, the possessor of steadfastness, that he was captive to the soul in the way that you fear? Was he weeping because of the soul's trouble-making? No, he was being the inspector in his own house,

so that the disbeliever would know that he would get no consideration.* He was speaking the words to himself; they were not
going anywhere else.

> I'm happy with myself—
>   after this it's I and I.

This indeed was another secret that the Messenger spoke, but he
kept it hidden from Umar. It was not that he was keeping it back
from him, but its time had not yet come. If he had spoken of it to
him, he would have been held back from the caliphate in perplexity. He would not have been able to keep the outward realm in
check and to spread the Shariah outwardly in the world. (764-65)

70.

*He said, "That is not what the shaykh says, and it is not a correct trans-
mission."*

The obedience and practice of the Messenger was immersion in
self. For practice is practice of the heart, service is service of the
heart, and servanthood is servanthood of the heart. It is immersion
in the Object of one's own worship.

Nonetheless, since he knew that not everyone had a way to that
true practice, and that few people would be given that immersion,
he gave them the commandments that are the five prayers, the
thirty days of fasting, and the rituals of the hajj, so that they would
not be deprived and so that they would be distinguished from others and be delivered. And perhaps they might even catch a scent of
that immersion. Otherwise, what does hunger have to do with
being a servant of God? What do these outward prescriptions of
the Law have to do with worship? (612-13)

71.

*He said, "Our debate is about these transmitted words, regardless of
whether or not the transmission is correct."*

*The seeker said, "O Object of my Seeking! Do not prescribe anything
for me, for I worship You many times more than You have prescribed for me
because of my love. Prescription is dreadful and heavy."*

The Sought Object said, "Your putting up with a little bit of prescrip-
tion* is a thousand, thousand times better for you than worshiping without
prescription. A dirhem that you give because of seeking the Sought Object
is better than a thousand dirhems on your own accord. 'And they did not
measure God with His true measure' [6:91]. They rejoiced in a little of
this world, and they did not rejoice in a thousand, thousand profound wis-
doms that would bring them near to everlasting life. They rejoiced in a
dirhem as soon as they found it; they humbled and abased themselves.
They wallowed and rolled in the dust: 'O everything that is trifling, come,
so that our affairs may have the correct appearance in everything, even in
food. We will not be hypocrites, not even in food.'"

The seeker said, "I asked my soul for obedience, but she did not answer,
out of forgetfulness or enmity."

The Sought Object said, "Seek from your soul red water, or white water,
or the vapors that are worthy of life, but do not ask her for obedience, for
she did not grow up in the growing place of males." That is why He said,
"Take not My enemy and your enemy [as friends, offering them love]"
[60:1]. (679-80)

72.

How is it that the Prophet said, "*God created the spirits before the*
bodies"? Suppose it was a hundred thousand years before the bodies.
It is still a veil, because it is newly arrived [*hadith*]. And of course one
must make an ablution after a "new arrival" [*hadath*].* Leave aside
new arrival so that you may find the way to prayer and service.

I don't know how he perceives the new arrival of the pure, eternal Speech. No, he must travel completely hidden—hidden in following. Then his spirit will come to naught and be annihilated,
and nothing will remain. Thus the Sage said—even if he said it fee-
bly and incompletely,

> Although Muhammad was there,
>   what sort of existence did he have?
> Other than God, anything there
>   had gone through plundering and annihilation.*

When he was annihilated, then He would have said, "I've
come—*peace be upon you.* I found you all alone. Everyone was busy

with something, happy-hearted and content with it. Some were spiritual. They were busy with their own spirits—some with their intellects, some with their souls. I found you without anyone. All the companions went after the ones they sought, and they left you alone. I am the companion of those without companions."

Of what happened between them, this became famous: "*He revealed to His servant what He revealed*" [53:10]. From the beginning of an-Najm* to here was put forth—though it was not put forth.

They ask, "What did He reveal?"

He says, "He said what He said."

His spirit comes along and asks, "What did they say?"

The Prophet answers it, "We said what we said."

Intellect comes along like this and asks. It is told, "Now a line has been written on his forehead." (282-83)

73.

The Prophet, upon whom be peace, said, "*There is no salat without recitation [of the Koran]*." He also said, "*There is no salat without the presence of the heart.*"

A group of people suppose that when they find the presence of the heart, they have no need of the prayer's form. They say, "*Seeking the means after obtaining the goal is ugly.*" In their opinion, they have taken the right position, because the state has shown itself completely, along with sanctity and the presence of the heart. Nonetheless, for them to abandon the prayer is a defect for them.

"Did the Messenger—God bless him—achieve this perfection that you have achieved, or not?"

If he says that he did not, then they should cut off his head and kill him. And if he says, "Yes, he did achieve it," then I say to him: "Then why don't you follow—such a noble messenger, the unparalleled good-news-giver and warner, the *light-giving lamp* [33:46]?"

If there happens to be one of the saints of God, whose sanctity has been established such that there is no doubt whatsoever, and there is also Rashid ad-Din, whose sanctity has not become manifest; and, if the saint abandons the outward form, whereas Rashid ad-Din is assiduous in the outward form, I will take after Rashid ad-Din and not even greet the other one.

Then he turned to Mawlana Salah ad-Din and said, "How's my talk?"

Mawlana Salah ad-Din said, "The judgment belongs to you. Whatever you say—there's no answer and no way around it." (140)

74.

He said, "Have they said the prayers?"*

He said, "Yes."

He said, "Oh!"

Someone said, "I'll give you all the prayers of my life—you give me that 'Oh'."

He said, "Now it's fitting for me too."

Look at this allusion—he's saying that he's the lover. That's a dervish.

Following Muhammad is that he went on the *mi'raj*—you also should go in his tracks. Strive to gain a settling place in the heart. When you are seeking this world, that is not in speech, but rather in engaging with the secondary causes. You should be seeking the religion. This also is not in speech, but rather in never leaving obedience. You should be seeking God by never leaving the service of the Men.

> Your sitting companion should be better than you—
>   then your position and rank will increase. (645)

75.

An hour's meditation is better than sixty years of worship. What is meant by this "meditation" is the presence of the sincere dervish—an act of worship in which there is no false show whatsoever. Certainly that is better than outward worship without presence. The salat can be made up for, but there is no making up for [lack of] presence.

Muhammadan fakirs strive in this: *There is no salat without presence.* It is not that they abandon its form so that the soul may be happy. In the outward Law, *There is no salat without the Fatihah.*

If Gabriel comes during presence, he will be given a slap. The Prophet had not yet reached presence when he said to Gabriel, "Come on!" Gabriel replied, "No, *if I approach another inch, I will be burnt to cinders.*" (208-9)

76.

Were it not for this bread-box, Gabriel wouldn't find the dust of this group. (638)

77.

There's a king in the house. The road to the king is by way of the door, that is, obedience, because the walls are very high. *I take refuge in God!* Whoever falls—the libertines. Only from the door!

There remains this objection: How is it that there are some who do not perform the acts of worship, yet they are great? We reply: That's a defect. However, these are dangerous words. Pay attention to this: When someone must come in by the door, he's outside the door. As for the elect who are in the service of the king, they're inside the door. But this is difficult, and extremely dangerous.

There remains the objection: Muhammad was one of the elect and performed servanthood.

The answer: He had complete strength and in his servanthood none of that meaning went away. In the meaning of servanthood, nothing escaped him. He had perceived the flavor of servanthood. When he was at the door, he saw himself inside. When he was inside, he also saw himself inside. However, in others there was weakness and that meaning was becoming less. Thus Abu Sa'id said about Avicenna, "What sort of man is this? 'Do it, but take it as not having been done.'"*

If [the time of worship] escapes me and Mawlana unintentionally when we are occupied, we are not satisfied with that and we make up alone for what we missed. When I don't go on Fridays, I become sad: "Why didn't I join them for this meaning?" Even though it's not a true sadness, it's there. (742-43)

78.

He said, "He placed the staff of worship in the hands of the blind: 'These people will not reach the reality of servanthood; perhaps they will catch a scent by means of supplication and prayer.'"

Why should it be like this? The Prophet himself, with his perfection, performed the prayer. If someone believes that he prayed to teach the common people, then he's an infidel, a know-nothing. He has no share, he knows nothing! On the contrary, the

Prophet did so out of love, *until his feet became swollen*, for, when he said, "*God is greater*," he would leave this world.

For example, there was that Companion from whom a hundred camels loaded with wheat were plundered. In his sadness he omitted the first *God is greater*. When Muhammad greeted him, he did not see him in that station. His face turned sour. He made his excuse to the Prophet, but his face remained sour—even though he was among the ten favorites—until he stopped making excuses. He said, "I repent."

He said, "That alone won't do it—send two thousand camels to bring wheat and distribute it." After that, he looked upon him with kindness. (696-97)

79.

Sayings are quoted from Ayn al-Qudat from which ice pours down. He said, "May my mouth be smashed if I say about something that has come to be, 'Oh, would that it had not been!'" Something of this sort has also been related from Ibn Abbas. But, from Muhammad, the opposite of this.

They did not reach Muhammad's secret, and they will not reach it. Moses and Jesus used to say, "*Make us part of the community of Muhammad!*" They knocked themselves out in all those ways seeking his station, but it didn't happen.

*Noble writers who know what you do** [82:11-12]. When you intend something, an angel is on the right hand, and an angel on the left. The angel on the right has received the commandment, "When he puts that intention into practice, write until seven hundred—until *without reckoning* [2:212]." We have verses for each of them.

[*So, whoever hopes for the encounter with his Lord, let him do*] *worthy deeds and not associate with the worship of his Lord any one* [18:110]. That "one" is himself. He should not make his existence his companion.

God guides to His light whom He will [24:35]. The Koran has made promises to us, and the severities are the portion of the others. The Absolute Apportioner has divided it.

He said, "Why aren't you doing the prayer?"

He said, "Because of God's words."

He said, "Where did He say that?'

He said, "*Do not approach the salat when you are drunk* [4:43]."

He said, "Read that. Everything has been given to everyone. The work is by apportioning. In the Koran, one verse is for the sake of the state of the believers. After that, He says a verse for the sake of the state of the unbelievers. However, in the world of love, all is gentleness. There is no severity. It's quite some time now that I have come out of severity. But, right here, severity is near. Hell is on this side. When you pass beyond hell, paradise is on the other side of the Narrow Path. The world of gentleness is without end and without shore." (663-64)

80.

They report that Abu Yazid didn't eat Persian melon. He said, "I have not come to know how the Prophet ate Persian melon." I mean, following has a form and a meaning. He preserved the form of the following. So why did he ruin the reality of following and the meaning of following? For Muhammad said, "*Glory be to You! We have not worshipped You as You should be worshipped!*" Abu Yazid said, "*Glory be to me! How magnificent is my status!*" If anyone supposes that his state was stronger than that of Muhammad, he is very stupid and ignorant.* (741)

81.

So-and-so* was saying, "*We have not known You.*" In other words, "*I have not known myself.*" "*We have not worshiped You.*" In other words, "*I have not worshiped myself.*"

He went out to the graveyard. He placed that big dome of the ego behind himself. He shot an arrow. One step *and he arrived*.

This happiness is because last year the beggar had no bread and this year he's been dying of hunger. It's humorous, isn't it? This year, he found a hundred dinars and happiness has come. But that dear, gentle prince who was born in good fortune and property and who has grown up with property laughs at his happiness. (227-28)

82.

The one who said "Glory be to me! How magnificent is my status!" *went astray.* Does this mean that the Real was speaking? How could the Real wonder at His own kingdom? How could wonder be permissible? The speaker was himself. But, he will not be taken to account for it, because he had become selfless. When he came to himself, he asked forgiveness. (657)

83.

How should I call him "king of the gnostics"?* He's not even the prince. Where is following Muhammad (upon him be peace!)? Where is following in form and meaning? I mean that the same light and brightness that was in Muhammad's eyes should be the light of his eyes. His eyes should become his eyes. He should be described by all of his attributes, such as patience and the rest, each attribute without limit. (738-39)

84.
O you who died trying to undo knots!*

That is the state of Athir Abhari and everyone like him. Whenever those fine points escape someone, he has died in trying to undo knots.

One man is the counterpart of the whole world—*Were the faith of Abu Bakr to be weighed against the faith of all creatures, his would be heavier.*

But what does it mean that the Messenger gained faith?* After all, that was another, higher state. *The ulama of my community are like the prophets of the Children of Israel.* He did not say, "*the fakirs of my community.*" That in which the prophets don't fit—he has pride in that.* How could they fit?

Having religion is a sweet thing when someone sees Him subtly and gains faith—not when he sees nothing and then has faith.

Sometimes one should be in the desert, sometimes before a sword, sometimes traveling in winter.

After all, it has come that He commands prayer toward the kiblah. Wherever you may be, you must pray toward the kiblah. Suppose that the world's horizons were all brought together, and everyone formed circles around the Kaaba and prostrated themselves. When you remove the Kaaba from the midst of the circle, wouldn't everyone be prostrating himself toward everyone else? They will have prostrated themselves to their own hearts.

He conveyed the message and he explained it: "I saw, I saw that all is He. No, not all—I pull down a mask so that I won't be like Hallaj." No, it has passed far beyond that you should be like Hallaj.

In the same way, that master said to the calligrapher, "It has long since passed that I should steal the teaching of calligraphy from you. That has passed, that has gone."

That would be a defect. With all that prophethood, would it be fitting that he be listed along with Abu Yazid and Zahid Tabrizi, with all their defects?

One day, he and his disciples were going to the hot springs. They had taken along a great deal of food. At the first way station, Zahid consumed it all—he left nothing. They stopped at the second way station. Zahid was hungry. The people of the village busied themselves with slaughtering sheep. One dervish went into the houses. He brought whatever there was of yoghurt, bread, and so on. Zahid ate and finished it. At night he set off without bread. He paid no attention. He said, "Rid yourselves of dispersion, let it go." (653-54)

85.

He said, "We want an invocation."

He said, "You must have an invocation that does not keep you back from the invoked. That is the invocation of the heart. The invocation of the tongue is not enough. Abu Yazid wanted to bring the invocation he had in his heart to his tongue. Since he was drunk, he said, *Glory be to me!* If someone is drunk, he cannot follow Muhammad, who is on the other side of drunkenness. One cannot follow the sober in drunkenness. *Glory be to me* is predestination. They all sank down in predestination." (690)

86.

What are those predestinarians doing? How could a strong man not know that all of this is from the Real? If you say to a child, "Who created us?", he says, "The Real." If you say to him, "Does the wheel turn without a turner?", he says, "What are you saying? Are you crazy?" If you say, "He who made us and gives us being and nonbeing—is He stronger and more dominating, or are we?", he says, "Surely He is. If He were not stronger, how could He give us being and nonbeing? Surely He dominates."

The Man is he who sees this dominating One, who sees the Giver of being, and who sees Him giving the being. He opens his eyes and he sees the Creator without imitation and without veil. He sees God. Then it is said to him, "Now go and see Muhammad. See the light of Muhammad. For infirmities sit on this sun and moon, but no infirmity sits upon that. It has no infirmity. The face of this sun becomes black, but the face of that sun does not become black. That sun has taken on the light of His majesty, but this sun stands in the station of *When the sun is darkened* [81:1]." (299-300)

87.

There may be one fault in a man that conceals a thousand excellent qualities, or one excellence that conceals a thousand faults. Iblis did not have any faults, except that he was spiteful, and that concealed his excellent qualities. What happened in the end? *Surely the curse is upon you* [15:35].

But indeed, how could a good man turn his gaze toward faults? A shaykh passed a corpse.* All the people kept their hands over their noses and turned their faces the other way, hurrying past. The shaykh did not hold his nose, nor did he turn his face, nor did he speed up his pace. They said, "Why are you looking?"

He replied, "How white and good are his teeth! That corpse is answering you with the tongue of its state."

The book of your deeds is variegated. This variegation comes from predestination. Do not write a variegated book. After all, this tribe knows better about predestination. If you try to deal with predestination, you will be held back from many benefits. It's not like you say: "Let's go to sleep. We'll see what God commands."

A good man has no complaints about anyone. He does not gaze upon faults.

When someone complains, it's he who is bad. Seize him by the throat—certainly it will be apparent that the fault is his. He complains about this side, the other one complains about that side. Both are variegated. They are predestinarians on their Companion's side, but free-willers on their own side.*

It is this tribe that knows predestination. What do those ones know about predestination? After all, predestination has a realization, and it also has an imitation. Why are you looking at imitation? Why don't you look at the realization? You increase your service, and we will increase our supplication. [*The weighing that day is true.*] *As for those whose scales are heavy*—[*they are the prosperous*] [7:8]. (90–91)

88.

He said, "The Sufi tore his clothing.* Someone said to him, 'Is tearing the clothing in the Book of God?'

"The Sufi said to him, 'Is there in the Book of God, "So he began to sever their shanks and necks" [38:43]?'"

These great ones, they all fell into predestination—these gnostics. But the Path is something other than that. There is a subtlety outside of predestination. God calls you "freely-choosing." Why do you call yourself predestined? He calls you "powerful" and He calls you "freely-choosing" because commandments and prohibitions, promises and threats, and sending messengers all demand free choice. There are a few verses on predestination, but not many.

He comes toward the servant, the servant quickly goes toward the Real.* (245–46)

89.

Until you give yourself totally to something, it will appear hard and difficult. When you give yourself totally to something, it will no longer appear difficult.

What is the meaning of *walayat* [sovereignty, sanctity]? Is it that someone should have armies and cities and fortresses? No! Rather, *walayat* is that someone should have *walayat* over his own soul, his own states, his own attributes, his own speech, and his own silence. Severity should be in the place of severity, and gentleness in the place of gentleness. He must not start being a predestinarian like the gnostics: "I am helpless, and He is powerful." No, you must have power over all your own attributes, over silence in the place of silence, over response in the place of response, over severity in the place of severity, and over gentleness in the place of gentleness. Otherwise, a person's attributes will be his affliction and chastisement, because he does not rule over them. Rather, they rule over him. (85–86)

90.

"You should hold to the greatest multitude,"* that is, the service of the perfect gnostic. "And you should avoid the villages," that is, companionship with the defective.

People are mines, like mines of gold.

A dervish wanted something. The owner of the shop sent him away: "There's nothing ready."

I said, "This dervish was honorable. Why didn't you give him something?"

He said, "God had not made that his ration for today."

I said, "God had made it his ration, but you prevented it. When I have seen something myself, how should I say that you speak the truth? If you had put your hand in the sack, and then the top of the sack firmly grasped your hand and injured it—on the basis of eyewitnessing, not interpretation—then I would say that God did not want it." (205)

91.

The fault was with the great ones, for they spoke words out of infirmity—*"I am the Real."* They left following. Then things like this fell out of their mouths. Otherwise, what kind of dogs are they to say these things? If the command over them was in my hands—killing, or repentance. (210-11)

92.

Rabi'a said, "I sent my heart to this world to see this world. Then I sent it to see the next world. Then I sent it to see the world of meaning, but it did not come back to me."

I wanted to bring these words forward for debate, and I would have voiced secrets in the debate. But you became warm and went into a state.

I have often raised objections to the words of the great ones, but I have never objected to the words of Muhammad. (643)

93.

A group of people found a taste in the world of the spirit. They dismounted there and settled down, and they talk about lordly things. Although this is that same world of the spirit, they fancy it to be lordly.

It may happen that the divine bounty will come, or one of God's attractions, or a man who takes them under his arm and pulls them from the world of the spirit to the lordly world. "Enter into following, because there is another subtlety. Why have you dismounted here?"

The beauty of the spirit had not yet completely shown itself to Hallaj. Otherwise, how could he have said, "*I am the Real*"? What does "I" have to do with God? What is this I? What are words? Even if he had been immersed only in the world of the spirit, how could letters fit there? How could "I" fit in? How could "am" fit in? (280)

THE RELIGION OF OLD WOMEN

94.

The Path is one of these two: Either by way of the opening up of inwardness, as in the case of the prophets and saints; or by way of acquiring knowledge, and that also is struggle and making oneself limpid. If both of these are put aside, what remains but hell?

Your creation and your uprising are as but one soul [31:28]. Where is the equal of this in the hadiths? *The believers are like one soul.*

So, the call of the prophets is just this: "O stranger in form, you are part of Me. Why are you unaware of Me? Come, O part, don't be unaware of the whole. Become aware, and become acquainted with Me."

He says, "I would kill myself rather than becoming acquainted and mixed with You!"

In short, in those outward seclusions, the more they go forward, the more imagination increases and stands in front of them. But in this path of following, the more they go forward—reality upon reality, and self-disclosure upon self-disclosure! (162-63)

95.

If you seek for the reality of the Law, it is the Shariah, the Path, and the Reality.* The Shariah is like a candle. The purpose and meaning of a candle is for you to go someplace. When there is a candle, you are right to be content with it. But if you keep on making wicks for it, changing it, and gazing upon it and you don't go anywhere, what good is it? How will you ever reach the Reality by doing that? In order to reach the Reality you must go by the Path.

For example, this pot is full of salt water. I say to you, "There's river water."

You say, "Give me some."

I say, "Empty it completely of that—heat to cold, cold to heat. As long as those things you know do not become cold, it won't be possible."

These words aren't finished. Sleep doesn't come. I'll put my head on you so that sleep may come. (741-42)

96.

This is separation [between you and me]* [18:78]. I said some words, but not the reality. Even if I wanted to, I couldn't go. No—one shouldn't be deluded by these words. *No one is secure from God's deception save the people who are the losers* [7:99].

> *I complained to a leader about the weakness of my memory,*
> *and he indicated to me that I should abandon sins,*

which means *to abandon existence.**

> *Surely knowledge is a bounty from God,*
> *and God's bounty is not given to the sinner.*

So, it is as if he is saying that memory is found in abandoning memory.

And seek God's bounty [62:10]. *Bounty* means having an increase, that is, increase over everything. Do not be satisfied with being a jurist. Say: "I want increase"—an increase over being a Sufi, an increase over being a gnostic, an increase over whatever comes to you. An increase over heaven.

They say, "Whatever is in the whole world is in the child of Adam."* Which are the seven spheres that are in the child of Adam? Which the stars, the sun, the moon? (220-21)

97.

Know that there is no God but He [47:19]. This is a commandment to knowledge. *And ask forgiveness for your sin* [47:19]. This is a commandment to negate this existence, because it is newly arrived. How can this existence, which is newly arrived, see the knower of eternity? Your body came to be only yesterday. Take the spirit as two or three days, take it as a thousand years. It's too little. (218-19)

98.

What the child of Adam knows is *There is no god but God.* Who has the capacity? What does Adam's child see? He is forced to talk of "tresses" and "moles." He declares God's similarity. Otherwise, how could there be tresses and moles?

> If I can seize Your tresses in hell
> I will scorn the state of those in paradise.*

What are "tresses" doing in hell?

He must return to God. He must open his eyes, open his ears, and turn his face toward the Men of God. He must let go of self-worship, because God-worship is to let go of self-worship. He's cold in the religion. He must become a bit warmer. (195-96)

99.

Someone said, "God is one." I replied, "So, what's it to you? You are in the world of dispersion—hundreds of thousands of dust motes, each of the dust motes scattered, withered, and frozen in the worlds. He indeed *is.* He is eternal Being. What's it to you? For you are *not.*" (280)

100.

"There is no God but God" is My fortress, and whoever enters My fortress becomes secure from My chastisement. Whoever comes into this fortress—He did not say "whoever mentions the name of this fortress." To say the name of the fortress is very easy. You say with the tongue, "I went into the fortress." Or you say, "I went to Damascus." If it's with the tongue, then in one blink you'll go to heaven and earth, you'll go to the Throne and the Footstool.

He said, "*Whoever says 'There is no god but God' purely and sincerely will enter the Garden.*" If you now sit and say it, your brain will dry out. He is one. Who are you? You're more than six thousand! Become one yourself—otherwise, what's His oneness to you? You are a hundred thousand dustmotes, each dustmote taken by a caprice, each dustmote taken by an imagining.

"*Purely*" through his intention; "*sincerely*" through his activity. There's no need for the promise of entering the Garden. When he does that, he will be in the Garden itself.

This speech of the foreteller* makes them a bit warm. It doesn't make them colder. I am the foreteller.

If the work could be accomplished simply by speaking or by a seven-colored cloak,* then you should mourn for the Verifiers.

Did you see the seven-colored prayer-carpet! Shaykh, you were told to leave the colors behind. (258-59)

101.

When a minstrel's not in love, or a mourner not in pain, they make others cold. They're here to make them warm.

Every rupture in the togetherness of the companions is because they do not watch out for each other. They should live such that they know themselves to be inseparable.

No one knows them other than I has two meanings. One meaning is straightforward, the second is that by this "other" He means the stranger.

From the world of meaning an *alif** charged out: "Anyone who understands this *alif* has understood everything, and anyone who does not understand this *alif* has understood nothing." The seekers are shaking like willow trees in trying to understand that *alif*.

They've talked at length to the seekers about those veils: "There are seven hundred veils of light and seven hundred veils of darkness."* In reality, they have not led them on the highway. Rather, they have been highwaymen. They drove them to despair: "How can we pass by all these veils?"

All the veils are one veil. Other than that one, there is no veil. That veil is this existence. (99)

102.

The dreams of God's servants are not "sleep." No, they are the same as events that occur in wakefulness. There are things that are not presented to them in wakefulness because of their frailty and weakness. They see them in sleep so as to be able to tolerate them. When he becomes perfect, he will be shown without veil.

He asked, "How long is the road from the servant to God?"

He said, "As much as that from God to the servant. If they say 'thirty thousand years,' this is not correct, for it has no end and no measure. To speak of the measure of the measureless and the end of the endless is absurd and false. One should know that the end-less is extremely far from what has an end. But this is all the form of the words, and it has no connection with endlessness. What do words have to do with God? *Speech 'is unto the day of the known moment'* [15:37]." (175)

103.

As long as the citadel belongs to the rebel, destroying it is incumbent and will lead to robes of honor, and helping the citadel to flourish is treason and disobedience. Once the citadel has been taken from the rebel and the standards of the king have been raised, or rather, once the king has come into the citadel, then destroying and ruining the citadel is treachery and treason, and making it flourish is an obligation, obedience, and service.

> Glorification, religion, and monastery are the pattern of asceticism,
>   sash, unbelief, and tavern are the basis of love.
> Until faith becomes unbelief and unbelief faith
>   no servant of God will become a true Muslim.* (160)

104.

God is greater. What is lesser? In other words, within himself someone conceives something that is the creator of the heavens, the Throne, the Footstool, the lights, and paradise. It means that He is greater than what you have conceived of. In other words, don't stand with that. Come forward and see something great. Seek so that you may find. (655)

105.

When you saw the pleasure of the obedience, you took your wage. It would have been better if you had not seen it and had not grasped it. Then you would have been drowned in the lordly world, and even greater than that. You should seek higher, and higher, and higher, for that is the meaning of *God is greater.* Lift up your thoughts from whatever comes into your imagination and your thinking. Hold your gaze higher, because He is greater than all those conceptions. Even if it is the conception of the prophets, the envoys, and the Possessors of Steadfastness*—He is greater than that. (647-48)

106.

He who knows his soul. When he breaks himself, that is *he who knows.* That is *he who knows.*

*You should hold to the religion of old women.** In other words, the old woman says, "O You! Oh, all is You!" Since she said, "all," the old woman is included too. This is better than saying, "*I am the Real.*" Although he arrived at God, he did not arrive at the reality of God. If he had been aware of God's reality, he would not have said *I am the Real.*

O guide and hand-grasper! He says, "So, *you should hold to the religion of old women.* Learn from an old woman."

The other offers proofs for the existence of God, that God is. He turned into a fine preacher. That's a long story. (262)

107.

He who knows his soul knows his Lord. Why didn't he say, "*who knows his intellect? Who knows his spirit?*"

I said, "Because the soul encompasses everything. The *soul* is a thing's existence."*

One must gain that disposition when one is little. *Thou knowest what is in my soul, and I know not what is in Thy soul* *[5:116]. (309-10)

108.

The meaning of speaking to someone is as if there is a veil like this before your eyes and heart, and I lift up that veil.

One must have need for the presence of the great ones. *You should have the religion of old women.* The need for them is better than anything. Fakhr-i Razi and a hundred like him should be proud to lift the corner of the face-covering of that needy, truthful woman so as to take blessing. And still—what a pity for that face-covering! (249-50)

109.

There's not much from *Ahad* [the One] to Ahmad—
    an *m* in the world veils the meaning.
Count that *m* as the world. When it disappears,
    Ahmad has the attributes of *Ahad.**

Listen to some words: "Every *j* is *b*, and every *b* is *j*. Hence it is necessary that *bism Allah* ["in the name of God"] becomes *jism Allah* ["the body of God"]." What an absurdity!

"That *m* is denial, and it is the veil of the state. When that *m* no longer remains, that is the state, and no absurdity remains. 'Count that *m* as the world. When it disappears'"—what tasteless words! What insipid speech!

Learn from that little old woman. She says, "O You, all You! O You, all You!" After all, she's in the midst—whether a little old woman, a youth, or a man. Where is she? Gabriel doesn't find her dust. What place is there for Michael? Her intellect does not find the way. How could there be a place for someone else's intellect?

You have been brought for this work. You have not been brought for denial. There's no room here for words. It's narrow. (641-42)

110.

If you pass beyond the body and reach the spirit, you will have reached a newly arrived thing. The Real is eternal. How can a newly arrived thing find the Eternal? *What does dust have to do with the Lord of lords?*

In your view, that through which you leap up and become free is the spirit. But, if you offer the spirit, what have you done?

If Your lovers bring the gift of the spirit to You,
    by Your head, they will have brought cumin to Kerman!*

If you were to take cumin to Kerman, what price, what value, what honor would it have? Since there is a Court like this, and He has no needs, take need to Him. He who has no needs loves need. By means of this need, all at once you will leap from the midst of these newly arrived things. Something from the Eternal will join with you, and that is love. Love's snare will come, and you will be caught by it, for *they love Him* is the trace of *He loves them** [5:54]. Through the Eternal you will see the Eternal, *and He perceives the eyes* [6:103]. This is the entirety of the words that can never be completed. Until the day of resurrection they will not be completed. (69)

III.

A dervish should have dervishhood and silence.

What's best for a fig-seller?
    Selling figs, brother.* (668-69)

112.

Seek someone lovely that you may become a lover.* If you don't become a complete lover of this lovely one, then another one. There are many subtle beauties underneath the chador. There is another heart-snatcher—you can become her servant and be at ease.

Are you free? You have to worry about bread. You must have clothes. I mean, the servant has nothing of these worries. His Lord arranges his bread and clothing.* How could he have love for bread? (651)

113.

The ocean of generosity moves its waves and gives you whatever you want from it. Each person worships something*—one beautiful women, another gold, another position. They say, "*This is my Lord*" [6:76], but they don't say, "*I love not those that set*"* [6:76].

Abraham says, "*I love not those that set.*" Where is someone who has the attribute of Abraham so that he may say, "*I love not those that set*"? The secret here goes back to another celestial sphere, for there are spheres in the world of the spirits. Inside the world of the spirits there are suns, moons, and stars.

When someone goes beyond these images, he knows that all of them have a Creator and are undergoing annihilation. When the

image of the Companion cleaves forth from the World of
Inwardness, self-disclosure becomes manifest. Then he says, "*I have
turned my face to Him who originated the heavens and the earth*" [6:79].

And when I am ill, He heals me [26:80]. He ascribes the illness to
himself in order to teach us. *Our Lord, we have wronged ourselves*
[7:23]. In other words, "I am ill, and my health is indeed from
Him." This is the negation of self, the negation of selfhood. When
you have negated yourself, you have affirmed Him.* (308-9)

114.

Speaking before a knower of speech is discourtesy, unless by way
of offering. Thus, they take cash to an assayer: "Pick out the counterfeit." But, if the assayer is a lover and devotee of the speaker, or
his disciple, then everything of him that is ugly will appear beautiful to him, and his counterfeit will appear as genuine. *Your love for
a thing makes you blind and deaf.* He is in fact in love with the sweetness of his talking.

I answered thus: All lovers are not such that they see the bad as
good. There are lovers who see everything just as that thing is,
because they see it with the light of the Real, for *The believer sees
with the light of God.* They in fact would never fall in love with
faults. Thus he said, "*I love not those that set*" [6:76].

If a beauty is apt to disappear
    the Men will never fall in love with it. (160-61)

115.

You said that they don't listen to a lover who gives news and
bears witness, because it is characteristic of love to show faults as
excellence. *Your love for a thing makes you blind and deaf.* Can't it be
possible that someone be a lover and still have the faculty of vision
and discernment? They say, "By 'lover,' we mean someone who is
totally snatched away and overcome."

I said, "The possibility cannot be denied."

In this question, let's take the words of the theologians that there
are three propositions. One is necessary, like the world of the Real
and His attributes. The second is impossible, like bringing together

two contradictories. The third is permitted, since it has both faces. It is fitting to be, and it is fitting not to be. Whoever takes this sort will be delivered.

They say that the Garden out of which Adam fell was only a hill, an elevation, right on the earth. It is not the Garden promised to the believers, which they show to be on the top of the spheres.

I said, "You said that you are talking philosophy. Well, you yourself have founded philosophy!" (164-65)

116.

I wonder what these people think friendship with God is. That God who created the heavens, who created the earth, who made the universe appear—is His friendship gained so easily that you come in and sit before Him, you talk and you listen? Do you fancy this is a soup kitchen? You come in and you drink it down? Then you just leave? (236-37)

117.

Become estranged from people, little by little. God has no companionship with people, He is not attached to them. I don't know what one gains from them. From what can they free you? To what can they bring you near? After all, you have the conduct of the prophets. You're going in their tracks. The prophets didn't mix much. They were attached to God, even if outwardly people gathered around them.

The words of the prophets have interpretations. It may happen that they say, "Go!", and, in reality, that "Go" is "Don't go." (231)

118.

"I'm burning up! I don't have the capacity for this suffering."

The Presence says, "I keep you for the sake of just this."

He says, "O Lord, but I'm burning up! What do You want from this servant?"

He says, "Exactly this—that you burn."

This is that same story of breaking the pearl.* The beloved said, "So that you would say, 'Why did you break it?'" The wisdom in this weeping is that the ocean of mercy must come to a boil. Your weeping causes that. As long as the clouds of your heartache do not rise up, the ocean of mercy will not boil.

Pity will not move the mother to suckle her child
as long as the child stays silent. (624)

119.

The vizier said, "How can I break this pearl?"*

The king said, "You speak the truth, how can you smash it?" He kissed him on the eyes. With this movement of kissing he was searching for an intelligent man. With this test he was searching for an intelligent man.

King Mahmud gave the pearl to the chamberlain, and the chamberlain imitated the vizier, especially since he had seen the kiss and the praise in the case of the vizier. He said to the chamberlain, "Is this a good pearl?"

He said, "It's not just good!" Again, discourtesy. "Is it good? It is a hundred thousand times good." He exaggerated in praising the king, another discourtesy.

"Now break it."

"How can I break it? The vizier says that the king's whole kingdom does not have one-fourth the value of the pearl."

"Then, is it fitting for the treasury?"

"Yes, by God, it's fitting for the treasury."

He said, "You've done well." He gave him a robe, and then another robe, and he increased his salary. This also was a test to see if there was anyone who would appear.

The pearl went from hand to hand toward Ayaz. Inwardly, the king was saying, "My Ayaz!" He was trembling for him—"Let him not say that!" Then he would say, "Well, even if he does say it, he's beloved. Let him say whatever he wants."

The pearl reached that side, and on the other side a board was put so that no one would be next to Ayaz. The king reached out his hand to take the pearl, in fear lest Ayaz do the same as the others. Ayaz looked at the king—"Why are you trembling for me? Is Ayaz someone for whom you tremble?" Inwardly he was ripened, his heart was perfected, his reality trained in courtesy.

The sultan said to Ayaz, "O sultan, take the pearl"—no. Rather, "O servant, take it," but beneath his saying "servant" was more than a thousand "sultans." He was a thousand times happier that it be hidden. If he had said "sultan," he would have been troubled— "Go, you've thrown me out to auction!" He took the pearl.

He said, "Is it good?"

He said, "It's good." He added nothing to that.

He said, "Is it fine?"

"It's fine, by God." He added nothing more.

He said, "Break it."

He had earlier had a dream, and he had brought two stones, hidden in his sleeve. He struck the pearl with them and broke it to bits. Everyone began wailing and sighing.

He said, "What is this sighing? What is this wailing?"

Someone said, "You've broken that valuable pearl!"

He said, "Is the king's command more valuable, or the pearl?"

They all looked down. This time they all brought out a hundred thousand sighs from their hearts—"What have we done!"

The king commanded the captains of the executioners, "Take them all, from this side to that! Clean away these fools!"

Ayaz said, "O clement king! *Pardon is better.*"

Your image came to me one day in a dream
and let me drink the water of your union.
My lover stayed all night long
and left when the face of morning appeared.

My all is given to your all, my all is busy with your all.* (87-89)

120.

Ablution upon ablution is light upon light. Once inwardness is perfected, certain people let go of outwardness. Some think they are granted that, and some think they are not granted it. They say, "*Ablution upon ablution is light upon light.*" They are not fit for leadership. These others, however, are the support and refuge of the world's inhabitants.

There is no doubt that inner filth must be purified, because a dust-mote of inner filth does what a hundred thousand outer filths cannot do. Which water purifies that inner filth? Three or four goatskins full of the eyes' water—not just any water of the eyes, but the water of the eyes that comes forth from sincerity. After that, the scent of salvation and security will reach him. Tell him, "Sleep easy!" But how indeed can he sleep? Sleeping is one thing, dozing something else.

As for water of the eyes without that need, and prayer without need, those take only to the edge of the grave. From the edge of the grave he will go back with those who go back. What is with need comes out inside the grave. It rises up with him at the resurrection, and so on to paradise, and to the Presence of the Real. It keeps on going before him.

If he has this sort of wakefulness in the heart, let him sleep. If not, beware! It is sleep that is in the channel of the flood. Even if he's asleep, it will be easy. Someone will poke him on the side and he will wake up. If he doesn't, someone else will hit him in the head. If he still doesn't, they'll pull at his beard. They keep this up until he opens his eyes. When he wakes up, they'll show him the flood from afar. Fear of the flood will take away the pain from his beard, and he'll take to his feet. But if someone is a heavy sleeper, the enemy will have halfway cut his throat and he still will not open his eyes. When he does open his eyes, the rest will have been cut. (131–32)

121.

There was a man who used to be thrown by everyone with whom he would wrestle, even a Jew. One day, by God's decree, he threw someone. That poor fellow came there and, as it happened, he fell, never having fought. When he threw him, he jumped down on him and grabbed him by the throat: "I'm going to kill him."

"Why? What did he ever do to you? Whenever you used to wrestle, everyone threw you down. This poor fellow fell down. Why are you going to kill him?"

"No, I certainly will kill him."

"But why?"

He said, "Should I throw down someone once in my whole life, and then not kill him?"

They went before the king, because the king had shown favor to him. They said, "For God's sake, pull him back from that poor man's head."

He said, "Bring them."

They brought them. He said, "Take one hundred dinars and let him go."

He said, "Every member of this man's body is worth a thousand dinars. Now, how many members does he have?"

When man comes by way of need, his price will never appear.

Man has two attributes: One is need. Through this attribute he is hopeful and he looks forward to reaching the goal. The other attribute is being without need. What hope can you have from being without need?

What is the utmost end of need? Finding what has no needs. What is the utmost end of seeking? Finding what is sought. What is the utmost end of the sought? Finding the seeker.*

He said, "I'm an unbeliever and you're a Muslim. The Muslim is included in the unbeliever. Where in the world is there an unbeliever that I may prostrate myself before him and give him a hundred kisses? Tell me that you're an unbeliever, that I may kiss you." (142-43)

122.

You shall see your Lord. What is this *shall* here? Is it a *shall* that indicates expediting? Will you tell them?

Right now, where is someone who has arrived?

I say: It depends on what one understands from this. The "arrived one" is he who sees face-to-face. *Whosoever is blind in this world shall be blind in the afterworld* [17:72]. After all, He doesn't mean the one who is outwardly blind.

He must see face-to-face just as he sees with these eyes. Where does that put the one who boasts, "*So my heart may see my Lord?*"

Someone may arrive and not know that he has arrived. He reaches Aksaray, but he doesn't know that he's reached Aksaray. As long as he has not reached it, he's in fear and hope: When does he know that he has arrived or not arrived? He's in doubt, he has not reached certainty.

They say, "As long as we haven't seen that thing, we won't set out."

That thing says, "As long as they have not gone ahead and expended freely, I will not show them. As long as they are like this, and as long as they do not first act themselves, that will not be." (207)

123.

Bind yourself to being a warrior, not a general, for the general can't battle much. He must make no mistakes lest the army scatter. Let your generalship be your warriorhood. In the army be a warrior who can defeat ten of those generals with a finger. (206)

124.

O sincere seeker, have a happy heart, for He who makes hearts happy is busy with your work and with completing your work. *Each day He is upon some task* [55:29]. He is either the seeker in the work, or He is the sought in the work. Anyone who says He is other than these two is speaking foolishness and stupidity, though he does not see his own stupidity. Those who have the divine discernment—for *they see with the light of God*—know that in the view that subsists after the annihilation of all views, what he now sees as excellence and subtle vision will be stupidity and veiling.

Now, O sincere man, the Real—high indeed is He—is busy with your work, both outwardly and inwardly. It is all for you. You will lose nothing. This is specific, for *You will not will unless God wills* [81:29]. And *you will not will*, O Muhammad! Whatever you will is what We have willed. It is not the soul, not caprice.

Some say that this *you will not will* refers to the Companions and the Community: "You will not be able to will and to seek the path as long as I, who am God's deputy, do not will."

Only for the hand and heart of Muhammad
does the storehouse of secrets open and close. (97)

125.

It wasn't out of eagerness. He purposefully drank it hot to open up the pores, so that something there should pass out of him. Heaviness goes out through the pores. This is medicine.

Were it not for *from one Wise, Knowing* [27:6], what would happen to the work of the saints? Their work would not be set straight in forty thousand years. If they lived twenty lifetimes one after another, that would not be enough. (235)

THE GUIDANCE OF THE SHAYKH

126.

If you enter under the shadow of God, you will become secure from all coldness and all death. You will be described by God's attributes, and you will be aware of the Living, the Ever-standing. Death will see you from a distance and die. You will find the divine life. So, at first, quietly—lest anyone hear. This science will not be obtained in the madrasah. If you study six thousand years—six times the lifespan of Noah—it will not come to hand. A servant may study a hundred thousand, but that is not as much as breathing along with God for one day. (716)

127.

One day a scholar awoke, and everything he had of clothing and possessions had been taken away. He wandered and lamented, saying, "*I have let my life pass by in the law of divorce,* and I have thrown the Book of God behind my back. What will I answer my Lord when He asks me about the things in which I have wasted my life, how I have seen what I have seen, how I have heard what I have heard, and the objects upon which my heart has pondered?!*"

By *the Book of God* he does not mean this bound volume. He means the man who is the leader. It is he who is the Book of God—he is the verse, he is the surah. In that verse, what verses there are!

After all, that Jew learned the outward volume and the outward book. He was judge for a long time in Baghdad. He had gathered treasuries, and built underground rooms. He had chosen manly men with weapons and had prepared an ambush to overthrow the caliph and take possession of Baghdad. The story is long. The upshot is that the caliph became aware of his plots and informed of his secrets, and seized him. So, he had taken judgeship and the knowledge of the Koran to the degree that they had made him the judge of Baghdad, and inwardly he was a Jew and a dog.

So, we come to know that what will save you is the servant of God, not simply that written book. *He who follows the blackness [of the ink] has gone astray.*

The "Night of Qadr"* is hidden among the nights, and the servant of God is hidden among the pretenders. He is hidden because

of his contemptibleness, or rather, because of his extreme manifestness—just as the sun is hidden from the bat. He is sitting next to
him but is unaware of him, because the veil of love for this world
has made him *blind and deaf*.* For, when love for this world is strong,
it is a magnet that attracts this world. When it is weak, it attracts the
image of the beloved, which is this world. The image of the beloved
veils everything other than the beloved, unless mercy comes down,
for *Verily We sent it down in the Night of Qadr* [97:1].

In [the surah] *We sent it down* there are several verses.

[*Better*] *than a thousand new moons* [97:3]: He is brighter than a
thousand full moons, and he is hidden in the midst of the moons.
He is hidden because of extreme manifestness.

On the day when he becomes aware he shouts, *Alas for me, that
I neglected the side of God!* [39:56], the region of God. What an
incomparable side! What a region without region! (316–17)

128.

He who follows the blackness has gone astray. His whole body is
tongue, questions and answers, eloquence—but he knows nothing
of the world of the Real! (624)

129.

When this person says, "I have gained faith," the meaning is that
caprice has died and the soul has died. Dying is that darkness
should not return, that the tasting should be continuous. Why is it
not continuous?

To all this I said, "All right. I have taken the soul as dead so that
indeed it may slowly die. Now, this depends upon the companionship of someone. God has connected this to a cause."

So, it depends on this person who has come. There was a wall
from heaven to earth in front of your path. He kicked the wall and
knocked it over. He taught you how to knock over the walls that
are in front. Now, your work depends upon him if it is to be
finished. Only with his help will you arrive at God's attraction.

So, what use is satisfaction with God's decree?* You must be
satisfied with his work. You must be satisfied with everything he
says and does. You must do nothing such that the helper will take

back his help. You must do what will increase his help and what will add to his love and willingness. (745)

130.

What is the shaykh? Being. What is the disciple? Nonbeing.* Until the disciple becomes nonbeing, he is not a disciple. (739)

131.

When he falls into the ocean,* if he moves his hands and feet, the ocean will break him, even if he's a lion—unless he makes himself dead. The custom of the ocean is that, as long as someone is alive, it swallows him down until he is immersed and dies. When he is immersed and dies, it picks him up and becomes his carrier. Now, make yourself dead from the first, and go forth happily on top of the water.

If someone wants to look at a dead man walking on earth, let him look at Abu Bakr as-Siddiq. He grew up from the dark dustbin, and he resides in the company of subtle, spirit-increasing water.

That ocean is one of God's servants.

After all, if all of this hasn't happened to you, some of it has happened, and some of it has happened to other companions. If at this time it has not happened, it will happen in the future. (148)

132.

When the water passes the mouth and nose and head, then he is secure. As long as mouth and nose are above the water, he still goes by himself and lives through himself. When he is completely immersed in the water and his mouth and nose go down into the water, then they say that he is dead. Others say that he has come to life. Both speak the truth. That borrowed life has gone, and the abiding, subsistent life has come. (210)

133.

Moses said, "Who in the world knows more than I?"*

Joshua said, "You're being deceived, you're being deceived! There is someone in the world who has more knowledge than you."

He did not become angry, nor did he become heated toward

him. He just said, "Well, well. How can you say that?" This is because he was seeking.

Joshua was also a prophet, but he did not give rulings. At the time, it was Moses who gave the rulings. And I also say this for my own part: I also, were I to find a sought one, I would do the same. I would hold on to him as long as I could so that no veil could come over me.

[*Moses said to his page, "I will not give up until I reach the meeting place of the two seas,] though I go on for many years"* [18:60]. One account says forty years, another says forty thousand years, another eighty years, and still another says eighty thousand years. Very coldly, they tell this story of Moses being hot, of the fact that his heat was burning the heavens.

When he arrived at *the meeting place of the two seas*—according to the folk of the outward sense, it is near Antioch, or near Aleppo— [he saw Khizr]* performing the prayer on a mountain. According to one account, he was on a horse, and he was driving the steed across the water. He saw him from afar.

Now God praises him: [*Then they found] one of Our servants unto whom We had given mercy from Us*, and no one else had that; *and We had taught him knowledge from Us* [18:65], such that it could not be gained in any madrasah or khanaqah, nor from a teacher, a book, or by means of any created thing.

Now Joshua said, "I know the subtlety of Khizr's work. I did not have the capacity to be his companion that I should be able to be it this time. You will fall out with him such that you will never see him again." Then he went back.

Now the two of them remained. They spoke together. He was asking him about many things. Then he asked, "*Shall I follow you [so that you may teach me]?* [18:66] What do you command? Shall I have following?"

Look at the need of God's speaking-companion, who had already arrived at the Real!

Now I will tell you [unabbi'u] [18:78]. "I will awaken you." He is speaking to one who awakens people. *Nabi* ["prophet"] means "awakener." He was already awake to the Real, but he was awakening him to the reality of the Real. Let the rest of it be a debt on me. I will tell it another time.

When he asked him the second time, he answered him in wrath: *"Did I not say to you [that you could never bear with me patiently]?"* [18:75]. This was not egocentric wrath. How could God's servants have egocentric wrath? *We seek refuge in God!* That is God's wrath. One must guard against that.

He could not make the same excuse again. He said, *"If I question you on anything [after this, then be my companion no more] [18:76]."* Khizr clapped his hands and danced in joy: "Speak quickly, leave me alone, deliver me!"

Moses said, "If you had taken the wage for this." He said, *"This is separation [between me and you] [18:78].* Now there is distance between me and you."

Moses woke up. He saw the heart-taker gone, the candle dead, the saki asleep.

Happy the one who finds a servant [of God], keeps the story of Moses and Khizr before his heart, and makes him his own imam! (758-59)

134.

They asked someone, "Is your shaykh better, or Abu Yazid?"

He said, "My shaykh."

They said, "Is your shaykh better, or the Prophet—upon whom be peace?"

He said, "The shaykh."

They said, "Your shaykh, or God?"

He said, "It is from him that I found oneness and *tawhid.* I know nothing other than that oneness."

Who is it that declares the similarity of the One—him and his little prostration and his declaration of similarity! *We are two spirits dwelling in one body.** This is the declaration of similarity. But, the road to this declaration of similarity is long. There's a great deal of road. And from this declaration of similarity to the world of *tawhid* is extremely far. (685-86)

135.

I was speaking some words in a dream. The shaykh reiterated them for me one by one.

When someone does not consider the shaykh truthful, neither in act nor in word, this is precisely the cause of being cut off. I wonder what the motive is for not considering the shaykh truthful? He should put that motive in the palm of one hand, and what he hopes for from the shaykh in the palm of the other. He should see whether this is worth that. The shaykh has a world tremendously full of tasting and is utterly occupied. The disciple will not be occupied with such delight. How can conformity and kindness be greater than this?

This is like those ten Sufis. One of them fell in love with a Christian youth. He kept around him, in the church and elsewhere. The Christian found him out. He said, "Why are you keeping around me?" He recounted his state. The Christian youth said, "I dislike seeing other than the folk of my own creed from afar. How can you crave that I allow you to come near?"

He saw no escape. He quickly went and bid good-by to his companions. They said, "It's for the best!"

He told them the story and then said, "Now I am going to buy myself a [Christian] sash."

They said, "We will conform ourselves to you. Let's buy ten sashes, and bind them around our waists. After all, we are one soul in many bodies."

When the Christian youth saw them, he asked about them. They recounted the story to him: "Among us there is oneness."

A fire fell into the Christian youth's heart, and he tore off his sash. He said, "I am the slave of a people like this, who have such kindliness toward each other. I've never seen such kindliness among the folk of any religion."

The youth's father and relatives all came together and began to blame him: "Are you going to destroy your own religion because of spells cast by the Sufis?"

He said, "If you saw what I see, you would fall in love with them a hundred times more than I." (153–54)

136.

Someone became a plaintiff in a case. They wanted witnesses. He took ten Sufis. The judge said, "I want another witness."

He said, "Your honor, *Call in to witness two witnesses, men* [2:282]—I have brought ten."

He said, "These ten are all one witness, and if you bring a hundred thousand Sufis, they'll all be one." (272-73)

137.

They said to Khwarazmshah, "The people are calling out for help in this famine because bread is so expensive."

He said, "How so? How so?"

They said, "One maund of bread used to be one grain of silver, and now it's reached two drams of gold."

He said, "Hey, what are two drams of gold?"

They said, "Two drams are this many coppers."

He said, "Fie, fie. What kind of stinginess is this? Aren't you ashamed?"

He thought it was cheap. He would have thought it was expensive if they had said that they'll give you a full stomach's worth of food for your kingdom. Then he would have been frightened. He would have said, "After filling my stomach once, where would I find another kingdom? A lifetime was necessary to gain this one."

Now, in religion it's the same way. An attribute or a station appears terrifying to the people, but for that one person it's easy. The heavens can't pull back his bow. *Surely We offered the trust** [*to the heavens and the earth and the mountains*] [33:72]. It was said that the heavens and the earths can't put up with the trust of our work, for their gaze is not upon [God's] success-giving. Otherwise, they would say, "Although the bow is hard, when we pick it up, there is someone behind us who pulls it." That strength of the gaze and of trusting in God belongs to Muhammad and the Muhammadans. (230)

138.

Some go backwards with the intention of going forward and jumping over the stream. If someone goes backwards with that intention, that's good. But, if he goes backwards with another

intention, then he will be abandoned. And of course, the water of
this stream has to be passed over, both by unbelievers and Muslims.
If you remain on this side, any forbidden act will bring you low.
But on that side, no forbidden act can hang on to you. On that
side of the stream, you will have strength, and strengths will come
to you, and assistance. Now, even if you go very far back, if the goal
is to jump to that side of the stream, none of your members should
be in pain because of the length of the road. It is enough that your
two feet land on the other side of the stream. If, however, one of
your feet falls in the water, the water is swift and will pull you
under. (106–7)

139.

He asked, "Is variegation that sometimes we are busy with acts
of obedience, and sometimes busy with food and drink? The former would be the discipline of the soul, and the latter the nurturing of the soul."

He said, "Didn't the prophets and saints have that? However, both
in the state of obedience and in the state of eating the prophets and
saints were nurturing the spirit, not the soul. In war, retreating is
counted like charging—there's no contradiction. But don't fancy
yourself as equal to them. If you were equal to them in acts and
worship, you would be equal to them in states and unveiling." (163)

140.

All those birds went to serve the Simurgh.* There were seven
oceans before them on the path. Some died from cold, others fell
down at the smell of the ocean. From all of them, only two birds
remained. They displayed their souls: "All of them fell back down,
but we will reach the Simurgh."

As soon as they saw the Simurgh, two drops of blood fell from its
beak, and they died. After all, this Simurgh dwells on the other side
of Mount Qaf. As for flying to that side, God knows how far it is.
All those birds gave up their souls to circle around Mount Qaf.

He claims to undergo states. If, in his whole life, the scent of one
state had reached him, his state would have been changed. (213)

141.

In a day whose measure is fifty thousand years* [70:4]. You don't understand the symbols of the Koran. If you die, according to the outward meaning, fifty thousand years are needed before you catch the scent of paradise.

If you think about what the world of the prophets has to do with the saints, you will become perplexed. You'll fall. Rather, clap your hands and move your feet from there.

When someone comes toward Me by a fathom. From this fathom to that fathom, this span to that span, this knee to that knee,* there are differences. *Two strides, and he arrived.* You do not have the Muhammadan stride. In you, Pharaoh has stuck up his head. Moses comes and drives him away. Again Pharaoh comes, and Moses goes. This is proof of variegation. How long will that be? Take Moses the way he is, so that Pharaoh may not come again. Variegation doesn't count in this work.

Surely those who say, "Our lord is God," then stand firm [41:30]. They say already in this world what the heedless will say in that world: "Do we not have a God?" They stand firm in that, without variegation. How could they be brought to undergo the resurrection? As soon as they reach the edge of the grave, they will see a hundred thousand rays of light. Where is *the angel of death* [32:11]? For them it is *the angel of life.* Where's the grave? They are delivered from the grave and the prison. *This world is the prison of the believer.*

Suppose someone is told, "As soon as you come out of this prison, you will be the companion of the sultan. You will go on the throne next to him and sit there forever."

He'll say, "Grab me by the throat and squeeze so that I may be delivered."

So *wish for death* [2:94], if you are sincere.

If they bring them to the resurrection, how can the resurrection remain? That is the day of the unveiling of the secrets.* Their secret is God. When God becomes manifest, how can the resurrection remain? They are fastened by chains of light so that they may not undergo the resurrection.

Whatever should be done, they do to the people. The paradise-dwellers are taken to paradise, the hell-dwellers to hell.

They tear apart the chains so as to enter the resurrection. Again, chains of light are fastened to them, till that time comes to an end. (130-31)

<h3 style="text-align:center">142.</h3>

This world is bad—but, only for someone who does not know what this world is. When he knows what this world is, then for him there is no "this world."

He asks, "What is this world?"

He says, "Other than the afterworld."

He says, "What is the afterworld?"

He says, "Tomorrow."

He says, "What is tomorrow?"

Expression is terribly narrow. Language is narrow. All these struggles are so that you may be released from language, for it is narrow. They go into the world of the attributes, the pure attributes of the Real. Strange, what the theologians say! "The attributes are the same as the Essence, or other than the Essence." They agree on this. No, they don't, because the world is variegated. One-colored words don't come out.

He was asking about that dervish who went on a pilgrimage to the sage, Sana'i, and then came back. "What did that variegated one say?"

The dervish threw down his head.

He said, "The worldlings are variegated—unless there be someone who is pure from these variegations and little by little goes toward his own house. In him there's none. Otherwise, the world is extremely variegated—that Jew, that Christian, that infidel." (125-26)

<h3 style="text-align:center">143.</h3>

The Messenger of God—God bless him and give him peace—said, "*When someone devotes himself purely to God for forty days, the springs of wisdom will come forth from his heart to his tongue.*" He was explaining this to his Companions. One of them busied himself with worship for forty days. Afterwards, he complained to Muhammad: "O Messenger of God! The companion so-and-so underwent states. His glance and his words acquired a different color. In explaining about him you said, '*When someone devotes him-self purely....*' I went and spent forty days and strived as much as I could. *God does not burden a soul save to its capacity* [2:286]. And your words are not contradicted."

The Messenger answered, "I said *devotes himself purely*. The stip-ulation is pure devotion. It should be purely for the sake of God, not for any other wish or purpose. You worshiped out of craving that those marvelous words should appear from you, just as you saw that they appeared from that companion, and you wished for that." (187–88)

144.

Forty days doesn't give benefit to everyone. It wants a man who is prepared, whose preparedness has been perfected, so that *forty days* may be the key that opens his heart. Otherwise, a hundred thousand days will have no benefit. (706)

145.

God's speaking-companion* said *Show me* [7:143]. Since he knew that this belongs to the Muhammadans, he asked, "*O God, make me one of the community of Muhammad!*" This is what he meant by *Show me: Make me one of the community of Muhammad*. When he saw that the radiance of manliness fell on that mountain, and the mountain was smashed, he said, "That's not my work, but *Make me one of the community of Muhammad*."

It was said, "Now go for a few days in the service of Khizr." Khizr also says "*Make me one of the community of Muhammad.*" There is another light that plunders Moses and Khizr. If you look at Jesus, you'll see him perplexed in that light. If you look at Moses, you'll see him transfixed by that light. Muhammad has a light that over-comes all lights.

After all, those forty-day seclusions and those invocations—are they really the following of Muhammad? Yes, Moses had received the instruction *forty nights* [2:51]. What then is the following of Muhammad that Moses did not dare to ask for it? Rather, he said, "Make me one of his fellow riders." (284)

146.

They said, "You have given all the scholars a bad name with this *sama*."

I said, "Didn't you know that without them, good and bad and unbeliever and Muslim do not become manifest?"

He says, "You reached God by dancing."

He said, "You try dancing too, you'll reach God. *Two strides and he arrived*." (214)

147.

The dance of the men of God is subtle and weightless. You'd say they're a leaf floating on top of the water. Inside, like a mountain and a hundred thousand mountains—but outside, like straw. (623)

148.

There was a *sama*. The minstrel was subtle and sweet-voiced and the Sufis limpid-hearted, but it just didn't take. The shaykh said, "Look and see if there are any others amidst us Sufis."

They looked and said, "There's no one."

He told them to search the shoes. They said, "Yes, there are some strange shoes."

He said, "Put those shoes outside the khanaqah."

They put them outside, and immediately the *sama* took hold. (180)

149.

The tambour-player brought out his tambour: "Now, before the food arrives, you are very generous, and the few dirhems that I have to spend come from playing the tambour." The shoes began to fly. He said, "I'm abandoning your food, your hospitality, and you. Give me my tambour, you're keeping me from my work."

They said, "This is a mosque."

He said, "Oh! It's many days that I haven't performed an ablution. Quick, give me the tambour so that I can go." (629-30)

150.

The vicegerent said, "The shaykh has prohibited *sama*." A knot appeared inside the dervish and he became ill. They brought a skillful physician and he took his pulse. He didn't see the causes that had brought him to this. The dervish died. The physician opened up his grave and his chest and brought out the knot. It was like an agate. At a time of exigency, he sold it. It passed from hand to hand until it reached the vicegerent, and he had it set in a ring that he kept on his finger.

One day during *sama* he looked down and saw that his clothing was stained with blood. When he investigated, he found no wound. He put his hand on his ring and saw that the stone had melted. He summoned those who had sold it until he reached the physician, and the physician told the story.

> When you see drops of blood making a path,
>   follow them and they'll lead to my eyes.*

How can the corporeal person do the *sama*? His *sama* is eating. He eats through his soul. He has become only feeding. *They enjoy themselves and feed as the cattle feed* [47:12]. You'd think that he was created for that and given existence for that. If someone found the scent of meaning, how could he eat anything? (80)

151.

Once, in the *sama* with the shaykh, a disciple of Shaykh Shihab ad-Din recited a verse. The shaykh said, "May they behead you and cut out your tongue! Who would have the gall to recite a verse here? Where God has disclosed Himself and thrown off the curtain, there is only seeing. What place is this for the tongue? Whoever has not gone into a state should leave. He has disgraced himself openly. He's become like a house full of defilement. Like a black man among beautiful women—naked, disgraced, full of caprice and appetite!"

All at once in my breast I saw a candle, a brightness—like a sun rising from my breast. I put my head down like this. When the shaykh saw that my turban had fallen off, he took off his own turban. You would say that I was looking into myself. Because of the brightness, I was seeing all my own veins, fat, bones, arteries, and entrails. When I was seeing that, I didn't see anything else. (649-50)

Avoiding Caprice

152.

Islam and faith are opposition to caprice. Unbelief is conformity with caprice. When someone gains faith, this means that he has made a covenant not to conform to caprice.

The other one says, "That's not my work. I can't do that. I'll pay the tribute* and stay alive." The Prophet also was satisfied. He accepted that and gave them safe-conduct. He said, "*When someone torments a zimmi,* *it is as if he has tormented me—and a possessor of a covenant in a covenant.*"

This one says, "I'm a believer, I'm disgusted with caprice." But he isn't. He wants neither to pay the tribute nor to abandon caprice. He says, "I'm a believer," but he's not a believer. He says, "I'm peace," but he's not peace. He says, "I'm a companion and a subject," but he's not. He says, "I'm white," but he's not, he's black. He says, "I'm a falcon." He's a crow. (607)

153.

Whoever lives as he sees fit will not die as he sees fit.

Did you see the bee that went around aimlessly? Wherever its opinion took it, it sat down. The butcher drove it back from the meat several times, but it didn't stay away. The third time, he lifted up the cleaver and cut off its head. It was rolling and twisting on the ground. The butcher said, "Didn't I tell you not to sit just anywhere?"

And that was a honey bee, which sits by the command, "*Eat from all the fruits*" [16:69]. This is why, whenever it eats something, *within it is healing for the people* [16:69]. (267)

154.

"Drunkenness" is of four sorts and four levels: First is the drunkenness of caprice. Deliverance from it is immensely difficult. Only a fast-going traveler will pass beyond the drunkenness of caprice.

After this there is the drunkenness of the spiritual world. He has not yet seen the spirit, but he has an immense drunkenness. He does not look upon the shaykhs, nor even the prophets. When he begins to speak, nothing of the Koran and the Hadith comes to him. He considers it shameful to speak of transmitted knowledge, unless by way of making understood. Passing beyond the second level is extremely difficult and arduous—unless the dear servant of the Real, God's unique one, should be sent to him so that he may see the reality of the spirit and reach God's road.

The drunkenness of God's road is the third level. It is an immense drunkenness, but it is linked with stillness, for God has brought him out of what he had fancied it to be.

After this is the fourth level—drunkenness in God. That is perfection. After that is sobriety. (700)

155.

Forgetfulness is of two sorts. One pertains to this world, because it's standing forth. This world makes you forget the afterworld. Another cause of forgetfulness is being busy with the afterworld, such that someone forgets even himself. In his hand this world is like a mouse in the hand of a cat. Because of being a companion of God's servant, he has become what no shaykh sitting thirty years on a prayer-carpet has ever become.

A third cause of forgetfulness is love for God, so he forgets this world and the afterworld. This is the level of Mawlana. *This world is forbidden to the folk of the afterworld, the afterworld is forbidden to the folk of this world, and both this world and the afterworld are forbidden to the folk of God.* That is the meaning of this—that is, that he should forget. The reason is that Mawlana is drunk in love, but he has no sobriety in love.

As for me, I'm drunk in love, but I'm sober in love. In my drunkenness I don't forget like that. How could this world have the gall to veil me? Or—to be veiled from me? (78-79)

156.

As for the explanation of "caprice": Know that by "caprice" I do not mean gold, women, and this world. Rather, [a person of caprice] does not dare to circle around this world, fearful lest the drunkenness of caprice should be lessened. Most monks have this drunkenness of caprice, and it is of such minds that they speak.

Imad and those like him, having become perfect in the drunkenness of caprice, caught a scent of the drunkenness of the spirit.

Awhad was closer to the completion of caprice. Pharaoh's sorcerers were complete in caprice, so the scent of the spirit reached them. Pharaoh was not complete. He was a logician* and well-born, but there was an excellence in the sorcerers that he did not have. Sayyid had the scent of the spirit and the drunkenness of the spirit more than Mawlana. His sciences were many, but he had no attachment to them.

Shaykh Abu Bakr* had the drunkenness from God, but he did not have the sobriety that comes after this drunkenness. I know this on the basis of knowledge. (700-1)

157.

These leaders also do not speak correctly about the outward meaning of the Koran, because that outward meaning can be known and seen only through the light of faith, not through the fire of caprice. If they had the light of faith, how could they pay out several thousand and take judgeships and posts? Does anyone give a skirt full of gold to buy a serpent from a serpent-catcher? I don't mean the water snake that doesn't have any poison, I mean the mountain snake that is full of poison. When someone flees from judgeships and posts—if he flees for God's sake and not for some other reason—that's from the light of faith. When he becomes a serpent-knower, he'll be a Companion-knower.*

The Koran-bride will throw off her veil
    when she sees the dominion of faith cut off from strife.*

The man who said that—I marvel how disengaged he was from himself! His speech is God's speech. God's speech is perfect, it's complete.

When grapes have not become ripe, they're kept between clouds and sun lest they burn. Again, the sun shows its face—lest they become withered. And so on until they're perfect. After that, there's no harm from the sun. Before they become sweet, the owner of the garden fears that cold will come. Once they're perfect in sweetness, they're nurtured even under snow.

The man who reaches this perfection is drowned in the light of God and drunk in the pleasure of the Real. He is not fit to be a guide, for he is drunk. How can he make someone else sober? Beyond this drunkenness there is a another sobriety, as I explained. When a man reaches that sobriety, his gentleness takes precedence over his severity. But the one who is drunk has not reached that sobriety, and his gentleness is equal to his severity. When someone's gentleness has become predominant, he is fit to be a guide. God's gentleness is equal to His severity. However, His Essence is all gentleness, so gentleness predominates.

The Prophet had revelation from Gabriel, and he also had revelation in the heart. The saint has only the latter.* (146-47)

158.

Now, grapes have a limit before which cold will harm them. After that, there's no fear. After that, they're nurtured under snow.

At first the fish went toward the water. Now, wherever the fish goes, water goes.*

Meat, wine, and melon have the characteristic that if the body is healthy, they aid the health, and if the body is ill, they aid the illness. That's why they tell a sick person to avoid meat. (644)

159.

The treatise of Muhammad* the Messenger of God would not profit me. I must have my own treatise. If I were to read a thousand treatises, I'd become darker.

They don't know the secrets of God's saints and they study their treatises. Everyone stirs up his own imagination, then makes accusations against the speaker of the words. They never accuse themselves. They don't say, "There's no mistake in those words—it's in our ignorance and imaginings!"

When you write metrical words next to each other, why does this make you happy? You should know that happiness is in the companions' togetherness, that they should live agreeably next to each other and display beauty. As for those who fall apart, caprice comes between them, and their light goes away.

When you put something in honey, it stays fresh and sweet, because the air of caprice does not find its way into it. If the pores become closed, it becomes turbid. (270-71)

160.

With all this, when a disciple has not become perfect so as to be secure from caprice, it is not in his best interest for him to be away from the shaykh, because a cold breath can turn him cold all at once. That is a mortal poison, breathed out by dragons, and it turns everything it touches black. But, when he becomes perfect, being absent from the shaykh does not harm him.

And glorify Him through the long night [76:26]. In other words, when a veil comes between the disciple and the shaykh, that is night. When darkness comes upon you, at that time you must glorify Him with seriousness. You must try to make that curtain disappear. The more darkness increases and the more the shaykh becomes disliked by you, the more you must strive in his service. Do not grieve and do not despair if the darkness becomes long, because *through the long night*. When the darkness becomes long, after that the brightness will be long. *When someone's debt is heavy, his affliction will be heavy, and when someone's debt is light, his affliction will be light.*

*The high places will be earned in the measure of diligence** because, when the veil has not come, this brings the self's tasting and light into movement, for, whenever someone finds, that is the influence of *I blew into him of My spirit* [15:29]. It is that which does the work. For a darkness may come in, a veil and an estrangement, such that he becomes unaware of the state of the companion. The soul begins to take control, and it starts to make interpretations,* because it is not able to breathe in the midst of that love and brightness. As long as the soul keeps on interpreting, make yourself a fool, because *Most of the folk of the Garden are fools.*

The majority of the denizens of hell are from among these clever people, these philosophers, these knowledgeable people, the ones for whom cleverness has become a veil. From everything they imagine, ten more imaginings arise, like the offspring of Gog.

Sometimes he says, "There is no road." Sometimes he says, "If there is, it's long." Yes, the road is long, but when you go, extreme happiness does not let you see the length of the road. Such is *The Garden is surrounded by detestable things.** All around the garden of paradise there are fields of brambles. But, the scent, which comes forth in welcome and gives news of the beloveds to the lovers, makes those bramble fields pleasant.

All around the bramble field of hell the road is roses and sweet herbs. But, the scent of hell that comes out makes that pleasant road unpleasant.

If I were to explain the pleasantness of this road, no one could bear it. (144-46)

161.

How can the folk of war be made the confidant of secrets? Abandon war and opposition! The stuff of war is caprice. Wherever you see war, it is because of following caprice.

If someone has tied himself to peace, would he carry on like that? Would he speak like that? He would speak and act such that, if it were to reach the ears of that person, he would wish for peace. He would say, "I am terribly ashamed of my own acts and words. They were the goadings of Satan, the deception of Satan. O Lord, what bad I did! What was it that I did! What an unfortunate whispering doubt—words came from me and an act came from me that troubled his mind!" His regret will throw gentle words into his heart, and his gentle behavior will let him know that those gentle words are seeking peace.

> Your teacher is love—when you get there
>> he'll tell you in the tongue of your state what to do.*

"Should I not tell you about a lawful sorcery through which you will enslave free men to you without dirhems and dinars?"
They said, "Tell us, O Messenger of God."
He said, "Gentle acts and soft words." (608-9)

162.

The trial of Abraham* is an account of the angels' jealousy—no, not the jealousy of envy and denial, or else they would be Iblis. Rather, "This is strange. We are substances of light. How is it possible for corporeal feet to pass beyond us in intimate friendship?"

He said, "He has abandoned caprice."

They said, "But he has all the causes of caprice, such as flocks and possessions."

He said, "He is free and pure of that."

They said, "*We have faith and we attest*. But this is strange."

He said, "Test him so that it may be apparent. In the test, another secret will be unveiled, and that is what makes him pass beyond you. Also, some of the secret of *Surely I know what you do not know* [2:30] will be unveiled to you. Gabriel, hide beyond a rock and say, 'Glorified! Holy!'"

Abraham heard. He looked, but he did not see the form of anyone. He said, "Say it once more, and all these sheep will belong to you."

He said it once more and came out from behind the rock. He said, "I am Gabriel. I don't require sheep."

He said, "I'm not a Sufi who'd come back to what he's left."

Through this action, some of the angels knew the state of Abraham. They knew that *a little indicates much*. Some still did not know. They said, "The business of possessions is easy. Now he needs to be tested with his children." (129)

163.

"A little bit indicates much." In other words, the utterance is little, but the meaning is much. For example, a sack of sugar is placed over there. They bring a piece of it. The little bit indicates much. A little bit of a man's truthfulness indicates much, and a little bit of his crookedness and hypocrisy indicates much. (122)

164.

Someone said, "Those who were moved were twisting in their state within themselves."

I replied: "Being moved" is of two sorts. If someone is tortured, he also moves. He's moving because of the whack of the stick. Someone else moves in tulips, sweet herbs, and narcissus. Don't go after every movement.

The same thing happened to the moth with the candle—
he went for the light but fell in the fire.

Since that one is fiery and his movement comes from fire, he thinks the same of all God's servants.

Whenever he saw that someone was bad
    he was looking from the circle of his own existence.*

He didn't know that the business of the other is backwards. He went for the fire and fell in the light. Don't look at him with those eyes, or you'll lose him. (92-93)

165.

When he speaks ill of God he is speaking ill of himself. How can he upset God? He is upsetting himself. How can words like this come out of their mouths? Don't they know God? Sana'i says,

O you whose gods torment God!* (701)

166.

Whenever something good is said about someone to you, or you are asked about the good of someone, you are being requested to do good. In the same way, when something bad is said about someone, know this: God is taking an account of your good and evil. You should abstain.

Thus, in Nishapur, when they want to straighten out a boy, they say to him, "What do you say about the boy so-and-so. Does he get along well with us? Does he have a good nature?"

If the boy says that he has a good nature and is not crooked, then he himself is subdued. But, if not, and he says that he is far from these things, then they say, "So, what is it with you?"

Sometimes someone becomes a Muslim inside when he hears a sermon, but then, when he comes out, he hardens, like tin that you bring out of fire. Another one also does not soften during the sermon. He can be softened with something else, with hard suffering. Still another becomes soft with something else. In the same way, in sensory things, each thing can be softened with the right tool. (107-8)

167.

Whenever anyone tells you something bad about one of your friends—whether the speaker be internal or external—saying that your friend is envious of you, know that the envious one is the speaker, and he is boiling out of envy.

Surmari said, "Who is Iblis?"

I said, "You, for right now I am immersed in Idris. If you're not Iblis, then why aren't you also immersed in Idris? And if you have a trace of Idris, then why this concern for Iblis? If you had said, 'Who is Gabriel?', I would have said 'You.'"

In the same way, someone asked, "During the prayer, if the imam does not keep his eyes on the place of prostration and looks left and right, is his prayer defective?"

He was given the answer, "The prayer of both is defective."

He said, "I was asking about the prayer of the imam. Are both the same?"

He was answered, "One is the imam, who looks around scatteredly and disturbs presence, and the other is the follower, who has become the guardian of and watcher over the imam's eyes and does not look in front of himself."

If anyone tells you that so-and-so praised you, say, "You're praising me, and you're making him the pretext." If anyone tells you that so-and-so called you bad names, say, "You're calling me bad names, and you're making him the pretext. He may not have said that, or he may have said it in another meaning."

If he says to you, "He called you envious," say, "Envy has two meanings. One is the envy that takes to paradise, the envy that warms people up in the path of good: 'Why should I be less than he in virtue?' Lady Kirra is also envious, and so is Mawlana. This is the envy that takes to paradise."

All day, my words are for the sake of this envy. But there is also the envy that takes to hell: "I came to serve him, and he was envious of me so that I would be denied and held back from something." (314-15)

168.

You have obstacles. Possessions are the kiblah of most people. The travelers have sacrificed that. For the worshiper of this world, one copper is more precious than his sweet soul.

You say, "But doesn't he have a soul?" If he did have a soul, possessions would not be more precious to him than it. By God, for the worshiper of this world, one copper is the kiblah. (128-29)

169.

Someone was complaining about the folk of this world.

It was said to him, "This world is a game and a frolic in the eyes of men. But in the eyes of children, it's not a game, it's incumbent. If you can't tolerate playing and frolicking, don't play. If you can, then play, drink, and laugh. The savor of playing is in laughter, not weeping." (312-13)

170.

Galen admitted only this world.* He had no news of that world. He said, "If I didn't die, and they placed me in a mule's stomach so that I could gaze on this world by way of its backside, that would make me happier than to die."

That's like the Kurd whose son came back looking sad. He said, "You're dying. Why are you sad?"

He said, "I killed a young man. I saw that he had a belt, and I fancied that it was gold. There was only one-sixth of a coin."

The father jumped up, slapped him hard in the face two or three times, and nearly killed him—"You whoring catamite! Why didn't you kill six of them for the whole dinar?"

Captains of ships are the same way. When they see that the ship is heavy, they look around to see who is fat, tie his hands behind his back, and throw him overboard. A cry goes up, "What was that noise?"

They say, "Nothing, the wind knocked a plank overboard." (237)

171.

I arrived among the blood-letters,* and this thought came to my mind: What a fine bunch of heedless people! A sun has come up, beginningless and endless. Indeed, what is this "beginningless and endless"? These are two attributes that appeared yesterday. They named the head "beginningless" and the tail "endless." What do beginningless and endless have to do with that place! A sun has come up, filling the whole world with light. What place is this for a "sun"! And all these people are in darkness. They have no awareness of that whatsoever. (223)

THE COMPANION OF THE HEART

172.

Nothing kills the soul that commands to evil like seeing the beauty of the heart. At once its members become feeble.

This is like a forceful king who has made someone helpless. They give him a bit of poison in something. His hands and feet become feeble, and all of his forcefulness is lost. (690-91)

173.

God says, "*Neither My heaven nor My earth embraces Me, but the heart of my believing servant does embrace Me.*" Anyone who says that the heart is this piece of meat is more of an unbeliever and worse than a Christian. He is worse than the one who says that Jesus is the son of God. (267)

174.

Whenever you see someone who has a spacious character and disposition, speaking broad and capacious words, and supplicating for the whole world, such that his words open up your heart, and you forget this world and its narrowness—not like the open-natured one who speaks unbelief and makes you laugh, but rather such that he speaks of nothing but *tawhid*, then, like Siraj ad-Din, tears will come to you on the outside, but inwardly you will be laughing. Such a person is an angel and a paradise-being. But, when you see constriction, narrowness, and coldness in someone and in his talk and you become cold from his talk, just as you had become warm from the talk of others, and now you do not find that warmth because of his cold, he is a satan and a hell-being.

Now, someone who has become aware of this secret and puts it into practice will pay no attention to a hundred thousand shaykhs. Why should he worry about death? Why should he pay attention to his head? An animal lives through its head, a man lives through his secret heart. When someone lives through his head, *No, they are further astray* [7:179]. When someone lives through his secret heart, *We honored* [17:70]. I mean, how can the secret heart fit in the head? If it won't fit here, what use is the head? (713-14)

175.

The son-in-law of Badr Zarir said, "Let's go to Shams ad-Din."

The son-in-law of Shihab ad-Din, the son of Warakani, said, "That's impossible, Jalal ad-Din is preaching."

These words are correct. Who knows the words of God and the tongue of God? The servant of God. Become the servant of God so that you may know the tongue and words of God. I do not say that you will become God. I do not utter unbelief.

After all, the various sorts of plants, animals, and inanimate things, and the subtleties like the spheres, are all within man. But what is in man is not in them, for that is in fact the reality of the macrocosm. After all, God says, *"Neither My heaven nor My earth embraces Me, but the heart of My believing servant does embrace Me."* (676-77)

176.

One must not be the companion of nature, one must be the companion of the heart. Seek for the heart, not nature. And what's the place of the heart? The heart is a mask. He is the companion of God. Out of jealousy they say "companion of the heart."

Doesn't the heart flourish when the ray of the Real's majesty comes, and when it's absent, the opposite? However, it becomes like this so many times that the heart is lost and melts. As much as the heart breaks and is removed from the midst, God remains.

He made allusion to this to David. When David asked the Presence, *Where should I seek You?*, He said, *Neither My heaven nor My earth embraces Me, but the heart of my believing servant does embrace Me.* These are His words, *I am with those whose hearts are broken for Me.*

When you say "companion of the heart," say *those whose hearts are broken.*

One must have the breaking of the heart. When the light of the Real takes you to the Real, then you will see the light of His majesty, for *No one knows them other than I.* (283-84)

177.

Two people are wrestling or battling. Of those two, God is with the one who is overcome and broken, not with the one who overcomes, for *I am with the broken.* (205)

178.

[*The station of Abraham:*] *and he who enters into it is secure* [3:97]. There is no doubt that this is the attribute of the heart. [*Have they not seen that We have appointed a sanctuary secure,*] *while all around them the people are snatched away?* [29:67]. Outside the sanctuary of the heart are whispering doubts, fears, and dangers, for *he whispers in the breasts of men* [114:5]—a hundred thousand times he whispers, frightens, and terrifies. But in the midst of the fire he remains like Abraham in the nurturing of the Real and the perfection of power. In the same way, He nurtured Moses at the hand of the enemy. (613)

179.

It is as if the resurrection has come and the Unseen has become visible. By God, the Unseen is visible and the veil has been lifted— but for that person whose eyes are open. (732)

180.

The vision of the Real for the folk of vision is a ray of manliness. Now, come in! Come in! Let God see Himself and see what happens. He looks upon Himself, He looks from the servant. Moses became selfless in that ray.* (227)

181.

What harm reaches a dervish from the sourness of the creatures? He takes the whole world as an ocean. How can it harm a duck? (90)

182.

He came, "Oh, the Tatars have arrived! A bad event!"
I said, "Aren't you ashamed? You've been claiming to be a duck for some time now. You tremble like this because of a storm?"

A duck seeking a ship would be surprising!* (269)

183.

A disciple entered in and said to the shaykh, "I've come like a rogue."
The shaykh said, "*God willing*, He will take you and me to the station of being a rogue."

Happy the one whose eyes sleep but whose heart does not sleep! Woe on the one whose eyes do not sleep but whose heart does sleep!

The doorway of the heart opened. Since there was crowding, someone had unintentionally banged against the door. Guard over it now so that it doesn't shut. When the door is opened, then you will see whoever passes by whether you want to or not. When it is shut, you will hear their voices and you will find a taste. But how can this be compared to that?

When the dust settles you will see
if you're riding a horse or a jackass.

Several times the dust has cleared, and I saw that I'm riding an Arabian stallion.

They don't say "*you will see*" to just anyone. How could it be correct to say it to everyone? It is not correct to say to a man blind from birth, "*you will see.*" They say it to someone when only a little bit of his existence is left, and the rest has all become spirit. In other words, "Come out of this dust of existence!" (265-66)

184.

Now, concerning the meaning of *When poverty is complete, he is God*, people have spoken a thousand inanities. It means that when poverty is complete, God is seen plainly. You find and you see— not that you become God. *When poverty is complete, you find God.* Otherwise, it's unbelief.

He said, "Maybe it doesn't mean that."

He said, "Then what is the difference between you and the Christian? After all, Jesus was subtler than Hallaj, Abu Yazid, or others. So why do you blame him for saying that Jesus is God? You say the same sort of thing. No, the meaning is *When poverty is complete, you find God.*"

In other words: When someone's soul dies and when his satan dies, when he is purified of blameworthy character traits, he arrives at God. God forbid! Rather, he arrives at the path of God. Otherwise, he has strayed from the path of God and the soul is still alive, the satan is still alive. If he does not distinguish between the light of God's path and the light of God, he is in

darkness and blindness. "Surely God has seven hundred veils of light," or
"seven hundred thousand veils of light. Were one of the veils removed, this
world and everything within it would be incinerated." Little by little you
pass beyond those veils until you arrive at the light of the Essence, at a light
that grows up from the Essence.

"Ablution upon ablution is light upon light." In other words, when one
makes an ablution on top of the ablution that is innate to the tempera-
ment, that is light upon light. It is not that someone should make the ablu-
tion twice. (732-33)

185.

Words are for the other. If they're not for the other, of what use
are they? As you see, the call of the prophets is for the other. If it
were not for the other, what was all this conversation about? When
unification and presence are established, how can you see conversation? Yes, there is talk, but without letters and sound. And, at the
moment when there is that talk, there is separation, not union, for
in union there is no room for talk, whether it is without letters and
sounds or with letters and sounds.

Yes, the bride talks with the groom. But, at the moment of pene-
tration, there's no room for talk. If there is talk in that state, the companionship provides no enjoyment. If you talk at that moment, it's
because the exercise of appetite is without eagerness and fulfillment.
If there is eagerness from the two sides, there's no room for talk.

When two companions meet, there is either senselessness, or
immersion in one another. Yes, from the midst of that immersion
there is a sobriety that gives you awareness of the work of the
world. The description of that awareness is a meaning that has
already been talked about. *And God knows better.* (770-71)

186.

These words that Mawlana wrote in the letter are motivating,
they're stimulating. If there were a stone or a stony object, it would
move inside itself.

The Prophet said, *In the days of your era your Lord has inblowings, so
expose yourself to them!* It comes to me that you should interpret this.

The meaning seems to be that these *inblowings* belong to the soul of one of the servants brought near to God who has the "alchemy of felicity"—not that book.* By God, this is neither alchemy nor felicity, for if you put one atom of this alchemy on a hundred million rooms full of copper, it would become pure gold.

He said, "So which is the inblowing of that man?"

Last night a shaykh told me in a dream
    that "I" and "we"* are the blight of love's path.
I said to him, "Which are 'I' and 'we'?
    It's you who solve all these problems."
He said, "Whatever is not the Real Himself
    is all 'I,' 'we,' and plain error."

"Speech" is an attribute. When He comes into speech, He veils himself so that the words may reach the creatures. As long as He does not enter into the veil, how can He convey words to the creatures, who are within the veil? However, it's in His hands. If He wants, He will leave the veil in front, and if He wants, He will throw it off. It is not that they will bring Him into the veil, nor that they will pull back the veil. This is why I say that when I speak, I have the most insipid of states.

Attributes belong to the Creator inseparably. Miracles and charismatic acts are the attributes of the servant. God has no miracles. The servant who is the most elect is shown the way to His attributes. (750-51)

187.

The world of God is very great and spacious. You've put it in a box: "It's only this that my intellect perceives." So, you've confined the Creator of the intellect inside the intellect. What you imagine is not the Prophet—that's your Prophet, not God's Prophet. You've read your own picture—read the Companion's picture. You've read your own page—read the Companion's page!

He said, "Then why did Sana'i say, 'That you may see the heart without avarice and miserliness'?"

I said, "Well done! After all, Mawlana gave that answer to Sana'i. Otherwise, did he want to answer Sharif Pa-sukhta? After all, he was talking about *Sayr al-ibad*.* That answer was for Sana'i, who spoke frigidly and had no news of the heart. Where is the heart? Is it this common heart that is addressed in preaching and that is given the advice, 'Purify yourself of vileness, miserliness, and blameworthy qualities so that you may be delivered from hell!' Of the attributes of the heart, say just this much: '*Neither My heaven nor My earth embraces Me, but the heart of My believing servant does embrace Me.*'

"'*The heart of the believer is between two fingers of the All-Merciful.*'
"'*But He looks at your hearts.*'"

That you may see the heart without avarice and miserliness.*

He said, "I thought a great deal and wrung out my mind to find this argument."
He said, "Then Sana'i says,

"O Sana'i, in this world, speak like a Kalandar—
   strew dirt in the eyes of all the pure who make claims."*

That is why he is deprived, that is why he is ignorant. At the end of his life, he asked for the sash,* for *I bear witness that there is no god but God and I bear witness that Muhammad is God's messenger.* Now, there are two opinions here: One opinion is that he died a Muslim. Another is that he died an unbeliever but found faith at that moment. Yes, he said, "O God, You are so generous that if an unbeliever should speak ill of You for seventy years, if he returns to You at this moment and gains faith, You accept him." (737-38)

188.

In his poetry Khayyam says that no one has arrived at the secret of love, and he who has arrived is bewildered. Shaykh Ibrahim objected to Khayyam's words: "If he has arrived, how can he be perplexed, and if he has not arrived, what then is this perplexity?"

I said, "Yes, every speaker describes his own state. He is perplexed, so sometimes he accuses the spheres, sometimes the passing days, sometimes luck, sometimes God Himself. Sometimes he negates and denies, sometimes he affirms. Sometimes he says 'if.' He speaks mixed-up, unmeasured, and dark words."

The believer is not perplexed. The believer is he for whom the

Presence has thrown off Its mask. He has lifted up the veil and seen his own goal. He acts in servanthood, face-to-face, and he receives pleasure from Him Himself.

If the disbelievers begin saying "No" from east to west* and they say it to me, doubt won't enter into me, because I see clearly, I eat, I taste.* What doubt could I have? I would say, "Say whatever you like." Or rather, I would be overcome by laughter.

It is as if someone were to come to you this morning, in one hand a cane and the other hand against the wall. He walks very shakily, and says, "Oh, Oh," and he moans: "Tell me what has happened. Why have we been abandoned? Today the sun did not rise!"

Then another one comes, "Yes, I have this same difficulty. How come day is not coming?"

You see that it is full morning. If a hundred thousand say that to you, your ridicule and laughter will simply increase.

Now, the believer is not deprived, but which one is a believer? (301-2)

189.

Come, tell me, how do you conceive of the rising of the sun and the turning of the spheres? The same way that the astronomers explain it? One would not understand it that way from the apparent sense of the Koran.

Come on, let's look—*The believer is an examiner*. Now, everything that is intelligible from the stars must be accepted.

For example, I'm a Shafi'i. I find something in the school of Abu Hanifa through which my work goes forward and which is good. If I don't accept it, that's being obstinate.

The gnostic is aware of everyone's state.* Whenever he hears words, he laughs. He knows which station that person is in. He sees the stations of everyone. He gives thanks that God has not made him captive to that station and has taken him past it.

God has many servants. From each of them He wants a meaning and a wisdom. The gnostic is aware of the state of everyone, and to him they are plain. And there is someone else who is aware of this gnostic and who sees him. But no one sees this one except God. (182-83)

190.

Recognizing this tribe is more difficult than recognizing the Real. You can do the latter through inference. When you see a carved piece of wood, you know that there is a carver. For certain it did not carve itself. But, this tribe, which you see just like yourself in outward form, have another meaning, far from your conception and thought. So, there is nothing strange about recognizing the Carver. However, "how" is this Carver? How is His majesty? How is His infinity? This tribe knows just that, but they do not make it manifest. (657)

191.

This is why he says, "*Oh the yearning to encounter my brothers!*"

They said, "O Messenger of God. Are we those brothers whom you wish for?"

He said, "No, you are my Companions."

They said, "Are your brothers the prophets of the past?"

He said, "By these brothers I don't mean them. Rather, they are dear servants who will come forth after me." (185)

192.

The servants who have God-given knowledge are of two sorts: The knowledge comes to one sort like a flood; they are the place over which the knowledge passes. The other group is rarer than this group, for they have the power to speak. Once they pass beyond the water, they show you a state adorned with form and meaning, a state that I haven't seen in you. All the prophets and saints hope to meet such as these, to see their form.

When someone is stuck in the idea that a hundred saints cannot reach the environs of a prophet, how can he reach this? When someone's belief is that the Koran is God's speech and the Hadith is Muhammad's speech, what hope is there for him? If this is his beginning, where will he reach in the end? All these things should be known by him in childhood, but he's remained in this narrowness.

The world of the Real has a spaciousness and an endless, magnificent expansion. For some it is exceedingly difficult, for some terribly easy. Because it's so easy, they are perplexed why anyone would even talk about it.

He's stuck in the idea that *The Koran has an outward sense and an inward sense up to seven inward senses.* The ulama know the outward sense, the saints the inward sense, the prophets the inward of the inward, and the fourth is the degree that *none knows but God.* Will he ever become human or reap the fruit of this path?

There are more secrets in the Hadith than in the Koran. Look at His words, *The heart did not lie* [53:11], and his words, *What no eye has seen and what no ear has heard.* This is just like a bow.

Although the secrets are in the Koran, Ali used to recite the texts of the Koran all day and he never became selfless. When he heard one word of the secrets, he became selfless, and all that commotion appeared.*

Abu Yazid's words appear the way they do because he himself spoke the secrets. The Prophet spoke no secrets, only preaching.

In a few places he has mentioned those Companions without explanation, like *the possessors of the kernels** [2:179], but he did not mention anything of their states.

They made themselves naked and disgraced, but he remained concealed and hidden.

Muhammad used to burn in wishing for them, but there was no opportunity. He used to say, "*Oh the yearning!*"

If Abu Yazid had been aware, he never would have said "I." Necessarily he wanted a sash, like that fellow Sana'i.* But he was better than Sayyid, and Sayyid was better than Mawlana. He had a better state and more knowledge. You see these people—Imad and others. You should take those in the past as a hundred times greater, two hundred times greater.

For example, there is a sack of wheat, and they bring a handful as a sample. All of it comes to be known. Take that as a hundred times more, a thousand times more—but it is of this kind.

Suppose there is a saint upon whom shine one hundred thousand limpid rays of sanctity, and he sees one of them in the desert. If he looks within himself saying, "Maybe he is this, who knows?", at once his head would go and he would be destroyed. All of his states would be plundered. He would fall from the roof and break his leg. In short, that meaning would go from him, faith would leave him, and he would congeal, because it was as if he had wanted to be that person, but he is the desired of God. (727-29)

193.

What no eye has seen and what no ear has heard and what has never passed over the heart of any mortal. This is stronger than *The heart did not lie about what it saw* [53:11]. This has passed beyond that like four pounding horses. There He mentioned *lie*, which is proof of a veil. This is Koran, and that is Hadith! He has spoken fewer secrets in the Koran, because it is well-known around the world—a watchman that is seen by the world and at which everyone points. There are more secrets in the hadiths. (650)

194.

The companion, then the path. On this path especially, you must have companions.

The whole universe is curtains and veils that have been wrapped around the child of Adam. The Throne is his sheath, the Footstool is his sheath, the seven heavens are his sheath, the sphere of the earth is his sheath, his bodily frame is his sheath, the animal spirit is the sheath, and the holy spirit also—sheath within sheath, veil within veil, up to the point where there is gnosis. And this gnostic is also a sheath relative to the Beloved. He is nothing. Since the Beloved is, the gnostic next to him is paltry. (200)

195.

You will see them all in yourself—Moses, Jesus, Abraham, Noah, Adam, Eve, Asiya, Antichrist, Khizr, Elias. You will see them in your own insides. You are a world without end. What place is there for the heavens and the earths? *Neither My earth nor My heaven embraces Me, but the heart of My believing servant does embrace Me.* "You will not find Me in the heavens, you will not find Me on the Throne."

Where's someone who declares His similarity so that he may shout, "What's this! God forbid!"

A preacher was saying, "Do not conceive of God within the six directions, nor on the Throne or the Footstool."

One of those who declare His similarity jumped up, tore his

clothes, and began shouting, "God forbid! Get lost from this world, just as you have made our God lost from this world!" (212-13)

196.

Someone said to a Sufi,* "Lift up your head: *Gaze upon the traces of God's mercy* [30:50]."

He said, "Those are the traces of the traces. The roses and tulips are inside." (642)

197.

He came to be concealed. After all, in the view of the philosophers, the microcosm is the human make-up, and the macrocosm is this world. In the view of the prophets, the microcosm is this, and the macrocosm is man.* Thus this world is a sample of the human world. (718)

198.

Glory be to God! All are ransom to man, and man is ransom to himself. Did God ever say, "*And We honored the heavens*"? "*And We honored the Throne*"?*

If you go to the Throne, nothing will be gained, even if you go beyond the Throne. If you go below the seven layers of the earth, nothing will be gained. The door of the heart must be opened. The prophets and the saints and the pure all knocked themselves out for the sake of this. They were seeking this.

The whole universe is in one person. When he knows himself, he knows all. The Tatars are in you. Tatars are the attribute of severity. That's in you. *Guide my people, for they do not know*, that is, *Guide my parts*. After all, these parts were unbelievers, but they were part of him. If they were not part of him and were separate, how could he be the whole?

You say, "*God knows the universals, not the particulars*."* When one says "universal," which part is left out? If He does not know the particulars, then He does not know the universals, because when you take the part from the whole, it is no longer the whole. (203)

199.

They told the assembly, "Welcome! Everybody place their heads on their knees and be watchful for a while."

After that, someone lifted up his head: "I saw up to the top of the Throne and the Footstool."

Another said, "My gaze went beyond both the Throne and the Footstool. I am looking from empty space into the world of the Void."

Another one said, "I see to the back of the Cow and the Fish,* and the angels that are entrusted with the Cow and the Fish."

Still another one said, "As much as I look at all the kinds, I see only my own incapacity. I'm the little bird about which they said, 'He's hanging by both feet.' Yes, I'm hanging, but suddenly I'm hanging in the trap of the Beloved. I say, 'Welcome, welcome.' This indeed is what I'm seeking. I didn't want a shop, I wanted two mines*—the mine of gold and the mine of silver. Or rather, I sought to rid myself of being and location, for I don't get along with any but Him. Just as others don't get along with poverty, but they do get along with existence. There's a poverty that takes to the Real* and makes one flee from everything other than the Real, and there's a poverty that makes one flee from the Real and takes one to creation."

When you don't get along with roses
    you'll along with thorns,
When you don't get along with pulpits
    you'll along with the gallows.

Beloved, cast a glance, there's a bit of breath left;
    worry about my work now, there's still twilight left.
The color of your lovely face, the shape of your rosy cheek,
    have put rose into rosewater and the moon into dawn.
Though my gold and silver have become less, why did you turn away?
    My love for you has left a golden orb on the door.
You claimed my heart, I sacrificed my life as well.
    Is there anything more to say? Have you still a right over me?
Let me trouble you for another two or three days—
    in the book of my life there's only one page left.*

Throw yourself into the water and become black.* Every joy and happiness that comes forth gives you the good news of grief. *So give them the good news of a painful chastisement* [3:21]. Joy and good news are appropriate for mortals—they are not the attribute of the hearing and seeing Lord. Joy is the messenger of grief, and expansion is the messenger of contraction. The wonder and marvel that make you love something, such as herbs, beauty, position, and so on, are the divine bud that blossoms. However, if you smell that blossom an hour later, you will be upset by its rottenness. Because of your grief and sadness, you want to flee from yourself. You seek a branch to latch on to, and that is children, excellence, and wonderful words. After an hour, that same rottenness of yours will start to strike, for you are aware. Your dreams have become empty like a plain. This awareness of yours is the blossom of a thornbush and a fire.

Take all these colors far from your eyes, so that you may see another wonder—a world from the He, different from and not similar to this happiness and unhappiness. (259-61)

THE SAINTS

200.

In the Koran, He called John a saint.* He was a great weeper. If I had been there, I would have dried his eyes. He was protected [from sin], and it is sin that demands weeping. Who is this saint? Come, tell me. In the Koran, He does not call the prophets themselves saints. And God knows best. (83)

201.

Whatever has been said of the saints—
provide me that and give me success!
Whatever has been said of the prophets—
*we have faith and we attest!**

There is a subtle meaning here. He did not seek for what belongs to the prophets. He just said, "*We have faith.*" He sought what belongs to the saints: "*Provide me that and give me success.*"

However, this was not his work, because a man's words become known through the context. If he had been aware of that, his

words would not be variegated. Everything he had was for the sake
of meter and rhyme. As for the rest: "How could I reach the state
of the prophets?" And as for that of the saints, yes: "*Provide me that
and give me success!*" (90)

202.

Uways Qarani—God be pleased with him—did not reach the
service of Muhammad during the latter's life in the form of water
and clay, even though he was not empty of that—the veils had
been lifted. His excuse was serving his mother, and that by God's
instruction. The Messenger—upon him be peace—gave Umar and
some of the other Companions news of his state. He said, "When
he comes after I'm gone, his mark will be such and such. Give him
my greetings, but say nothing more to him."

When he came after the death of our Prophet, his mother had
passed away. The great ones among the Companions were not
present. When he visited the grave of the Prophet, the
Companions asked many questions from him. He told of his state
and offered his excuse. They said, "What are mother and father that
a person should fall short in serving the Messenger of God? We
and our companions considered killing our relatives out of love for
Muhammad as easy as killing flies and lice."

As much as he offered excuses, saying that it was by the instruction of Muhammad and not by the demand of the soul and nature,
they of course considered him a sinner, and they spoke at length.

He turned to them and said, "How long were you in the company of Muhammad's presence?"

Each of them said for so many years. That had a measure, they
said, such that each day was worth more than a thousand years.
How can it be calculated?

> When you're the confidant of the companion for a moment,
>   you'll find your whole life's share at that moment.
> Beware, don't waste that moment!
>   A moment like that is rarely found.*

Uways Qarani said, "So, what was the mark of Muhammad?"

Some of them said that he was this tall and his face like this, and his color like that. Uways said, "I am not asking about that. What was Muhammad's mark?"

Some said that his humility was like this, his generosity like that, his acts of obedience night and day such-and-such—*Stand through the night, except for a little* [73:2]. He said that he was also not asking about that. Others said that his knowledge was such and his miracles such. He said that he was also not asking about that.

If the great ones among the Companions had been present, he indeed never would have asked this question, because he would have seen Muhammad's mark in them. *Reports are not like seeing face-to-face.*

> Look at my face yellow as gold and don't ask.
>> Look at these tears like sparks of fire and don't ask.
> Don't ask me what's inside the house—
>> look at the blood on the threshold and don't ask.*

When they had become helpless, they said, "We don't know any marks other than these. Now you tell us."

He opened his mouth to speak, and seventeen of them fell down on their faces unconscious, without his having spoken. Weeping and sympathy appeared in the others. He had no permission to say anything, and no one was settled enough to listen. (276-78)

203.

Abu Yazid—God's mercy be upon him—was going on the hajj.* It was his custom, when he entered a city, to go first and visit the shaykhs, then any other business. He arrived in Basra and went to the service of a dervish. He said, "O Abu Yazid, where are you going?"

He said, "To Mecca, to visit the house of God."

He said, "What provisions do you have for the road?"

He said, "Two hundred dirhems."

He said, "Stand up, circumambulate me seven times, and give me the money."

He stood up, undid the money from his waist, kissed it, and placed it before him.

He said, "O Abu Yazid! Where are you going? That is God's

house, and this heart of mine is God's house. But, by that God who is the Lord of that house and the Lord of this house, from the moment they built that house, He's never gone inside, and from the moment they built this house, He's never left." (264)

204.

When Abu Yazid went on the hajj, he insisted on going alone. He didn't want to be anyone's companion. One day he saw someone who was going on in front of him. He looked at him, and a taste came to him from his way of walking lightly. He was hesitating inside himself whether or not he should walk along with him. "Perhaps I should let go of the custom of going alone, for he would be a fine companion." Then again he'd say, "*The Highest Companion!* Let my only companion be the Real." Again he'd see that the taste of becoming the companion of that person was overcoming the taste of going alone. He remained in this dispute: "Which should I choose?"

That person turned around and said, "First, investigate whether I will accept you as my companion."

He went into himself in wonder: "How could he tell about my inmost mind?"

The man picked up his pace. (229-30)

205.

Alms in secret [*extinguish the wrath of the Lord*] are that you are so immersed in sincerity and in preserving that sincerity that you have no pleasure in giving alms. I mean being busy with regret— "Too bad that it's not better than this" or "more than this."

Abu Yazid—God's mercy be upon him—mostly went on the hajj on foot. He had gone on the hajj seventy times. One day he saw that the people on the road of the hajj had become extremely distressed because of water and were perishing. He saw a dog near a well of water at which the hajjis were crowded and crushed together. The dog cast a glance at Abu Yazid, and inspiration came: "Get water for this dog!"

He called out, "Who will buy a pious, accepted hajj for a drink of water?" No one paid any attention. He added to it: "Five accepted hajjes on foot. . ., six . . ., seven . . ?," until he reached seventy. Someone called out, "I will give it to you." It passed into Abu Yazid's mind, "Good for me—I've spent seventy hajjes on foot for that drink of water!"

When he put the water in a bowl and placed it in front of the dog, it turned its face away. Abu Yazid fell on his face and repented. A call came, "How long will you say to yourself, 'I did this and I did that for the sake of God?' Don't you see that a dog doesn't accept that?'"

He shouted out, "I repent, I will no longer have such thoughts!" At once the dog put its face into the water and began to drink.

Despite a hundred intercessions and a hundred laments,
    You won't let me kiss Your foot even once!* (216-17)

206.

So, this is the meaning of *None knows its interpretation except God and the firmly rooted* [7:3].

The explanation is that Abu Yazid saw his own soul as fat. He said, "Why are you fat?"

It said, "Because of something that you cannot cure. It's that the people come and prostrate themselves before you, and you see yourself as deserving that prostration."

He said, "So, you have overcome in the end. I will not be able to overcome you at the time of death." He wanted a sash* to see what its secret might be, so that [he could say], "*Join me with the worthy*" [12:101]. (647)

207.

After all, they don't consider Abu Yazid one of the complete saints, for that sincere dervish passed by his grave, bit his finger and said, "Oh! Between this dervish and God a veil has remained!"

This same Abu Yazid was passing by the village of Kharaqan. He said, "After one hundred and fifty years a man will come out of this village who will pass five degrees beyond me," and that's what happened. On that date, Abu'l-Hasan Kharaqani became a seeker and put on the cloak at his gravesite.*

So, it is even more appropriate that God make the perfect saints aware of secrets: "So-and-so has said this bad thing about you."

I say to God, "Was that not from You? Did You not want that from the first?"

He says, "No. He said such a cruel thing about you."

I say, "What will You do with him now?"

He says, "Whatever you say."

I say, "Let him be for now." (117-18)

208.

They said, "For the sake of God, give us a mark by which we may know with whom you have the most solicitude and mercy."

He said, "The one who remembers my God the most."

There's a remembrance on the tongue, and there's a remembrance in the spirit.

Whenever Abu Yazid—God sanctify his spirit—would enter a town, he would go to the town's graveyard when he wanted recreation.

Someone asked Ibn Abbas, "O cousin of God's Messenger! When I want recreation, where should I go?"

He replied, "If it's daytime, go for recreation in the graveyard. If it's night, go for recreation to the heavens."

When Abu Yazid was wandering in the graveyard, he was finding human skulls. Inspiration came to him: "Pick them up in your hand, and look inside very carefully."

He saw that the ears of some of the skulls were stopped up and had no holes. In others he saw that the hole went from one ear to the other. In some he saw that the hole went from the ear to the throat.

He said, "O God, people see all these as the same, but You have shown them to me as different. Now solve this. Why do those skulls have these attributes?"

Inspiration came: "The skulls that have no holes heard nothing of Our speech. Those in which the holes go from one ear to the other listened with one ear and let it out the other. Those that have a way from the ear to the throat accepted it." (194)

209.

Children were pointing out Junayd—God's mercy be upon him—to each other: "This is the one who remains awake for God all night long."

Junayd said, "It would not be fitting for me to prove their opinion wrong." He had been staying awake until midnight, and now he accustomed himself to staying awake until daybreak. So, it may be that the beliefs of those who believe in someone have an effect upon him.

The Men employ stratagems to keep themselves hidden. But that one tries in a thousand ways to make himself known. This was the first wakefulness of Junayd's soul. After all, it was said to him that he was weak, that he should rest at night, that he should sleep. In any case, one first must strive. (265)

210.

Something like this is the account of Ahmad the Heretic* [*zindiq*]. Junayd was sent to him from Baghdad: "In such-and-such a city is Ahmad the Heretic, one of Our servants. Your difficulty will not be solved without him, even if you perform a hundred forty-day seclusions."

He got up and set off for that city. He said to himself, "It would not be courteous to ask where the house of Ahmad the Heretic is." He interpreted [the vision], and asked for Ahmad the Sincere [*siddiq*].

There was so much gnosis inside him that it became an obstacle to the goal. In the apparition, words were said to him that had no interpretation, but he heard them as having an interpretation. For sixty days, he wandered perplexed in that city, asking "Where is the lodging of Ahmad the Sincere?" His misfortune was that he had been spoken to without [the need for] interpretation, but he was asking with an interpretation. Finally it came to his mind to pass by the ruined mosque. When he set off in that direction, he heard the sound of the recitation of the Koranic story of Joseph, and it took his heart away. A youth came out of the ruined mosque. He said to himself, "I'll ask this man without interpretation." He asked.

The youth said, "Well, you just heard the sound of his reciting the Koran." Junayd gave a shout and fell down senseless. The youth fell at his feet.

From the blessing of speaking truth, Junayd reached the goal. When he came to himself, he went into that ruin, and he sat far away. He was not so bold as to greet him and speak, nor did Ahmad give him an opportunity until late.

Afterwards, he felt sorry for him. He looked again at him and said, "Welcome, Junayd."

Junayd said to himself, "I wonder how he knows I'm Junayd."

He smiled and said, "How should I not know? From the day you had that knot and fell into that difficulty, I have been turning around in myself: 'When he comes, what shall I say to him?' I don't find anything to say to you. Do you have anything to recite? Snap your fingers, recite!"

Junayd began reciting something.

Ahmad the Heretic stood up and spun around several times. The holy spirits came: "If you spin one or two more times, the spokes of the wheel will break apart." He was ashamed, and sat down. (123-24)

211.

Ahmad Ghazali—God's mercy be upon him—and Muhammad Ghazali, and that third brother, all three came from pure seed. Each in his own field was such that he had no equal. Muhammad Ghazali, in the custom of the sciences, had no equal. His compositions are clearer than the sun. Mawlana indeed knows this. In gnosis, Ahmad Ghazali was the sultan of all the notables. And the other brother—in munificence and generosity, for he was the companion of blessings and great charity. That third brother was called Umar Ghazali.* He was a merchant and a man of wealth. In munificence and generosity, he had no equal.

Ahmad Ghazali had not studied these outward sciences.* The criticizers criticized him before his brother Muhammad Ghazali: "He talks, but he knows nothing of the different sciences." Muhammad Ghazali sent the books *Dhakhira* and *Lubab*, both of which are his own compositions, to his brother on the hand of a jurist. He gave him this advice: "Go, enter in with courtesy, and, from the moment your gaze falls upon him, watch for any movement that he makes—a smile, a movement of the hand or the head, or of any limb. Record all his acts, such as shifting the position of his feet, and moving his fingers."

When the messenger entered, Ahmad was sitting happily in the khanaqah. His gaze fell upon him from afar, and he smiled. He said, "Have you brought the books for me?"

The messenger began to tremble.

After that he said, "I am unlettered.* 'Unlettered' is one thing, 'unlearned' is something else. The unlearned man is indeed blind. The unlettered man does not write." Then he said, "You read, so I may listen."

He read from all the parts of the books.

Then he said, "On the front leaf of the book, write these lines that I will dictate:

"In searching for the treasure, my body is ruined,
    in the fire of love, my heart is roasted.
"What use to me are *Dhakhira* and *Lubab*?
    The balm of the Beloved's lips is my wine."*

Iblis is a pretext, Adam a mark; Iblis a darkness, Adam a light; Iblis terrestrial, Adam celestial. (320-21)

212.

Ahmad Ghazali was faced with a difficulty that had become his veil. No one was able to lift the veil for him, but he showed a great deal of manliness in himself. He was a man who, when he would gaze on heaven in the direction of the spheres, would *make it crumble to dust* [7:143], and in himself he would find *When heaven is split open* [82:1]. He underwent concealed ascetic disciplines of which no one was aware. Whatever has been transmitted about his outward discipline is all lies. He did not sit in any of these forty-day seclusions, for that is an innovation in the religion of Muhammad. Muhammad never sat in a forty-day seclusion. That's in the story of Moses. Read, "*And when We appointed with Moses forty nights*" [2:51].

Don't these blind people see that Moses, with all that grandeur, used to say, "*My Lord, make me one of the community of Muhammad!*"? In other words, "Make me one of the folk of vision!" This is the secret of those words. Otherwise, why would Moses want to be with me and you with our stinking armpits? What he meant is this secret—or that unique one in the community of Muhammad who belongs to the folk of vision. He meant either that, or this. This too is a place of denunciation.

In short, Ahmad Ghazali was striving to repel that veil. He heard a voice, or an inspiration came to his heart: "This veil of yours will be dissolved with the Master of Sangan."* He got up and went. On the very day that he arrived there, the Master had a *sama*, and during the *sama* the difficulty was solved.

He turned back to Tabriz. When the people of Tabriz heard he was coming back quickly, they said, "He's surely coming for the sake of that lovely boy."*

They hired an old woman to go and meet him. The old woman sat sadly in the road on which he was coming. Ahmad Ghazali reached her. He said, "What's the matter with you? Why are you sitting sadly in the road?"

She said, "Why shouldn't I sit sadly? Such and such a boy, who was a piece of my liver and the light of my eyes, has died."

He said, "He died?"

She said, "Yes."

He said, "O caravan. Will you conform with me in this place for a time? Will you dismount so that I can think whether this woman is speaking the truth or not?"

They said, "We are at your service," and they all dismounted. He put his head down for a time. The next day at sunrise, he lifted up his head and said, "The woman is lying. I have just examined one by one, from the era of Adam to this moment, every spirit that has separated from its frame and gone from this world. But the spirit of that boy's body was not among them. Let's get going."

When he came to Tabriz, the whole city was upset, saying that this is not good.

He didn't incline to these beautiful forms out of appetite. He saw something that no else saw. If they had taken him apart piece by piece, they wouldn't have found an iota of appetite. However, because of this behavior, some people acknowledged him and some denied him. During the time he was there, there was someone who acknowledged him a hundred times, and denied him a hundred times.

One day they took news to the Atabeg:* "You will not believe it from us, but come, look through the window of the bathhouse. He is lying down, and he has put his leg next to that boy whom we are talking about. He is burning a brazier with aloes-wood and incense."

The Atabeg came and furtively looked in from the window and

the sky-light. He wanted to open it to reject him completely. The shaykh shouted out, "You little Turk, look carefully!" Then he turned his gaze toward him, lifted up his other foot, and placed it in the middle of the burning brazier. The Atabeg was astonished and asked forgiveness. He went back astonished.

That scholar and professor, the learned master in various fields, had become his disciple and his servant. He had come to believe because his pulpit had lifted into the air. Many times, in the case of this lovely boy, he had acknowledged him and then denied him. He would place the saddle-cloth* of the shaykh on his neck and walk in front of his mount. That boy would hold the shaykh's saddle-straps. On the road the shaykh would speak to the boy of mysteries and allusions, while he was carrying the saddle-cloth on his neck. By the time they reached the house, he would have denied him ten times, wanting to throw away the saddle-cloth and go. Again he would acknowledge him. He would walk bare-headed, and would fall to walking behind the shaykh's horse in asking forgiveness for these whispering doubts. He would seek refuge from these doubts. The shaykh was aware of both states. In the grasp of the shaykh, he was like an infant—sometimes he would make him cry, sometimes he would make him laugh. (323-25)

213.

Look at his fairness—how fairly he acted. With all this learning, he was walking among the retainers of the shaykh. This student was qualified in the various fields. The learned group was blaming him. He said, "By that God who is the Creator of the creatures, if you were aware of one hair of his the way that God has made me aware of him, you would steal his saddle-cloth from my hands, just as you steal each other's positions and you envy each other."

He went among his retainers with all this belief. But when they arrived at the house, he kept on acknowledging him and denying him: "Why is the shaykh so humble before that youth, who is the place of appetite." Then he would say, "But what harm does it do him, for he is the source of the antidote. He is the source of *God forgives your prior and later sins* [48:2]. He is the ocean of *God changes their ugly deeds into good deeds* [25:70]."

> Though the mountain be full of serpents, don't fear—
>   in the mountain you'll also find the antidote.*

When he looked upon the shaykh with solicitude, these good thoughts would shine within him. But, when he went into the shadow, the whispering doubts of darkness would appear—"I take it that this is his station. How can one be manly by leading people astray and throwing them into doubts and thoughts?"

The shaykh saw all this. He said, "Peace be upon you. How are you in thinking about me? Have you forgotten again? Do you fancy that I will just release you into acknowledgment or denial? *He turns about the day and night* [24:44]. How many times does He turn the light of the day upside down in the ocean of darkness? How many times does He burn away the darkness in the rays of light? *Do the people reckon that they will be left to say, 'We have faith' and not be tested?* [29:2]. Is there anything in the world that is accepted without testing, or rejected without trial? However, *God willing*, in the end you will stand up correctly, take the right road, and know who you are." (285-86)

214.

That learned man, with all his worthiness, carried the shaykh's saddle-cloth and would run before his horse. In the road, at every moment he would lose his belief and deny the shaykh. Shaykh so-and-so had come before him and greeted him, and he had paid him no attention. Following that shaykh, so-and-so, a catamite, had arrived and greeted him, and the shaykh had offered his salutations.

"How should I not lose my belief?" Again he would ask God's forgiveness in himself. He would keep on carrying the saddle-cloth, but he feared that the shaykh would shun him. Thus he went on, one moment a Muslim, the next an unbeliever, until he arrived at the door of the shaykh's house, the saddle-cloth on his shoulders.

The next day, saying, "*There is no power and no strength but in God*," he pulled himself to visit the shaykh. With a thousand tricks, he blinded Iblis. When he arrived at the door of the shaykh's house, he saw that the shaykh was playing chess with that son of the headman. He lost his belief, and he went back. He saw

Muhammad in a dream, and he tried to run to visit him, but Muhammad turned away from him. He began weeping: "O Messenger of God, don't turn away from me."

Muhammad said, "Why do you deny me? How long will you deny me?"

He said, "O Messenger of God, when did I ever deny you?"

He said, "You have denied my friend. *A man is with him whom he loves* is for the sake of a friend like him. *The believers are like one soul* is for the sake of one like him."

He fell on his face, he wept, and he repented. Muhammad placed a handful of raisins and filberts next to him. He woke up. He ran, he came, he saw that they were still playing chess. Although he had the raisins in his pocket, he still lost his belief and wanted to return. The shaykh shouted out, "How long will this go on? At least have shame before the Master."

As soon as the shaykh came out, the man fell at his feet. The shaykh said, "Bring that plate!" He saw that it had raisins and filberts in it, but the place of a handful of raisins was empty. He said, "Put that handful of raisins on the plate, because Muhammad took it from here."

One time a group went to the king saying that he was a libertine: "How is his religion and his state? He spends a whole week in the bath-house, night and day, one leg next to a servant and the other next to the son of the headman. He's set up a brazier and is making kabob. He takes a kiss from this one, and a kiss from that one! What is left?"

The Atabeg came and looked through the window of the bath-house. He quickly wanted to return. The shaykh shouted out, "You little Turk, look carefully! Then go." He lifted up his leg from beside the servant and placed it in the brazier. The Atabeg struck himself in the head two or three times.

They said, "He came up to the top of the pulpit, and this was how he spoke of *tawhid*:

"That idol, the beauty and adornment of our assembly—
      he's not in the assembly, I don't know where he's gone.
He's a tall cypress, with a straight stature—
      without his stature, I'm overcome by calamity.*

"He said this, then he said, 'As long as the boy doesn't come, I won't preach.'"

The headman commanded them to bring the boy. He was in the bath-house shampooing his hair. He rinsed his head, came out, and made himself present at the assembly. He sat in the front seat. Then he began preaching. (617-18)

MY INTERPRETATIONS OF SCRIPTURE

215.

Above the Koran there's nothing—above God's speech there's nothing. However, this Koran that He's voiced for the common people concerning commandments, prohibitions, and showing the way, has one taste, and the one He voices for the elect has another taste. (184)

216.

There are people who observe rhyming prose and end their sentences with rhymes. There are people who speak poetry. There are people who speak only prose. Each of them is a part. The Speech of God is the whole. Grab on to the whole, so that all the parts may be yours, in addition to everything else. Don't grab on to the part, lest you lose the whole.

A tree appears in someone's house and grows up. He must embrace the whole of the tree if all the branches are to be his along with the trunk. However, if you grab on to one branch, the rest will be lost. There is also the danger that the branch will break and you will be cut off from the branch and be held back from it, and that you will also be held back from yourself. (172-73)

217.

If he keeps away from the sciences, that's no wonder. "*There is many a reciter of the Koran [whom the Koran curses]!*" He said "*reciter*" along with the word "*many,*" so it is not all-inclusive.

There remain other reciters, who are *the folk of the Koran, the folk of God and His elect,* who are aware of the seven meanings. For *The Koran has an outward sense and an inward sense, and its inward sense has an inward sense up to seven inward senses.* These seven are not necessarily what is customary and agreed upon among the people. He knows something other than these and beyond these, and that has become his practice. He knows seven and a hundred thousand—the one who is a seeker and God's elect.

Beyond this there is still another level, and that is the most elect. People like him are not mentioned in the Koran except through allusion, and they have no connection with *There is many a reciter of the Koran.* They are not of this sort, nor of that sort, because they are *the folk of God and His elect.*

Before I said this, was this the meaning with you?

I said, "No."

He said, "Don't stand on ceremony, there's none of that here." (698-99)

218.

Someone was seeking to learn the Koran. He had taken great trouble in memorizing the Koran, but he was still eager. He was asking where he could find a qualified, good-reading reciter. He requested from God that he would find a reciter who was of *the folk of the Koran, the folk of God and His elect.* All of a sudden he found one. In Baghdad a reciter came before him, and he presented to him each verse that he had read. The reciter would say, "Read it like this."

When he looked, he saw that he had wasted his life and would have to begin over. He said, "Let be what must be!"

The son of the reciter said, "My father stipulates one dinar for every ten verses." He replied that he would be happy to pay.

He was learning the Koran and gladly giving the gold. But then one day there was no gold left. He wandered around sad. He saw an old man, who said, "Why are you sad?"

He recounted the situation. The old man laughed. He took him to his house and made him a guest. He was so sad that he would not eat food. The old man said, "After all, that reciter is my son, and that gold of yours is all under that carpet. He has no need for gold. *Whoever is not rich through the Koran is not one of us.* Our gold is the Koran. Our property is the Koran. We did not learn the Koran such that we would need anything other than the Koran. This was only to test you. Look, all your dinars are right here. Take them and go." (253)

219.

Humam is indeed a great man. He reads Koran exegesis.

Whoever becomes a completely learned man is completely deprived of God and completely full of himself. An Anatolian who becomes a Muslim right now finds a scent of God. But when someone is full, a hundred thousand prophets can't empty him. Many a weeping is a veil that takes far from God.

My ears have become dull. Say to my ears,

> I played deaf when the gazelle was speaking,
> > hunting lions with her glance.
> I'm not really deaf
> > but I wanted her to glance again.

Thus the Prophet said that the angels plead with the Presence: "The believing servant, so-and-so, has pleaded and asked so much. He is weeping, and You accept the supplication of the estranged. Why not take care of his request?"

He says, "*Leave Me and My servant, for I am not less merciful than you. Surely I love him and I love his voice.*"* The reason for the delay in response to the supplication of some people is the perfection of love.

Sometimes, the praising is a trouble and a veil, and the words just bounce back. Sometimes, if he does not praise, this nearly tears him to pieces.

There is a time when He likes weeping, and a time when it troubles Him. Laughter is the same. (206-7)

220.

Ibn Mas'ud—God be pleased with him—said that Muhammad used to speak of the secrets of the Koran.* He related, "He would tell the meaning of such and such a verse to the Companions, and he would whisper a second meaning in my ear. If I were I to tell it to you, O Companions, you would cut my throat." It would have appeared to them as unbelief, so they would have cut his throat.

I am only a mortal like you [18:110]. You should know that the occasion for the descent of this verse is that Ali was conforming to Muhammad during the ten days of Ashura.* He did not eat for nine nights and nine days. Muhammad looked upon him and saw the traces of weakness. He said, "*I am not like one of you.*" The verse came: "*I am only a mortal like you.*" The difference is only this little bit: "*It is revealed to me*" [18:110]. I do certain things that no one knows. I do this among them such that the nose is unaware of the mouth, unless I should want that. (667-68)

221.

The Companions never raised objections to Muhammad. They viewed him with belief and became drunk with his words. Abu Bakr narrated no more than seven hadiths. If he had been asked, he would have given them numerous other benefits and unveiled many secrets. From this can be caught the scent of my words.

I am the Real is extremely disgraceful. *Glory be to me* is a bit more hidden. There is no mortal who does not have some measure of egoism.

Moses said, "*I am more knowledgeable than anyone on the face of the earth.*" Something came into him, and this is what he said. He was turned over to Khizr. He was with him for a few days, and that left him.*

Muhammad said to Ali, "Why have you conformed with me in continuous fasting? You have become too weak. *I am not like one of you. I stay the night with my Lord—He feeds me and gives me to drink.*"

The verifiers say that this was the occasion for the descent of the verse, "*Say: I am only a mortal like you*" [18:110]. In other words: "Say this, and throw that extreme fullness with self to the side. Say this!" Then, so that his fragrant mind would not be beaten down, He said, "*It is revealed to him.*"*

This is the same as *He who hopes for the encounter with his Lord* [18:110]. This is the same as that—*I am not like one of you.*

[*Let him not*] *associate with the worship of his Lord* [*any one*] [18:110]—this also is the same as that. (621-22)

222.

We shall show them Our signs in the horizons [*and in themselves until it becomes clear to them that he is the Real*] [41:53]. What do they say about this? About *horizons*? "Winter and summer." About *in themselves*? "Illness and health." A fine exegesis! Well done, O exegetes! Another opinion about *horizons*—"splitting the moon, and miracles." *In themselves*—"expanding the breast." *That he is the Real* means that God is the truth, or that Muhammad is true. A fine exegesis! This exegesis is granted.

But, for the travelers and wayfarers, each verse is like a message and a love-letter. They know the Koran. He presents and discloses the beauty of the Koran to them. What kind of talk is this: *that he is the Real* means that they should know who God is, that is, that He is the Real?

There's the exegesis of Wahidi Qudsi. And what about Tusi's?

The All-merciful taught the Koran [55:1-2]: Listen to the Koran's exegesis from God. If you listen to any exegesis other than God's, that is the exegesis of the speaker's state, not the exegesis of the Koran. A literal translation of the Koran's words? Any five-year-old can tell you that. (634-35)

223.

They said, "Make an exegesis of the Koran for us."

I said, "As you know, my exegesis is not from Muhammad, nor is it from God. My 'I' also denies it. I say to it, 'How can you deny it? Leave me alone, go away. Why do you give me headaches?'

"It says, 'No, I won't go. I'll just keep on denying.' And that's my own self—it doesn't understand my words.

"This is like the calligrapher who used to write three kinds of calligraphy. One, he read but no one else. Another, he read and others too. The third, neither he nor anyone else could read. That's me when I talk. I don't understand, nor does anyone else." (272)

224.

One day Asad the theologian was offering an exegesis of the verse, *And He is with you wherever you are* [57:4]. With all his learning, when I would ask him something in public, he would break down. One day I asked him, "You say *He is with you*—God is with you—how is that?"

He said, "You are spilling things. What is the motive in this question?" As much as he took the side of clemency, he also took the side of anger. He kept on letting it pour out.

I said, "What do you mean? This question is not the place for asking about motives. You've tied a dog to your tongue and made yourself accustomed to tormenting people. How do explain the meaning of *He is with you*? How can God be with the servant?"

He said, "Yes, God is with the servant through knowledge."

I said, "Knowledge is not separate from God's Essence, and no attribute is separate from the Essence."

He said, "You're asking old questions."

I said, "What's the meaning of 'old.'? Does He die from something new?"

The people say that this is what a "theologian" is. (294-95)

225.

What has he said in that exegesis about *The All-merciful sat upon the Throne* [20:5]? Anything other than what has been said in these outward texts? Thus they say that *"sat" means to gain authority over, as in the verse,*

> *Bishr has sat upon Iraq*
> *without sword or spilled blood.**

Even Abu'l-Hasan Ash'ari said, "*We have faith in his words, 'He sat upon the Throne' without asking how,* and we believe this without examination.*" What comes to be known from these words?

Did he say anything in that exegesis about *taha** [20:1] other than what the folk of the outward sense say? Thus they say: *Taha is a name of Muhammad, or its meaning is, "O man,"* or it is diacritical marks used by the astronomers; or, that it means, *Tread the ground,* put your feet on the ground, because the Messenger was standing on one foot during the night vigil after the commandment came, *Keep vigil as a work of supererogation* [17:79]. He stood so long on one leg that his blessed foot became swollen.* So the commandment came, *taha*—"Put your other foot on the ground too; don't stand on one foot, for We did not send the commandment of keeping vigil for the likes of you."

I'm not asking about these outward explanations that they have given. Other than these, what have they said? Won't you say? So, it is known that the exegesis of this must be read from the Guarded Tablet. That Tablet doesn't find room along with imagination.

The King said, "Don't do service, you shame Me."

He replied, "Don't dispute. This prohibition of Yours makes my heart's love for You cold—You become cold in my heart."

The King said, "If that is so, then I won't speak." Then another time He says, "By your spirit and secret! There's no requirement. Don't do that! *Surely We have opened up for thee a clear opening* [48:1]."

He says, "By Your soul and secret! I'll do it." He stood so long that his feet became swollen.

The King says in anger, "Enough! I don't want this. *Taha. We did not send down the Koran on you so that you would be wretched* [20:1-2]. I have placed you next to Myself and speak to you. I don't speak so that you will fall into suffering, *only as a reminder to him who fears, a revelation from Him who created the earth* [*and the high heavens*] [20:3-4]."

He is explaining this proximity for the sake of the common people. *Earth* is Muhammad's body, *heavens* are his luminous faculties of reflection, conception, and imagination.* *The All-merciful sat upon the Throne* [20:5]—He has settled down upon your heart.

How long, how long will you keep on saying, "I'm independent of Muhammad, I've reached God"? God is not independent of Muhammad! How is that? It is He who brought him first. And what do you say about this: *If We had willed, We would have sent forth in every city a warner* [25:51]. He didn't do anything? He wanted nothing? With *If We had willed* He is talking about Muhammad himself. "If I had wanted—*If not for thee*."* This He said about Muhammad.

Muhammad said, "I also." *His eye swerved not* [53:17]. "You chose me out from all—I also want nothing other than You." (319-20)

226.

The All-merciful sat upon the Throne [20:5]. That Throne is the heart of Muhammad.* If there had not been sitting before that, what was it like in its moment?

He tells him his own story: *Taha:* "Don't suffer, don't suffer, don't see any suffering. I did not bring this story so that you should suffer."

To him belongs what is in the heavens and what is in the earth [20:6]. The heavens are his brain, the earth is his existence. All is his story. "Sitting" is his state.

He who follows the blackness has gone astray—whoever looks upon his form and not upon his meaning. (657)

227.

The All-merciful sat upon the Throne [20:5]. This is the same as *He who knows his soul.* In this one person a treasure has come to sit, and there's nothing left of agitation. He who busies himself with Him attends neither to himself nor to anyone else. *Though you be loud in your speech, He knows the secret and what is more hidden* [20:7]. However, he flees. You'll find the One in Muhammad, but you won't find Muhammad in the One.

When the Sufi comes out of the house, he places a piece of bread in his sleeve.* He looks at the bread and says, "O bread, if I find something else, you're delivered. Otherwise, you're in my hand."

They're all Oners,* but we're Muhammadans. Someone wanted to fly above the Kaaba.* Then he said, "No, following is better." Praying on the roof of the Kaaba doesn't have that. Their hidden egoisms tie them down. (257-58)

228.

Give an interpretation of *My heaven does not embrace Me.*

He said, "It is the same as the meaning of *Surely We offered the trust to the heavens* [33:72]. It means gnosis of God. Gnosis has degrees, and the meaning of that hadith is connected to this."

He commanded, "Don't you have anything more about the meaning of this hadith, *My heaven does not embrace Me?*"

True embracing is impossible.

They became quiet.

He commanded, "This is a place for debate. They flee from here. If they were to debate here, the benefit would be more." (125)

229.

I dreamed that I was saying to Mawlana, "*Everything is perishing but His face* [28:88]. What remains is seeing the friends."

Many a beloved has come to me drunk,
  blear in his eyes, sleep in his head.

*You will not see Me** [7:143], because He is in front of you and you don't see Him. If that's the way you want to see, *you will not* *see Me.* He is so subtle that He passes by the sight, for *eyes do not perceive Him* [6:103]. However, His subtlety charges like horses on the double—*and He perceives the eyes* [6:103]. When He passes by and you cannot see Him, *Look at the mountain* [7:143], which is your own existence. Learn from Muhammad at the end of time: *"He who knows his soul knows his Lord."*

I have repented [7:143] from asking things like this. *This points to his words,"And I am the first of those who have faith"* [7:143].

Since water allows filth into itself and does not forbid it, how could He forbid someone who is thirsty for Him? There is a water that does not put up with filth and becomes filthy. Hence it forbids things from itself out of fear of becoming filthy. But, there is another water which, even if you put all the world's filth into it, does not become filthy. (762)

230.

There is no fault in the blind, there is no fault in the lame [24:61]. So, since He has provided the excuse for them, for whom is the advice? After all, everyone is blind and lame in relation to Him,* for He is the seeing—it is He who walks well. Even Gabriel does not reach His pace. He says to Gabriel, "Come on!", and Gabriel says, "I can't do it. *If I approach another inch, I will be burnt to cinders."* The one who is healthy without any illness is He. His color is right and His constitution is right. Hence He Himself is talking, and He Himself is listening. He's not talking to anyone. What is the exegesis of this?

In my hell, all are gnostics. That's what my hell is like. He's the one about whom hell complains. It says, "Hell has come!" Hell sees him and says, "Hell has come!" Hell wishes the believer well. It says, *"Cross over, O believer, for your light extinguishes my fire!"*

The narrations tell us that a great man came to the grave of a dear one.* He saw that he had gone from this world veiled. He sat at his grave for forty days until his work was completed. (182)

231.

Captain wind came, bringing the rebels to the royal court. When heaven's clouds are sleeping at the shore of the ocean or on top of the mountains, no drop of rain falls anywhere. They arrive at the command, and they rain.

In the same way, the wind of caprice and appetite begins to blow, bringing the loins into movement and sending the drop of sperm to the womb. From that seed, the leaves that are ears and the branches that are hands stand firm on the body.

God has not placed two hearts in any man's breast [33:4]. It belongs wholly to us—it belongs wholly to Him. These two statements are one.

The Real never says "*I am the Real.*" The Real never says "*Glory be to Me.*" *Glory be to Me* is an expression of wonder. How could the Real wonder at anything? If the servant says "*glory be to,*" which is an expression of wonder, that's correct. (185-86)

232.

What, did you think that We created you only for sport? [23:115]. Some say that this is severity—no, rather gentleness. It means, "I've charged like a hundred horses, I've turned My face toward you, and you busy yourself with something else. You hold yourself back, but I don't hold Myself back. I have turned to you totally. *My all is busy with your all* is the response to *My all is given to your all.*"

Someone is loudly weeping by the door: "Let me inside the house for a moment."

They say, "We'll certainly not let you in."

Someone else weeps: "Let me go out for an hour."

They say, "No, how can that be?"

Sir, everyone speaks of his own state, and then he says, "I'm explaining the meaning of God's speech." (281-82)

233.

Surely the squanderers are brothers of Satan [17:27]. The "squanderers" are those who take their dear life, which is the capital of everlasting felicity, and say: "I guess there will be no resurrection or punishment."

Don't you regret placing a pearl like this under a stone and destroying it? Even though there are proofs giving witness that the sun will disappear? What place is this for doubt? But he puts on his sleeping clothes. They've brought him here so that he can sleep.

It is certain that this pearl is not in everyone. Otherwise, it would show itself during the preaching, and everyone would move. Invite everyone! But some don't have the legs. Some have never heard of legs. Their legs are asleep. When everyone moves, they will benefit by virtue of conformity. (651-52)

234.

What is the meaning of *houris,* cloistered in cool pavilions... untouched [before them by man or jinn]* [55:72, 74]? Come on, such a houri is the world of God. He said, "This is how you should judge it."

I said to him, "'Man and jinn have not reached them.' Does this mean that these wines do not reach us in this world in the measure of the level of each—ginger, Salsabil,* camphor, pure wine?"

So, what is this *They fulfill their vows* [76:7]? Does this apply generally? These people* say that it applies to Ali.

The occasion for the descent is understood from the verse. It may be that they will speak of an occasion that is frigid, and they become cold. (667)

235.

He found thee astray and guided thee [93:7]. What's the meaning of this verse? "God found you having lost the road and He showed you the road." Everyone has said only this. When did He lose him that He should find him? Is He like a shepherd who lost a calf yesterday and is running this way and that to find him? On the contrary, *Muhammad found himself astray*; or, *your soul found your soul astray, and it guided. The verb is not feminine because the gender goes back [not to self] but to the meaning of self, which is essence and existence.* (694–95)

236.

But those who struggle in Us, surely We shall guide them on Our paths [29:69]. This means what it says if you read it in reverse order: *We shall guide on Our paths those who struggle in Us.* This is what is meant. Those who struggle in this road struggled without His guidance, then He showed them the road and they struggled with His guidance. Otherwise, why is there the repetition of *We shall guide them*?

Or, it may be from the tongue of the Messenger: "*Those who struggle in us,*" that is, the servants that are our outward body, "*we shall guide them on our paths,*" that is, the paths of our spirits and our realities. (238–39)

237.

They asked, "What was the occasion for the descent of *Surely We have opened up for thee [a clear opening]* [48:1]."

I said, "When the verse *I know not what shall be done with me nor with you* [46:9] was sent down, they understood only the outward sense of *I know not*. They began to criticize: 'So, you turn your face to someone who doesn't know what will be done with him or his people?' Then *Surely We have opened up for thee* was sent down."

They asked me how this answered their question.

I said, "The implication of the words was like this: The *I know not* was not ignorance and perplexity. Rather, the meaning was this: 'I do not know in which robe of honor the King will dress me or which kingdom He will give to me.'"

They said, "But the difficulty remains. When someone like him does not know what will be bestowed upon him, that is a defect. Moreover, since some of the robes had arrived, how come the rest were not known? *A little indicates much.*"

I said, "This is not ignorance. This is to stress the greatness and infinity of the gift. Thus, in another place He says, *And what shall make you know what is the steep!* [90:12]. *And what shall make you know what is the Day of Doom?* [82:17]." (167-68)

238.

Buhlul threw a stone at a Koran-reciter. They said, "Why did you throw it?"

He said, "Because he was lying." A riot began in the city.

The caliph summoned Buhlul. He replied, "I'm talking about his voice, not about what he's saying."

He said, "What kind of words are these? How can his voice be separate from what he says?"

He said, "Suppose you, who are the caliph, write out a firman, saying that when the agents of such a region hear the firman, they must come as soon as they can, without any delay. The courier takes the firman there, and they read it. Every day they read it, but in fact they don't come. Are they truthful in the reading and in their saying *We hear and we obey* [2:285]?" (130)

239.

God's Messenger said, "*Do not prefer me over Jonah, son of Amittai,* because he had a *mi'raj* at the bottom of the ocean in the stomach of the fish, and I had it above the seven heavens. Beware, do not prefer me in this respect!"

If the encounter with the Real belonged to location and became defective through location, then the Real would be subordinate to location. (189)

240.

[*I have a moment with God*] *in which neither proximate angel*, that is, his own pure spirit, *nor sent prophet*, that is, his purified body, *embraces me*. If they don't fit there, what lies beyond them? Who dares to open this up but this child of Tabriz?

This is not the station and state of Muhammad—it's an invitation. Here he counts out numerous things—*I have*—*with God*—*moment*. What kind of state is this? I say that this is not his state. (701)

241.

I have a moment. This is an invitation. Otherwise, it's a state that passes. In that state, where's *I have*? Where are *with*—*proximate angel*—*sent prophet*—three or four diverse things!? And these words! Whatever enters into words is an invitation.

But there is never hopelessness. If two breaths remain, there is hope in the first breath. Shout out in the second, and you'll pass on. And in hope there are many hopes, there is much laughter—one never laughs out of grief. That is beyond all joys. Everyone has a joy—the ascetic, the scholar, the worshiper, the saint, the prophet.

After all, if the secret of speech is eternal, the secret of the secret of speech is more eternal. The form indeed has been brought down on the neck with a sword. The speech is good, but it has been unsheathed and brings hopelessness. *The best of speech is short and to the point.* There's not much. The speech of Muhammad is the best. (693-94)

242.

[*I have a moment with God*] *in which neither proximate angel nor sent prophet embraces me*. In the road I said some words. That Armenian was saying, "Happy and fortunate is he who is with you every day."

The other unbeliever was saying, "What you're saying is that we and all the people are cows, donkeys, and quadrupeds!"

That was of the same kind as *The Real speaks on the tongue of Umar.* (147-48)

243.

Someone sewed a beautiful pair of shoes for the Prophet, and he was pleased. He said, "You have sewn beautifully! You have sewn well!"

The man did not remain silent. He said, "I have sewn better than that, O Messenger of God, and I can do it again!"

He said, "So, for whom are you keeping the better pair? If you haven't sewn them for me, for whom did you sew them?" (664)

244.

Keep yourself new so that you won't deserve to be addressed by *Visit at intervals*. If you hear this address from the tongue of the state, go into seclusion and weep your heart out: "I mean, what is it with me and what has happened that I should be addressed by these words? This address is not for Abu Bakr, nor for the other Companions." Rain down those tears until you find tasting and ease. "*Visit at intervals*. Go, for you do not have the gaze, and what you do have will be harmed if you see any more."

The occasion was this: He used to take Muhammad's shoes and place them on his eyes and head. This time, he straightened his sandals on his feet. No one has said this—this is a secret, I'm saying it.

He said, "Well! At first, you placed them on your head and eyes. I myself was complaining to the Lord: 'Have my shoes become so lowly that they should reach his head and eyes?'

"Have you now become stale that I appear to you as stale? Don't look at me as if I'm stale."

The purpose of this *Visit at intervals* was that he meant, "Look at me with the gaze with which the ignorant look at me after an interval. See me as fresh and new, for in no way have I become old. Don't become old yourself. And, if something old comes into your gaze, turn back: 'I wonder why that is? Have I sat with the folk of caprice? What happened?'

"Place the fault on yourself, for *Visit at intervals* means go quickly, see me in reality. Renew your own burning. I am new. Affirm yourself, for I am affirmed. If you want to affirm me, it's because of your lack of firmness. How could I become firm through your affirmation? Are you strong in affirming? You've said to me that you have affirmed me. The angels stand on their feet and say, 'God give you long life!'

"How would it be appropriate to say to the Being of God that God is? You should gain existence. The angels will praise you all night—you have set God's existence aright!"*

Happy is he who sees me, and happy is he who sees him who has seen me! If you say that a hundred times, it will be the same: "Whenever someone has seen me, I have seen him, and he is like me." These words are spoken by the speaker of words. He looks to see if they've understood. He's speaking deceptively. The last is just that, and the first just that. Necessarily, everyone who drinks becomes drunk—unless he pours it down his sleeve, or has a strong constitution. If you had understood these words, you would have come to naught and been effaced. (688-89)

245.

A Sufi, a seeker, struggled for many years. He served shaykhs and others, all in one hope. But the moment had not yet come.

> Until the appointed time, whatever the work,
> you'll get no gain, whoever the companion.

After old age and despair had come, once he went out to the cemetery and remembered his hopes. He wept a great deal. He put a brick under his head and slept. In that sleep, his work was completed and his desire was obtained. He stood up and placed the brick on his head and face, and wherever he went he took it with him—banquet, mosque, toilet, bath, recreation, *sama*, market. That frail and weak man kept the brick under his arm every day. They asked him, "Why don't you put it aside?"

He said, "In the grave also this will be my pillow, for I had lost something for a long time. I had despaired, become hopeful, again despaired, thousands and thousands of times. One day I put my head on this brick, and I found what I had lost."

The Prophet said, "*When someone is blessed by something, he should cling to it.*"

They might object and say, "How should we consider '*Visit at intervals*' next to '*He should cling to it*'?"

I say: That was said in the case of Abu Hurayra and others who had obtained a certain discourtesy through companionship, and they felt sated. He would have never said that in the case of Abu Bakr. He would not even let him go out on raids, lest he become absent from the Messenger and busy with the raid.

One day in battle a warrior charged into the field, and the Companions jumped back. No one went before him. They asked, "How is it that the self-deniers of *as though they were a solid building* [61:4], the sacrificers of *So wish for death* [2:94], those who seek death like a poet seeks rhyme, a sick man health, a prisoner deliverance, and children Friday—why and from whom is this flight and holding back?"

They said, "It's not out of fear for life. However, that warrior who charged into the field is the light of the eyes and the child of Abu Bakr Siddiq.* The Companions are ashamed to go forward."

These words reached the ears of Abu Bakr Siddiq, who was in the camel-litter with the Messenger. He asked, "What's all this uproar?"

They said, "It's your son who has attacked."

He immediately mounted up and went out in the field of *I am quit of you* [8:48]. When the son saw his father's face, he returned. Siddiq also returned.

The Messenger put his blessed hand on Siddiq's shoulder and said, "*Save yourself for us, O Siddiq!*" In other words, "Your self has no value for you, but for us it has tremendous value. For our sake watch out for it. Don't go into the fighting, don't go out on raids, and cling to companionship with us."

How could he say to him, "*Visit at intervals*"?

Raiding was incumbent for the other believers, and it was the most precious act of obedience. But for Siddiq it would have been disobedience. *The good deeds of the pious are the ugly deeds of the proximate.* (158-60)

246.

"The effort of the hand and the sweat of the brow" means the food of the spirit. *Eat from the effort of your hand and the sweat of your brow*, that is, from the food of your own spirit.

How should they know the meaning of the Koran and the Hadith? For them the Koran puts on a hundred veils.* *None touch it but the purified* [56:79], only a few. Why would the beauty of the Koran throw off its veil?

It's following that I'm explaining, but he doesn't know it. To himself he says, "I wonder what this following is?" Following is standing before him, opened up right in front of him, but he doesn't see the following.

Moses was a prophet—I don't ask the difference between a prophet and a messenger, other than the difference that the folk of form say, which is that the messenger is the one who has a book. Nor do I ask the difference between the messenger and the possessor of steadfastness,* through which the folk of the outward sense have become arrogant. I am speaking about following.

He's bemused, where is his mind going? Following has come to the door of his house, but he doesn't know. Moses gives it a pot, "Go, get some water."*

When Moses went to Khizr, he did not see the following. Muhammad recognized following. When Muhammad saw that dervish, he gave him the needful and suitable gaze and spoke suitable worlds. (197-98)

247.

One day some of the Companions came to see the Messenger. They said, "There's a man here who mixes with neither the unbelievers nor the Muslims. We don't see the attributes of mad men in him, nor do we see him seeking his own portion like the rational." Another group then began to describe him.

Tenderness toward him entered into the Master. He said, "When you see him this time, extend to him my greetings, and tell him that I am eager to see him. But do not invite him, and do not trouble him more than that."

When they came, at first he gave them no opportunity to greet him. After a time he gave them the opportunity and he paid attention. They extended Muhammad's greetings to him and the Messenger's eagerness. He remained silent, and they did not dare to repeat what they had said, for the Prophet had instructed them not to bother him more than that. After a time, they saw that he had gone to visit Muhammad, and he sat rather late. God's Messenger was silent, and he was silent. Muhammad stood up before him with deference, both when he came and when he went. He said, "*You have been poured upon abundantly*"—you have been poured down upon with an immense pouring.

This is our madrasah—these four walls of flesh. The professor is great. I won't say who it is. The heart is the tutor. *My heart spoke to me of my Lord.* (263-64)

248.

When someone eats with one who has been forgiven, he is forgiven. What is meant by this *eating* is not the eating of bread, not the eating of food. It is the eating of the food of that world. Concerning the martyrs whose throats have been cut He says, *provided, rejoicing* [3:169-70]. Once the soul that commands to evil has been subdued, it has become a martyr and a warrior already in this life. When anyone eats of that food with someone who has been forgiven, *he is forgiven.* Otherwise, a thousand hypocrites and Jews ate food with Muhammad.

He said, "But they did not believe that he was forgiven."

I said, "Belief in the forgiveness of Muhammad will become correct when one eats with him from the same pot. This is the recompense for belief and the mark of correct belief." (318-19)

249.

He said, "The meaning of Iblis is not newly arrived, though his form is indeed newly arrived."

Someone said, "That's unbelief."

He said, "No, it's not unbelief, it's Islam, because when I say that the meaning of Iblis is eternal, I mean that his existence was in God's knowledge."

He said, "His existence was not in God's knowledge. It was in God's knowledge that he would come into existence."

He said, "In any case, Iblis's meaning preceded his form, just as human spirits are prior to their forms. *The spirits are ranked troops.* God says, *'Am I not your Lord?' They said, 'Indeed You are'** [7:172]. This happened before the bodily frames."

Muhammad also said that Iblis enters into the veins of human beings.* He flows in the veins just like blood. Certainly, that ugly form that they make out of a tall hat,* saying "This is Iblis," does not flow in the veins of Adam's children.

Iblis enters into the veins of Adam's children, but he does not enter into the speech of the dervish. After all, the speaker is not the dervish. The dervish is annihilated. He has been obliterated. Speech comes from that side.

In the same way, you make a goatskin into a bagpipe,* you put it to your mouth, and you blow into it. Whatever sound comes out is your sound, not the sound of the goat, even though it comes out of the goatskin, for the goat has been annihilated. The meaning that used to cause the goat to make sounds has been annihilated. So also, when you beat the skin of a drum, a sound comes. But when the animal was alive, if you had beaten its skin, would that sound have come?

> The man of intelligence knows
>> the distance from this sound to that.

It was necessary to bring this example because the one who speaks from the perfect dervish is God. How then can anyone object to the speech of the dervish?

He said, "Not hearing the question, and becoming disturbed by the question, are defects."

I said, "Anyone who has perfect understanding knows that this is perfection, for no defects can fit on the side of God. The defect comes from his impatience. Are you not like this because of impatience? When someone deliberates, then the answer will come, and the answer of the speaker. Even if you don't hear the answer and it does not come, the meaning does come. When the blessing of patience becomes the listener's strength, and another knowledge helps your knowledge—'Up until now, he has been giving one answer to the difficulty; after this, he will speak a hundred answers'—then the assembly will go well. In his mind the dervish will imagine that the assembly has gone well and been carried out well, and he will be inclined to come again to that gathering. That inclination will do many things for him and yield various fruits."

After all, the dervish was not taught on this side. He was taught from that side. Through God's bounty, the teaching of that side falls to this side. How can you object to him with the narratives of this side?

He said, "*The eyes do not perceive Him* [6:103] is despair."

He said, "*And He perceives the eyes* [6:103] is complete hope. When
the reality of vision turned its face to Moses* and took over such that
he was immersed in vision, he said, *'Show me'* [7:143]. He replied,
'You will not see Me' [7:143]. In other words, if you want to see like
that, you will never see. This is to stress denial and wonder: 'Since
you are drowned in seeing, how can you say, "Show me so that I may
see"?' If this is not so, how can we suppose that Moses was God's
beloved and His speaking-companion? For most of the Koran mentions him, and, *when someone loves something, he mentions it often.*"

But, look at the mountain [7:143]. That mountain is Moses' own
essence. He calls it a "mountain" because of its tremendousness,
stability, and fixity. In other words, "Look into yourself and you
will see Me." This is near to *He who knows his soul knows his Lord.*
When he looked into himself, he saw Him.

He disclosed Himself [7:143]. Then his self, which was like a mountain, crumbled to dust. Otherwise, how can you consider it permissible that He would reject the supplication of Moses, who was His
speaking-companion, and show Himself to an inanimate object?

After that, he said, *I have repented to Thee* [7:143]. In other words,
[I have repented] from the sin of being drowned in vision and then
asking for vision. (173-75)

250.

These people have become confused by the reality of Iblis. If
Iblis is that form, then how can it be true that *he flows in the veins
of Adam's children like blood?* So, he is related to meaning, and there
is another meaning that repels him. For example, wrath comes to
you, then again ease comes to you. The first is related to meaning,
and the second even more so. When it takes precedence, know that
mercy has taken precedence.*

He's speaking philosophy, intellectual and delicious, *but with God
there is a philosophy more delicious than this philosophy.*

By the pure Essence of God! What they have said, that he must
have a shaykh—those words should not be repeated. They do have
an interpretation—they are not like *I am the Real* in being without interpretation.

Here there is doubt, for, when he said "I," how can there be

God? And when there is God, to say "I" is terribly naked and disgraced. (762-63)

251.

One day I was speaking by allusion about the meaning of this verse: *This is of Satan's doing** [28:15]. I said, "The Messenger of God says, '*Satan flows in Adam's children just as blood flows in the veins.*' So, this Satan is not the form of the Turkoman with the tall hat that they draw. When heat came into Moses so that he punched the Egyptian, that was Satan's heat."

I twisted into the son of Jalal Warakani:* "In fact then, what is this Satan, other than what I've explained concerning the killing of the Egyptian?"

He said, "What you say is good. But you should also accept the form of Satan that I am talking about. I'm making him intelligible. What you're saying has been given to all of them. Muhammad is the last of them, for you admit that all the sciences connected to the basis of the religion were known to Muhammad, and you say that Muhammad had them all." He kept on repeating that it was good, but it's been given to all of them. (214-15)

252.

Adam was forgetful. He said, "*Our Lord, we have wronged ourselves*" [7:23]. He spoke no more and did not busy himself with any other words. Iblis began saying, "*I am better than he* [38:76]."* The child of the vicegerent knows that He wants excuses for the just, but that excuse was worse than the sin. He denied the Creator—exalted is He. "Don't You know that I know better than You?"

*By Your exaltedness, I shall lead them all astray** [38:82]. The prophets, saints, and great shaykhs are included in this. He will not let go of his own act. When will he bring his act to pass?

He placed His solicitude on one side and him on the other. He wanted to see what he would do. "You can keep him from Me, but how will you keep Me from him?" (639-40)

253.

A severe and hot-headed man is needed to bring a people like this, a community like this, to worthiness—someone like Muhammad, or Ali, who was a swordsman.

One day Muhammad was asking each of the Companions indi-
vidually about his nature and his inclination: Is he inclined toward
war, or toward peace? Is he inclined toward gentleness, or toward
severity? Is the inclination toward peace because of faint-hearted-
ness, loving the soul, and searching for safety, or is it because of
wanting the good, generosity, patience, and forbearance?

He asked some things from Abu Bakr. He saw that he was no
swordsman, because of extreme clemency and mercy.

Each of them was described by one of the attributes of
Muhammad.

He asked them one by one, "If you were the caliph after me,
what would you do?"

He asked from Umar. He said, "I would be just, I would be
impartial."

He said, "You're speaking the truth—it's raining down from
you." He would kill his own son to enact the punishment for fornication and to close the door of corruption. He would kill his
own father for criticizing Muhammad.

He asked Abu Bakr, "What would you do?"

He said, "As long as I could I would keep the curtain down and
pretend not to hear and not to see."

He said, "You speak the truth—it's obvious in you." (616-17)

254.

From the lash of Umar's whip, the earth used to give back milk,
and in fear of him, wine would turn into vinegar. He said, "What
do you have in your hand?"

That fellow said, "Vinegar."

If the sun was affecting his shoulder, he would look with a wink
at the sun, and the sun would turn black. I acknowledge this. If the
philosopher does not acknowledge it, what can I do?

One day Umar came into the mosque. He saw that Muhammad
was speaking to someone quietly, and he found no opportunity,
because his blessed insides forbade him to come close. He was
thinking, "How is it that I'm not the confidant of this talk?"

The Messenger was aware of his thought, for *I was told of it by the
Knowing, the Aware** [66:3]. He said, "O Umar, did you hear anything of

what I was saying to that companion? Did you understand anything?"

He said, "No, O Messenger of God. I just saw that your blessed lips were moving."

He said, "You saw a lot—you may have guessed by the shapes of the letters."

Umar fell on his face. (219)

Even if it be after a thousand
years, these words will reach
those for whom they're intended.

My Time
with Mawlana

OUR ENCOUNTER

I.

I used to plead with the Real Presence: "Allow me to mix with and become the companion of Your saints." In a dream it was said to me, "I will make you the companion of one saint."

I said to myself, "Where is that saint?"

The next night it was said to me, "He's in Anatolia." When I finally saw him after a long time, it was said to me, "It's still not time." *Affairs are in pawn to their times.* (759-60)

2.

This is a symbol for the state of the sought one who has no mark in the world.* Every mark is a mark of the seeker, not a mark of the sought. All is the speech of the seeker. Nothing becomes manifest except through the seekers. When the seeker gazes on someone's forehead, he knows by the light of his own seeking whether that person is felicitous or wretched.

The seeker has come to look around and see if there are any seekers who have the attribute of being sought, who are looking at the seekers, who are ill at ease and agitated. He will say that this is the unique pearl—"I am the sought. I've come to the world to look around."

They say, "We're at ease, now we'll settle down."

He says, "What place is this for settling down?"

They say, "Let's go."

He says, "First let's look around together for a few days."

Now, with my light, we'll look around every day.

When the friend is at hand, does anyone still say "seeker"? The seeker is boiling and speaks quickly like Jesus.*

After forty years, the sought! The one sought for sixteen years gazes upon the face of the friend—after fifteen years the seeker has found him qualified to speak. (763)

3.

In the whole world, words belong only to the seekers.* What mark is there of the sought? I heard—did you hear the dispute of the sought one with God at the time He intended to create the world?

"After all, where are you going, My dear?"

After the dispute—well, what can I say? "*God be with you*"—not by way of farewell, but rather on the sofa of solicitude and gentleness.

Stop, my camel—joy is complete,
the time has arrived, the journey ended.
The earth has become like paradise in beauty,
the festival has come, affairs are in order. (764)

4.

Now, there's no doubt that in the world there's an intended one, a sought one. There is someone for the sake of whom this tent has been raised up. The rest are his subordinates and servants. The building is for him—he's not for the building.

For example, someone has a dear guest. For his sake he builds a lodging. He's in one residence, and he sets up this building for him.

There are those who are intent on reaching the intended one. Not every one of those intent on him are given the way to him, only the one whom he wants. The one who has the intention will never reach him on his own—only if the intended one shows himself to him. The one who has the intention has trampled the world underfoot and tossed it behind his back. He has tossed knowledge behind and thrown away worlds subtler than that, because he is prepared, he is thirsty for him. When he starts presenting himself to him, he will not be let go.

This knowledge cannot be gained by struggle.* Were someone to exert the struggle of heaven and earth for this knowledge, he would become more abandoned and disgraced. Unless it happens that he undertakes servanthood and struggle in the world of God—but, his intention will not be gained by this purpose.

Now, what if I were to say that I'm the sought one and Mawlana has remained far from me? What marvelous felicity he has now that he has found and reached me! And the contrary would be the contrary. (704)

5.

Beyond these outward shaykhs who are famous among the people and mentioned from the pulpits and in the assemblies, there are hidden servants, more complete than the famous ones. And there's a sought one, who is found by some of them. Mawlana thinks that I am he. But that's not my belief.

If I'm not the sought one, I'm the seeker. In the end, the seeker will bring up his head in the midst of the sought. Right now, God is seeking me.

However, the story of the sought one is not known in any book, nor in the explanations of the paths, nor in the treatises— all those are explanations of the road. About that one person, we've heard this, nothing else.

That day I was recounting the saying of Junayd, "If it's ten cucumbers for a copper, how much is it for me?" He went into a state from this, such that ten ill people would not reach the weakness he had from these words. In my view this is unbelief. Judge the rest in the same way. Since he is that, the story that gives his mark is true. (127)

6.

There is the story of that gnostic in Baghdad. He heard, "One hundred cucumbers for a copper." He beat his clothes and fell down senseless and ill. He's not of my line. Why would you say my words and state are like his? I have none of that. I am seeking the One. Where did a hundred cucumbers come from? If you say to the seeker of the One, "One hundred cucumbers for a copper," wouldn't that be unbelief? Would he put up his hands and say, "Why did you say that?"? No, why would he put up his hands? He would leave him as he was. Why do you bring this as the like of my words? (110)

7.

This tale has not yet grown in the world. Now it has grown, and even if it hadn't grown, the goal is advice. That cruelty has to be corrected. We commanded that it be corrected, and we taught the Path. The Path is to give away this world, *for whoever is guarded against the avarice of his own soul—those, they are the prosperous* [59:9]. He is saying, "Try so hard to rectify things that the cruelty I keep in front of Me for the sake of separation may be cast aside."

When he turns away from God in the time of testing, and he serves Him in the time of blessing, the Beloved says, "When I enter pleasantly, you enter pleasantly. When I turn sour, you turn sour. That's not much. The gist of it is sourness."

This sourness is pleasantness. This road is backwards. What I said in wrath is clemency. Pleasantness is in my disbelief, my heresy. It's not so much in my Islam. Those words that I said about the cruelty that happened in the time of separation—I take them like a mirror and hold them in front of me. You accepted that, you wrote it down, you put in all the punctuation. Now you see that those words were for someone else. The way to put that talk and advice into practice was not to offer any opposition after the advice, but you did.

The tale of that merchant who had fifty factors—I mean agents—has already been told. They went in every direction, land and sea, trading with his possessions. He had gone seeking a pearl, at the fame of a diver. He passed by the diver, and the diver came after him. The merchant and the diver kept the states of the pearl secret between themselves.

The merchant had seen a dream about that pearl, and he had confidence in the dream. In the same way, when Joseph* had confidence in the dream of the sun, the moon, and the stars prostrating themselves before him, and he had knowledge of its interpretation, then for him the well, the prison, and the lice were all pleasant.

Today, the diver is Mawlana, I'm the merchant, and the pearl is between the two of us. They say, "The path of the pearl is between the two of you. Will we also find the way to it?"

I said, "Yes. However, the Path is this: I don't say, 'Give something to me.' Rather, come in need. In other words, with the tongue of your state,* ask which is the road to God. Say that."

I say, "This is the Path of God. Of course, it goes by way of Aksaray.* And that is to pass over the bridge of *Struggle with your possessions and your souls* [9:41]. First, give away your possessions, and after that, there's much work to do. However, first you must go to Aksaray. There is no way to pass except by way of Aksaray, unless it be the desert. But, as soon as the ghouls and the wolves see that you have left the road, they'll come like an arrow shot from a bow and be your companion. They'll make one bite of you and swallow you down.

"What will you do today and what will you give? What is before your heart? Say whatever there is! If there is an obstacle, tell me about it. If you tell me about the obstacle, I will teach you the Path. It will become easy, because I know the Path better than you.

"I'm speaking of the pearl, and you're not letting go of the bridge." (113-15)

8.

He says, "If you would have patience, if you wouldn't speak cruelly. . . ."

How could that thought fit into the house of my heart? The house is full, there's no place for a needle. He's brought a stove for the warehouse: "Put it there!" Where can I put it? Show me the place!

I said, "How can you deceive God with the world, for it's a worthless thing. God's servants become bored even with precious things."

There was a pearl in a shell. He was wandering around the world, seeing shells without pearls. They were telling stories about the shell and the pearl, and he told stories along with them. They said, "That shell with the pearl that we've heard about—do you have it?"

He said, "By God, I hear the same things you do."

"You cunning knave! You have it, you're speaking deceptively!"

He said, "No, by God, I don't."

He went on his way, and the shell was in the world just as it was. One day, he found the unique pearl. He said what he said. *He revealed to His servant what He revealed* [53:10].

If you call this one a shell, don't call that one a shell. When there's a shell in which the pearl of God's secrets has boiled up, how can you call it by the same name as a broken piece of pottery? (107)

9.

With that great, everlasting, never-ending Pearl, I warmed up and became impetuous. I became hot. The Pearl responded with clemency and softness: "I'll do whatever you like."

When I was able to do so, I said, "I must have that well-known pearl. I want You to accept it and not throw it away."

It became hot and impetuous, I responded with clemency and softness.

If It receives my softness, It will bring forth clemency. Then I will bring forth clemency for Its softness. I said, "All right, I've given up. I don't want anything. The judgment is Yours."

Again It began: "What do you really want?"

I said, "You know."

It said, "No, you say it."

I said, "Right there—that's the reason. If You make peace, I'll make peace."

It said, "No, be exact, say what it is."

I said, "I mean, action is stronger than words. I spoke, and You forbade it."

It said, "For Me, your words are better than your action. Say it."

I said, "No, it's what You know. Until it's done, there's no use. It's given over to You. It's Yours." (109)

10.

The forms are diverse, but the meanings are one. I remember Mawlana sixteen years ago. He was saying that the creatures are like numerous grapes. They have number in respect of form. If you squeeze them in a pot, will any number be left? If anyone can put these words into practice, his work will be complete. (690)

11.

I hardly mix with anyone. Even with a chieftain like him—if you sift the whole world, you won't find another—it was sixteen years before I ever began with "Peace be upon you." He went.

Dip the pot in water, fill the table with bread, pull the knife across the lamb. *Intentions are through works* of this sort. *Through opposites things become clear.*

If I said to them, "If you give it to the dead, it will go from grave to grave, and if you give it to the living, it will go from dump to dump," they would flee.

That property which they steal and then bring to me is permitted in my eyes. What difference does it make to me? All the more so for property that comes from something permitted.

This is not a water that is less than two basins,* or a jug that you have to fear will become polluted and changed. But, it's not fitting for others to be so bold.

For example, a falcon comes and sits on the wall of a fort. Someone picks up a stone to throw at it, and it flies up and goes. But, if a donkey stands on the wall—"If a stone comes this way, I'll jump like him"—he'll fall down and break his neck. Or he'll fall down in the muck, and he'll go down and down and down—like Korah. (290)

12.

The other day you said that this eye-ache had given you a limpidness. Again I wanted to steal away my words and remain silent, but my insides had warmed up, so I said, "This time I won't hold back." Strange—the person who possesses tasting, the moment the tasting arrives, does not let himself talk. So, the words remain inside me.

You left early, and I found someone else who didn't have much understanding. I was speaking with him. He became perplexed and bewildered. I didn't have much patience with a friend and beloved—how could I have had patience with a stranger?

From the beginning, I inclined strongly toward you. But, I saw from your talk at that moment that you were not receptive to these symbols. If I had spoken, nothing could have been done during that time, and we would have ended up wasting it. At that moment, you didn't have this state. (618-19)

13.

I had heard that in Konya there were many *sama*s and invitations. *I haven't seen it*—I mean there are no states, no words.

He said, "You will see."

From the day I saw your beauty, inclination and love for you sat in my heart. If you had known nothing of writing, I would have taught you how to write. But you know. I want someone who knows nothing. I want to teach.

Now that I am saying this, you're being humble. How come? Didn't it reach you? Didn't you hear what I said?

[The meaning of Koran 93:7 is] *Your soul found your soul.** Then you will not have attributed "losing" and then "finding" to God.

You shouldn't be perplexed by the many opinions. Although its meaning is obvious, it unveils a hundred million secrets. The road is long, and it is blocked by the wall all the way to heaven. It disappears with this—with this kick. And He also taught him how to knock over other walls.

God did not consider it feminine* because "I can conceal so many things; I can also conceal the feminine gender."

Does anyone ask a corpse to pray?* Someone comes across a corpse and says, "Hey, stand up, say your prayers!" Everyone rational will say that he's mad: "He should be taken to the asylum, locked in chains, and beaten a hundred times a day until he becomes rational." Even a man half mad, hearing him, will say, "You should take him to the asylum, or kill him."

> When your holy bird flies up from the body's well,
>   it will be freed of fasting's shame, rid of prayer's disgrace.*

I never tell anyone to stay away from something until I see that he's not attached to it. Otherwise, it will turn into a wound. I let him be until I see that nothing of it remains. When a wound heals, the cotton falls off.

When it was time for playing with bats and sticks, I used to have the states of Junayd and Abu Yazid—what they used to do. Now, the sultan's child is the sultan. How could he play with balls in the square? Everyone knows the difference between playing tipcat and playing with the ball of the dynasty. The ball of good fortune is won and lost in the square.

God willing, things worth seeing will be seen. (752-53)

14.

I have nothing to do with the common people in this world— I haven't come for them. I've put my finger on the pulse of those who guide the world to the Real. (82)

15.

The goal of the existence of the world is for two friends to meet and look upon each other for the sake of God, far from caprice.

The goal is not bread, not the baker, nor the butcher-shop and the butcher. It's just like this hour, when I'm at ease in the service of Mawlana. (628)

16.

I speak beautifully, I speak happily. On the inside I'm bright and luminous. I was water bubbling in itself, twisting in itself and beginning to stink. Then Mawlana's existence struck against me, and the water began to flow. Now it goes forth happily, fresh and splendid. (142)

17.

Joining with you is extremely exalted—too bad life does not suffice. I should have a world full of gold to give away for the sake of joining with you.

I have a living God—what would I do with a dead God? *Meaning is God**—this is the same meaning that I said.

God's covenant does not become corrupted—unless someone becomes corrupted or is corrupt. (665)

18.

It's the sun that brightens the whole world. It sees the brightness—"It's falling down from my mouth. Light's coming out of my talk. It's shining underneath the black words."

The sun has turned its back to them and turned its face to heaven, but the earth's brightness comes from it.

The sun's face is turned toward Mawlana, because Mawlana's face is turned toward the sun. (660)

19.

I was sent because this fine servant of ours was caught in the midst of unfit people. It would be a pity if they were to take him to harm.

Two companions sit with each other, look at each other, and speak—how can the savor of that be compared with gazing from afar? The distance veils you. Even if you have such limpidness that it does not veil you, where is the savor of nearness? If someone has presence from afar, what then will nearness be like?

They say, "We're going to such and such a place. Find out if Shams will be there. If not, say we're busy right now."

He said to me, "Is he better, or that goldsmith Akhlati, who has become the shaykh?"

I said, "Everyone is great in his own station. But how is he related to him? I wouldn't detract from anyone, but his world is something else. He's a dervish whose wishes are still raw. What kind of a place would let this child be the shaykh! He still needs to serve the Men for years. Night and day he needs to burn and melt like beef fat on a frying pan. Then—perhaps, maybe." (622-23)

20.

Two people entrusted something to someone. When the first came out of the bath, he asked for the sack, took it, and went. The other one came. The adversary said, "I have the gold, but you bring the other fellow and then take it."

In short, those Men of the Real who were hidden—it was never required that I speak to them. They offered their salutations if possible, and they went. I never spoke to anyone, except to Mawlana.

Come, let me tell you in your ear: When I want to do something, if God forbids me, I don't listen.

When someone sees me, he becomes either a complete Muslim, or a complete disbeliever. When he does not become aware of my meaning, he sees only what's on the outside and he sees shortcomings in these outward acts of worship. He has a high aspiration, but now he fancies that these acts of worship are not required. He falls far from the acts of worship, which are the means of deliverance for everyone. (739)

21.

This was a vat of divine wine, its mouth stopped up with clay. No one was aware of it. I put my ear to the world and listened. The vat was opened because of Mawlana. When anyone benefits from it, the reason is Mawlana. In short, I belong to you. What makes me happy, my goal, is the profit that opens up through you.

If they say, "You're happy," I become happier. I snap my fingers in *sama*. If the state is to be, let it be however it's to be.

That day I had come to stay overnight. Mu'id Hariwa began talking, "I'm the Pole, and the world inside me is such-and-such."

Mawlana jumped up: "I'm not going to listen to this," and that made us leave. That was last night.

You said that the disciples say he's arrogant to us, he doesn't mix with us, and he craves things.

Mawlana prepared himself to go. I wanted to stay there two or three days.

I don't want anything from anyone for the sake of judgment. If they bring something as a gift for the cloak, I don't reject it. That's my custom. If I judge, that will be for his good and his deliverance.

When someone says, "We tried to get Shams to come in the hope that he would persuade Mawlana to preach," that's not right. What's the remedy?

The answer: When they have heard ten times that the others want to hear Mawlana preach one time, I want it a hundred times over. These little jobs will go wrong if it's like that dervish says. They interpret the situation and say that a hundred advantages are to be found in it. (773-74)

MY SPIRITUAL MASTERY

22.

Mawlana has good beauty, and I have beauty and ugliness. Mawlana saw my beauty, but he did not see my ugliness. This time I will not be hypocritical. I will be ugly so that he may see all of me, both the fineness and the ugliness.

When someone finds the way to be my companion, his mark is that companionship with others becomes cold and bitter for him—not such that it becomes cold and he continues to be a companion, but rather such that he can no longer be their companion. (74)

23.

My existence is an alchemy that does not need to be put on the copper.* When it's placed in front of the copper, it all turns into gold. The perfect alchemy should be like this.

God has servants who, as soon as they see that someone is wearing the clothing of worthiness or the cloak, judge him to be a worthy person. And when they see someone wearing robe and cap, they judge him to be corrupt.

There's another group who look with the light of God's majesty. They've let go of war and they've left behind color and scent: "If you bring that one out of the cloak, he'll be suitable for hell. Hell is ashamed of him. And there's someone in the robe who, if you bring him out of the robe, will be suitable for paradise. Someone is sitting in the prayer-niche busy with work that is worse than what is being done by the one who's fornicating in the tavern.

"*Backbiting is worse than fornication.* If the latter becomes apparent, they punish him, and he's free. If he repents, *God changes their ugly deeds into good deeds* [25:70]. But this one, even if through ascetic discipline he becomes so subtle that he flies in the air, will not be delivered."

If someone has both the clothing of worthiness and the meaning of worthiness—*light upon light* [24:35]. (148–49)

24.

He said: The Man appears outwardly the same whatever he is on the inside. I'm all one color* on the inside. If that became manifest and I had sovereignty and ruling power, the whole world would be one color. There would be no more swords, no more severity. But it is not *the wont of God* [33:62] that the world should be like that.

Long words have become short. If I had outward influence, it would mean that whatever is inside me would fall outside, but then this world would not be. That indeed would be another world.

So, if I had the power, when he began telling the story of Abu Yazid and the seclusions yesterday, I would have said, "This is innovation in Muhammad's religion. Don't talk about innovators." I would have brought Judge Izz, and I would have recounted his faulty judgments and investigations. Just that, and no other revenge. I would have said: "Get up, go, and don't do anything like this again—listening to other people's words, and quoting the sayings of faulty transmitters about God's servants." (106)

25.

I have a heated state. No one has the capacity for my state.

However, my words come and put a plaster on him. They intervene between my state and him, so he gains strength. Some day, if
that state should strike against him, he will have the capacity for it.
A man should be prepared for the work, not for sorrow or grief.
He should be bored with sorrow and grief.

When someone enters the Path, he should watch out not to
keep on slipping. His father's tradition is once.* Once is enough,
and then he should regret it. He should be skillful and wakeful so
that it doesn't happen again. And if it does happen, he should pay
no attention and not think about it, for the days are passing, and
there's no profit in sorrow and grief.

For example, someone wounds his arm in battle. If he weeps and
sorrows over it, what's the use? Rather, he should take some silver
and go to a sage, a physician, a surgeon. He should not weep. Or,
he should send the silver to the surgeon so that he will come to
him and quickly heal the wound. He will be so relieved that he
will fancy that he is well. (766-67)

26.

Moses, with all his majesty, wanted to perfect the attribute of
gentleness by being the companion of Khizr. He kept on repent-
ing until he gained that attribute.

The Men make excuses once in their whole lives, and then they
regret that once. A dervish should repent once in his life, and then
be regretful: "Why should this happen in my road? The policeman
should have come from inside. When something is going to veil
me from myself, why should I let it come forth? When I let that
disturbance go so that it can come forth, it keeps me busy fending
myself off so I can't be busy with myself. A cat steals meat from
me, and I keep myself busy chasing the cat. I'm held back from
eating the meat." (248)

27.

Which arrow is it? These words. Which quiver? The world of the
Real. Which bow is it? God's power. This arrow has no end. *Say:
Were the sea ink. . .* [18:109]. Happy is he who is struck by this
arrow! This arrow will take him to the world of the Real. It's in

the quiver, but I can't shoot it. The arrows that I do shoot go back into the quiver from whence they came. (115-16)

28.

When something needs to be said, I'll say it even if the whole world grabs me by the beard and tells me not to. Even if it be after a thousand years, these words will reach those for whom they're intended. (681)

29.

When Mawlana has some God-given words, he speaks them without being concerned with whether or not anyone will benefit. But ever since I was small, God has inspired me to use words to train people so that they may be delivered from themselves and go forward. Such is the true shaykh.

Some of God's servants are "active," some are "speaking." *You need an active leader more than you need a speaking leader.* However, He decreed that when someone who has the power of activity speaks, the speech takes on the power of acting. It acts. (767)

30.

I mean, don't you know that whatever words I use, I take them forward and put them right? The speaker is strong—no weakness is allowed for him.

I never had the custom of writing. Since I never write anything down, the words stay with me. At every instant they show me another face.

Words are a pretext. The Real has thrown off His mask and is showing His beauty. (224-25)

31.

I said explicitly that Mawlana should go to them, because they don't understand my words. "You talk to them. God hasn't told me to speak in these lowly similes."

I talk about the root. This is extremely difficult for them. As a simile for that, I talk about another root. One thing conceals another right up to the end. Each word I say conceals another. In Mawlana's case, nothing is concealed.

I went to great lengths with them. How could they see face-to-face? When Mawlana spoke, they submitted and apologized. They hung their heads in the manner of dervishes. He went. (732)

32.

If everyone in the inhabited quarter was on one side and I was on the other, I would answer every one of their difficulties. I would never flee from speaking. I would not change the words around, or jump from branch to branch.

The inhabited quarter is where the people reside. The other three quarters burn from the shining of the sun, so people don't live there.

No matter what the difficulty the people of the inhabited quarter come up with, they will find a ready answer with me—whatever it may be. Answer upon answer, fascicle upon fascicle! That is my speech. For each I have ten answers and proofs that have never been written in any book with such subtlety and salt. That's why Mawlana says, "Ever since I became acquainted with you, none of these books has any taste." (186)

33.

By God, those who instituted the seclusion would be perplexed by the form of my words—so what about the meaning of my words?

For example, I should have a line of poetry, or a verse of the Koran—I don't have any words of my own with which to warm myself up.

Even that poor poet wasn't in the world, so what about me? Indeed God created me all alone. Or, I was taken up all alone to the top of a mountain. My father and mother died and I was raised by wild animals.

After all, the plain of speech is extremely spacious,* so meaning is narrow in its spaciousness. And still, there are meanings beyond the plain of meaning, such that the spaciousness of expression becomes narrow. It pulls it down, it pulls it under, both its words and its sounds, so no expression remains.

He's silent not because he lacks the meaning, but because it has filled him up. (97-98)

34.

When I recite poetry in the midst of talking, I blossom, and I speak of its secret meaning. Some people become dumb because they are overwhelmed by the meaning—Mawlana is never dumb except because of being overwhelmed by the meaning—and some people because of the lack of meaning. I don't have any of that.

These people have a right not to find my words congenial. My words all come by way of greatness. They all appear as pretension. The Koran and the words of Muhammad all came by way of need, so they all appear as need.

They hear words that are not in the path of seeking or need. The words are so high that if you look up at them, your hat falls off. But, it's no fault for God to claim greatness. If they find fault, it's as if they're saying, "God claims to be great." They speak the truth. Where's the fault? (138-39)

35.

Yesterday, I was coming to see you, but Izz ad-Din, Imad ad-Din's disciple, saw me passing. He came out and invited me to the khanaqah: "Let's go in for a while." It's my custom always to treat the companion's commandment and suggestion with the highest regard.

Knowledge is seldom accompanied by practice.* Both exist here. That's strange.

Right now, it's the inclination of my heart. What can I do?

I preach well, and I never become dumb at the end of the sermon. Khujandi becomes dumb at the end of the sermon. How can you compare the beginning of his sermons with their end?

Whenever I recite a line of poetry, I blossom and speak of its meaning.

You also fail for words at the end of your sermons. But that is because of being overcome by meaning, not dumbness.

How could he have this state? In any case, I don't have it. (347-48)

36.

He said, "Saying that he shouldn't speak is like saying, 'O sun,* don't give light, for you're upsetting the mind of the bat.' Of course it will go on giving light. It won't stop because the bat's upset."

He said, "Even though the sun doesn't worry about bats or blind men and keeps on scattering light, the sun-worshipers fear that it will be disappointed with them. Then it will deceive them, and they will remain far from the sun."

He said, "However, the sun-worshiper must believe that no one would have the gall to transgress the honor of the sun. The strength of belief must be able to take the one who has it over a mountain. If he sees a seven-headed lion, he'll grab it by the ear. He won't be worried—because of the strength of his belief in the sun and his love for it. Belief and love provide boldness and take away all fear." (693)

37.

I have never twisted around any saying of the Prophet except the hadith, *"This world is the prison of the believer."* I don't see any prison.* I say, "Where's the prison?" However, he didn't say, *"This world is the prison of the servants."* He said, *"prison of the believer."* The servants are another group altogether.

What I mean is that you shouldn't keep yourself in narrow thoughts. Whatever the state that comes, you should quickly tell the companion about it and be done with it. Don't think, "How can I talk like this to the companion?" The companion will see it, even if you don't talk about it. (610-11)

38.

I wonder at the hadith that says, *"This world is the prison of the believer."* I've never seen any prison. All I have seen is happiness, exaltedness, and good fortune. If an unbeliever should piss in my hands, I will forgive him and thank him. Bravo for me!

Why then do I make myself lowly? For a long time I did not recognize myself. What exaltedness and greatness! I'm like a pearl that you find in a toilet.

I fancied that I had been released from that. No, not at all, no indeed!

Now I speak happily, and it makes you happy. Give me your hand so that I can take it. With a brother Muslim, you shake hands. You shake like this, and then the sins fall away. Now let's shake. Always shake, O Muslims, so that we may shake! (317-18)

39.

The heart is greater,* more spacious, more subtle, and brighter than the heaven and the circling spheres, so why do you constrict it with thoughts and whispering doubts? Why should you make the pleasant world your narrow prison? How can you make this garden-like world into a prison? Like a caterpillar, you weave a web of thoughts, whispering doubts, and blameworthy images around your own make-up. Then you become a prisoner and suffocate.

Me, I've made the prison a garden for myself. If my prison is a garden, just think what my garden must be! (610)

40.

Their clothing in [the Garden] is silk [22:23]. Right here I'm wearing silk, but you don't see its fineness, just like an animal, which does not see and does not know the fineness of silk. My skin has become fine, it has become silk. My skin is silk. But how can the softness of silk be compared to this skin? How far apart they are! *Today I have perfected for you your religion* [5:3]. These are his words, "The spirit has found perfection in your frame."*

Either be manly and man-colored
   or be left with a thousand shames.* (189)

41.

Paradise is created. It is a created place that is seen by created things. For the sake of understanding, it needs to be given a beginning—so that understanding may grasp it. I say that it is endless, but not beginningless. It is God who is both beginningless and endless.

I will tell you the mark of the folk of paradise and also the mark of the folk of hell.

From the day that He created paradise, like an arrow flying from a bow, every day and every instant the door has been wide open. It is so thoroughly without limit that intellect is lost in it. (713)

42.

When someone is born in the sun* itself, from birth he opens his eyes to the sun and becomes accustomed to it. They tell him, "Speak of the moon, speak of Mercury."

"How can I speak of them? Does the sun even know that there is a moon in the world?"

It is the moon and the planets that are helpless. Everyone sees the moon and gazes upon it. Although nothing can be compared to the light of the sun, no one can see the disk itself—the eye cannot tolerate it.

The *sisfur** is a marvelous bird. It doesn't burn in fire, but it does drown in water. A duck doesn't drown in the ocean and isn't harmed by it, but fire burns it. The bird that is neither burned by fire nor drowned by water is extremely rare. (218)

43.

God's in my hand—God is not "with me." All these attributes that you spoke about in the sermon—*The Seeing from whose sight nothing escapes*—I see them all as my own attributes. They are my attributes.

> Aren't you ashamed of these stinking dogs?*
> > Aren't you contemptuous of these unbridled asses?
> Look at him—"Ornament of Religion"—
> > he's giving color and scent to unbelief!
> Look at him—"Pride of the Empire"—
> > he's putting shame and disgrace on the empire!

The poet means to say that you should grab the reins and pull them tight. Now the speaker says,

> The knower is different from the ignorant
> > because he's pulled in the reins, he's not let them loose. (623)

44.

Everyone talks about his own shaykh. The Messenger—upon him be peace—gave me a cloak in a dream. It wasn't the kind of cloak that gets torn after two days, then becomes a rag and you throw it in the trash, or that you use to wipe yourself. No, it was the cloak of companionship—not a companionship that fits into understanding, but a companionship that has no yesterday, today, or tomorrow. What does love have to do with yesterday, today, and tomorrow?

If someone says, "The Messenger slept,"* I reject that. If he says, "He was not a lover"—then the Jews will find deliverance and have every hope, but not him.

If they ask me, "Was the Messenger a lover?", I will say, "He was not a lover. He was the adored and the beloved." However, intellect becomes perplexed by the explication of the beloved. So I'll call him a lover in the sense of a beloved. (133-34)

45.

Abu Najib*—God sanctify his spirit—was sitting in a forty-day-seclusion because of a difficulty. He saw several apparitions: "This difficulty of yours will not be solved except by shaykh so-and-so."

He said, "I'll go visit him. I wonder where I'll find him."

A voice came, "You will not see him."

He said, "Then what should I do?"

It said, "Leave the seclusion, go to the mosque, and wander the rows one by one with need and presence. It may be that he will see you—you'll fall into his gaze."

Now, this was the state of Abu Najib.

If I had remained without a shaykh, I would not have remained so. When I showed opposition, it was because of relying on something else—I had confidence in something else. (179)

46.

My heart is nobody's storehouse—it's God's storehouse. Why would I put down the goods of a camel-driver here? I throw them all out. Other people's minds are something else. My mind has no capacity except to be the King's storehouse.

Strength comes from the other side because of selflessness, and it is full of self. This is the state of Muhammad. Did he ever become selfless? No, everything's best interest was apparent and obvious to him.

Now, some people fancy that this state is less than immersion, but many people have immersion. This is another subtlety—that you should have all those immersions, and still see everything's best interest. When the Messenger struck others with a tiny bit of that state, they become headless and footless. That is why Abu Bakr narrated only seven hadiths.

"It is only through them that good and evil, unbeliever and believer, become manifest." These words are true. (627-28)

47.

Let's go for a time to the tavern and see those poor wretches. It's God who has created those women, whether they're good or bad. Let's look in upon them. Let's go to the church too, and look in upon them.

No one has the capacity for my work. It would not be fitting for anyone to imitate me in what I do. They're right when they say that people like these should not be followed. (302)

48.

Let's go out and flatten those mustachios. I don't mean a raid such that the unbelievers would be frightened by my mustache. The unbeliever inside, even if every hair became a spear, would not fear that. I don't mean mine—it's been a long time since my soul's work has been finished. (235-36)

49.

We were quaffing and drinking—cup, flagon, pitcher, pot. The saki was helpless. The saki makes everyone helpless, but this fellow made the saki helpless. They always say that wine is "man-throwing"—if not with ten cups, then with twelve cups; even supposing you have to drink the whole vat.

The wine-seller says, "If the tavern becomes empty, there are many taverns in the city." That's exactly what I'm saying. Anyway, who drinks the whole vat? A hundred people can't drink it.

But, it has never been celebrated in the world that there is a man who is "wine-throwing." The more he drinks, the more he becomes sober. The drunker he becomes, the more sober he is. He's filled up to the gullet, but still sober—and he brings sobriety to the whole world and to the universe!

That would be strange. But why is it so strange? Don't you see
that this man is immersed in the Lordly wine? He's been completely taken over by the wine. His existence has become wine. He
came, and he threw it. Don't you see that he threw the wine? But
such falling is better than a thousand risings.

They nodded their heads, "Yes, yes." I too nodded my head,
exaggerating the yeses.

Someone may say that he was swallowed down by the wine. He
was protected by the wine and couldn't speak. He was talking gib-
berish and they didn't understand it. So his head is not in danger.

But this one is not swallowed by the wine. He does not have the
capacity for the wine, and he's lost himself in its light and its
aroma. His head is in danger—like Hallaj.

As for the one who swallows down the wine, he has not been
celebrated in the world. No one has talked about him. He's a
stranger. He came into the world, took a look around, and went.
But there are a hundred thousand like him. (745-46)

50.

God has servants whose grief can't be tolerated by anyone and
whose joy can't be tolerated by anyone. If anyone else were to
drink the cup that they fill up and swallow down each time, he
would never come back to himself. Others become drunk and
then leave. They're sitting on top of the vat. (302)

51.

"First measure the dress, then cut the cloth." I'm very cautious
in acting.

[We made] Your sleep rest, and [We made] night a garment—that's
the state of sobriety—and [We made] day a livelihood [78:9-11]—
that's the state of intoxication.

It's fish that eat fish. A brightness appeared in the ocean's water.
The captain said nothing. We went on in that brightness for a day.
Then another brightness appeared. After all that, the captain prostrated himself in prayer—a prostration of gratitude. He said, "If I
had said anything at the first one, your liver would have burst. That
was one of the fish's eyes, and this was the other one. If we had

turned back for one instant, it would have destroyed us. The other fish are all tiny.

Fish are always perplexed in the sea, but the sea is perplexed in that fish—"How can it be so big? What is it that's inside me?" (666)

52.

I was talking to myself like this yesterday and wandering around the moat. Talk was pouring down over me and I was overwhelmed. I was standing beneath the talk and being totally overwhelmed. I said, "What will I do if talk overwhelms me like this on the pulpit?"

I don't go up on the pulpit, sir, it was a lie. I was lying and talking wrong. The talk is inside me. Anyone who wants to hear my talk should come inside. However, there's a doorman sitting there—a frightful, fearless Turk. He's killed a hundred thousand friends and companions. He's fearless, and he doesn't care. He won't even ask who you are. He'll give you no chance to say who you are: "Listen, I'm an acquaintance, so-and-so, son of so-and-so." Just like that he'll strike you down and cut you in two—"I don't know anything about that."

They petitioned the commander with a complaint: "He did this and that." The commander ignored it. He didn't accept the petition, because he greatly loved the doorman. They brought the petition forward, but he left it hanging right there.

He said, "What is this petition? Look at this!"

I looked, but I wouldn't read it. He wouldn't do anything that he shouldn't do.

When alone, I said to the doorman, "Why did you do that? I mean, he was an acquaintance."

He said, "That was bad. I won't do it again. But, he went. Will he come back with fine courtesy, quick, and full of need?"

After you pass this doorman, there's another door and another doorman. Others are in the road, and there's long work ahead, until finally you reach the world of the heart. The one taken to the world of the heart has the secret. The reason they make him drunk is so that he will voice the secret in his drunkenness. But the listener must recognize which one of all those words is the secret.

There are little things that he had never spoken of, but which were voiced in the midst of all this talk, and then hidden once again. Perhaps, when Mawlana writes it down, he will find it—or maybe not—with the light of God. Then I will examine it.

While seeing myself I was thinking about the way God takes charge of me and turns me all around. But when I opened my eyes, I saw the prayer-ground just as it was. There was nothing left of His taking charge. I became angry. I was coming from obliteration to existence. I wondered at this business and laughed. Smack in the middle of this diversity of states, you must gaze on the wonders of God's workmanship. In one instant He keeps you like this, and in the next instant like that! He keeps your eyes closed like this, and your eyes open like that!

Man is more than all existent things and all newly arrived things, for his gaze contains the Throne and the Footstool, the heavens, the earth, and everything between the two. It penetrates into every attribute. But "the He" is greater than many thousands of gazes. Why should it be strange that "the He" is with all attributes and newly arrived things? *And He is with you wherever you are* [57:4].

So, in this world everyone's insight* is opened toward one direction such that it does not see the other directions. One sees the activity of a goldsmith; one sees the fine points of jewelry, or alchemy, or sorcery, or offering pretexts, or two-facedness; one sees the realities of disputation, jurisprudence, and theology; one sees otherworldly ease and comfort and the light of God; one sees appetite and beauty and love; one knows only jesting and tricks. In each case a different view and a different porch has been opened up in this little pavilion. This one knows nothing of that one's state, and that of this. And porches have been opened up for a hundred thousand—infinite—living things, animals, crawling things, angels, and others. The physicians, astronomers, and others—all who go higher have more porches. (321-23)

53.

Let's take the divine speech with all seven of its inner senses.* There is no "secret" here. The secret is something else. Even the secret is for the sake of the other, for *alif* itself is manyness; it is for the other.

Look how many words there are in the speech. The second speech breaks the first and conceals it, and the third conceals the second. Then things begin to appear again and turn back to the first speech. The other ones cling to its skirt. These are all a hundred thousand variegations and colorations.

Whatever He says, reply very quickly, for *Gratitude to the Blessing-giver is incumbent.*

My spirit was in a station and went no further. I was saying that there is no station beyond this. He took charge of my spirit, and it went even higher, flying in gentleness and mercy itself.

If someone comes one day and says that the secret of speech is one thing, and speech without words and sounds is something else, ask the difference. Once he finishes that and you have fallen at his feet, let him say what the secret of speech is, that it also is for the sake of others. Let him show you the proofs so that they become clear to you and you see in him the traces of God's awesomeness, tremendousness, and power. He's my younger brother. In any case, it wants a man who has a pain that burns away and rips apart supposition, imagination, and hesitation.

Whenever I speak to others, you should know what is meant for you in what is appropriate for you.

There is no monasticism in Islam. This doesn't mean that you should sit with people. Look at people from a distance. Otherwise, speak true words, sweet and fine.

I have a moment with God. This is an invitation to the state. In other words, do something so that this state may become yours. (691-92)

54.

There was an ascetic in the mountains. He was of the mountain—he was not of Adam. If he had been of Adam, he would have been among the people.

Such people have understanding, they have imagination, they have the capacity to know God. What was he doing in the mountains? He was mud, so he inclined toward stones. What does man have to do with stones?

Be among the people, but be alone. Don't go into seclusion, but be solitary.

Muhammad said, *"There is no monasticism in Islam."* According to one interpretation, this is a prohibition of cutting oneself off, of coming out from among the people, and of making oneself notable among the creatures because of knowledge. Another meaning is that it is a prohibition of refusing to take a wife. Take a wife, but be disengaged. In other words, be separate from all and be rid of all in your heart.

Every year all the people of the city and the king went to visit the mountain man. The sweetness of being accepted by the people was such that it had taken all appetite away from him—he had totally cut himself off from food.

One day a man, a stranger, a dear one, a dervish, passed by there on purpose. He said, "It's not the festival, it's not New Year's—what's this gathering?"

Someone said to him, "Are you crazy? Are you mad?"

What does Layla know of Majnun's state?
Majnun knows what state he has.

The fellow said, "You're a mad man."

He said, "Don't say that."

He said, "I repent. Forgive me." He fell at his feet. He was saying to himself, "There's the scent of tasting in these words. I repent and will be humble because of the blessing of that." The blessing of humility let the taste of those words reach him. He said, "In these mountains, there's an ascetic whom the people come to visit."

In short, the dervish went to visit the king. He greeted him and said, "Listen to one word from me."

The king pulled back his reins. Because of the sweetness of the dervish's words and talk, the king's heart began to boil. He dismounted and said to himself, "I'll sacrifice whatever he wants—if he wants the kingdom, if he wants my beautiful daughter. If he wants my wife, I'll divorce her and give her to him." He said, "O dervish, whatever you want I'll do, for you have a sweet breath."

He said, "That's why I came."

The king said to himself, "Well, from these words there's no scent of that—that he should have none of these desires." He said,

"O dervish, you have a very sweet breath."

He said, "It's because of a dervish's sweet breath. He spoke some words to me, and the sweetness of his words have made my words so sweet that you have dismounted and become obedient like this. If you give those words access to your own existence, the work will be completed. For a time, O king, send the people away right in the midst of the people. Then I will tell you."

The king came to the dervish, in a house where it was not apparent that one was a dervish and the other a king, and not the other way around. (721-22)

MAWLANA'S EXALTED STATION

55.

Mawlana's attributes are such that not one of them can be reached by any fast-going wayfarer with a hundred thousand struggles—whether we talk of his clemency, his knowledge, his humility, his generosity. That would be impossible. There would be no profit. Let him claim his rightful share. (129-30)

56.

Come, O sheer spirit! We're water beneath the straw. Slowly, slowly, the water moves beneath the straw, but the straw is not aware. Suddenly, it throws the straw into the air—*a scattered dust* [25:23]—and flows on.

By God, seeing your face is a blessing. If someone wants to see a prophet sent by God, he should see Mawlana without formality and free, not with all the formality. If he wants something else, he does not know how to live.

Happy is he who finds Mawlana! Who am I? Well, at least I have found him. Happy am I!

When your belief is variegated, where is the certainty of the road? You'll pass the time only in doubt. What I mean by doubt is that for a time you flourish, and then for a time coldness enters into you. This doesn't count in the work, it doesn't count in companionship. This road goes to the other side of certainty.

May Mawlana's day pass in good and your night in felicity! What is the meaning of these words?

One day someone asked about *Glorify Him dawn and evening* [33:42], [*Glorify Him*] *through the long night* [76:26]. I said, "When a Jew learns the script, he understands this literally. You also understand it literally. What's the difference? Since you have not known realization, you have the station of being a Jew. What's the difference between you and him?"

He said, "'Night' is for a cloud to come in or a veil to intervene."

Since it is permissible for a disciple to see a saint seventy times in a day, how could he not consider it permissible to see a prophet sent by God?

He said: What is apparent to the ulama is that every prophet is singled out for something—Abraham for intimate friendship, Moses for speech, Muhammad for vision. What he says is that sanctity and prophecy are for seeing. To preserve the side of the common people this was said with different words, such as "effusion of lights," "unveiling," and "contemplation." They did not speak explicitly.

Now, the reality is what the ulama agree upon—that the saint does not reach the prophet.

If the saint sees—or rather, even the disciple of the saint—how could that be veiled from a prophet? *Whoever is blind in this world shall be blind in the afterworld* [17:72]." (749-50)

57.

Arshad the Sufi was saying to his disciple, "Bring the invocation up from your navel."

I said, "No, don't bring the invocation up from the navel, bring it up from the midst of your spirit." My words threw him into bewilderment.

Whenever I turn my face toward someone, he turns his face away from the whole world. To whom should I show myself? But I don't turn my face toward him.

Someone said, *And what is the mark of that?* The Prophet said, *Withdrawal from the abode of delusion.*

I have a pearl within me. Whenever I show its face to anyone, he becomes estranged from all his companions and friends. This is another subtlety—this is no place for prophecy, no place for messengerhood. Indeed, what can I say about sanctity and gnosis?

Those curtained by the Presence said, "How should we appear? What should we say about who we are?"

He said, "Show your heads from Muhammad's collar: 'We are following him.'"

Otherwise, how can this be the place for following? The ray of their light reached Muhammad, and he nearly became senseless. What kind of following is this?

Mawlana was seated, and Khwajagi said, "It's time for the prayer." Mawlana was busy in himself. We all stood up and performed the night prayer. Several times I looked and I saw that the imam and the others had all turned their back to the kiblah—"We have left the prayer and turned away from the kiblah." (222-23)

58.

The devil was always in the bathhouse, but now the angel's in the bathhouse.

Has Mawlana made the journey to the kiblah?

He said, "Has he ever been empty of the kiblah? What business does he have other than traveling to the kiblah, visiting the Kaaba, and making the hajj? You're mistaken about the kiblah."

In the same way, a dear one saw the Prophet [in a vision] after twelve years. He said, "O Messenger of God! Every Thursday night you used to show yourself to me. You've left me like a fish out of water for all this time. What happened?"

He said, "I've been busy mourning."

He said, "For whom?"

He said, "For my own community. In these twelve years, seven persons turned their faces to the kiblah and came to me, no more. All the rest turned their faces away from the kiblah." (647)

59.

At another time, I would tell the story that I told last night, and you could darken the moon. But now, what darkness? Brightness upon brightness!

First ask—"We're eager, let's stay away from tedium."

I'll give him such a thrashing that you'll say, "Well done!"

I say, "In knowledge and learning Mawlana is an ocean.

However, generosity and manliness are that you listen to the words of the helpless."

I know that, and everyone knows it—he's famous for his eloquence and learning. When a king proudly sends a representative somewhere, would he send someone who's not eloquent and learned? But if Mawlana won't deign to listen to the words of a helpless man, the dervish won't be able to speak.

I'll make him so subdued and incapable in my hand that, with all that eloquence, he'll be like knuckle-bones in the hand of a trickster.

It will become clear that the heart of the saint encompasses the spheres. All the spheres are beneath his heart. (648-49)

60.

You have so much strength that others take strength from you. How can you say that you're weak? Yes, a great man, in the perfection of his greatness, will say that he's weak. Now be quiet, or you'll take away my belief in you.

If I'm as great as you believe, that's all good, and if I'm not, at least I'm clever. With this cleverness, I believe in your seeking—that you are a seeker.

If a sick man comes to a physician and says, "Cure my dropsy," he should not be seeking anything other than the cure. Or a thirsty man who comes seeking sweet water—if they bring bread and sugar candy for him and he eats, he's a liar in his claim to be thirsty. Or a hungry man who claims to be hungry—his test is to bring pure water for him. If he drinks it, he's a liar.

You tell the story of the sultan and the other stories so beautifully!

I was voicing a symbol—a symbol of Hajjaj. I said to Mawlana that yesterday Hajjaj had come like someone covered in sweat who goes from the heat out into the cold. The outside cold strikes against him, and he shrinks and freezes. I indicated to Mawlana that he should speak, even though Mawlana was immersed. He obeyed the command and spoke. Hajjaj left with his state changed, and surprisingly, his tears were flowing. I told the story of the command and the breaking of the pearl.*

I was busy with nothing but supplication for my dear companions: "O God, protect them!" This is the Sunnah of Muhammad. This is following him: *Guide my people, for they do not know.*

How could Mawlana put someone into seclusion and say, "Disciple, what sort of apparitions did you see?" Have you seen a shaykh who is so unaware of the states of his disciple? What would that mean? "What doubts did Satan whisper to you? I'm the other half of his work. You tell me, then I'll complete his whispering. Then you'll go so far away that you'll never catch the scent of God's road." (712-13)

61.

Right now in the inhabited quarter, Mawlana has no equal in all the fields, whether it be theology, or jurisprudence, or grammar. In speaking of logic with its masters, he voices the meaning strongly—better, with more flavor, and more beautifully than they—if he must do it, if he wants to do it, and if boredom doesn't prevent him.

What is distasteful here is that, if I were to become young again and strive for a hundred years, I couldn't gain one-tenth of his knowledge and excellence. But he pretends not to know that. When he's listening to me, he fancies himself—this is so shameful that I can't say it—like a two-year old child before its father, or like a new Muslim who has never heard anything about Islam. What submission! (730)

62.

The prophets long for his presence. I say this only because it pleases Mawlana, and this is what I think.

I do not see myself having any virtue such that words would emerge from me that are pleasing to Mawlana. That is not my state. But, one day I was bored with the discussion. I grabbed the neck one of those words passing through me and said, "From whence?"

It said, "From God."

I said, "Where to?"

It said, "To a great man, Mawlana."

I said, "What am I doing here? Why are you passing through me? Pass through someone else's house—Imad, or Arshad, or Zayn Sadaqa. Either begin with me, or stop passing through my house."

Right now, it doesn't make me bored when it passes through. I even fear doing things that would make it stop passing by way of me. I would regret that.

Is he more excellent than the recent ones? I don't speak of Muhammad, for his affair is magnificent. God doused Muhammad once in the ocean of generosity, then brought him out. Droplets of light fell down from him, and from each of these a prophet emerged. A few drops were left over, and from those He created the saints. So, how could I compare him with him? I say that Muhammad is more excellent than those after him, so how can anyone be compared with him? Whatever has reached me without studying the sciences, without intellect or effort, has all come from the blessing of following him.

The first words I spoke* to Mawlana were these: "Why didn't Abu Yazid cling to following? Why didn't he say, 'Glory be to You! We have not worshipped You [as You should be worshipped]'?"

Mawlana understood those words completely and perfectly. But what was the outcome and end of the words? The purity of his secret heart made him intoxicated, for his secret heart was immaculate and pure. So, that became manifest to him. I knew the pleasure of these words through his intoxication. I had been heedless of the pleasure in them. (684–85)

63.

When you serve the shaykh and are in the presence of the most outstanding of the shaykhs, you will have a permanent seclusion without sitting in seclusion. A state will come over you such that you will always be in seclusion. God has servants such that, when someone joins their service, he has a constant and continuous seclusion.

I don't take disciples. Why then should I bind myself to talking such that no one will be troubled and fall away from the Path? Well, Mawlana has to take some, no doubt.

That day I didn't know that the words I began would stir up that fellow's egoism. If he had been my companion, I would not have said anything.

If Mawlana were to set out to show humility, I would say, "No, Mawlana. First let me do what is necessary and incumbent for me, and that is to show humility before the most outstanding of the shaykhs." (751)

64.

Sometimes in Mawlana's preaching subtleties appear that would not have been found in the preaching of Mansur Hafada, with all his charisma. One day during Mansur's preaching, someone stood up and asked, "What is the mark of the saints?"

He said, "It is that if they tell dry wood to move, it moves." At once the pulpit pulled itself up from the ground—and it had been embedded in the ground two feet deep. He said, "Pulpit, I'm not talking to you, be still!" It sank back down.

God has hidden servants.

He said: From head to foot, God has taken all of me.

These know-nothings, these people without taste, how frozen they are, how rejected they are, how lacking in taste are they! *"I am the Real." "Glory be to Me."* Who has my capacity for these words, for this talk! Where do you see God?

They take some people accepted by the whole world and then warm up their own preaching and they flavor it by mentioning them. It's not that they know anything about their states. They heat themselves up just by mentioning their names! (284-85)

OUR COMPANIONSHIP

65.

The first stipulation I made with Mawlana was that life should be without hypocrisy, as if I were alone. For example, if I am alone, I go to the toilet. This body is my mount, everyone has one. Sometimes it eats fodder, sometimes it breaks wind. You may say it doesn't matter, but I can't do that. (779)

66.

They say that two friends were together for a long time. One day they came to serve a shaykh. The shaykh said, "How many years have you two been companions?"

They said, "So many years."

He said, "Have you ever had a quarrel during this period?"

They said, "No, only agreement."

He said, "Know that you have been living in hypocrisy. You must have seen some act that stirred up trouble and dislike in your heart—there's no escape from it."

They said, "Yes."

He said, "Fear prevented you from mentioning that dislike."

They said, "Yes." (273)

67.

When I came to Mawlana, the first stipulation was that I was not coming to be a shaykh. God has not yet brought to the face of the earth someone who could be Mawlana's shaykh. That would not be a mortal. And I am not such that I could be a disciple. Nothing of that remains for me.

Now, for the sake of friendship and ease, I must not have any need to speak with hypocrisy. Most of the prophets spoke with hypocrisy. Hypocrisy is that you should make something manifest that is not in your heart.

He who knows his soul knows his Lord. This was "who knows my soul," but he was ashamed to say that. He said, "*knows his Lord.*" He turned over all the states to Moses, Jesus, and others. If he had not been hypocritical, Abu Bakr would have left in disgust.

His hypocrisy was not of the sort that would take him to hell. Rather, it took others to paradise. His sincerity conveyed them to paradise. Whenever someone becomes qualified, his sincerity increases and he joins more closely to the world of the Real.

Right now, I am Mawlana's friend, and I am certain that Mawlana is God's saint. In this I make no oath of repudiation or honor. Now, the friend of God's friend is God's saint—this has been established. (777-78)

68.

Whenever Muhammad was asked about faith, he would speak in agreement with the state of the questioner—whatever was suitable for the questioner. One time he said, *"The Muslim is he from whose hand and tongue the Muslims are 'safe' [salima]."* Another time he said, *"He who 'performs the salat and gives the alms tax' [2:177]."* (240)

69.

I stipulated that I would not be hypocritical. After those words that I spoke, speaking lesser words would have deprived us of those words and would not have acknowledged them.

What would be appropriate for Amin Qimaz after this talk? In two days he'll be going to hell. In fact, he's already in hell, but two days from now it will become apparent to him that he is in hell.

Right now, talk of paradise-dwellers finds no room. How could talk of hell-dwellers find room here? Whenever I talk to someone with hypocrisy, it takes him to paradise. And whenever I speak truthfully to someone, it takes him to what he deserves. Which of the two is suitable for you?

He's begging pardon for Amin ad-Din. Why shouldn't he beg pardon from me—a hundred pardons? What were those words he spoke after I had spoken?

"I fancied that you had finished talking."

No, I hadn't finished talking. I wanted to tell another anecdote. Now he's gone away and fled. Now he won't be coming.

"No, I'll bring him by force. He'll be helpless: 'Of course you'll come.'"

Those upon whom the rays of my words fall sometimes see visionary things—wonders and apparitions, visionary light on hands or on walls. Could I be empty of that? What things I see! By God, if the scent of my words were to reach you, you would jump up, tear your clothes, and utter a hundred cries.

If I had played the hypocrite, you would have felt sympathetic, gone into a state, and wept. Since I spoke the truth, you didn't do any of that, you were just bewildered. The very state that overcame you overcame Abu Bakr. He was bewildered when he heard the truth. He said, "I have nothing but bewilderment in my hands. *Increase me in bewilderment!* Indeed, add to it!"

The hypocrisy that I voice is a marvelous hypocrisy. Nothing but this hypocrisy came to most of the prophets, except for Muhammad and Khizr, to whom the truth was spoken. It's a difficult hypocrisy of which I speak. What would Abu Yazid have shouted out here? And the one who ate the roots of herbs for fifteen years—if he had eaten them for a thousand years, the path that he took would not have brought him here. (775-76)

70.

There are many great ones whom I love inwardly. There's affection, but I don't make it manifest. Once or twice when I made it manifest, I did something while keeping company with them, and they didn't know and recognize their duty in companionship. I took it upon myself not to let the affection become cold. When I made it manifest with Mawlana, it increased and did not lessen.

I cannot speak truthfully. If I begin speaking truthfully, I'll be thrown out. If I were to speak the complete truth, all at once the whole city would throw me out—young and old, and Mawlana would help them. Ask me why. Because, when he saw that they were all being excessive, he would go out with them on the pretext of helping them. He would see where I was going, and then he would follow along after me.

I said that these words are half hypocrisy. If I were to speak the truth, all of you in this madrasah would aim for my life. But you would not be able to do anything. The harm of that would fall back on you. If you want, try. (121–22)

71.

In short, let me say one word: Hypocrisy makes these people happy, and truth makes them sad.

I said to someone, "You're a great man, unique in the era."

He became happy, he took my hand. He said, "I was eager, I was remiss."

Last year, I spoke the truth to him. He became my antagonist and enemy. Isn't that strange? You have to live with the people in hypocrisy to stay happy among them. As soon as you begin to speak the truth, you have to go out into the mountains and deserts. There would be no way to stay with the people. (139)

72.

He said, "What a happy state so-and-so has! I wish I had that state!"

I said, "You claim friendship. Aren't you ashamed to say such things in front of me?"

He said, "Do you mean that it's not an elevated station?"

I said, "It is an elevated station and it is a high state, but anyone

who is my friend would not be satisfied with it. Your words make
you like someone who is the favorite of a vizier. He talks happily
with him and becomes the confidant of his secrets. Then he says,
'I wish I were the police-chief of Konya!' The vizier has taken him
as a close friend and believes in him. The high aspiration of the
vizier, who is the sultan's deputy, has said to him, 'I'm just a name,
the command belongs to you!' The police-chief might come with
a hundred thousand flatteries and kiss the ground ten times, but he
still wouldn't dare go near him." (695-96)

73.

Do you see Mawlana? He has egoism and Pharaonic pride, so he
turns down his head. You see those others? Heads high in the air.
If they were not ignorant, it would not be necessary to take all this
trouble and seek all that knowledge.

If this stupid fellow had not said to his wife, "You are my mother
and my sister"*—does any intelligent man say that? Only someone ignorant.

These scholars have sacrificed themselves to the ignorant. They
have become sacrifices to them and their work.

If for one instant you speak to people without hypocrisy, they
no longer greet you like a Muslim. First and last I wanted to exercise the way of truthfulness with the companions on the Path, and
then all of this happened.

I was playing the hypocrite with Fakhr ad-Din: "I must take lessons from you."

He said, "You've found Mawlana, and you've left me!"

Without hypocrisy, I would have said, "How can you compare
yourself with Mawlana?"

These are our words, and Mawlana knows that it is like this, and
he is troubled.

Right now shaykhhood and discipleship are set up. Look at this
master of all learning, deeply read in jurisprudence and the principles and branches of theology. These have no connection with the
path of God and the path of the prophets. Rather, they've covered
it over. First, you have to become disgusted with all of these—lift
up your finger and say, *I bear witness that there is no god but God.*

He should be rid of those sciences and be like a poor Russian, cloaked in a sheepskin, wearing a tall hat, and selling sulfur for a while. Let him be slapped around to reduce some of that egoism so that the path of Islam may become clear to him.

You can't say this to him, so it's necessary to be hypocritical. And shaykhhood and discipleship are set up around him. There are a hundred thousand roads beyond shaykhhood and discipleship for Mawlana. (778-79)

74.

What's it to you if the world is eternal? You must make your own eternity known—are you eternal or newly arrived? The measure of life that you do have should be spent in investigating your own state. Why do you spend it investigating the eternity of the world? Recognizing God is profound, idiot, you are profound. If there is something profound, it is you. What kind of companion are you if you don't know the insides of your companion's veins, feet, and head like the palm of your own hand? What kind of servant of God are you if you don't know all His secrets and insides?

What I have done with you I did not do with my own shaykh.* I left him with severity. I went. But he used to say, "I'm the shaykh." Mawlana says something else.

Yes, by God, the shaykh. And he opened my eyes.

He was just like this for everyone. As long as I did not bring them, they didn't come. If I didn't want it to, it didn't happen.

If Joseph the Sincere were alive, he would remove your stupor in *the interpretation of narratives** [12:101]. How is it that you do not know? Or is it that you do know, but you speak deceptively? (221-22)

75.

If the Men of the Real should come to you, that's no defect. It's for the sake of a wisdom.

Religious prescriptions are not difficult, and there's no hurry. When there's elation, there's no boredom.

He was preaching good sermons, but he was still in the midst. He was full of his own existence.

When his eyes were like that—even though he did that so as

to accept and attest—my words fled. Don't turn your eyes and head away.

What do you have from the world of *tawhid*? What's it to you that He is one? You're more than a hundred thousand—each part of you in a direction, each part of you in a world. May you lose and expend those parts in His unity, and may He make you the same color as His unity—may your head and your secret heart remain for that! Then your prostration will be accepted.

Now, as you know, when a guest arrives, you retell the story so that he may not remain without share. It is even more fitting to say welcome to me. (638-39)

76.

You cannot preach before a preacher or sing before a singer unless you're a great master. He'll say, "This is a strange tune."

If you have not yet been opened up, you will be. Since you have turned to me, many openings lie ahead of you. They'll come.

Whatever veils there are, they're on your side. Whenever there's a difficulty, complain of yourself: "This difficulty is in me." God will act with the servant as he acts with Him. Whatever he does, He will do the same. Despite all this, what good things, what pleasures are ahead!

If someone talks about love for this world, he's in the midst of it. Love for this world is what he's in. (234)

77.

The son of Ala asked what happiness is. I said, "At this time, your presence." I spoke deceptively.

He shouted, "*God willing*, I'll belong to paradise."

I said, "In any case, there's no *God willing* for me. It's been a long time that everything has been known to me. It's past beyond being known—it's become my state."

As for the novice disciple whose seeking is new, he's hung up on secondary causes and marks. Suddenly a grief overcomes him, unpleasant news reaches him, and he becomes feeble. Suddenly opening and joy come to him. Someone brings good news to him and he finds it pleasant.

When he said to that fellow that his insides are boiling, and he said it in order for him to become warm, he himself became cold. If this shaykh were aware, why did he give this false testimony? I see that he is not boiling. No fire has reached me. Perhaps that shaykh said so because of deficient knowledge, and he thought that he would become warm with this. Perhaps he said it so that he would be frightened, and he said it on purpose. (146)

78.
Should I be hypocritical, or talk without hypocrisy?

Mawlana is moonlight. Eyes do not reach the sunlight of my existence, but they do reach the moon. Because of the extreme radiance and brightness of the sun, eyes do not have the capacity for it. Even that moon will not reach the sun, unless perhaps the sun reaches the moon. *The eyes do not perceive Him, but He perceives the eyes* [6:103]. (115)

79.
When I saw you in that state and that station, I tried several stratagems to bring you out of it. My whole heart was with you: "Why is he standing in that station? Why is he sad and sour?"— just so that you'll know what my kindness to you is like.

Now, rub my little hand like that. It's a long time since you've rubbed it. Do you have something to do? Rub like that for a while.

Peace be upon you! May your festival be blessed!

Forgive me, I made you suffer. My "peace be upon you" is a fortress. You will be secure from all suffering when you enter it.

If a person's fortress is God's help
  even a spider can be his gate-keeper.*

You've come into the world unique, and you've stolen the ball from the whole world. You've taken the ball away from the whole world and left the playing-field.

He said, "Some lovers have a great drumming, but the objects of their love and affection stay still."

I said: "That drumming, that celebrating and inviting—it's as if someone takes you to a garden: 'Come on, let's go eat walnuts.' He goes up the tree, and then the sound of cracking the walnuts begins. He says, 'Come on, eat them with your own little hands.' The guest's hands and sleeves become black.

"Someone else takes the guest to the garden. He has him sit down in a pleasant place. He tells the servants, 'Go, bring the walnuts down from the tree, clean them, shell them, and also remove that fine skin.' They do so. Then they bring the cleaned walnuts before him and tell him to eat.

"He says, 'What kind of walnuts are these? I didn't hear any cracking, my hands aren't becoming black, and my sleeves are staying clean. I won't eat them—God knows what they are. These aren't like walnuts. I've never seen anything like this.'" (300-1)

80.

"O people, pass beyond this house of newly arrived things!" This is not talking, it's an admonishment to talk, an invitation to talk, an invitation to come to that world. He's saying, "There's a world there—be steadfast in that. You busy yourself with this prayer, but the prayer goes. You busy yourself with being steadfast, but the steadfastness goes."

How happy I am with your friendship—that God has given me such a friendship! My heart gives me to you—whether I have that world or this world, whether I'm in the pit of the earth or above the heavens, whether I'm up or down. (188-89)

81.

I wanted someone of my own kind so that I could make him my kiblah and turn my face toward him. I was bored with myself. What do you understand of these words—that I was bored with myself? Now that I have a kiblah, he understands and grasps what I'm saying.

Come on, let's take the most difficult and abstruse sayings of the Prophet and designate their real sense and intention like the palm of your hand. For example, we'll take his words, his meaning, his grammar, and his vocalization.

Particles, for example, have no interpretation. Negations are unqualified. However, our particles are negations and declarations, and other things as well.

But, if I were to think about these details, I would see what he has come to see through effort. If I wanted to be the companion of Muhammad, God's messenger, I would see all the verbal and practical details, and I would give him an account of them.

I set out to be your friend, audaciously and boldly. Was I worried that people would be suspicious about these words? Did I think that I should be cautious? Or, that from this exchange, such things would come to mind so that I should be cautious? I walked into this boldly and audaciously. Either I should have no companion—but that would be chastisement. Or, I suddenly need to be knowledgeable—or else just stay an ignorant villager.

However, when wet firewood smokes, I say, "Kill it," but I don't want to. Either let it catch fully, or let it die fully.

He says, "These are virgin words." Yes, they're virgin, but for you—not for the needle-maker.* (219-20)

82.

Whatever the speakers said, they were just scratching the skin of *alif*. They did not understand the meaning of *alif*, because they did not have a Man. If you put a beautiful woman in bed with an impotent man, what will he do? There will be this tasteless touching—he can't have intercourse. He'll just put his face on her face. He will be deprived of that for which this is the means and the motive.

That's the story of the needle-maker who had an impotent friend. But the people and his relatives were not aware of his impotence. They were deceived by his beard and mustache.

His tool gives witness that his beard's a liar—
    pull out the bastard's beard—that's what he deserves.

They made him a marriage contract with a girl like a hundred thousand pictures, and then they married the two. Of course he was not able to have relations with her. When he became totally helpless, he came to his friend the needle-maker, to whom he had

told his secrets from childhood. He said, "You're my confidant—
my states are such and such. Tonight, you come with me, put on
my clothes, and deliver me from this headache. However, when
you go into the private chamber, don't say anything, or else she'll
understand. Turn out the light, because it's my habit to turn out
the light at the time of sleep."

He said, "I would do a thousand acts of service." When he went
into the private chamber, he killed the light, and quickly went into
the bedclothes. The girl fancied that this was her impotent husband. When the bold man sat on her, she opened her legs, and he
put it in. She began to shout and weep, saying "Oh, Oh, Oh!"

From outside the door the husband said, "You whore! You fancy
it's me that has turned your liver into blood. It's the needle-maker.
He's the one who splits iron and makes holes!" (295-96)

83.

Why does Mawlana say that he is not happy that I should go
alone? The fact is that by myself I'm free—I wander anywhere and
sit in any shop. I can't take him along—a well-born man, the mufti
of the city—to any shop and any place, looking in on every dump.

You should know that I have never acted with the I-don't-care
attitude of the shaykhs—"I'm going such-and-such a place,
whether you want me to or not. If you want to belong to me,
come along." Rather, whatever is difficult for you is unnecessary
for you. When you sit here like this, that's on loan to me—my
heart is frightened. (760-61)

84.

It occurred to me that you shouldn't drink from every spring, so
we should not be separated. What would that be like? But you did
not say "*God willing*," and of course I did not like that. Yes, and
when you did say it, I said that you are like Shaykh Muhammad
in this.

That is the cause of the friendship. There was indeed that, but
the root cause was something else. It fell to me from the first. I
filled a cup: "I can't drink it, I can't pour it away." My heart does
not allow me to let go and leave, as I did with the others.

I repented: Let go of that disposition! *"The metaphor is the bridge to the reality"*—and the reality is the bridge to the metaphor.

If I had not come tonight, something would have gone from between us. There would have been estrangement in this state. If, in other than this state, we had slept apart, no harm would have been done. But, in this situation, it's like this. Guard the words of the dervish, because he can't tell you the reason.

When God gives feathers and wings, *This world is a bridge.* Then the bridge collapses, and beneath it there is obviously fire upon fire. He built his house and family on the bridge; he settled down and leaned back.

Concerning women it was said, *"Consult with them, and oppose them."* This is what they do with God.

Right now, this world is this very body. Why are you building it up? *The amount necessary*, and that's all—the rest is nothing. (650-51)

85.

Exert effort so that no veils may come into the midst. I have taught you the Path. Lament to God: "O God, You have shown us this good fortune. We had no way to this. You have been generous— be generous again! Do not take this good fortune away from us!"

The one who will ambush you here is not Satan, but God's jealousy. For, just as He has shown His generosity, so also His jealousy wants Him to steal it away. If a few days of separation happen, quickly and heatedly strive to arrive again.

Where I am, a child would not be veiled. No veil can come. Be so heated in seeking that whenever the heat of your seeking falls on someone, he will become your companion—not cold, cold, such that it becomes a burden.

If an apparition comes down on you in this—what a fine, blessed apparition! Whenever someone prevents this, it is Satan who finds a way in. That is the first sign of God's jealousy. Once it goes to work, Satan finds a way in.

If you're not in fact able to accompany me on the Path, I am carefree. I don't suffer in separation from Mawlana, nor do I become happy when joined with him. My happiness is from my own make-up, my suffering from my own make-up. Right now, living is difficult for me. I am not this! I am not this!

> Gamble your soul—they won't put union with Him in your hands.
>> The drunk won't get wine from the Shariah's cup.
> When the men of disengagement drink together
>> they don't give one gulp to the self-worshipers.*

> When it's spring and I'm far from the face of the Friend,
>> what good is the garden, what use are the herbs?
> Let thorns grow up instead of herbs!
>> Let stones fall down instead of rain!

I'm much happier with you than in a place where I would be given property and a post. If I went to Tabriz, I'd have a magnificent position. But it's more pleasant sitting here with you. If someone gave me position and property but did not understand my words, how could that be pleasant? It's pleasant with someone who understands and grasps my words.

Now then, seeking and searching must be like this—heated, so that no veil will have the gall to step forward. (756-57)

86.

If you accept these words—just as, on that day, you felt sympathy—much good fortune will come to you. This is because when you show reverence, and when you listen by way of need, the gathering will go well. The dervish will think that it was a good gathering. Whenever he remembers the gathering, his heart will incline and he won't flee. That inclination of the heart will give him ease.

Your goal in asking and talking is to be accepted by their hearts—it is for you to become sweet in their hearts. When the work turns out the other way and it results in disturbing their hearts, the suffering will come back to you. The heart won't allow it. (139-40)

87.

If you want to know whether someone's thirst for water is truthful or false, place some sugar candy before him. If he pays any attention, it's not truthful.

Yesterday I ate a bit of stew. I ate nothing else. If I did not abstain, illness would come to me every day. My existence is weak, and I burn things away with abstinence. As soon as I see an excess, I quickly burn it. Woe on the day when my heart does not want to abstain—when God makes that illness so sweet to my heart that I do not seek health.

I wouldn't have come, but if I hadn't come when Mawlana had this susceptibility, that would have brought about loss for the religion. A coldness and frigidity had come to him in the Path, because on that day he was unhappy about the silver that had been brought. When Mawlana confirmed that dislike, he became cold. But even if he did not have that susceptibility, I would have come happily, just as I have come many times. (768)

88.

The Muhammadan is broken in heart. The early ones were broken in body, and after that they would arrive at the heart.

There are people who recite the Footstool Verse* over the ill, and there are people who are the Footstool Verse.*

When I'm inviting people, there are both severity and gentleness, but when I'm alone, it's all gentleness.

I don't want to explain it to you. I'll just speak in symbols, that's enough. It would in fact be discourtesy to offer explanations to you—but you've given me this audacity.

The springhead is one, but it branched off into two branches. Sometimes all the water is in one branch, sometimes in the other. Sometimes this branch empties that branch, pulling all the water into itself, and sometimes that one empties this. Anyone who passes beyond the two branches will reach the headwater. He will plunge in and be immersed, free of branches.

It's the same with trees. If you grab a branch, it will break and you will fall down. If you grab the tree, all the branches will belong to you.

In the Beloved's lane there's a kind of hashish. People eat it and lose their intellects. Then they can't find the Beloved's house and they fail to reach the Beloved. (646)

89.

Iblis has spent a great deal of effort and wrestled a lot with you. After this it looks like he will have difficulty whispering his doubts into you. He'll have to undergo a lot of suffering and striving if he's going to throw you into trouble. (706)

90.

When I was a child, I read a story in a book.* Once when a shaykh was near death, his disciples and those who believed in him had gathered around. They were asking him to say the Shahadah— "*There is no god but God*"—but he turned his face away from them. They went to the other side and recited it to him. He turned his face away from them to this side. When they implored and insisted, he said, "I won't say it."

The disciples began to wail and cry: "Oh, the root is this very hour! What's happening? What is this darkness? What will our own state be?" They lifted up their weeping and clamor to God.

The shaykh came to himself. He said, "What's happening? What is it with you?" They recounted the state.

He said, "I was not aware of that. Satan had come, and he was shaking a goblet of ice water in front of me. He was saying, 'Are you thirsty?' I was saying, 'Yes.' He said, 'Say that God has a partner and I will give it to you.' I turned away from him. He came to the other side. He said the same thing. I turned away from him."

> By day I wait for you to scatter pearls,
>> from night to morning I wait for the heavens.
> I don't wait for you to spill my blood,
>> but if you're going to spill it, I'll wait for it.

This in fact is true. However, when that moment comes for the servant of God and the elect of God, how could Satan have the gall to come around? Even angels will come around with trepidation.

They say that Umar struck out an eye of Satan. Other than the apparent meaning, there is another meaning, a secret that they themselves know. Otherwise, this Satan is not something embodied. *Satan flows in the children of Adam just as blood flows in the veins.*

One day Satan came: "Umar, come along and let me show you a wonder." He took him to the door of the mosque. He said, "Umar, look through the crack in the door." He looked. He said, "Umar, what do you see?"

He said, "I see someone standing and performing the prayer."

He said, "Look again, carefully." He looked. He said, "What do you see?"

He said, "The same person is performing the prayer, and someone else is sleeping in the corner of the mosque, his feet pulled up."

He said, "Umar, by the God who made you exalted by having you follow Muhammad and who delivered you from me! Were it not that I fear and think about the one who is sleeping, I would do something to the one saying his prayer that a hungry dog would not do to a bag of flour!"

Nothing can burn this Satan—only the fire of the love of the man of God. All the other ascetic disciplines that people perform do not hold him back. Rather, he gets stronger. He was created from the fire of the appetites, and light alone puts out fire. *Your light extinguishes my fire.* (231-33)

91.

Two gnostics were trying to outdo each other in boasting and arguing about the secrets of gnosis and the stations of the gnostics. One said, "You see that man who's coming on a donkey—I see him as God."

The other said, "I see his donkey as God."

In short, most of them fell into predestination. Abu Yazid and the others—it's obvious in their words. There's not much there, and if you busy yourself with those words, it will veil you from going forward on this path, which is something else.

He said, "What sort is this 'something else'?"

I said: For example, you've heard my words. They've become cold in your heart. The veil is something like this.

They are near to incarnationism. They say, *"Two spirits dwelling in one body."** How could you perceive that? You're full of caprice. By this "caprice" I don't mean appetite. I explained this caprice before—caprice cuts off appetite. Caprice is such that, when it gets stirred up, a hundred houris could display themselves but that would appear to you like the adobe in the walls.

When you hear words of wisdom or you study, you become drunk, and that stirs up caprice. Caprice is the rays of the light of the veils, for God has "seventy veils of light."* Right now, you are drowned in caprice. How can you debate about rays of light? And if you did debate about them, that would all be caprice.

That Sufi, Imad, is drunk. Look at him move his head. That's the movement of caprice. How can caprice be compared with the rays of the light of God?

When they use their possessions to serve God's servants, a kindness comes into motion. Then their work opens up because of that kindness. But a copper given by someone sincere is equal to a hundred thousand dinars given by someone else. Whatever is accepted from the others follows on that, because the alms of the sincere open closed doors.

Beware, do not be satisfied with the shaykh just because of this beautiful form, beautiful words, and beautiful acts and character traits, because beyond all these is something else. Seek that.

One copper given by Mawlana is equal to a hundred dinars given by anyone else or by those connected to him. And anyone who finds the way to me becomes his follower, because a door was closed, and he opened it.

By God, I am incapable of knowing Mawlana. There's no hypocrisy in these words, no standing on ceremony or interpretation, because I am incapable of knowing him. Every day I come to know something about his state and acts that was not there yesterday.

You need to grasp Mawlana a bit better than this, so that afterwards you won't be astounded. *That is the day of mutual defrauding** [64:9]. He has this beautiful form and speaks beautiful words, but don't be satisfied with those. Beyond them is something else. Seek that from him.

He has two sorts of words—one hypocrisy, the other truthfulness. As for his hypocrisy—all the souls and spirits of the saints are yearning to meet him and sit with him. And as for his truth and lack of hypocrisy, the spirits of the prophets are yearning for that:

"Oh, would that we had come in his time so that we could have been his companions and listened to his words." Now that you have that companionship, don't waste it. Don't look at him like that. Look at him with the gaze with which the spirits of the prophets look—that of sighing and longing.

Harun ar-Rashid* said, "Bring Layla for me so that I can see why Majnun's love for her has thrown such fervor into the world and why from East to West the lovers have made the story of his love their own mirror." They spent a great deal of money and used many tricks, and they brought Layla. The caliph entered into her private chamber at night, the candles all lit. He gazed upon her for a time, and then for a time he looked down. He said to himself, "I'll get her to talk. Maybe whatever it is will become more apparent in her face when she talks." He looked at Layla and said, "Are you Layla?"

She said, "Yes, I'm Layla, but you're not Majnun. The eye in Majnun's head is not in your head.

> How will you see Layla with an eye that sees others
> and has never been purified by tears?

"Look upon me with the gaze of Majnun."

You should look at the beloved with the eyes of the lover, for *He loves them* [5:54]. The flaw is that people don't look at God with the gaze of love. They look at Him with the gaze of knowledge, the gaze of gnosis, and the gaze of philosophy. The gaze of love is something else. (103-5)

92.

I can speak to myself. If I see myself in someone, then I can speak to him.

You're the one who shows need, not the one who has no need and appears as a stranger. That one was your enemy, and I was making him suffer because he was not you. After all, how could I make you suffer? If I were to kiss your foot, I would be afraid that my eyelashes might scratch and wound your foot! (99-100)

93.

We've turned out to be two marvelous people. It's been a long time since two people like us have fallen together. We're extremely open and obvious. The saints didn't use to be so obvious. And we're extremely hidden and secret. This is the meaning of *the manifest, the nonmanifest: He is the first and the last and the manifest and the nonmanifest* [57:3].

In fact, it's because of your belief that it appeared to you like this. If he had understood those words, how could he have said, "Your words have no basis?"

When you give an answer, speak in "consonance" [*mutabiq*]. In other words, the two "leaves" [*tabaq*] should correspond, just like the two leaves of a door. When you put one leaf next to the other, it is neither more nor less.

A king said, "I want someone to come to me who will not speak until I speak, and if I do speak, he will answer in consonance, without any addition."

When someone came, he said to him, "Do you have a wife?"

He replied, "I have a wife and two children."

The king paid no attention to him and said, "Don't let him in."

The man wrote a letter to the king, saying, "After all, Moses was asked, *What is that in your right hand? He replied, It is my staff. I lean upon it and with it I beat down leaves* [20:17-18]."

The king wrote in answer, "There was another wisdom in that."

As for the intelligent man, he is the one who answers in consonance. Someone was asked, "Where are you?"

He replied, "In the dumps." That was a lie and not in consonance. He was not in more than one dump. It is impossible for one spatially located thing to be in two locations. (93-94)

94.

We should travel together to Mosul—you haven't seen those places—and then on to Tabriz. You could preach on so-and-so's pulpit, and you would be able to see that group and their seclusions. Then to Baghdad, then Damascus.

Right now you're too set on collecting money. If I go, you'll be satisfied, no? But I won't stay away more than two years. I'll come back, in short, in a day or two less than two years.

Let me give you headaches for another two or three days—
there's only one page left in the book of my life.* (353)

My Instructions to the Circle

95.

Sir, it's my habit that when someone comes to me, I ask him,
"Sir, will you speak or will you listen?"

If he says he'll speak, I listen continuously for three days and
nights, unless he flees and leaves me alone. If he says he'll listen, I
talk. Otherwise I don't put up with beginning to talk and then
having him interrupt. (760)

96.

Someone said to a hairdresser, "Pick out the white hairs from my
beard."*

The hairdresser looked and saw many white hairs. He cut off his
whole beard with the scissors and handed it to him. He said, "You
pick them out—I have work to do." (180-81)

97.

If he's going to listen to my words like this—with disputation
and debate about the sayings of the shaykhs, or the Hadith, or the
Koran—he won't listen to my words, nor will he reap the fruit. If
he wants to come with need and to take benefit—because a person's capital is need—then he will benefit. Otherwise, one day—
ten days—no, a hundred years. He'll talk, and I'll put my chin on
my hand and listen. (83)

98.

When a dervish begins to talk, no one should make objections
to him. Yes, it is the rule that the profit of whatever words are spoken in the madrasah and whatever is studied in the madrasah
increases through debate. But these words are far from that profit
and debate, and this has nothing to do with that.

A man brought an Indian sword to someone and said, "This
sword is Indian."

He said, "What's an Indian sword?"

He said, "It slices in two whatever it strikes."

He said, *"The Sufi is the son of the moment."*

He said, "Let's test it against this stone over here." He lifted the sword and struck it against the stone. The sword broke in two.

He said, "You said that an Indian sword's characteristic is that it slices in two whatever it strikes."

He said, "Well yes, the sword was Indian, but the stone was even more Indian."*

Moses was more Pharaoh than Pharaoh.*

This one was a saint, but that one was more of a saint than he.

He said, "Then what was his form?" (175-76)

99.

Whoever becomes my friend must worship more than he did at first. But I'm not talking about companions.

It's best to give alms such that no one else sees that you're giving them. The least of it is, if he does see, he should immediately envy you. (150)

100.

If an Anatolian should come through this door, see me, gain faith, and turn to me, he'll take more benefit from me than these shaykhs. They're full of themselves. The passing days have blown away their capital, which is need. Time has scattered them. (697)

101.

Since you left me my eyes have darkened
and my eyeballs' clouds pour down rain.

The speech of the lovers has an awesomeness. This is why He swore by it with His words, *"By the blaming soul!"* [75:2]. He does not put *the soul at peace* [89:27] out to auction, nor does He make it manifest.

I'm talking about the love that is true, the seeking that is true. The other's not seeking, it's wishing. "Oh would that…". What good is that?

I wouldn't give you the dirt off the old shoe of a true lover for the "lovers" and "shaykhs" of these days. Even the shadow-players who show images from behind the screen are better than they. They all admit that they're playing and they admit that it's not true. "We have to do it for the sake of bread." Because of this admission, they're better.

"Wishing" is nothing but caprice that has taken over above and below, layer upon layer. At that time, a ray from that person, or a ray from his words rising out of caprice, makes caprice strike against him. A part of him opens up, the words reach him, and he becomes happy. Once again the caprice blows up and overcomes him. He becomes happy with the words and goes after his own work. That itself is the proof against him.

He has to have a stipend from the madrasah to acquire his caprice and desire. He must acquire learning from Siraj, and he brags and blusters with Jamal. He puts on new clothes and shoes, and talks like an idiot with Lady Kirra and others. He's not preserving the dignity of a dervish: "Who is more intelligent than I am? Who can teach me about intelligence?" He puts seeking for God on top of the pack, as an overload. Has anyone ever seen seeking for God as an overload?

When the top shaykhs of the Tribe's classes reach me, they have to start practicing all over from the beginning.

When someone stays in caprice, you can't call him "variegated." Sana'i is "variegated," Sayyid is "variegated"—and then he is "variegated"? That's absurd. A mad man wouldn't say that. Even a totally mad man wouldn't say it.

Come on, for a year say good-bye to these character traits. Go in pleading and need, and wear the cloak. Let them buy you like a new Armenian slave. Stop eating simply because of caprice. You were not created for caprice. Take this advice to heart. And don't be intent on repeating these words, broken and patched up, to make people upset.

A lover who reaches the Beloved acts disdainfully. Before you reach the Beloved totally, disdain is not good. (91-92)

102.

Seeking God as an overload!—the God who created this heaven, in which imagination and intellect become lost. They can't even perceive one star. Whatever their philosophers, their astronomers, their natural scientists say, the star is not that.

Now, the world from which this world appeared—what sort of world is that? A little worm wriggling on a pile of dung wants to see and know God! And that as an overload!

They knocked themselves out until their livers were torn to pieces. They fell short, and they kept on gazing on that. Afterwards, God gave them new life. The stomachs of some of them bled, and after they reached death, God gave them life. They threw away kingdom, wealth, position, and life. Such was Ibrahim Adham,* the king of a city, and Mawlana, the seeker on the road of the Real.

After all, someone who is seeking and in love with a woman or a youth doesn't know his own shop, his business, his world. They tell him, "You're totally hung up."

He says, "I'm seeking because I want to be hung up."

For him, his life has no importance, his wealth has no significance, even though he loves someone who has no subsistence. Both will die and be placed under the earth.

So, he seeks love for the beginningless, endless, pure, faultless, and incomparable God as an overload.

For the sake of this seeking, Ibrahim Adham had sacrificed a great deal of wealth. Whenever he saw a dervish, he sacrificed his life. Beneath his clothing he wore coarse wool, and by day he would fast in secret. He would secretly sit in seclusion. Then his heart would become tight, because no opening would come. (89-90)

103.

Before Ibrahim Adham left the kingdom of Balkh, he had spent a great deal of wealth in this desire. He had done many acts of obedience with the body. He was saying, "What should I do? How is it that no opening comes?"

One night he was sleeping on the throne, sleeping and awake. The watchmen were beating their sticks and drums, playing their pipes, and calling out. He was saying to himself, "Which enemy are they keeping back? The enemy is sleeping with me! What I require is the gaze of God's mercy. What security comes from you? There's no security save in the refuge of His gentleness."

In these thoughts his heart was being taken by madness. He would lift his head from the pillow, then put it down again. "What a wonder! How can the lover sleep?" All of a sudden the loud sound of quick walking on the roof of the palace came to him, as if a group was coming and going, and the sound of their footsteps was coming from the palace. The king said to himself, "What happened to those watchmen? Don't they see the people running on the roof?"

Again, the sound of footsteps gave him a strange perplexity and dread, such that he forgot himself and the house. He couldn't shout or give news to the armed guards. In the midst of all this, someone looked down from the roof of the palace and said, "Who are you on this throne?"

He replied, "I'm the king. Who are you on this roof?"

The man said, "We've lost two or three strings of camels. We're looking for them on the roof of the palace."

He said, "Are you mad?"

He replied, "You're the one who's mad."

He said, "You've lost camels on the roof of the palace? Is that where you look for camels?"

He replied, "You look for God on the throne of the kingdom? Is that where you look for God?"

That was it. After that, no one saw him. He went, and they were looking for him. (84–85)

104.

He said, "Come with us so that we may keep the night alive together."

I said, "Tonight I'm going to that Christian, because I promised I would come at night."

They said, "We're Muslims, and he's an unbeliever. Come with us."

I said, "No, he's a Muslim in his secret heart, because he has submitted. 'Islam' is to submit."

They said, "Come on, because submission is gained through companionship."

I said, "From my side there's no veil and no curtain. *In the name of God*—try me."

One of them began: *"We honored the children of Adam and We carried them in the land and the sea"* [17:70].

Words jumped out of my mouth—"Quiet! You have no share of this verse. What do you have to do with *We carried them in the land?"*

He wanted to ask something. I said, "How can you question me? How can you object to me? I don't take disciples. Many people have stuck around me, 'We'll be your disciples, give us the cloak.' I fled. They followed me home and put down whatever they had brought. It was no use. I went. I don't take disciples. I take shaykhs—not every shaykh, the perfect shaykh."

On the day I was warring with that shaykh in the gathering, I cursed him, and he stayed silent. I broke his head, but he stayed silent.

The other one was rolling and rubbing his face in the dirt, coming toward me. They were saying to him, "You're mistaken, mistaken!" The one who is wronged here is the one who has been patient and tolerant for so long.

He said, "Leave me be! I'm not mistaken." This is the one who is wronged in meaning.

They were shouting because of the heat of his words. That broken-head kept on coming forward and smiling. He was rolling and shouting. (226-27)

105.

The rule is that when you consider true words variegated and you interpret them, people are hardly troubled. For the most part they feel sympathetic, enjoy themselves, and undergo states. But, when you speak without interpretation, people don't sympathize or undergo states—except the one whom God has singled out for receptivity. True pleasure reaches him.

In that station, you must not ask any questions. What kind of questions come to the people when the speaker himself is bewildered? "What am I saying? With whom am I speaking? If they don't understand, I won't speak." Then again he says, "I'll speak."

This is like the fellow who was beating the dawn drum in the daylight by the door of a house.* For him, night had become day.

Someone said, "There's no one in this house. For whom are you beating the dawn drum?"

He said, "Quiet! People build khanaqahs and inns for God. I too—I beat something for God."

I'm talking for God—how can you ask questions? You and I are like the flutist who was playing the flute. In the midst of it, he broke wind. He put the flute on his nethermost and said, "If you play better, play!"

You must go forward on the Path. What is this debating with the guide? Go forward, jackass! You're not the jackass that crosses a bridge, nor are you the sort of Egyptian jackass that in a day takes you to the way station and then returns on the same day. You can't even go halfway to the way station with a thousand urgings and words. *Surely God will not change what is with a people until they change what is with themselves* [13:11]. Complain and lament about yourself! *Surely, you do not guide him whom you love* [28:56].

He said, "I know this. The truth was hard for me."

He said, "What are you saying? I don't get any benefit from you."

He said, "Then what is your intention in turning around this work?"

He said, "Nothing. Get up! Get up!"

I've done many useless things like this. I turned away from truthful words and began reciting poetry. He felt sympathy and wept, saying "This bad soul of mine!"

I said, "You won't be deprived," but he still didn't become quiet.

He said, "Yes, Sayyid also said that I wouldn't be deprived."

I said, "He said that, and I said that. Now listen to the explanation of that and the explanation of this: When someone is in the special guest-house of the king, the king takes a morsel and puts it in his mouth. He's not deprived. What does this have to do with the fact that when bread crumbs and bones are left over, they throw them out the door so that the dogs won't be deprived?" (124-25)

106.

You say, "Show the proof." They want proof from me? They want proof from God. But they shouldn't want proof from God.

How are you with these words? Are you happy? You say, "I'm happy." That's it? Happy and nothing more?

A Man is the one who makes others happy. What kind of Man is he who makes himself happy? Yes, the servant can do just that, make himself happy. It is God's work to make others happy.

They said, "We don't get any opening from Mawlana Shams ad-Din." Anyone who seeks opening from me is an infidel. He finds me, and then he wants opening?!

You aren't that. You're a Muslim, a believer. A Muslim does little harm, he's forgiving. For example, a priest kills a Muslim. He comes to your door, "I'm fleeing from the officers. I've found you. Give me sanctuary!"

Wouldn't you say, "If a Muslim kills a Muslim, he won't be released unless he's given sanctuary"? Then he would incline toward Islam.

Even though you're a Muslim, you shouldn't be content with this. More Muslim, and more Muslim! Every Muslim must have disbelief, and every disbeliever should be a Muslim. What flavor is there in Islam? There is flavor in disbelief! You'll never find the mark and road of Islam from a Muslim. You'll find the road of Islam from the disbeliever.

When you said, "The utmost end of the sought is the seeker," you should have said it better. Otherwise, they won't become aware of the style of my talking, and they'll become perplexed. (143-44)

107.

In my view, no one can become a Muslim just once. He becomes a Muslim, then he becomes an unbeliever, then again he becomes a Muslim, and each time something comes out of him. So it goes until he becomes perfect. (226)

108.

A man full of self came and said, "Tell me the secrets."

I said, "I can't tell you the secrets. I tell the secrets to the one in whom I don't see him—I see myself. I tell the secrets of self to myself. I don't see myself in you, I see someone else."

When someone comes to someone else, he's one of three sorts: either a disciple, or a companion, or a great one. Which sort are you? Haven't you come to me?

He said, "It's obvious how I am in relation to you."

I said, "It's obvious. I see him in you. Since he's in you, I'm not in you, for I'm not he." (105-6)

109.

The words of Mawlana are a blindfold, they're a great joke. They're sorcery.

Two people are sitting together, and the eyes of both are bright—in them there's no blear, no dust, no knots, no pain. This one sees, the other one doesn't see anything.

Yes, the words of the possessors of the heart are sweet. They haven't been learned, they've been taught. It's the teaching of the Knowing, the Wise.

He says: He's full of himself and his own excellence, like a pot full of salty water. He tells him to pour it out so that He can fill it with fresh water—a spirit-increasing water that reddens your face and brings you to health. Whatever you have of choler, melancholy, phlegm, and unhappiness will be taken away. But that first has to be poured out. It has to be washed with water seven times—but not this water. If you wash it with this salty water, how will it become clean? Wash it with this fresh water, then it will become clean. When this has been washed, He Himself will see, and He will fill it up at once.

But he says, "Right now I see that this has been poured out, but I don't see the filling up."

He says, "Come on, you see My generosity—that I'm Generous. I'm Bestowing, I'm Truthful in My promises."

So, it should be obvious to this fellow. He should pour it out without delay. As long as he delays in pouring it out, he will not come to know these meanings.

No doubt it's because he's full of himself. How can a stomach full of water have appetite for cool water? His existence has pulled a hundred thousand veils over his face and eyes. How can these words reach him? How can he see me? (710-11)

110.

When I am with someone, how could he grieve? He has no fear in the whole world.

You said, "How come your tears are rosy?"
            Since you ask, I'll tell you what happened in truth:
My heart was bleeding in madness for you—
            all at once it came out from my eyes. (76)

III.

The point of a story is for it to set you to the work, not its out-ward sense—as if you were going to repel boredom with the story's form. No, you repel ignorance. (273)

112.

Remember this advice: My words are not to be repeated. They should be put into practice. Whatever happens, it will happen because of repeating my words. Repeat nothing.

If someone says something, say, "We heard some words—sweet, spirit-increasing, delicious. What they were I can't repeat. If you want them, go and listen."

When he comes, I'll know. If I want, I'll speak—if he's worthy of that. If not, I won't speak. (743)

113.

If it's unbelief to call a scholar's shoes "booties,"* what about the shoes of a dervish? If you spent a hundred thousand dirhems on me, that wouldn't be equal to having respect for my words. You who have respect, come! You without respect, go! Take away your disrespect.

If you have respect, how come you're telling everyone what you hear from me without my permission?

He said, "A new vat leaks, but it keeps the water cool."

[Someone] said, "I've taken many steps on this road."

He said, "They take someone on a long ramble, twenty farsangs this way, twenty farsangs that way, and the city's nearby, but they never reach the city. They bring him near, and then they take him far away again."

He said, "I've spent a lot of time seeking with the small and the great."

He said, "Did you go because you wanted to be at ease, or because you wanted to memorize some words?" (288-89)

114.

The one who's a seeker, who claims to be seeking—when will he come out of caprice and catch a scent of the spirit?

Some are truthful, and some are pretenders. Let's look: If his inclination is more toward the works of this world, then he's a liar and a pretender.

These words are warm, but next to the heat that's inside me and that I wanted to make apparent, they're frigid and cold.

Right now, we have me and you. You might think it's the resurrection, because the dervish—the servant of God—has this state: This hour and the resurrection are the same for him.

One day Abu Yazid Taqawi* was saying this from the pulpit—I mean an assembly in which there was discussion, not this pulpit made of wood.

A woman immediately stood up and uncovered her face in front of him. He said, "Sit down, lady!"

She said, "O shaykh! O pretender! You at least don't have this state. Your words are true, but who are you to speak them? They're not yours, this is not your practice. The attribute of the resurrection is awe and terror, and no one can tell the difference between man and woman. Everyone will be mixed together."

Abu Yazid stayed silent. (701-2)

115.

Mawlana doesn't let me do my work. I've got one friend in the whole world. Am I going to deprive him of what he wants? Am I going to listen and then not do what he wants?

You aren't my friends. What do you have to do with friendship with me? It's only because of the blessing of Mawlana's presence that you hear a few words from me. Has anyone ever heard anything from me? Did I ever say anything to anyone? You, Ibrahim, you used to come to the school—you saw me as a teacher. It often happens that you meet someone without recognizing him. How can meeting someone you recognize be compared with meeting someone you don't recognize?

When I talk in public, listen carefully, because it's all secrets. Anyone who puts aside those public words of mine—"Those words are obvious, that's easy"—will not benefit from me or my words. He'll have no share. I voice most of the secrets in the public words. There are great secrets that jealousy makes me put inside a joke. (729)

116.

I have a good opinion of friends. I don't have the capacity to think anything other than what I see with my own eyes. I don't even think ill of unbelievers at first. I say, "Who knows? He may be a Muslim in reality and in outcome."

The Commander of the Faithful, Umar—God be pleased with him—served an idol for forty years. He would ask his needs from the idol. He would say, "O idol!" The Eternal would say to him, *"Here I am."* (209)

117.

Friendship is that when your friend is asleep, and then someone comes and pulls back his bedclothes, lifts up his cloak, and exposes his private parts to the people—like Noah's son*—you give him a manly punch in his black face and pull down the sleeper's cloak. It's not that you also begin to laugh—"If I don't laugh, the one who exposed him will be upset!" Such agreeableness is not part of manliness or friendship. (609-10)

118.

There's the story about Abu Yazid—he took the wrong road and arrived at the city. He was mistaken, but he found the road. This is like the story of Moses,* who saw a light but it appeared as fire.

The same thing happened to the moth and the candle—
he went for the light but fell in the fire.

Here it's the opposite. It's like the shaykh who said, "The people are coming back from church." He meant that they never saw the mosque. What do they have to do with mosques?

A group who were outwardly Muslim and inwardly unbelieving invited me. I offered excuses. I was going to the church. They were unbelievers who were my friends—outwardly unbelievers, inwardly

Muslims. I used to say, "Bring me something to eat." With a thousand thanks they would bring something and break the fast with me. They would eat, and it as if they had been fasting. (628-29)

119.

I like unbelievers, because they don't claim friendship. They say, "Yes, we're unbelievers, we're enemies." Now I'll teach them friendship, I'll teach them oneness. But the one who claims to be a friend but is not is full of danger.

Someone who looks at a tavern with the eye of pity knows that this is forbidden and that it necessitates punishment and prohibition. But pity makes water pour from his eyes: "O God, deliver them from sin—and me, and all the Muslims!"

Now, if you have the strength to see the shaykh in the tavern, sitting and eating with a regular, and be just the same, and then you see him in whispered prayer, and you stay the same in your belief in the shaykh—that itself is a great work. If you're not like this, at least, when you see him in the tavern, say, "I don't know the secret of this—he knows, and his God." If you see him in whispered prayer, say, "Well, I know this; this at least is good." This is also good, for you don't have the strength to see the shaykh there in the tavern in whispered prayer itself, in the Kaaba itself, and in paradise itself. (298-99)

120.

He said, "I know it's bad, but I can't. My heart won't let me."

What kind of words are these? "I know this ocean drowns people, but I'll throw myself in. Or, this fire burns, or this well is a hundred cubits deep, or this is the hole of a serpent, or this is deadly poison, or this desert destroys people—I know and I go." Don't go if you know! So, you don't know. What kind of knowledge is this? Is this intellect? How can you call this "knowledge" and "intellect"?

I have given so much advice and admonition to you that, if I had given it in the city, a hundred thousand people would now be observing it. Great groups of them would have become my disciples. People would wail and cut off their hair. They would sacrifice their sweet souls and possessions. But none of it has had any effect on you. Your stone-like heart does not become soft. (241-42)

121.

Whenever a new fruit comes, the taste of the previous fruit does not remain. First there are cherries and *maruls*,* then apricots, then melons and grapes. In the same way, when Muhammad came, the shariahs of the other prophets were overthrown. Muhammad didn't invite people for forty years, only for twenty-three years. What great things became apparent! Yes, it wasn't long, but when someone breathes with God, that breath remains.

Yes, bravo you Muslim unbelievers! Once you've tried and tested something once, even if it be the soul, have nothing more to do with it! Suppose it's your soul. The soul is that from which you should be at ease. How can it make you suffer? When you say that, my heart pains me, as if someone were tormenting me. Don't say it, lest my heart become tight.

If it were mine, I would have torn it into a hundred pieces. I would have burned it all up, both the suffering and the physician. You're making it worse. You're making it difficult for yourself. Suffering upon suffering! When you see something that the heart can't bear, why do you put it there? One suffering becomes a hundred.

I said, "Why don't I see the end? Why don't I see the outcome so that I can put away the suffering?"

He said, "So, what has happened to *we are satisfied with God's decree and destiny*? You must be satisfied. He created Shuaib blind, and he was satisfied. He did not see the faces of his dear ones, though he did see their meaning. The outward aspect would have been sweet too. But it was not there, so he was satisfied. Satisfaction is that you be still and you not lose your intellect in the suffering. Despite all those worms, Job stayed still. He made it the resting place of his heart. He didn't think, 'How long will this be?' He didn't say, 'O God, tell me exactly how long!'"

Everyone has had a suffering without cure. The cure is this: I do not suffer. You too should not suffer. It is not part of manliness for me to keep on telling you not to suffer, for you have tried it several times.

I said, "I can abstain from something that's absent."

What is it that's absent, and what is it that's present? You've seen something specific that brings harm. That's harm and suffering. You yourself say that from the day that it began, you have no comfort in *sama*, no comfort in talk, states, or discussion. What's left? Don't take something and say, 'If I hadn't done that, I would be happy.' Or you say, 'I wish I hadn't done that.'"

He said, "Perhaps a remedy will come from the Unseen."

He said, "Yes, of course we have faith in the Unseen. We are believers in the Unseen, in what is absent. Everything comes from the Unseen. All opening comes from the Unseen." (662-63)

122.

He said, "That's like so-and-so, who will never be your confidant."

I said, "How are you supposed to know that he won't be my confidant? You'll need to be more perfect than this to know that."

He said, "Because he says, 'It should be like this, and it should be like that.' How can the station of submission be achieved if you keep on saying that it should be like this and it should not be like that?"

I said, "This criticism you're making of him—aren't you saying 'It should be like this, and it should not be like that'? You do it yourself, and then you say that no one should do it. This is like the Indian slave who spoke during the prayer.* Another Indian, who was also in prayer, said, 'Hey, quiet! You're not supposed to talk during the prayer.'

"There was also the fellow who went to the judge. He was told that there was no witness for his complaint and that he had to swear an oath. He said, 'By God, I'm not going to swear an oath, by God, I won't do it!'"

"The people of Ahlat say, 'You bastard, get out of here, or we'll call you bad names!'" (305)

123.

When the shaykh commands you to do something, you should consider it like a walnut. Of course it will give fruit. He's not making a mistake. Some turn away from it, so it doesn't give any fruit. Someone of that sort blames the shaykh. But he himself is the one who didn't do what was commanded. He fancies that he's bringing the work closer. The work had come closer and he's taken it a hundred leagues away.

When you seek a bit of lightness and alleviation at the beginning of the work, that will make you lose a hundred alleviations. If a child knew that it was acting like a child, it would never act that way.

> *Everyone's intelligent in his own eyes—*
> *I wish I knew who's stupid!*

> I take it you've been released from fancy at last—
> but the idol released from fancy is still there.*

He sees himself as better than someone else and becomes happy. He's like the fellow who was saying, "That woman who passed away used to laugh at her husband's body."

A wise man said, "She was laughing at his thing. Otherwise, why would she laugh at his body?"

I commanded you to do something. Why didn't you do it?

He said, "I already told you my excuse."

He said, "I was not satisfied with that excuse. I was being hypocritical. On the inside I wanted you to do exactly as I said, so that you would be delivered from suffering. If I do not deliver you from suffering in this world—such that your insides become happy, opened up, and full of tasting—it will be too late to help you in the next world. Everyone there will be totally helpless before his own beard." (150-51)

124.

Tomorrow I have to preach. That's difficult. The door has opened, so there's no escape. If you shut the door—shouts and denunciation!

I wish they'd take some benefit from it. I've said all those things, both explicitly and allusively, but it's as if they have never heard any advice. They grasp neither the outward meaning of the words, nor the point. If they don't understand the words, how are they going to put them into practice? *Works without knowledge are misguidance.*

I'm going to wash my head. What are you going to do? Are you going or staying? (622)

125.

I don't need your praise. I know. You just stop the praise.

I say this because, to praise Mawlana, you should observe whatever causes him to be at ease and content. You shouldn't do anything to disturb or trouble him. The fact is that whatever troubles me troubles the heart of Mawlana. (629)

126.

This talk of Mawlana is not for my sake—it's not for me. I know Mawlana's state in myself. If his eyebrows go sour, I know that's not for me. I examine Mawlana's state inside myself. I know it's so that others will take benefit. (303)

127.

Shaykh Ibrahim knows our oneness. When I say something, it's as if Mawlana said it. Both of us say it. So, if I say it, it doesn't occur to Mawlana to say it too.

He said, "They're offering their excuses: 'Mawlana was laughing like that with us, and he didn't take us to task—"Do it quickly, put it into practice." He didn't shout at us or threaten us, and he didn't command us to do anything. If Shams had acted the same way, we wouldn't have been prevented from coming. We put a lot into that without feeling burdened at all.'"

He said, "There you go. That's the saying of the Sufi:* 'If I find something, you're delivered, and if not, I have you in hand.' My intention in coming and the reason I came was that, if the disciples were faithful, good. If not, fine. I have Mawlana in hand."

The one who brought him to Aksaray could have taken him further, but my heart did not want to. Now my heart wants to. After all, I'm the object of desire, and Mawlana is the one desired by the object of desire. Whether father or mother, no one would act as gently or speak as sweetly as I do." (769-70)

128.

Seeing the ruler* won't harm me, and it will benefit him. As for these shaykhs, seeing rulers is very harmful.

God has servants who can pass over—not pools or rivers—but

oceans, without getting their clothes wet. But not them—not only will their clothes get wet, they'll drown too. And the rulers will be harmed by seeing them, for the aptitude and the emulation that they do have will be covered over by becoming the companions of these highwaymen of the religion. (702-3)

129.

Most of these shaykhs have been the highwaymen of Muhammad's religion. All these mice in the house of Muhammad's religion have worked ruin. But, God has cats among His dear servants, and they clear away the mice. If a hundred thousand mice were to gather together, they wouldn't have the gall to look at the cat, because the cat's awesomeness does not leave them any togetherness.

The cat is togetherness itself. If the mice were to come together, they would cooperate. Some mice would be sacrificed. But when the cat caught one, it would be kept busy. Then another would scratch out its eyes, and another would attack its head. They would kill it, or at least it would flee. Otherwise, it's just that their fear doesn't allow the mice to have togetherness, but the cat is togetherness. (613)

130.

In confirmation of my words that you should not listen to the bad things about people that are quoted: Yesterday, so-and-so came, and my words had been narrated to him. He jumped in my face—"How could you have said such things about me? I have often served the great ones, and they all admired me. They didn't want me to leave them."

I said, "Ask me that with more courtesy so that I may answer you."

He said, "Let me sit for an hour so that my ego may become quiet and I can speak with more courtesy."

I said, "Sit for two hours."

He sat for an hour. Then he began the same thing: "I was admired by everyone, I was illustrious. They all called me by beautiful titles. How come you consider me different from that? Right now, tell me, by what title do you call me?"

I said, "If you become a Muslim, 'Muslim,' and if not, then 'unbeliever,' 'apostate,' and even worse. Now, if you can speak without ego, speak. Otherwise, I will not answer you again." (202-3)

131.

I'm still not qualified to speak. Too bad there's no one qualified to listen. There should be total speaking and total listening. "On the hearts is a seal, on the tongues is a seal, and on the ears is a seal."*

A few rays are coming. If you show gratitude, they'll increase. Gratitude is to say with the tongue of your own state, *"Show us things as they are."* Then the answer will come: *"If you are thankful, I will increase you"* [14:7].

I was coming with extreme kindness to tell you that we should go once again alone to visit that shaykh. Then you recited that poem:

Though I sit and laugh with another,
    I'll not brand my heart with anyone's love.
When someone sees the sun go down,
      it's then that he lights up the lamp.*

I said to myself, "He means that it's night, and the sun has set. But I see that it hasn't set, the sun's right in its place."
Someone said to someone, "Is so-and-so qualified?"
He replied, "His father was qualified, he was learned."
He said, "I'm not asking about his father, I'm asking about him."
He said, "His father was very qualified."
He said, "Aren't you listening to what I'm saying?"
He said, "You're the one who's not listening. I'm listening, I'm not deaf. I know what you're asking."

Come back, so that you may be more than you were.
    If you were not before, you will be now.
You're the soul and the world in the time of war—
      think what you'll be in the time of peace.* (233-34)

132.

Today Shaykh Hamid was explaining unbelief and faith. I was looking at him and seeing that he's not going to catch a whiff of faith and unbelief in a hundred years. If he had understood all that, then wisdom and courtesy would have demanded that he conceal it in the presence of a dervish.

You said that I was seeing my own words.

My words don't go anywhere until I see the other. Maybe he will say it better and more completely. The Sufi says, "If I find another better than you, you're delivered of me and I'm delivered of you. Otherwise, I have you in hand." Then he hides the bread in his sleeve.

Conceal your going, your gold, and your school.

God's Messenger said, *"He who conceals his secret owns his own affair."* Yes, but then there's a servant—and why should I say this in secret? Mawlana Shams ad-Din Tabrizi—God elevate his mention—says, *"He who tells his secret owns his own affair."* But where is a servant like that?

> How long will you keep on talking, sweetheart,
> about the one whom you do not see? (191-92)

133.

Mawlana has said many times that he is more compassionate than I. He's happy in his drunkenness. When someone falls into deep water, or fire, or hell, he places his hand under his chin and gazes upon him. He doesn't jump into the water, or the fire. He just gazes.

I also gaze, but I grab him by the tail: "You too, brother, don't fall in! Come out with us. You too should be gazing." Grabbing him by the tail and pulling him out are these talks.

There's a hadith: *"Were the dead man to reveal some of it. . .".*

He lifts up his head. You say, "But, you were dead."

He says, "What was that breath that Seraphiel blew into me? What was that *I blew into him of My spirit* [15:29]?"

He says, "It was nothing."

He says, "It wasn't? All right, I'll die again. I've fallen."

The peace of God be upon you, the mercy of God be upon you. (774-75)

134.

I was not remembering my own head and beard, and I'm nearer to me than anyone. How should I be aware of you? You were imagining things to yourself, and you were troubled by your own imagination. An imagining was born from an imagining and became the other's companion, and then another and another.

Three times say, "O imagination, go!" If it doesn't go, you go.

Whenever you fear eating something or doing something, don't eat it and don't do it. (267)

135.

Our companions warm themselves up with hashish.* That's the devil's imagination. Even an angel's imagination is no great thing here—much less the devil's imagination. We would not be satisfied with the angel itself, much less the angel's imagination. What is a devil, after all, that there should be its imagination? Why indeed don't our companions have a taste of our pure, infinite world? That stuff makes people understand nothing and become stupefied.

He objected, "The Koran forbids wine, but it doesn't forbid hashish."

I said, "Every verse had an occasion, and then it came down. In the time of the Prophet, the Companions didn't eat this hashish. If they had done so, he would have commanded that they be killed."

Every verse came down as required and it descended at an occasion. When the Companions recited the Koran loudly near the Messenger, he was disturbed. Then a verse came to his blessed mind: *"O you who have faith, do not raise your voices above the voice of the Prophet"* [49:2]. (74-75)

136.

You can answer him with his own words: How do you say Mawlana has a splendor, a light, a gravity? I mean, when he believes in something, emulates it, and follows it wrongfully, what kind of splendor and light is that?

You say that fifty unique saints should walk in Mawlana's train. I mean, how could they emulate a blind man?

You say that the saints have marks. Who are you that you should know the marks of the saints?

When someone is made "helpless" [*'ajiz*], from that helplessness either brightness or darkness appears. Iblis became dark from helplessness, and the angels became bright. A "miracle" [*mu'jiza*] does exactly this, and God's signs are the same way. When they are made helpless, they prostrate themselves.

He says, "When I first gaze upon a man, I recognize him," but he's making a great error, he and his like. What they have found, what they rely upon, what makes them happy and drunk—that's an infernal, fiery gaze. One must go deeper and pass beyond that, because that's caprice. (81-82)

137.

A tribesman in whom Malik Adil believed was warring with a muleteer in Persian: "This donkey doesn't walk well. It keeps on falling on its face. The other day you showed me a good donkey and you gave good donkeys to the others."

The people said to him, "O Shaykh, speak Arabic to him—he doesn't understand Persian."

He paused for a while to summon the Arabic words. The muleteer walked further away. The shaykh shouted before forgetting the Arabic words: "O muleteer!"

He turned towards him and said, "What do you want?"

He said, "Tomorrow, I, a good donkey."

He said, "Today also, O Shaykh!"

Because of envy, the jurists wanted to pray the night prayer with him. Then Malik Adil would come to know that he did not know the Fatihah. They began telling him stories so that the time of prayer would arrive. He saw what they were doing. He turned his face to Malik Adil and said, "Do you know how a stork moves?"

Malik Adil said, "No, I don't."

He motioned to the servant with his eyes to bring his shoes, and he jumped up. He lifted up one foot, came to a stop, then lifted up the other foot. And so he went. (611-12)

138.

He said, "Living in this world is preferable to going to the afterworld."

I said, "Why?"

He said, "Because he is directing a group of people and enjoying himself in God's bounty."

I said, "Yes, the Prophet did not know directing and God's bounty, so he said, *'The Highest Companion!'*"

He said, "You're sitting just like that in the bazaar, but it seems you want to burn up the bazaar."

I said, "You fool, you yourself are burning. You are now being burned. This is what burning is—you are burning, and nothing will remain of you."

Yes, there's a group among the saints who fall into the outward fire and don't burn. There is a group who are hidden, and everything of them is hidden. (614)

139.

I said to the group who believe in you, "God has created you lucky, for such people come to you, and you know the value of serving them. When He creates someone fortunate, his moon opens up before him, the moon enters by his doorway."

> I indeed will lay down the law in the way of love
> so that the ignorant won't set foot in it.

Companionship with the unaware is terribly harmful. It is forbidden. Companionship with the ignorant is forbidden, their food is forbidden.

Forbidden food from the ignorant won't go down my throat. If I were to eat their food, it would be like a stone from a catapult coming into a glass-maker's house full of glass to the ceiling—glass utensils, glass containers.

> *Every one of your sins is forgiven*
> *save turning away from Me.** (188)

140.

A Muslim falls in love with a young unbeliever and shows his need to him. The Christian youth says, "I'm an unbeliever and you're a Muslim. This can't be. You join my religion." He too becomes an unbeliever. After this, should they call him an unbeliever or a Muslim?

And so also the opposite: an unbeliever falls in love with a young Muslim like the moon. He says, "If you want me, I'm a Muslim, you become a Muslim." He becomes a Muslim, and if anyone doesn't call him a Muslim, he's an infidel. Rather, whosoever says he's an infidel is himself an infidel.

Why is there mention of this? Right now, this world possesses beauty, and it's an unbeliever. When it saw God's servant, it fell in love. It became a Muslim, it became the afterworld. It became *My satan has become a Muslim at my hand*. And, *How good is worthy property for a worthy man!*

When the soul says, "I'll become a Muslim gradually, I'll become good," that's plain deception, that's the same as seeking separation. It's become weak and doesn't have any other choice. It's begun to dissemble.

What do you say about the fact that everyone agrees that the *soul at peace** [89:27] is better and more exalted than the *blaming soul*? Why then did He swear an oath by the blaming soul? *No, I swear by the blaming soul* [75:2]. Why didn't He pronounce the oath with the better one? Because He didn't want to expose it to mentioning. He kept it hidden because of its utmost exaltedness. In the same way, someone says, "O king, by the dirt under your feet!", even though his soul is more exalted.

In the exegesis of this verse another answer was also given: *And the wrongdoers, He has prepared for them a painful chastisement* [76:31].

That shaykh in Tabriz was saying, "What's this that they say in a funeral procession—*Glory be to the living who does not die!* They fancy that they are talking about the exalted God. God is far greater than that they should mention His name along with death! Rather, they are addressing the dead person. It means, 'You have now come to life such that you will never die.'"

When morning shows its light, we'll be brought together.
What bliss—not illumined by Time!

He says, "Islam is necessary, Islam!" Indeed, he knows nothing of Islam, not even of the form of Islam. He says that the words of so-and-so are harsh. For a month and two months, he's listened to the truth of these words, and he hasn't caught a scent, not least because he says so simple-mindedly, "God has bestowed something tremendous on me. I have found something great from God that the early and the later folk were not aware of."

I say, "God has bestowed something tiny on me, and I have so much intimacy with that tiny thing that I cannot busy myself with you. You say that He's given you something tremendous, but you offer no proof of that. I say that He's given me something tiny, and I offer the proof."

He says to Mawlana, "I love you, and I love the others for your sake," and he calls in witness the poem of Majnun:

In my love for her I love all the blacks—
in my love for her I even love black dogs.

Tell me if you are talking about other than Mawlana Shams ad-Din Tabrizi. If you love me for his sake, that is more excellent and will make me happier than that you love him for my sake.

What is this that you say—that other than the beloved is loved in subordination to the beloved? How is that done? Only when the beloved is satisfied to have that other as a subordinate.

He said, "A dervish had a cloak that spoke to him. He used to consult with his cloak and ask it to talk."

I say, "It's not God's custom to bring other than man into speech, unless it be established by traditions of undoubted authority—for the sake of the miracles of the prophets. Moreover, how is it that you, who are human, have no talk? You have no rational speech except the tales of old women and Arabic poetry. Now, where's your own talk?"

He said that there's poverty, above poverty there's shaykhhood, above shaykhhood there's being a Pole, and above being a Pole there's such-and-such. I wanted to say, "You've turned this poverty into nothing. You've put this fakir behind those know-nothing shaykhs. So, the elder of the world, the lord of the world and of Adam—for *Adam and everyone beneath him is under my banner, without pride; I am the most eloquent of the Arabs and the non-Arabs, without pride; Poverty is my pride*—what do you want with this poverty? What do you want from this poverty that you put it behind being a shaykh?" But I didn't say a thing. The answer to him was silence.

He said, "If they were thorns, it would have been necessary to set them on fire."

I said, "That would be following Noah, not following Muhammad. Noah said, '[*My Lord,*] *leave not on the earth even one of the unbelievers!*' [71:26]. Muhammad said, '*O God, guide my people, for they do not know.*'"

These people who do the forty-day seclusion are followers of Moses—they have not tasted the following of Muhammad. Far from it! Rather, they do not have the following of Muhammad according to its stipulations. They have a bit of the flavor of following Moses, and they've taken that.

He says, "The saint is solitary, and everyone looks at this world. I mean no one goes along with him front and back. It's as if they look down on a king who goes mounted alone, and they look on a police-chief with reverence, because he goes with clubs before and behind." (169-71)

141.

The house of the cosmos displays man's body, and man's body displays the other world.

A bald man said to another bald men, "Give me the cure."

The bald man replied, "If I had the cure, I would have cured my own head."

Someone says, "O God, do this! O God, do that!" This is exactly as if he were to say, "O king, lift up that pot and bring it here!" He's made the king into his own blessed butler! He commands Him, "Don't do that, do this!"

The Prophet said, "But what do I have in my hands? I'm the messenger. *You do not guide him whom you love* [28:56]." He's speaking deceptively. (266)

142.

A preacher was encouraging the people to take wives and get married, and he was reciting hadiths. He was encouraging the women from the top of the pulpit to ask for husbands. He was encouraging those who had wives to act as go-betweens and to try to bring about unions. And he was reciting hadiths.

He said so much that someone stood up and said, "*The Sufi is the son of the moment.* I'm a stranger here, and I should have a wife."

The preacher turned toward the women and said, "Ladies, is there anyone among you who would wish for that?"

They said that there was. He said that she should stand up and come forward. She stood up and came forward. He said, "Uncover your face so that he may see you, for the Sunnah of the Messenger is that they should see once before marriage."

She uncovered her face. He said, "Young man, look."

He said, "I've looked."

He said, "Is she suitable?"

He said, "Yes."

The preacher said, "Madam, what do you have of this world?"

She said, "I have a little donkey who carries water, and sometimes it takes wheat to the mill, or it pulls firewood. I get a little something from its wages."

The preacher said, "This youth looks like the child of a gentleman of distinction. He can't be a donkey-driver. Is there anyone else?"

They said that there was. She came forward the same way, and showed her face. The young man said, "She's acceptable."

He said, "What does she have?"

Someone said, "She has a cow, which sometimes draws water, sometimes ploughs land, and sometimes turns a wheel, and she receives some of its wages."

He said, "This youth has distinction. It's not fitting for him to drive a cow. Is there anyone else?"

They said that there was. He said, "She should come forward and show herself." She showed herself.

He said, "What sort of trousseau of worldly things does she have?"

Someone said, "She has a garden."

The preacher turned to the youth and said, "Now, you have a choice. Accept whichever of the three that is most agreeable."

The youth began to scratch his ear. The preacher said, "Hurry up and say which one you want!"

He said, "What I want is to sit on the donkey, drive the cow up front, and go to the garden."

He said, "Yes, but you're not so fine that you should be given all three." (157-58)

143.

My advice to Baha' ad-Din* was three things so that he could find the way to meaning and keep all his attributes beautiful. If he were to have a hundred thousand dirhems, he should give them away immediately.

If an infidel were to take a few seeming steps in the way of manliness, that would not go to waste. In the end, it would take his hand—not to mention the son of a chieftain who walks that much road on foot with such belief—a two-month road.* That will not go to waste.

However, I gave him these three pieces of advice: First, do not lie. Second, he eats the weed,* but the stipulation is uprightness. He should not eat it. Third, mix little with the companions.

As for lying, that is the worst of sins. *"Does the believer lie?"*
He said, "He does not lie."

So, how can I lie? Especially in dreams. The work of dreams is full of danger. But, I have said that I will teach the Path.

Someone on the road reaches a river—deep, swift water. If he enters, he'll drown, and if he jumps, he'll fall in the middle of the water. The cause of his heaviness must be repelled, *so kill your souls* [2:54], just as Abraham killed those four birds.* The very same four birds came to life again. But here, the same four birds don't come to life. Rather, they'll come to life in another way. For, the journey of the saints is through these four birds. The four birds have been killed and have come to life.*

Here words open up, a door is opened: What I have from Mawlana is enough for me and three more people. Supposing that it were not from Mawlana, there are friends who would say, "Since you're far from Mawlana, be with us. But the side of the opening is your business, so something may open up."

Something else: *What differences there are between him who lives through his soul, him who lives through his heart, and him who lives through his Lord!* There's no escape. Of course, the road is this: [*Perform the prayer, and pay the alms, and] lend to God [a good loan]* [73:20].

I mean, what requirements could God have?

"O Moses, I was hungry, and you did not feed Me. O Moses, when I

came to your door, what did you do?"

He replied, "O Lord, You are incomparable with that."

He said, "O Moses, if I had come to your door. . . ?"

As much as Moses said, "How can this be?", He kept on replying, "If it had happened, what would you have done?"

In the end He said, "I'm very hungry, stop disputing. Go and prepare food, because I'm coming tomorrow."

Moses prepared the food. In the morning he looked and everything was ready, except that there wasn't much water. A dervish arrived: *"Something for God*—give me some bread."

Moses said, "Welcome," and then placed two pots in his hands: "Bring water."'

The dervish replied, "I will serve you a thousand ways," and brought the water. Moses gave him some bread. The dervish thanked him and went.

Moses went to a great deal of trouble for the sake of God. How is that? And Moses had real knowledge of the science of alchemy, for he had been commanded to write the Torah in gold. The day became late, and Moses was waiting. He divided the food among his neighbors, all the while stuck in the puzzle. "What was the secret of that? Perhaps the secret was that all these people should receive some bounty. Or the devotion itself—the fact that I did what He asked?"

Finally, the time of expansion arrived and he asked: "You promised, but You didn't come."

He said, "I came, but you wouldn't give Me any bread until you commanded Me to bring two pots of water." (101-3)

144.

Oh, all the world's sated are hungry for union with you!

The world's heroes tremble in separation from you!

With your eyes, what do gazelles have to show?

Oh, your tresses have bound the legs of all the world's lions!*

It may be that the one who composed this knew nothing of this or of the state. He might be a farmer, a villager, someone who knows neither poetry nor prose. It was Sana'i, Nizami, Khaqani, and Attar who had a share of that speech.

Cheese is the food of a leopard.* Would a lion eat cheese? He eats the heart and liver of his prey. Everyone has a food.

I knew that it was poison, but I tasted it. It didn't harm me at all. It made me sweat a bit, and that passed. It's the same as the account of Umar—he drank a cup full of poison and it didn't harm him at all. (655)

145.

In my view, if someone throws off a cloak at the time of *sama*,* he can't take it back, even if it's worth a thousand pearls. Otherwise, in that *sama* and that state, he will have been defrauded. He will be like this: "I imagined that this taste was worth the cloak, so I gave it away. Now that I look again, I've been defrauded. It wasn't worth it."

Some people find these words bitter. If they bite hard on that bitterness, sweetness will appear. When anyone laughs in bitterness, it's because he's looking at the sweetness of the outcome.

The meaning of "patience"* is for the gaze to fall on the end of the work. And the meaning of "impatience" is for the gaze not to reach the end of the work.

> The first in line will be the man
> who knows that all will be well in the end.

The mule asked the camel,* "How is it that I often fall on my head, and you seldom fall on your head?"

The camel answered, "When I come to the top of a pass, I look to see the end of the pass, for my head is high, my aspiration is high, and my eyes are bright. I take one look at the end of the path and one look in front of my feet."

What is meant by the camel is the shaykh who is perfect in gaze. You become more closely joined with him by stealing his character traits.

Without doubt, whenever you sit with someone and are with him, you will take on his disposition. On whom have you been gazing that tightness should have come into you? If you look at green herbs and flowers, freshness will come. The sitting companion pulls you into his own world. That is why reciting the Koran purifies the heart, for you remember the prophets and their states. The form of the prophets comes together in your spirit and becomes its sitting companion. (108-9)

146.

The mule said to the camel, "You seldom fall on your head. How is that?"

He said, "Because I have three points of superiority. This superiority does not allow me to come down on my face. First is the largeness of my body and the height of my stature. Second is the brightness of my eyes. I look down from the top of the hill to the bottom of the pass. I see everything, low and high. Finally, I'm a legitimate child. You're illegitimate."

The mule confessed before the camel, and his illegitimacy did not remain. His illegitimacy was denial. Illegitimacy is not an inseparable attribute. (272)

147.

Let's tell jokes, because Mawlana is a man of the Real. In front of him one must speak subtle words. Don't you see? Up until now we have been talking about love. In front of the folk of this world, one must talk about fear.

For example, you tell the story of those two fellows, one of whom had gold strapped around his middle, the other was waiting until he slept so that he could strike him. But he was sleeping lightly, so this one couldn't win over him. He was someone whose disposition was wakefulness—otherwise, he couldn't have forced himself to stay on guard.

When they reached the last way station, he was in despair. He said, "The man is awake. If I try to strike him while he's awake, it may be that he has thought up precautions. Well, let me give up. I'll joke with him."

He said, "Sir, why don't you sleep?"

He said, "Why should I sleep?"

He said, "So that I can strike your head with a stone, beat you in the head, and take your gold."

He said, "Are you speaking the truth? Now I can sleep with a happy heart."

Right now, someone is sleeping in the midst of a dangerous road. One of God's servants has come along to wake him up. However, that sleeper is sleeping in relation to him. If I tell you the attributes of this sleeper, you will despair of yourself. I won't tell you, lest you despair. Don't despair, because there is hope. (132-33)

148.

Are you busy with something else? Well, in whatever you are, don't turn away from me, don't leave me. In whatever state you may be, give what you have. If you don't have anything, then set out to obtain it. When you do something so as to invite other companions, save a bit for me. A penny, two pennies, for the loan that you owe to me, for *a promise is a debt.*

Surely the covenant shall be asked about [17:34]. As for the covenant that is made with God, how will that be? In the same way, of everything conceal a portion for that loan from me, if it be only the amount of a penny—until the time that you yourself suddenly have an opening from the Unseen. Then you'll be finished with all this. In the same way, don't put me aside all at once and forget.

For example, intellect commands something, and caprice commands something that contradicts it. This is as if the master says, "Bring pickles," and the slave says, "No, bring sweets, because sweets are better." This is not appropriate. First he must say, "Bring what the master said. In truth, whatever the master commands is sweet."

The master says, "I am going to such-and-such a place."

The slave says, "*God be with you.* I'm not coming."

"Why aren't you coming?"

"I'll come when it's time to come. Right now I have an excuse."

This is not appropriate. This is to learn opposition. One must learn agreement in this path, not opposition. Or rather, you teach me opposition, I'll teach you agreement. In other words, you teach me disdain, I'll teach you need.

Thus, a jurist said to a lute-player, "I'll teach you [the chapter]

Yasin, you teach me the lute." *He buys from the believers* [9:111] is this. They give the false and fleeting to Him, and He gives them the subsistent.

In this Tribe, the tale-bearer is God.* He says, "So-and-so, for whom you make requests from Us and intercede—you want good fortune and elevation for him, and he said such-and-such about you." (116-17)

149.

The Mu'tazilites say, "If Speech were eternal, that would necessitate the eternity of the world." This is not the road of debating with the Mu'tazilites. It is the road of brokenness, being dust, helplessness, and abandoning envy and enmity. When a secret is unveiled for you, you must show gratitude for that.

Shall I tell the meaning of gratitude with hypocrisy, or with truthfulness?

God's be the praise—don't despair! Vision is through limpidness and pure light, and you are turned toward rightness, repose, and ease. Sufferings have passed, opacities have passed.

Although I seldom came, I was always here. Mawlana knows. I was busy with supplication night and day. My heart's suffering didn't let me see you in that state. Now that the state has finished with the good, I have come to you. You are *The best of people, those who give benefit to people.* Your existence will remain and subsist among the people for many years. You are going toward a youthfulness to which old age will not find a way. Every day you will become younger.

The best of people are those who give benefit to people. If someone does not know what good is, how will he do good? Since they do not know what years are and what lifespan is, why do they wish years of life for each other?

If one dirhem of your property goes to a companion of the heart,* that is better than a thousand dirhems that goes to a companion of the soul. I cannot explain this to you, because your soul is living and moving. If I talk, you will say some words, and I will cut myself off from you. (126-27)

150.

He was complaining a great deal about his own child. From my tongue this came out: "His outcome will be good. He's a child. He's doing what he does because of childhood, not because of the root. In the same way, unripe grapes and immature apricots are bitter and sour. That is because of the childhood and immaturity of the grapes, not because of the root. There is another sort of unripe grapes whose sourness is from the root, the ones that ripen hard. Those don't become sweet. Otherwise, unripe grapes must be put in the sun." (302)

151.

That one came and said, "Excuse me, we haven't cooked anything today."

I said, "What would I do with something you have cooked? You must be cooked."

He said, "How do I become cooked?"

I said, "What kind of disciple are you if you don't understand my allusions?"

He said, "If understanding did not waver in the allusions and the expressions, the ulama of Islam would not have disagreed. They would have understood one meaning from the texts."

I said, "How can the ulama of Islam have duality and disagreement? Seeing two and being a fanatic is your work. If Abu Hanifa saw Shafi'i, he would take him by the head and kiss his eyes. How can God's servants disagree with God? How is disagreement possible? You're the one who sees disagreement. Sacrifice yourself so that you may be released from duality."

He said, "When will I be released from the story of sacrifice?"

I said, "Sacrifice yourself, and you will be released from the story of sacrifice. The *God is greater** of the prayer is for sacrificing the soul. When will He be greater? As long as pride and existence are within you, you must say *God is greater*, and you must intend the sacrifice. Until when do you want to take the idol under your arm and come to the prayer? You say, *God is greater*, but, like the hypocrites, you firmly hold that idol under your arm." (303-4)

152.

Mawlana was saying, "I see trees and gardens, and an ocean of pure, sweet, spirit-increasing water. The water is so gentle and subtle that its description does not enter into words. The trees are not such that their roots are on the lower plane. Their branches pass beyond the Lote Tree of the Far Boundary,* with much shade, and sweet herbs."

But they don't see anything, because of their love for chieftainship and leadership. (710)

153.

You must seize the root. [Let go of] weeping for the sake of clothing, bread, and enmity: "They're looking down on me," or "So-and-so has become estranged from me," and all the other branches. Weep for the sake of the root, sit in sorrow for the sake of the root, lament, complain. Then you'll see that those branches will come to you and fall at your feet. All the chieftainships, the sovereignties, and the headmanships, and all the top people in every field of learning will come and put their faces on the ground in front of you, and you will pay no attention to them. As much as you drive them away, they won't go. But, if you seize the branch, the root will go away and you won't have gained the branch.

I want to give advice. However, I gave advice several times. He heard some of it happily, and some of it troubled him. The fact that he is troubled comes to me and strikes against me. I said, "When advice cannot be given, I should begin making the supplications of little old women and the helpless, so that they will turn toward that without my speaking."

You're weeping for every branch. In the same way, that young man fell at my feet: "I've left my home and family in search of so-and-so. I haven't been able to do anything. All I expect is just to greet him once, that he should answer my greeting. Then I'll return home. Or, that he should look upon me with his gaze."

I said, "I won't do anything that you ask. Why don't you be such that a thousand like him come to you and bind their belts in serving you?"

He said, "What should I do?"

I said, "Belong to that which is the root and the goal—the root of all roots and the goal of all goals, not the root that one day will become the branch. Be serious in seeking that. Whatever troubles your mind and keeps you far from the goal, consider that enormous. If you take rectifying it lightly, you will have looked down upon the goal." (181-82)

MY CRITICS

154.

He says, "The son of so-and-so has become a follower of a man from Tabriz! Does the earth of Khorasan follow the earth of Tabriz?"

He claims to be a Sufi and pure. He doesn't have the intelligence to see that earth is of no account. If a man from Istanbul should have that, then it would be incumbent upon the Meccan to follow him.

Love of the homeland is part of faith. How could the Prophet have meant Mecca? Mecca belongs to this world, but faith is not of the world. That which is part of faith is not a part of the world, it comes from that world.

Islam began as a stranger. Since it is a stranger and comes from another world, how could he mean Mecca? When they say, "Probably he meant Mecca"—probably he meant something else, and he certainly meant something else. That "homeland" is the Presence of God, which is beloved and sought by the believer. (736-37)

155.

It was his own asininity that made him say that people from Tabriz are jackasses. What has he seen? When he hasn't seen anything and knows nothing, why does he speak these words? There were people there of whom I am the least. They threw my ocean out just like flotsam that falls to the shore of the sea. I'm like this— what were they like! (641)

156.

Crowing belongs to the rooster, and morning to God. I mean, this is exactly what He said to Moses when he asked, "O Lord, what use is that? Pharaoh will not accept."

He said, "Do not put down what is yours. Tell him!"

God has servants whose speech they themselves hear and understand. (215)

157.

They said, "Mawlana is detached from this world, but Mawlana Shams ad-Din is not detached from the world."*

Mawlana said that this is because you do not love Mawlana Shams ad-Din Tabrizi. If you loved him, he would not appear to you as wanting anything, nor would he appear as disliked.

> *The eye of satisfaction is dull to every defect,*
> *the eye of displeasure brings out every ugliness.*

Your love for a thing makes you blind and deaf, that is, toward the defects of the loved thing. When someone begins to see defects, you know that love for it has decreased. Don't you see how a mother loves her child? If he dirties himself, with all her gentleness and beauty she does not hold herself back. She says, "Good for you!"

These words are susceptible to weakness. Mawlana Shams ad-Din Tabrizi says that Mawlana has given his answer. Now, listen to me: Someone binds up a lame donkey, feeds it fodder night and day, and the donkey defecates on him. This is one thing. Another is that someone is sitting on an Arabian stallion, and that stallion brings him out from a hundred thousand dangers and blights and highwaymen and delivers him. Even though he has confirmation from the other side, the Real has thereby proven the mount for him.

I want nothing at all—only the need of the needy. *Alms are only for the poor* [9:60]. Only need—not just its form, but its form along with its meaning.

For one thing, need is that you not become sour-faced and contracted before the shaykh. O master sourpuss! Do you want to rebuke me? Are you fighting with me?

He said, "No."

Now, a person is sour with someone who has caused him trouble, and with others he's laughing and happy. He sees this one, he turns sour; he sees that one, he smiles. If none of that torment remains for him, he becomes totally happy. If he is still troubled, that is a war that he has with himself. He looks at himself and becomes sour. He looks toward his friend, and he smiles.

Knowing this is perfection.* And not knowing this is the perfection of perfection.

I want to call someone for the sake of his meaning, and I want his meaning for the sake of the call. (100-1)

158.

When I'm joyful, if the whole world were to be full of grief, it would have no effect on me. And when I feel grief, I don't allow anyone else's grief to influence me. (303)

159.

O ass, O ass! O dog, O dog! O corpse! You can't give any news of my outwardness. How can you give news of my inwardness? O ass, O ass! No, no—whatever belief makes you warm, keep it. And whatever belief makes you cold, stay away from it.

The Man is the one who is happy in unhappiness and joyful in grief. He knows that the object of his desire is wrapped up in being deprived of his desire. In deprivation is the hope of having it, and in having it is the worry that deprivation will arrive.

On the day that was the turn of my fever, I was joyful that health would arrive the next day. And on the day that was the turn of health, I was grieving that fever would come tomorrow.

When you say, "If I had not eaten that yesterday, I would not have this suffering today," you put yourself into it. The Man is he who puts all into himself. That's his perfection. Then he becomes great. (640-41)

160.

At first, God's Messenger firmly avoided people because of his extreme intimacy with God. He shied away from good and bad, lest acceptance by the people should become a veil for an instant or an hour. At the end, when he reached perfection, he had passed beyond being affected by the acceptance of the eighteen thousand worlds,* or anyone's rejection. He used to say, *"Sell me to the people!"*: "O Companions, sell me to the people, for I myself won't come to sell, and how can I suffer loss?"

Since Muhammad said this, look how God says "Sell Me" a hundred times: *Make Me beloved in the hearts of My servants. Remind them of My bounties and My blessings, for hearts are disposed to love those who act well toward them and hate those who act badly.* The soul that commands to evil says, "He's selling himself to you."

This is why many of the great ones became weak because of me: "He's bound himself to silver." I have not bound myself to money [*pul*], I have bound myself to making the donkey* pass over the bridge [*pul*]. They are the great ones, the shaykhs. What can I do for them? I want you because you're like this. I want someone needy, I want someone hungry, I want someone thirsty! Out of its own gentleness and generosity, sparkling water seeks a thirsty man.*

The soul has the nature of a woman.* Or rather, woman herself has the nature of the soul. *Consult with them, then oppose them.* O Messenger of God, you commanded that we consult, especially in a business whose profit and loss is general. Now, if we do not find a man with whom to consult and there are women, what should we do? He says, "Consult with them, but whatever they say, do the opposite." (287)

161.

A woman will never be a shaykh.

He said, "Yes, that would be cold."

He said, "I don't understand. Does 'cold' mean that she could do the work, but it would be better for a man to do it? Or that she couldn't do it at all, whether hot or cold? If Fatima or A'isha had acted as shaykhs, I would have lost my belief in the Messenger. But they didn't. If God opens the door for a woman, she'll remain silent and concealed as she was. A woman should stay with her work and her spindle." (755-56)

162.

It's best that a woman sit behind the spindle in the corner of the house, busy in the service of the one who takes care of her. (668)

163.

In the same way, someone asked my friend about me: "Is he a jurist or a fakir?"

He said, "Both jurist and fakir."

He said, "Then how come he only talks about jurisprudence?"

He answered, "Because his poverty is not of the superficial kind that he could properly speak about it with this group. It would be a pity to speak of it with these people. He brings out words by way of knowledge, and he speaks the secrets by way of knowledge and in the curtain of knowledge, so that his own words may not be spoken."

As for "worldly," Mawlana knows that in this city there is an important man who wishes to see me. Even today, if I were to command him, before this evening as much gold would reach me from him as belongs to the richest of you seated in this assembly. I don't crave knowledge, I don't crave gnosis, I don't crave the worldly. Whatever I make obligatory for you is in your own best interest. If someone speaks the words of the dervishes to you, listen while believing. Don't listen any other way. When you have listened, do not become deniers. And if you do become deniers, this silly formality of asking for forgiveness will be worthless. They defile themselves a thousand times, and then they put forth their stomachs: "*Our Lord, we have wronged ourselves* [7:23]—we have purified our breast." No, that wants a protector and a helper. (326-27)

164.

I don't want anything from anyone for worldly reasons, only because of following—the Prophet used to accept gifts.

If you have a hundred thousand dirhems and dinars—a citadel full of gold—and you bestow it on me, and if I look on your forehead and don't see there a light and in your breast a need, that gold would be the same for me as a hill of dung.

For me Mawlana would be enough—if I had any wants. Remember this, for you are reading your own pages. Read also something of the companion's page. That will be useful for you. All this suffering is because you're reading your own page and not reading anything of the companion's page. Imagination arises from knowledge and gnosis, but after that imagination there's another knowledge and gnosis, and that knowledge and gnosis has another imagination. This becomes long.

There's another, shorter road, which has none of that, but that road also has been given a bad name. It should have another name. It has put down a good rule: One day you burn, one day you don't. That is the good rule for him who has never wanted worldly things. His mind has never inclined toward the worldly and he's paid no attention. But now, because of me, he's had a hundred regrets—"Would that I were thousands so I could sacrifice myself! Alas!"

In the same way, if someone were to fill the storehouses and rooms with millet, and one grain of millet fell out, why wouldn't his heart let it go?

It's been said a hundred times, "Alas, if only the Amir were alive, if only he still had life, so he might bestow something great, like a village!" For he would have wished that I request something from him. (731-32)

165.

All of you are sinners. You said that Mawlana is detached from this world, but Mawlana Shams ad-Din Tabrizi is busy gathering things. Bravo this taking to task! And bravo this deprivation!

If this person doesn't absolve you, then I'll ask from God: "Did he say it or not?"

He'll say, "Do you absolve him, or should I take care of him?"

I'll say, "What do You want? My want is included in Yours."

He'll say, "From My side, it's a hundred times more so!"

In short, the discussion will be long. If there is pardon this time, and if it happens again, they will never benefit from it again, and at the resurrection they won't see me, especially in paradise. Were it not for those few dirhems, I would leave this place naked and barefoot. Then what would your state be? There would never be any hope for my return. (79-80)

166.

One dirhem in the hand of a truthful and sincere man is better than a hundred dirhems that you give to them, for that one dirhem will go in good. *Lend to God* [73:20]. It is concerning these that he said that *He has a hand: "Alms fall into the hand of the All-Merciful before falling into the hand of the poor man."*

And one dirhem in the hand of him whose face is turned in service toward that man is better in the same way, because he also will spend it in this good. Good is the servant of God, good is God, and *God is good.* (200)

167.

When someone calls me bad names, that makes me happy, but I am troubled when someone praises me. Praise should be such that afterwards no denial comes. Otherwise, that praise is hypocrisy. Someone who is a hypocrite is worse than an unbeliever—*Surely the hypocrites will be in the lowest reach of the Fire* [4:145]. (319)

168.

A shaykh in Baghdad was sitting in a forty-day seclusion. It was the night before the New Year's festival.* In the seclusion he heard a voice not of this world: "We have given you the breath of Jesus.* Come out, and present it to the people."

The shaykh thought, "I wonder what was intended by this call. It's a test. But what does He want?"

A second time the sound came, with more awesomeness: "Leave aside these whispering doubts! Come out! Go to gatherings! We have given you the breath of Jesus."

He wanted to think about this with watchfulness so that what was intended would be unveiled for him. The third time, a shout came that was terribly awesome: "We have given you the breath of Jesus. Come out, without hesitation, without delay!"

He came out. It was the day of the festival, and he set off among the crowds of Baghdad. He saw a candy-seller who had made little birds of sugar candy and was shouting, "New Year's sugar!"

He said, "By God, I'll test it." He shouted to the candy-seller. The people stood there wondering what the shaykh was doing, for the shaykh had no interest in candy. He took the bird-shaped candy from the tray and placed it on his palm. He blew upon the bird the breath of *I will create for you out of clay as the guise of a bird* [3:49]. At once it turned into flesh, skin, and wings, and flew away.

The people gathered around at once. He made a few of those birds fly away. But the shaykh felt constricted by the crowds of people, prostrating themselves and showing astonishment. He set off for the desert, and the people followed after him. As much as he tried to fend them off—"I have work to do in seclusion"—of course they kept on coming after him.

He said, "O Lord, what kind of charismatic act was that? It has imprisoned me and made me helpless."

An inspiration came to him: "Do something so that they will go."

The shaykh broke wind. They all looked at each other. They nodded their heads in their denial of him, and they went away. One person remained. In fact he wouldn't go. The shaykh wanted to say to him, "Why didn't you conform to the group?" But, because of the radiance of the person's need and the splendor of his belief, the shaykh was ashamed, or rather, the shaykh was in awe. Nonetheless, he voiced those words harshly.

He answered, "I didn't come because of the first wind that I should go because of the last wind. In my view, this wind was better than that wind, because this wind put your blessed essence at ease, and that wind gave you pain and trouble." (243-45)

169.

O master, the house is yours—don't go. I will go with gratitude.

Those who exercise enmity toward the saints of God fancy that they are doing bad to them. That's wrong. Rather, they're doing good. They're making their hearts cold toward them. The saints are those who devour the world's grief. Their loving kindness and their concern for someone is their burden, and when he does something that cuts off the loving kindness, it is as if Mount Qaf has been lifted off of them.

So, they cannot act with enmity. Enmity would be for them to make Mount Qaf more firmly fixed on his neck and shoulders, and for them to increase this—I mean that they would do something that would add to the loving kindness and he would devour even more of their grief. But then they throw his burden of loving kindness and his thoughts from him. That is the ease of his soul. (315-16)

170.

Now, be fair: Who can live like this? If you show humility toward someone, he flees, and then becomes your enemy. How can harming yourself do any good to anyone? Come now, this must be repelled.

There is the story of the king who was mounted on an Arabian stallion. He was passing by, heading for a destination. In this road he suddenly passed by a village. The dogs were barking from every side. How does this harm the king? On the contrary, it benefits him. He goes faster, so it makes him reach his destination quicker. The dogs are pissing in the latrine. However, out of mercy, he says, "The louder you bark, the more I benefit. Nonetheless, I'll leave aside my own benefit so as not arrive sooner." (659-60)

171.

When you oppose the shaykh, it's like the slave who kills himself over a quarrel with his master. "Hey, why are you killing yourself over a quarrel?"

He says, "So my master will suffer loss." (274)

172.

They came and made a denunciation before Judge Baha: "Such-and-such a dervish has said contemptuously that you're indigent."

The judge became angry. He said to one of his deputies, "Well, let's go and see."

When he came, he said, "How is it that you have mentioned us with contempt."

I said, "What did I say?"

He said, "You said that he is indigent."

I said, "Well, that's what gets the work done. With all that majesty, Muhammad begged from the Presence, '*O God, give me life as an indigent, give me death as an indigent, and muster me among the indigent!*'" (263)

173.

I had a hope—if there should be some talk among those who criticize me, or those who imagine things about me, while some are hesitating about me: "I wonder if it's what the friends say, or if it's what these criticizers say—which should I accept?" They were waiting to hear something so as to prefer one of the two sides. My hope was that you would speak some good words among these people, but you didn't say anything. You should have spoken right out. It was because of this that I cut off from you and broke off the companionship—the dervish was troubled by you. Such words would have given them gain, for they don't understand that you avoid them out of love for me. They attribute it to boredom and frailty and other things.

When something comes to mind such that [you think], "If I say something, the result will be such-and-such a loss," whatever has come to mind must not be kept to yourself. You must quickly tell the companion. (610)

174.

In order to see once the eyes of the friend, I must see one hundred times the eyes of the enemy.

Yesterday, I placed your image in front and was debating: "Why don't you answer these people openly and clearly?"

Your image said, "I am ashamed before them, and I don't want them to be troubled."

I was answering you. The debate became long. What was left that we didn't say? No, what indeed did we say? In fact we said nothing. I mean that we spoke in relation to the defective and said nothing about our own talk. (187)

175.

In short, I seek to be with Muhammad only in fraternity. I'm in the path of fraternity and brotherhood, because beyond him is someone else. After all, God has not gone. Sometimes I mention his greatness for the sake of showing respect and reverence, not because it's required. The station of *He is the Real* is far above that of *I am the Real*.

If this does not become known, that will be because our friendship has its feet in the air. Why don't you say outright who it is about whom he spoke badly? Bring this fellow here so that he may say it in my presence. In order to soothe their hearts, lest they be troubled and wounded, you chewed up the words: "Even if he spoke badly, I am satisfied." You've affirmed the bad talk about me!

After all, how can he talk bad about sheer good? God has servants who are sheer evil. Whatever they say is bad.

God is He that does not speak but brings everyone into speech through His strength, even if it's an inanimate thing. Suppose everyone agreed that God is someone who speaks with words and sounds. I would say, "Another God is necessary to bring Him into speech, for 'God' is that strong one who brings all things into speech, but He says nothing in words."

After all, the Prophet said, *"Assume the character traits of God!"* In God's character there are both severity and gentleness. There's no flavor if everything is gentleness. *Hard toward the unbelievers, merciful among themselves* [48:29]. (242-43)

176.

Today, for example, Mawlana was advising the companions and telling them about my attributes. The companions felt sympathy. Mawlana said, "When you look at this little bit of deprivation and cruelty that you see from Lord Shams ad-Din Tabrizi—may God elevate his mention—my counsel and your sympathy will be concealed from you. Satan's wolf will once again scatter snow in the eye of your moment."

The companions said to themselves, "No. Let's go and ask forgiveness from Lord Shams ad-Din and offer our services. After that, we will not turn away from this."

They came to the door of the house and were not let in. Immediately, all that sympathy went. The reason for not letting them enter was that I had been thinking to myself: "This is not a pigsty, such that any time someone wants, he can come in with a bit of regret, and then, with a bit of coldness, anguish, and restlessness, go back out."

After all, look at that great one in relation to Ahmad Ghazali.* The crime was simply that he sent books to him, for the sake of repelling the denunciation of the people: "Sometimes you should quote from this book, so it will stop the tongues of the criticizers."

He didn't let his brother into his khanaqah. One report is that he commanded him to travel for seven years, another that it was fifteen years. He was saying, "Is this a pigsty so that, as soon as a state overmasters you, you come in here?"

I mean, I have no wish from these companions. First, I don't gain any knowledge from you. On the contrary, you will grasp my words well when you make yourself totally present through need and when you empty yourself of your own knowledge. Even then, you may not grasp my words. (325-26)

177.

Before the promise comes, what will he do? He'll do the same thing that they do to me because of lack of recognition. But I'm happy. How could I not be happy? No one has ever denied me without a hundred thousand proximate angels acknowledging me. No one has ever been cruel to me and called me bad names without God's praising me a thousand times in place of those bad names. No one has ever become estranged and gone far from me without the Lord giving me a thousand proximities and bounties. And I have never given advice to anyone and had that person reject my words without a hundred thousand souls of the sincere and the proximate coming to me and hanging down their heads. (317)

178.

But those who struggle in Us, surely We shall guide them on Our paths [29:69]. This is reversed in terms of order.*

The master of this house made me sit here. There's no place for a meddling guest. Mahmud said to Ayaz, "Sit here." Can you object to Ayaz? Does anyone object to what the king wants?

The king said, "Since it's I, he's killed a hundred fine men so that they'll learn the lesson."

A Qazvini became the chief inspector. He killed his mother* so that the disbelievers would know that they'd get no consideration.

I mean, there was a minstrel who had a bad voice. Someone said to him, "Don't you hear your own voice?" Now, don't you hear my explanation? This is not from the master of the house, it's from elsewhere. Haven't you thought about my finding my way into this house? Or the fact that he has made me familiar with his wife? That he would be jealous if Gabriel were to look upon her? But he sits in front of me like a son sitting in front of a father who's feeding him a piece of bread.*

Don't you see this strength? I will tame them all such that you will be perplexed. Since I have been truthful for one person, I will be truthful for all.

In the same way, for Muhammad to bear witness once was counted as two people's bearing witness. The reason was that Muhammad gave witness in a case. They said, "We need another witness so that there will be two."

Dhu'l-Yadayn said, "I was also a witness to this case."

After the judgment was made and everyone left, the Messenger said to him, "I know that you were not a witness to this case. How could you be a witness?"

He said, "O Messenger of God, there are many thousands of unseen things, of the states of the beginning and end of the world, of which I had no awareness. Because of your words I have acknowledged their truth. I have accepted them and bear witness to them. Wouldn't you be a speaker of truth in such a trivial affair?" (660-61)

My Harshness with Friends

179.

He keeps on holding His own servant dear. If I sometimes put on bad clothes, that's by my own choice. Toward me God is gentleness upon gentleness, and generosity upon generosity. However, in myself sometimes I have gentleness and sometimes severity—I become bored with gentleness. (740)

180.

The men of God have more of this disclosure and vision of God in the *sama*. They have come out of their own existence, and the *sama* brings them out of other worlds, so they reach the encounter with the Real.

In short, there is a *sama* that is forbidden. In fact, he was kind to say that it is forbidden. A *sama* like that is unbelief. A hand that is raised without that state will certainly be chastised by the fire of hell, and a hand that is raised with that state will certainly reach paradise.

There is a *sama* that is allowable, and that is the *sama* of the folk of ascetic discipline and asceticism, which brings them to tears and tenderness.

There is a *sama* that is incumbent, and that is the *sama* of the folk of states, because it is an aid to their life.

If one of the folk of *sama* has a *sama* in the east,* another possessor of *sama* will also have a *sama* in the west, and they will be aware of each other's state.

Someone said, "Mawlana is all gentleness, and Mawlana Shams ad-Din has both the attribute of gentleness and the attribute of severity."

So-and-so said, "Well, everyone is the same way." Then he began to offer an interpretation. He said, "I wanted to reject his words, not to diminish you."

You idiot! Those were my words. Why do you interpret them? What excuse can you offer? He described me with the attributes of God, who has both severity and gentleness. Those were not his words, nor the Koran, nor the Hadith. Those were my words passing over his tongue. How does it come to you to say that everyone has that? How can the severity and gentleness that are attributed to me belong to everyone?

Then, with intellect and courtesy like this, they want to reach Abu Yazid, Junayd, and Shibli in two days and drink from the same cup! If the practices of those shaykhs were to be fully described to them, they would lose their intellects without having done a thing—simply having heard about it.

Nonetheless, with all that, when he died he was veiled from God.* A dervish was passing by his grave. He said, "Oh! One veil remained between this man and God!" That indeed was because of the generosity of that dervish. Ask another dervish. (73-74)

181.

Most of God's elect are such that their charismatic acts are hidden. They don't appear to everyone, for they themselves are hidden. There are things that I don't dare say—a third of it was said.

They insist on saying that so-and-so is all gentleness. He is sheer gentleness. They fancy that perfection is in that. It isn't. He who is all gentleness is defective. It would never be allowable for this attribute to belong to God—that all of Him should be gentleness. You would be negating the attribute of severity. Rather, there must be both gentleness and severity, but each in its own place. The ignorant man has both severity and gentleness, but not in their place, because of caprice and ignorance.

So-and-so had said that this indeed belongs to everyone—both severity toward enemies and gentleness toward friends. But not everyone recognizes friends and enemies. If everyone recognized friends, He would not have said, *Take not My enemy and your enemy as friends, offering them love* [60:1]; nor would He have said, *Among your wives and children there is an enemy to you, so beware of them* [64:14]; nor would He have said, *Ha, there you are—you love them, and they love you not* [3:119].

There are also the words of the Commander of the Faithful, Ali: *"Love your friend with some easiness, for perhaps one day you will come to hate him. And hate the hateful person with some easiness, for perhaps one day you will come to love him."*

It may be that God will establish between you and those of them with whom you are at enmity love [60:7].

For you to tell the difference between enemy and friend
     you'll need to live your life once again.
Many are the enemies with faces of friends—
     you need a friend who's true to you.

So, "You'll need to live your life once again" is for the person who has not died to the first existence and found a new existence. The one who has found a second life—for *We shall assuredly give him to live a goodly life* [16:97]—sees with the divine light. He recognizes the enemy, he recognizes the friend, his severity is in the place of severity, his gentleness in the place of gentleness. His severity is suitable, and so also is his gentleness, even though, in reality, both go back to the same thing. (615-16)

182.

You've seen only one birth. All the animals share with you in this birth. If you had only this one birth, you would not be distinct from them. *None treads on the carpet of the All-Merciful and none ascends to the celestial realm unless he has been born twice.* (679)

183.

I am not one of those who go out to meet someone. If someone becomes angry and flees, I will flee ten times more than he. If God were to greet me ten times, I wouldn't answer. After the tenth time, I'd say, "and to You too." I'd make myself deaf.

Right now, all right, I must stand. Become angry, and I'll become angry. (273)

184.

Sometimes I'll pass by and not greet the companions. This is not to torment.

Let me also say this: They do not know what I am thinking about them. If they knew what limpidness, purity of heart, and good fortune I seek for them, they would give me their lives. I never think badly. What does a mind pure of the devil and whispering doubts think about? The devil has never come into this heart. The angel has always been inside it. God said, "I have made this the house of My own mercy. You be kind enough to leave."

After all, minds are of three sorts. One mind is always the house of the devil. Another mind is the house of the devil and the angel together. Sometimes the angel leaves and the devil enters, and sometimes the angel comes in and drives the devil out. Still another mind is specific to the angel; the devil does not enter into it. (211-12)

185.

Yes, one group remained in doubt, another group remained in certainty.

You say that this is the level of a group—Hallaj went into doubt, a group was between doubt and certainty. *The spirits of the martyrs are in the craws of green birds, the spirits of the believers are in the craws of white birds, the spirits of children are in the craws of sparrows, the spirits of the unbelievers are in the craws of black birds.*

For the elect, *sama* is permitted, because they have unblemished hearts. *Love in God and hate in God* are in the unblemished heart.

If my name-calling reaches a hundred-year unbeliever, he will become a believer, and if it reaches a believer, he will become a saint. In the end he'll go to paradise.

I mean, you saw the apparition: In your dream I said to you that when my breast reached his breast, he came to possess this station. He has many more apparitions ahead of him. In the end he'll go as a Muslim, he'll go without blemish.* (77-78)

186.

Being the companion of the folk of this world is fire. There must be an Abraham if the fire is not going to burn.

Nimrod* built up a fire from the outside, and Abraham also built up a fire: "Let's see whom the fire will burn. Nimrod, you are the result of severity, I am the result of mercy. Let's see who gets burned in the end."

He said, *"My mercy takes precedence over My wrath."*

Abraham said, "Since the precedence is known, why is the test required?"

He said, "No, there has to be the transaction."

He said, *"In the name of God."*

He said, "The foot of mercy is such that it is severe toward severity. So, mercy is severe to severity."

He said, "Is that what severity is like?"

Yes, friends will have many tests. If you act like this toward your friend, how will you act toward your enemy?

He threw down his friend, then went, to see what his state would be. His state is known by the one who threw him. (109-10)

187.

Whenever I love someone, I bring forth cruelty. If he accepts that, I belong to him like a morsel. I mean, if you act with kindliness toward a five-year old child,* he believes in you and loves you. It's cruelty that does the work. (219)

188.

If they gave that child to me, I'd bring him up such that he would want neither this nor that. Anyone who saw him would say that he's an angel, not a human being.

If he asked me for an almond, I would slap him in the face: "What! Are you hungry? Eat bread! Otherwise, don't talk nonsense." It's like when a cat shits and makes a pollution, they strike it and rub the stuff in its face.

The food of people is bread, and every once in a while stew with meat—the rest is games. Should I let him grow up playing games? When he's big, then he himself will know. Tell him, "Go ahead and play games."

I would bring him up in a short time such that he would be a wonder. He wouldn't die, he wouldn't become ill, and he wouldn't put a morsel in his mouth without permission. A finger would go into his mouth and bring it out. The reason is that if he grows up in self-absorption, advice will be of no use—unless you kill him, or beat him so much that he dies.

My purpose in this harshness is to see where his soul comes forth. Yes, there is a time when you put up with a child's nonsense, not for the sake of teaching him courtesy, but for the sake of the soul's fury. Right there I would intercede: "Enough! Teach courtesy to your own soul, don't kill the child!" (234–35)

189.

What grief do I have? For the Real does not withhold His secret from the servant. Which secret does He hold back? However, if He voices the secrets of this world in a sheath, no harm is done. That's why the Prophet said, *"I know better the affairs of your religion, and you know better the affairs of this world of yours."* There's a reason for that, and for this too, for *No soul knows what it will earn tomorrow, and no soul knows in which earth it will die* [31:34].

That shaykh was saying, "Such-and-such a shaykh, Bu Latif, exceeds God by a Bu." In other words, God is called "Latif," and the shaykh is called "Bu Latif." "Exceeds God by a *Bu*"!

I said, "Shove that *Bu* into your wife's cunt and up the arse of her procuress!" What a jackass! He was voicing his own asininity.

Another one said, "I was in a ship. A jewel like the sun appeared on top of the ocean. I looked into that pearl and it almost took away the light of my eye. I covered my eyes with my hand." Then he talked about the spectacles and wonders of the ocean.

I said, "You're looking for a spectacle? You want a spectacle? Come inside me—you'll see a spectacle. You've gone for recreation into your own world and your own insides. Come for recreation into my world and my insides!"

Still another one fancied that my state had become defective. He said to his companions, "He's our enemy. Did you see what he did to my aspiration?"

You little woman, what do you know about aspiration? Go, make an ablution, say your prayers, and repent. Say, "I was an unbeliever and I've found faith. I've passed beyond unbelief." Buy some cotton and a spindle, and sit and spin! Who are you? The most manly of men hope to put a couple of pots of water at my door! (183-84)

190.

If a stranger beats me a hundred times with a shoe, I won't say a thing. But someone special I'll call to task for the tip of a hair.

These others have tossed on their tongues the story of Hallaj—ice rains down from it. The only ones who will like this story are those who have the same state.

They tell that when he was strung up, the sheriffs of the Law commanded that the folk of Baghdad stone him. Everyone threw a stone fit for a catapult. They required that from his friends as well. There was no choice, so they threw bouquets of flowers instead of stones. He immediately began to lament. The gaze that perceived that state asked in wonder, "You didn't lament from all those stones, why did you lament when they threw bouquets?"

He said, *"Don't you know that cruelty from friends is hard?"* (252-53)

191.

If this Christian talks for a hundred days, I won't become bored. When someone becomes boring and quarrelsome, I burn him, for getting along is found in burning. I ruin him, because buildings appear after ruins.

He knows so many sciences, but he knows nothing of the worthiness of his own work. He does something, and he fancies that the path of bringing about worthiness is his own work. He's got the wrong hole. He's reciting *"Refresh me with the fresh fragrance of the Garden"** while cleaning his anus. He's got the right supplication, but the wrong hole. (309)

192.

They're all in love with this word—"Bravo!" They kill themselves for the sake of "Bravo!" (622)

193.

All of them are this world. They live through this world. Did you see how he was sitting that day, all broken, because he was not the deputy and had been dismissed—and how he's sitting today? The clothes he's wearing! *I see that the length of the era is forgotten.* That little infidel's the one who's forgotten. Once I will go with steadfastness so that he may see the divine awesomeness. That state of his will fall apart. No ecstasy will remain, no apparitions, no watchfulness, no words, no state. All of it will be plundered. (692-93)

194.

The great ones and perfect ones for whom He gave existence to the world also have a veil. It is that from time to time they voice secrets with God so as not to come to naught. They don't have this veil at any other time.

I voice secrets, but I don't voice the Speech. I marvel at the great ones, because even Speech appeared from the great ones. Abu Yazid was not one of them. They are the prophets and the messengers. It is as if they became drunk from the Speech and are not able to hear.* A hundred thousand vats of wine do not do what is done by the Speech of the Lord of the worlds.

The knowers of the Koran are themselves in extreme narrowness. The first person who became a knower of the Speech was not even aware that there was a Koran in the world. If someone passes by the Koran after he has come to know the Speech, he won't be in narrowness, because, before he found the Koran, he had found spaciousness. He knows how to explain the Koran. Thus the poet's words:

I said to my night, "Come down,
for my moon has gone to bed."

By "night" he means the veil that is between the two of them and others,
or the veil that is between him and his beloved, if there is a veil between them.

Someone said, "O Messenger of God, because of darkness and cold, that bedouin hypocrite was not able to voice the attribute of your prophecy."

He replied, "You should not let the nomads all become veils. Are you veiled by a nomad?"

He said, "O Messenger of God, he is a denier and an enemy."

He replied, "So now, how does your blaming benefit him? Rather, perhaps you can lift off his head with the word of Truth. Put it in the air. Maybe that will benefit him."

I said to my night, "Come down."

The veil of that little student of ours is this half-done job. That's his night—despite the Jealous One—and it is between us. *I ask forgiveness from God*—I'm letting fly. *And praise belongs to God*—though I'm letting fly, he's flying. (94-95)

195.

The reason for speaking harshly in answering is so that the roughness may come out from the inside and not increase. *He who torments without having been tormented is a jackass.* Nonetheless, the strength of toleration and clemency is perfect, and I have no relation with suffering. My existence does not remain, and suffering comes from existence. My existence is full of happiness. Why should I take the outside suffering upon myself? I repel it with an answer and a curse. I throw it outside the house. (268-69)

196.

Did you see Ala' ad-Din*—how I threatened him behind the curtain?

I said, "Your coat is in the chamber."

He said, "I'll tell the merchant to bring it."

I said, "No, I've forbidden him to come into the chamber and disturb me. I've chosen that place for my seclusion and solitude. I upset the merchant: 'Why have you come? Don't come again!'"

That woman came to bring water. I said, "Come when I tell you to. Otherwise, take the penny. That's what you want. But don't come until I ask. I may be naked or clothed. *Three times of nakedness for you* [24:58] *And if they had patience* [*until you come out, that would be better for them*] [49:5]." (198)

197.

I said, "The sweetness of faith is not such that it comes and then goes."

I saw that Zayn Sadaqa had become deranged, like a galloping horse that sets its head to the desert and loses the road. This fellow Imad, at least, is better than he. He knows the difference between a grammarian and a philologist.

The grandson of Shihab Suhrawardi was saying to me, *"To hesitate is to show love."*

I said, "Well, not in your case, you brother of a whore."* (82-83)

198.

Some are given opening in the going, some are given opening in the coming. Beware and look carefully: Is your opening in the going or the coming?

Beware, they won't put union with Him in the hands,
    the drunk won't get milk from the Shariah's cup.
When the men of disengagement sit together
    they don't give one gulp to the self-worshipers.*

When Imad was weeping while reading the letter of Nasir, I wanted him to look at me so that I could weep as well, because it appeared that he was weeping out of mercy and sympathy. No, he was weeping because of his great love for rank. (138)

199.

Grasp what I am saying! When I think of shortcoming, I become angry. Why should you be in my anger? Why should you come into my anger? I'm terribly humble with the sincerely needy, but I'm terribly prideful and arrogant with others.

They always talk about Junayd and Abu Yazid. When I talk, Junayd, Abu Yazid, and talking about them appear to the heart as cold and frigid. It's like when someone eats rock candy, which is the best and purest sugar. Grape syrup tastes sour to him. "I wish the grape syrup were sweet. That Baalbaki grape syrup is really good—when you stick your finger in, a whole ounce comes up."

And now that professor, Siraj ad-Din,* has been wondering all his life whether his four-by-four pool has become polluted. (275)

200.

You have to gain that disposition when small so that you can come to the work more quickly. A fresh branch can be straightened without fire. Once fire has dried it out, it's difficult. You must put on the shoe when it's wet, so that the foot can open up its place and not be troubled when it's dry.

He said, "Troubling people and making them cold doesn't do that—instill willingness, not aversion."

I said, "If I do not test him, he will not know who he is. Haven't you seen these people who displayed belief and self-sacrifice—as soon as I began to test them a little bit, did you see their belief? I made them naked in front of you, and you saw them naked. One of them claims to love from the bottom of his soul, but if I ask him for one dirhem, his intellect goes, his soul goes, and he loses both head and feet! I tested them so that they would see a bit of themselves. They began to revile me, saying that this fellow has made all those who believe in you cold.

"I said, 'He didn't do it, it was God's jealousy towards his existence. He doesn't want people to be informed of him. The brand of *No one knows them other than I* is on his forehead. How could you see him? He is still under God's gaze. If you come into God's gaze, you will see him. How can the creatures grasp God? How can they see Him? So also is this person who is in His gaze.

"Wonderful the way they all fell apart! Just like something all together that falls apart. Each of them has a state. The preacher on top of the pulpit has a state, the Koran-reciter on the seat has a state, the listener has a state, the shaykh has a state, the disciple has a state, the master has a state, the lover has a state, the beloved has a state. *There is no god but God.* Bravo the misguidance and blindness that does not know that it is blind! I'm not one of them, but I'm informed of them.

"There's another group who see and who know that they see. They themselves know who they are."

"How long will you talk of the one you don't see, lover?"

He said, "But I'm your father, you're my child."
I said, "Is a jackass lying here that you think I'm your child and you're my father? When Muhammad is there, how can Adam compete?'" (306-7)

201.

Look at him whose face is shining with the light of faith, pure of hypocrisy—the light that does not become dark or lessened by any test. That's different from a light and taste that becomes dark with a bit of testing.

There was someone who showed himself to be my friend. He claimed to be my disciple. He would come and say, "I have one soul, and I don't know if it's in your body or mine."

To test him, one day I said, "You have some property. Find me a beautiful wife. If they want three hundred, give them four hundred." He dried up right there. (290-91)

202.

What grief do I have? There are the folk of this world, the folk of the afterworld, and the folk of the Real. Shibli is of the folk of the afterworld, and Mawlana of the folk of the Real.

Last night, I was bringing the friends to my mind one by one— the belief of each, the need and understanding of each. So-and-so arrived. I said, "Why should he be like this?" I felt sorry for him— he's one of ours. He is indeed.

You're happy-hearted because you're one of ours. That's why I greeted you. First I do such as that, then I greet. First I bring about the person's worthiness, then I ask.

I've said it a thousand times: Whenever I love someone, I act cruelly toward him. For a tiny slip, I give him a hundred thousand retributions. As for the others, I don't call them to account for a mountain of sins.

Whenever someone has been chased into the desert, that's because of estrangement. I show him consideration and serve him, for he's a stranger and far away. Don't you see the great length I go to in magnifying and being kind to those who are not fit to pick up your old shoes? Don't you see that I overlook several thousand bad acts from them? Don't you see that all the tribulations of the prophets and the saints were because they were His elect? (759)

203.

The difference between me and the great ones is just that—what I have inwardly is exactly what's outward. God has given it to me to sit with strangers—and with friends, even better. When someone finds benefit from a designated way, he takes that way seriously.

When someone's perplexed in his own work
    it's better for him to start over.

In other words, he should take that tested path and be true in companionship. He should not fancy that his companion is ignorant and foolish.

Abu Bakr Rubabi had heard of the fame of Juhi. One day they met but did not recognize each other. Both of them stole from one person—his donkey, his bags, and his clothing. Out of grief, that fellow hung a little drum around his neck and was beating it: "So that they won't steal me too." They stole the drum.

Then, in rivalry, each showed the other his art. Every time one of them showed a skill in knavery, the other one showed a skill that would overcome that skill. Then, one day he said, "Who are you with all this skill?"

He said, "Juhi."

He said, "Ah, you speak the truth!"

In the same way, two dervishes, possessors of the heart, happen to meet. One of them shows reverence toward the other, because he knows that he has reached various goals by that path. The other knows what the first is doing. He starts acting cruelly, because he knows that the path of felicity is to put up with cruelty, and he sees and knows the path of felicity more clearly than the disk of the sun. (155–56)

204.

I'll not put you in the heart or you'll be wounded,
    I'll not keep you in the eye or you'll be lowly.
I'll give you a place in the spirit, not the eyes or the heart,
    so you'll be my companion at the last breath.*

Severity looks upon gentleness with its own eyes and sees only severity. When this servant of God calls someone an "unbeliever," he means that you belong to Him, and I belong to Him, but you are the attribute of His severity, and I am the attribute of His gentleness. Gentleness has a precedence. Pass beyond the fact that He is severity and join with the gentleness. It has a better taste.

In other words, the Prophet does not place among his community anything that is not there. Rather, he casts a spell on what is veiled so that the veil may be lifted. The gist of all the words of the prophets is this: "Acquire a mirror." (93)

205.

A mirror has no inclinations. If you prostrate yourself to it a hundred times—"There's this one fault on his face, conceal it from him, because he's my friend"—it will answer in the tongue of its state, "That is certainly impossible."

He said, "Now, friend, you're asking me to give the mirror into your hand so that you may look. I can offer no excuses, I cannot break your words. In my heart I'm saying, 'I'll certainly offer excuses, I won't show him the mirror.' For, if I say there's a fault on your face, you won't tolerate that, and if I say that the mirror is faulty, that would be worse. But still, love does not let me offer a pretext. I'm saying, 'Now I'll give the mirror into your hand, but if you see a fault on the face in the mirror, don't think it's from the mirror. Know that it is incidental to the mirror, and know that it is your own reflection. Place the fault on yourself, don't place it on the face of the mirror. And, if you don't place the fault on yourself, well, at least place it on me, since I'm the owner of the mirror— don't place it on the mirror."

He said, "I accept, I give you my oath. So, bring the mirror. I have no patience." But still, he didn't give his heart.

He said, "O master, let me be excused in this." Maybe he'll leave aside this pledge, for the work of the mirror is delicate. But love didn't allow it.

He said, "Once more I renew the pledge."

He said, "The pledge and promise is that whatever fault you see, you don't throw the mirror on the ground, you don't break its substance—even though its substance can't be broken."

He said, "Far be it from me! Never! I would never try or think that. I won't imagine any fault in the mirror. Now give me the mirror so that you may see my courtesy and kindliness."

He said, "If you break it, the price of its substance will be such-and-such, and the fine will be such-and-such." He made him swear to this. Nonetheless, when he gave the mirror into his hand, he fled. He was saying to himself, "If it's a good mirror, why would he flee?"

He was about to break it. In short, when he held it in front of his face, he saw a very ugly picture. He wanted to throw it on the ground—"He turned my liver to blood for this?" Then he remembered the fine, the recompense, the money, and the sworn oaths. He said, "Would that there weren't the witnessed pledge and the money. Then I'd make myself happy and show him what has to be done." He was saying this, and the mirror, with the tongue of its own state, was rebuking him: "Don't you see what I've done to you and what you've done to me?"

Right now he loves himself. He's making an excuse for the mirror. If he loves himself, he'll be kept from himself, but if he loves the mirror, he won't be kept from either.

The mirror is God Himself. He supposes that the mirror is someone else. In any case, just as he inclines toward the mirror, the mirror inclines toward him. It's because of the mirror's inclination that he inclines toward the mirror. Or it's the opposite. "If you break the mirror, you've broken Me—*I am with the broken.*"

In sum, it's impossible for the mirror to incline and be cautious. In the same way, when a touchstone or a scale inclines toward God, if you say to it a hundred times, "O scale, make this crooked-ness straight," it will only incline toward God, even if you attend to it and prostrate yourself to it for two hundred years. (69-71)

206.

The woolen sack is big. It disputes with the pearl: "I'm bigger than the cotton sack!"

The pearl says, "Let's ask the mad, not the rational."

The mad man will have heard that there is a pearl. He'll say, "Even if you fill the sacks with gold, they will not be able to tell the price of the pearl. The pearl will tell its own price."

The rational man says, "He's mad. The unique pearl will never have a price." (763-64)

207.

The accusation of that big-bearded, little shaykh is like the woolen sack's disputation with the pearl. And what sort of wool? Polluted, stinking wool. I won't refute him with my own state-ment. I won't pollute my words with him. I'll refute him with his words—that lie with this.

Jesus began speaking immediately, Muhammad started speaking after forty years*—not because of defect, but because of perfec-tion. For he was the beloved. To a servant they say, "Who are you?" He replies, *Verily I am the servant of God*" [19:30]. No one says to the sultan, "Who are you?"

The person who thinks about defects is reading his own page. He's not reading the page of the friend. Were he to read one line of the friend's page, he would say nothing of these things. He's reading his own page, only that. In his page, all the writing is crooked, bent, dark, and false. He's conceiving of himself and com-ing up with suspicions. He has carved his self like an idol, and now he's its servant and helpless before it.

These holidays, like those idols, say, "O unaware of yourselves! You are seeking blessings from us, but we ourselves hope that you will look upon us, so that the day will no longer have dayness, the hour hourness, and the inanimate thing inanimateness."* (98-99)

208.

"On these days one must worship, for God is gazing upon His servants on these days, but on other days He does not gaze like this on His servants and does not see them like this." These people talk like that. I mean, as long as God is, He sees. He is hearing and seeing. How can you say that during Ramadan He sees, so don't commit acts of disobedience, and in Sha'ban He sees, so abstain.* But, when Shawwal arrives, busy yourselves with ungodliness and corruption. With the tongue of the state you are saying, "He's gone. God no longer sees and He doesn't want to know. Until next Ramadan, come on, bring the games and the wine so that we can enjoy ourselves." (768-69)

209.

I gazed on someone, and he pointed at me. I said, "You may become a Muslim a thousand times, but something of that unbelief will stay with you. Otherwise, why do you look upon me from your helplessness?"

A shaykh was there. He began to give me advice: "Talk to people in the measure of their capacity, and be nice to them in the measure of their purity and unification."

I said, "You're right, but I can't give you an answer, because you gave me advice, and I don't see in you the capacity for the answer." (279-80)

210.

When you see that the shaykh is sour, stick to him, flee to him, and then you may become sweet. Your ripening is in those clouds. Grapes and fruit ripen under the clouds.

There's a good man without knowledge. A good man says, "I trust in God." He does not have the knowledge to recognize the place of trust. After all, "following" is what he said: "Tie the camel's leg and trust in God."*

Didn't the Messenger have trust when he exerted himself so much in struggle? Wasn't he a gnostic? Wasn't he a knower? Wasn't he a good man? (199-200)

211.

Those who flee from cruelty are like the grammarian who fell down in a lane that was deep with muck. Someone came and said, *"Give me your hand,"* but without proper vocalization. The grammarian became upset and said, *"Pass on. Thou art not of my folk."*

Someone else came, said the same thing, and again he became upset. He said, *"Pass on! Thou art not of my folk."*

The people came one after another, and he was seeing tiny distortions in pronunciation, but he didn't see that he was staying in the filth. He remained in the filth all night long until morning—at the bottom of the garbage-dump, and he wouldn't take anyone's hand, or give his hand to anyone. When day arrived, someone came and said, *"O Abu Umar, thou hast fallen into uncleanness!"*

He said, *"Take my hand. Thou art of my folk!"* He gave him his hand, but the man himself was not strong. When he pulled, they both fell in. They started to laugh at their own state.

The people were astonished: "Why are they laughing in this state? This is not the place for laughter."

One person goes into a state at a sound, because this sound is similar to the sound of so-and-so. But he has no awareness of the reality of the sound. Someone else goes into a state because of conformity, but he does not know what conformity is.

Once a grammarian heard a singer sing, *"In every delight and in an illumination!"* He tore his clothes to pieces and was shouting out. All the people in the assembly gathered around him. The judge remained perplexed about him—"This man has never been one to go into states."

The singer fancied that he liked the verse, so he was singing it again, and the grammarian kept on shouting out, and motioning toward the people, "Listen, O Muslims!"

They fancied that he had probably heard a marvelous voice from the Unseen. "He's trying to wake us up!"

When the day became late and everything was finished, the grammarian had torn his clothes to shreds, thrown them away, and become naked. They gathered around him and sprinkled water and rosewater on him. When he calmed down, the judge took him by the hand and brought him to a private place. He said, "By my soul and secret heart, speak the truth! How did this state come over you?"

He said, "Why shouldn't a state come over me? Why shouldn't a thousand states come over me? From the time of Adam to the era of Noah, from the era of Abraham to the time of Muhammad, the pronoun 'in' has made nouns take the dative case, but just now, he made it take the accusative!"

Now, since everyone falls into this much of state, each with a corrupt purpose, if they were to expend that strength in the reality of the subsistent, spiritual, everlasting purpose, what would that taste be like? That strength is one's capital. *Whoever buys what he does not need has sold what he does need.*

Someone has moisture and dust in his eye. Someone tells him, "You should cure that."

He goes off: "I'm busy. I'm patching my old shoes. Sir, I wear these old shoes in the bath—this is what's important to me."

He's saying, "No, that other is what does the work." (156-57)

212.

A mouse took the reins of a camel and started walking.* The camel, unhappy because of recalcitrance toward his master, was obedient to the mouse—because of the quarrel with the master. The mouse fancied that it was the strength of its own hand. A ray of that fancy struck the camel. He said to himself, "I'll show you."

When they reached water, the mouse stopped. It said, "What has caused this halting?"

The mouse said, "A great stream of water has come forth."

The camel said, "Let me see how deep the water is. You stand back."

He placed his feet in the water and took a few steps, then came back. He said, "Come on, the water's shallow. It's only up the knees."

The mouse said, "Yes—but from knee to knee. . ."

He said, "Do you repent? Don't be so bold and, if you are, be so with someone whose knees are like yours."

He said, "I repent, but take my hand."

The camel lay down: "Come on, climb up on my hump—whether it's a stream or the Bactrus, even if it's the ocean, I'll swim. I have no fear."

Now, this camel, compared to Og son of Anak, is the same—"from knee to knee." Og was not drowned during Noah's flood. The ocean's water came up to his knee. Moses killed him.

Then this Og son of Anak has the same property—"from knee to knee"—before Adam and the children of Adam's soul and heart—no, the children of Adam's water and clay—especially the one concerning whom it came, *"Two strides, and he arrived."* That's the Muhammadan stride—one stride to the afterworld and the second stride to the Lord. As for me and you, if we take a hundred strides, we'll go no further than the edge of the bench.

The servant has been promised resurrection and paradise so that he may have the vision of God. When he sees all in this world, what spectacles and wonders he'll see! What pleasures he'll find! When someone does not see these things, but he sees the seer and believes in his truthfulness, what he will taste simply by supposing that truthfulness! This tasting is precisely his showing consideration and his asking. For the outward show of consideration is general for Jews, Christians, and Muslims. Everyone has this outward asking, and they deceive each other with it. But this show of consideration lasts until the edge of the grave.

Right now, I am wrathful and cruel to the friends so that they won't rely on the outward asking and shows of consideration. With the tongue of their state, they say, "Gentleness with strangers, and severity with acquaintances?"

With the tongue of my state I answer, "Don't you see the gentleness of companionship? It's with friends, and it lasts forever." It is such that, were the prophets sent by God alive, with all their majesty, they would wish to be their companions. "Oh would that I could sit with them for an instant!"* That cruelty is so that the friend may become the confidant of truth, and hypocrisy may leave his disposition, for God's servant has no hypocrisy in his make-up.

In any way possible he wants to speak the truth so that the dark-thinking antagonist will find no means to interpret it away, and so that he will know the reality of the state. For he has much gentleness and mercy, and these don't allow him to conceal the state's reality. Then that person may find release and deliverance. (134-36)

213.

He was criticizing the preaching of the shaykh. "What kind of preaching was that? He sings two or three tunes from the pulpit and wags his hips. Why doesn't he preach to himself? Why doesn't he talk to his children—'Beware, don't do that!' Why doesn't he tell his wife to watch out?"

Mawlana himself is detached from preaching. Through God's instruction, and with a thousand intercessions and pleadings, large and small, he says what he says. The shaykh's preaching brings a stone into movement.

If they say to a physician, "You're curing this ill person. Why didn't you treat your father, who died? Why didn't you treat your own child?" Or they say to Muhammad, "Why didn't you bring your uncle Abu Lahab out from darkness?"

He will answer them, "There are illnesses that can't be treated.* For a physician to busy himself with them is ignorance. There are illnesses that can be treated. To let those go to ruin is not to be merciful."

Someone is planting something in the ground. They say to him, "Why don't you plant in the land around your own house?"

"Because, it's salty. It wouldn't be appropriate."

Those words of mine do no harm at all. On the contrary, they have a hundred benefits. But, are there any benefits in the world from which some people are not deprived? If the Egyptian finds that the Nile's water* has turned to blood, the Nile can't be criticized. If David's voice sounds ugly to the denier, there's nothing wrong with his voice.

*The sun's ray is not harmed when it strikes
an envious denier blind to its light.*

If my words right now don't appear the way you like, don't flee from this state. Honor my words so that you may find honor. Then you will have confirmed the claims that you made to faith and belief, and you will have given witness to your own vision and that of your fathers. In contrast, if you're discourteous and act with contempt toward me, you're the one who's contemptible, because you will have given witness to your own blindness and falsity. Then the service and respect that you undertook earlier will have been blind, and you will have led others astray—"He deserves contempt. Why did they show reverence to him?"

I fear that at this hour, you're heedless of the noxiousness of separation. You're sleeping happily in the shadow of kindness. If you do something that cuts off the kindness, you won't see this state in your dreams. Nor will you see the shaykh in your dreams. You can't see the shaykh except by the shaykh's choice, whether in sleep or in wakefulness.

Anyone who just hopes will rot—I mean a hope cut off from secondary causes. This is like a castrate who hopes that God will give him children. Compare that to the hope of a young stallion of a man who has a young wife. How can you compare this hope with that hope? Becoming a castrate and unmanly comes from being cut off from the shaykh's kindness.

Alas for the ill person whose business falls to [the recitation of] Yasin!* In other words, he finds tasting from the shaykh when the shaykh is hypocritical towards him and speaks soft and sweet words. Then he rejoices, and he does not know that this is where he should fear. When a king speaks rashly and harshly, there's no fear. He's simply speaking words fit and appropriate for the state of his own kingship.

> When you see the lion's fangs jutting forth,
>   don't think for a moment he's smiling.*

You should fear kings when they treat you with respect! (151-53)

214.

A king was coming with a thousand shouts of "Make way!" A tramp came out and spoke harshly. He stood in the road calling the king bad names. The king arrived, but said nothing to anyone. If he had said anything to anyone, they would have cut him into little pieces. He turned around and said, "Let's go that way."

They said, "Why, lord?"

He said, "My heart wants it so."

Against whom should he act with severity? Against a tramp? Was he at root a tramp that he should quarrel with a tramp? Kings strike out at those who lift up their heads in pride—Pharaoh, Nimrod. *You shall hear [from those who were given the Book before you and] from those who associate others with God much hurt, [but if you are patient and godfearing, surely that is true constancy]* [3:186] (621)

215.

Sultan Mahmud became separated from the army and was very hungry. He said to a miller, "Peace be upon you! Do you have anything for me to eat?"

He said, "Sure." He was about to get food, wondering where this heavyweight had come from. "Right now, there's only bread. Will you eat that?"

The king said, "Bring it."

On the way he had regrets. He came back and said, "We would eat it too, if we had any. There's no bread, but there is flour. Will you eat that?"

He said, "Hey, bring it, whatever there is."

He left, and said to himself, "That would be a shame. That stupid fellow has a stomach hanging out." He came back saying, "There's barley flour." Again he came back, "It's mixed with millet." Again he came, "It's promised to the orphans." In short, in the end he brought a skin and shook it in the king's face: "This is all that was left—so that you'd believe me. I fancied that there was something."

The king's eyes were wounded. He sat by the edge of the stream, holding his eyes with his hands for a long time—those fine eyes. And so on.

He went from there, and he saw a small boy, a Turk. He said, "Do you have anything for me to eat?"

He replied, "I do, but is that the way to ask? Say, 'Peace be upon you. Would you like a guest?'"

He said, "By God, he's right." He pulled back the reins and returned: "Peace be upon you."

"And upon you be peace."

"Would you like a guest?'

"Join me." He quickly brought pastry, milk, cheese, and other things.

He ate. Then he said, "Take this ring, because I'm a favorite of the king, and with this I will get something good from the king for you. If he won't give it, I'll give it."

He saw a beautiful ring. He said, "It's a pity. I didn't kill a sheep. What did I do?"

The more the king thought about him, the more he saw the beauty of his act and the more his worth went up. Finally the king reached the army.

The child came and presented the ring, and they all fell down on their faces. They brought him down. He saw that the princes and kings were lined up in rows. Other mounted soldiers and kings were standing opposite. He was looking all around, wondering which one was that prince. He saw the king in that shape. He said, *"There is no power and no strength but in God!"* Again, he looked at them all, and said, "Oh! Is this the king? Oh, what did I do!" The king spoke. He said, "By God, it is the king!"

He commanded that forty slaves with golden belts should serve him. Judge the rest of the bounties by this.

He said, "Bring that stupid miller here so that I can freeze his heart."

A hundred armed men went off. He had told them where the village was. They were looking around, having arrived at the skirt of the mountain in those parts. One of them said, "That's it." They said, "Yes, that's it."

The stupid fellow said, "Hey, they've come." He fled and locked the door. They banged at the door. He stayed silent. "I'm dead."

"How can you be dead if you talk?"

"No, this is my last breath, I'm dead."

"Get up!"

He didn't get up, so they broke down the door. They came in: "Get up! The king is summoning you."

He said, "O lords! What do I have to do with the king? I'm just a miller. If the king has wheat, he should bring it, I'll make flour."

"Hey, get up! The king is summoning you!"

"But I make fine flour."

"Get up, don't talk so much!"

"I'll give you flour, I'll give you bread, I'll give you pastry and yogurt." Before this, he wouldn't give anything to the sultan. Now he wanted to give it to a hundred men!

"Get up! Why are you talking nonsense?" He didn't get up. They tied a rope around his neck and pulled him out.

In the royal court, he was looking all around expecting to see the chief servant. Of course, he saw no one like that—only the sultan. He was saying, "Oh, if I had a thousand heads, I wouldn't make off with one of them!"

The king said, "Little man! I've brought you because my ring has fallen into the latrine. Bring it out!"

He said, "At your service."

Secretly the king said, "When he goes in, lock him up tightly and don't open the door for three days, so that he can suffer the grief of hunger." The miserable fellow used to eat five maunds of bread a day. He had a stomach as greedy as hell itself. For three days he was in that stinking place, with nothing to eat. He set his heart on death.

After three days, he said, "Bring him!"

"Get up! Come out!"

He said, "Now what do you want? I've only one breath left in me. Let me die!"

They said, "Little man, are you such that we would let you die one death?"

He was saying, "Woe, woe on me!"

They brought him. The king said, "Little man, will you eat plain rice?"

He said, "Oh, yes!"

He said, "I would too, if we had any. Will you eat cumin stew with sugar cane?"

He said, "Yes."

"Will you eat rice pudding spiced with sugar?"

He said, "Yes, how could I not eat it?"

He said, "We would eat it too, if we had any." And he kept on listing foods.

He said, "O lord, go ahead and kill me!"

Once he had become severely pitiful and oppressed, the king's kindness came to a boil. The effect of the kindness made him remember this verse:

If I do bad, and you do bad in return—
    what's the difference between me and you?

He began to laugh. He commanded that he be given a thousand dirhems, and a robe of honor, and he sent him happily on his way. Then he commanded that they call him back. They ran after him and told him to come. He said to himself, "Oh, he made me feel secure so that he could seize me even worse." He said, "Now take my gold and give me my life."

They said, "Come. Answer over there." They brought him.

The king said, "Promise me and lay down the stipulation that, if the greediness of your own throat makes you fail to give something to someone, at least don't shake that floury skin on him, because you blinded me."

The miller fell on his face and wept a great deal. He promised that he would never hold back what there was, and he would never look at any guest with contempt. (630-33)

My Return from Aleppo

216.

From the time I left my city, I have never seen a shaykh.

Mawlana is fit to be a shaykh if he wants to. However, he does not give the cloak. It's one thing when they come and push themselves upon him—"Give me the cloak! Cut off my hair!"—and he is forced to do so. But it's something else when someone says, "Come, be my disciple!"

Indeed, Shaykh Abu Bakr did not have the custom of giving the cloak.

I haven't seen my own shaykh. He's there, but I came out of my city looking for him, and I haven't found him yet. However, the world is not empty of a shaykh.

He says that the shaykh gives a cloak without the person knowing it. He gives the kingdom, and he passes on.

I haven't seen my own shaykh, not even this much: someone before whom you can quote and he doesn't become troubled, or, if he does become troubled, he becomes troubled with the one who is quoting. I also haven't seen anyone like that. From the station of having this attribute to being a shaykh, there's a hundred-thousand-year journey.

I also haven't found that. But I did find Mawlana with this attribute. The fact that I returned from Aleppo to his companionship was built on this attribute. If they had said to me, "Your father has come out of the grave and wishes to see you. He has come to Tel Basher* only to see you and then to die once again—come and see him." I would have said, "Tell him to die. What can I do?" I wouldn't have left Aleppo. Only because of that did I come. (756)

217.

What can be said about Damascus? If it weren't for Mawlana, I wouldn't have wanted to come back from Aleppo. If you had brought news that my father had risen from the grave and come to Malatya, saying, "Come and see me, then we'll go to Damascus," I certainly wouldn't have gone. I would have gone to Damascus though. What do I care whether it's flourishing or in ruins? That place at least would be there—that congregational mosque.*

Yes, for mankind, there's an intimacy with other people.

As for the root, they haven't exaggerated—"Paradise is either Damascus, or right above it."*

They write these lines for qualified scholars, not for weavers. I need it to be vocalized to understand it. Without vocalization I don't understand. (168-69)

218.

The Koran is all commandments and prohibitions. He who is qualified for the Speech says, "We hear and we obey" [2:285]. Otherwise he says, "We hear and we disobey" [2:93]—not with his tongue, but with his state. If he carries out the command, then he says that by putting it into practice. If he should say outwardly, "We disobey," it doesn't matter after he has said "We obey" by putting into practice. This is the exegesis.

Interpretation is your business. Most of your words are of this sort. Why be perplexed at that? Hurry, say "Yes, that's the way it is." My spirit is tormented, it is variegated—for an hour like this, an hour like that.

I'd like some of those kabobs of Zahra. She makes good kabobs—fresh, fine, full of moisture. Why does Kirra make kabobs so awfully dry? Zahra's food is good, Kirra has no food. Zahra has food, she has kabob, she washes clothes.

I remember in Aleppo, I was saying that I wished you were there. When I was eating, I would have given you some as well. It's a wonderful city, Aleppo—the houses, the streets. I looked around happily, seeing the tops of the battlements. I looked down, I saw a world and a moat. (340)

219.

In Aleppo what supplications I said for you in that caravanserai where I stayed! It was not right to show my face to the people when you were not there. I should have busied myself with a work, or turned to a khanaqah.

I mean, what I make and build up in twenty days, you kick over and destroy with one blink. None of that counted toward the work. All that was the destruction of the work. And the suffering came back to me. You saw what the training did indeed bring. But I had begun. The work of a fakir is not in vain. Did you see how much light you found on that first day? If that had become permanent, think what it would have been by now! So, none of that counted toward the work.

Going to Damascus was not your work, it was mine. With what wonder Mawlana looks at me!

He said, "He's seeking for God in someone like me. My belief in him has increased."

I said, "What he said first is wrong. I am not seeking for God in him, I am seeking for him in God." (766)

220.

Be impartial so that impartiality may take you somewhere. Preserving health is easier than seeking health. Preserving oneself from sin is easier than repentance. When you are afflicted by illness after abandoning abstinence, then you start having patience and you start saying, "Why didn't I have this much patience before? This much patience is nothing."

If you can, act such that I don't have to travel for the sake of your work and your best interest, and so that the work may be accomplished by the journey that I took. That would be good. I am not in a situation where I could command you to travel. I'll put the travel on myself so that your work may become worthy, for separation cooks. In separation you say, "That amount of commandments and prohibitions was nothing. Why didn't I do it? That was an easy thing compared to the hardship of separation."

What I was not saying—I was speaking hypocritically and watching out for the minds of both sides. I was speaking riddles. I should have been explicit. What's the worth of that work? For your best interest I would make fifty journeys. My journeys are for the sake of accomplishing your work. Otherwise, what difference does it make to me whether it's Anatolia or Syria? Whether I'm at the Kaaba or in Istanbul, it makes no difference. However, it is certainly the case that separation cooks and polishes.

Now, is the one polished and cooked by union better, or the one polished and cooked by separation? How can the one who is cooked by union and whose eyes are opened be compared with the one who is standing outside, wondering when he will be allowed inside the curtain? How can he be similar to the one who has taken up residence inside the curtain? (163-64)

221.

They said to a Sufi, "Do you want a slap in cash, or a dinar in credit?"

He said, "Hit and leave."

There is a blessing in the leaving. He feared the pain and regret of losing the blessing. (760)

222.

He replied, "Yes, they don't become secure and they don't accept the path of security."

He said, "When you throw words far from yourself, give advice to others, and forget yourself—what's the profit of that other than dispersion?"

He said, "Yes, they throw words far from themselves and they give advice to others, but not to themselves."

Why did you go away from me so that you would have to say, "In the end I regretted it—why did I go?" I also should go away from you in the same measure for the sake of taking to task. You've regretted this much. How could I have claimed that we have a conjunction whose dirt is sweeter than others' gold? You don't know the worth of this conjunction, so you need to be taken to task. (678-79)

223.

When anyone claims to be my friend, I rebuke him for the tip of a hair. I don't rebuke an enemy at all, even if he curses me. If you say those words, that's bad. If someone else says them, whatever he wants to say—I'll live with whatever he wants, however it is for him. This is that same story: If he doesn't come to me, he won't be a man, but if I were to go to him, I'd be a catamite.

I won't go on foot. I'll ask for twenty dirhems from this brother and say that I'm going to Aksaray. He'll give them, and there are other friends as well. One of the blessings of empty pockets is that they took me to Egypt.

That time they saw: Was Mawlana ever happy from the day I left? And, from the day I came back, I have lived in another way, such that one day of this companionship is equal to a year of that companionship.

The more there is union, the more difficult and arduous is separation.

When you came to Aleppo,* did you see any change in my color? And if that had been a hundred years, it would have been the same. It was so unpleasant and difficult for me that it would be ugly to speak of it. In another respect, it was pleasant. But unpleasantness predominated except on this side. I preferred Mawlana. (772-73)

Abû Nu`aym al-Isfahânî, *Hilyat al-awliyâ'*, 10 vols. (Cairo: Matba`at as-sa`âda, 1971-79).

Aflâkî, *Manâqib al-`ârifîn*, edited by T. Yazici (Ankara: Türk Tarih Kurumu Basimevi, 1959-61).

Arb. A. J. Arberry (tr.), *Discourses of Rumi* (London: John Murray, 1961).

`Attâr, *Mukhtâr-nâma*, edited by M. Shafî`î-Kadkanî (Tehran: Tûs, 1358/1979).

Bihar. Muhammad Bâqir Majlisî, *Bihâr al-anwâr*, 110 vols. (Beirut: Mu'assasat al-Wafâ', 1983).

Chittick, W. C., *A Shi'ite Anthology* (Albany: State University of New York Press, 1981).

Chittick, W. C. and P. L. Wilson, *Fakhruddin `Iraqi: Divine Flashes* (New York: Paulist Press, 1982).

Conc. A. J. Wensinck et. al., *Concordance et indices de la tradition musulmane* (Leiden: E. J. Brill, 1936-69).

D. *Diwan* of Rumi. Published as *Kulliyyât-i Shams yâ dîwân-i kabîr*, edited by B. Furûzânfar (Tehran: Dânishgâh, 1336-46/1957-67).

Ebn-e Monavvar, Mohammad, *The Secrets of God's Mystical Oneness*, translated by John O'Kane (Costa Mesa: Mazda, 1992).

FAM. B. Furûzânfar, *Ahâdîth-i Mathnawî* (Tehran: Amîr Kabîr, 1347/1968).

FP. W. C. Chittick, *Faith and Practice of Islam: Three Thirteenth Century Sufi Texts* (Albany: State University of New York Press, 1992).

Fih. Rumi, *Fîhi mâ fîhi*, edited by B. Furûzânfar (Tehran: Amîr Kabîr, 1348/1969).

Hujwîrî, *Kashf al-mahjûb*, edited by V. Zhukovsky (Tehran: Amîr Kabîr, 1336/1957),

Ibn al-Jawzî, *Talbîs Iblîs* (Beirut: Dâr al-Kutub al-`Ilmiyya, 1368/1949).

Ibn `Arabî, *al-Futûhât al-makkiyya* (Cairo, 1911).

Khalidi, Tarif, *The Muslim Jesus* (Cambridge: Harvard University Press, 2001).

Khâqânî, *Dîwân*, edited by `A. `Abdur-Rasûlî (Tehran: Kitâbkhâna-yi Khayyâm, 1978).

Kisa'i. *The Tales of the Prophets of al-Kisa'i*, translated by W. M. Thackston (Boston: Twayne, 1978).

Knysh, Alexander, *Ibn `Arabi in the Later Islamic Tradition* (Albany: State University of New York Press, 1999).

Lings, Martin, *Muhammad* (London: Allen & Unwin, 1983).

M. *The Mathnawî of Jalâlu'ddîn Rûmî*, edited and translated by R. A. Nicholson, 8 vols. (London: Luzac, 1925-40).

Maq. *Maqâlât-i Shams-i Tabrîzî*, edited by Mohammad-Ali Movahhed (Tehran: Khwârazmî, 1369/1990).

Maybudî, Rashîd ad-Dîn, *Kashf al-asrâr wa `uddat al-abrâr*, 10 vols., edited by `A. A. Hikmat (Tehran: Dânishgâh, 1331-39/1952-60).

MSM. Attar, *Muslim Saints and Mystics*, translated by A. J. Arberry (Chicago: University of Chicago Press, 1966).

Murata, Sachiko, *The Tao of Islam* (Albany: State University of New York Press, 1992).

Murata, *Vision*. Sachiko Murata and W. C. Chittick, *The Vision of Islam* (New York: Paragon, 1994).

Mustamlî Bukhârî, Abû Ibrâhîm, *Sharh-i ta`arruf* (Lucknow: 1328/1910).

Raghib. Ar-Râghib al-Isfahânî, *adh-Dharî`a ilâ makârim ash-sharî`a*, ed. T. `A. Sa`d (Cairo: Maktabat al-Kulliyyât al-Azhariyya, 1972).

Râzî, Najm ad-Dîn, *Mirsâd al-`ibâd*, edited by M. A. Riyâhî (Tehran: Bungâh-i Tarjama wa Nashr-i Kitâb, 1352/1973).

RPP. Franklin D. Lewis, *Rumi: Past and Present, East and West* (Oxford: Oneworld, 2000).

Ruba'iyyat. Rumi, *Rubâ`iyyât*, printed in D.

Safi, Omid, "Did the Two Oceans Meet? Connections and Disconnections between Ibn `Arabî and Rûmî," *Journal of the Muhyiddin Ibn `Arabi Society* 26 (1999), pp. 55-88.

Sanâ'î, *Dîwân*, edited by Mudarris Radawî (Tehran: Ibn Sînâ, 1341/1962).

———. *Hadîqat al-haqîqa*, edited by Mudarris Radawî (Tehran: Sipihr, 1329/1950).

———. *Sayr al-`ibâd*, edited by M. T. Mudarris Radawî in *Mathnawîhâ-yi Hakîm Sanâ'î* (Tehran: Dânishgâh, 1348/1969).

Schimmel, Annemarie, *The Mystery of Numbers* (New York: Oxford University Press, 1993).

SDG. W. C. Chittick, *The Self-Disclosure of God: Principles of Ibn al-ʿArabí's Cosmology* (Albany: State University of New York Press, 1998).

Shahrazûrî, Shams ad-Dîn Muhammad, *Nuzhat al-arwâh wa rawdat al-afrâh fî taʾríkh al-hukamâʾ waʾl-falâsifa*, edited by Khurshid Ahmed, 2 vols. (Hyderabad: The Daʾiratuʾl-Maʿarifiʾl-Osmania, 1976).

Signs. *Signs of the Unseen: The Discourses of Jalaluddin Rumi*, translated by W. M. Thackston (Putney: Threshold, 1994).

SPK. W. C. Chittick, *The Sufi Path of Knowledge: Ibn al-ʿArabí's Metaphysics of Imagination* (Albany: State University of New York Press, 1989).

SPL. W. C. Chittick, *The Sufi Path of Love: The Spiritual Teachings of Rumi* (Albany: State University of New York Press, 1983).

ST. Mohammad-Ali Movahhed, *Shams-i Tabrízí* (Tehran: Tarh-i Naw, 1375/1996).

Sufism. W. C. Chittick, *Sufism: A Short Introduction* (Oxford: Oneworld, 2001).

Sultan Walad, *Walad-nâma*, edited by J. Humâʾî (Tehran: Iqbâl, 1316/1937).

NOTES TO THE PASSAGES

PART I

4.   With me you're like duck eggs. Compare Rumi's story of the ducklings raised by the hen, M II 3766 ff.

6.   Otherwise, it might have fallen on you. Rumi explains how lesser afflictions fend off greater afflictions in the story of the man who asked Moses to teach him the language of the animals (M V 3266 ff.).

   From the reed. Ruba'iyyat # 689.

9.   If a Muhammadan believer is dancing in the east. Compare passage 3.180.

13.   In your lane. Ruba'iyyat # 731.

17.   Surely your soul. Shams's point can be clarified with the help of the full hadith. In one version, the narrator tells us

that the Prophet addressed the following words to Uthman ibn Maz'un, "who was one of those who had left aside women." He said, "O Uthman! I was not commanded to monasticism. Have you turned away from my Sunnah? . . . Surely, included in my Sunnah is that I pray, I sleep, I fast, I eat, I marry, and I divorce. Anyone who turns away from my Sunnah is not one of us. O Uthman! Surely your spouse has a right against you, and your soul has a right against you" (Darimi, Nikah 3). In many versions, the hadith ends, "so give to each that has a right its right!" In the Sufi vocabulary, the word "soul" (*nafs*) was usually understood to designate the fleshly or animal soul. It is interesting to note that Ibn Arabi tells us he had no interest in women or sexual intercourse for the first eighteen years after he entered the Sufi path. Then God made him love women, just as he had made the Prophet love them (see Murata, *Tao*, p. 186).

Qipchaq. A region in Turkistan. In general, Turkish women were famous for their beauty.

18.　Like the Sufi who turned to his loaf of bread. For a fuller version of this anecdote, see 2.227.

Five-year old child. Shams also makes this point in 3.187.

19-22. I have placed passages 19-22 in the section on the early years, but one or more of them may pertain to the time spent in Aleppo after the initial parting from Rumi. Passage 1.22, for example, mentions "the road to Homs," which is a city rather close to Aleppo.

24.　The child of Adam must slip once in his life. Adam, it should be remembered, is not looked upon as a sinner in Islam; rather, he is the first prophet and the model of human perfection. His "slip" (*zallat*) was that he ate of the tree. Before and after that, he was a faithful servant of God. Compare passage 3.25.

25.　Shams ad-Din Khunji. The printed text—as in passages 1.28-30—has Khu'i, which would make him a scholar of Damascus who had been a student of Fakhr-i Razi, was on good terms with Ibn Arabi, and died in 1239-40. However the editor of the text provides evidence in ST (54) that the text should be read as Khunji, not Khu'i, and I have followed his revision. If this is correct, he is an unknown teacher of Shams. The editor tells us that the manuscripts are not reliable enough to know whether Khunji and Khu'i are two different names or the same name badly written.

27. A dervish set something down, i.e., the Prophet. On Muhammad as a "dervish" and a poor man, compare 3.140.

28. "God's work is this—deceiving." This statement is not nearly as bold as it may sound. In two verses, the Koran says concerning the unbelievers, "They deceived, and God deceived, and God is the best of deceivers" (3:54, 8:30). Metaphysically, God's creative act both conceals and reveals, both deceives and delivers. Sufis commonly discuss God's deception in terms of the "veil." See Sufism, Chapter 10.

30. "Believer" is one of the Koranic names of God. Sufis often interpret this hadith to mean that the believer is a mirror of God (e.g., Chittick and Wilson, *Fakhruddin Iraqi*, p. 86). Another version of the hadith has, "The believer is the mirror of his brother Muslim," and Rumi typically interprets it this way (M I 1328, 3147, II 30).

31. Shams-i Khujandi. Weeping for the Household of the Prophet, especially the martyrdom of Imam Husayn, is an activity typical of Shi'ites. Rumi makes a parallel point in an anecdote about the Shi'ites of Aleppo (M VI 777 ff.): "If you are not aware, go, weep for yourself ... Mourn for your own ruined heart and religion!" (M VI 801–2).

32. On Shihab Hariwa, see the introduction.

36. Splitting of the moon. A miracle attributed to the Prophet, said to be referred to in Koran 54:1.

Ali. The text is in Persian, making it difficult to trace the Arabic original. Perhaps Shams has in mind something similar to the saying of the eighth Shi'ite Imam, Ali ar-Rida. In debating with an atheist he said, "If the correct view is your view..., then are we not equal? All that we have prayed, fasted, given of the alms and declared of our convictions will not harm us." Chittick, *Shi'ite Anthology*, p. 49.

"He saw in himself." In other words, Shihab understood

such verses about the resurrection as references not to external, cosmic events, but to the internal experiences of the
soul. The typical position of the later philosophers is to take
such verses as references to both external and internal trans-
formation and to speak of two resurrections, the "greater"
and the "lesser."

37. He's reading his own page. Compare 1.47, 2.69, 3.164, 207.
     Rumi's best known anecdote to illustrate the error of judg-
     ing others from the standpoint of one's own limitations is
     that of the greengrocer and the parrot told at the beginning
     of the *Mathnawi* (I 247 ff.).

38. "Seventy-two veils of light." Probably a reference to the
     commonly cited hadith, "God has seventy veils of light and
     darkness. . . ."

     "The weeping of inanimate things." Sufis such as Ibn Arabi
     commonly talk about the speech of all things, animate or
     inanimate. The "weeping" is probably a reference to the
     Moaning Pillar, mentioned in the next selection.

     Do you have any idea where in your body or your heart.
     Rumi often offers this sort of argument, as in Fih 212 (Arb
     218-19; SPL 111-12)

39. The Moaning Pillar. A tree stump that began to moan when
     the Prophet ceased using it as a pulpit. Rumi tells the story
     in the *Mathnawi* (see especially M I 3280).

     His words, "If a man speaks. . ." In M VI 4900, Rumi puts
     this sentence into the mouth of a character in an anecdote,
     without suggesting that it goes back to an early saying.

40. Angel's jealousy. As the following passage suggests, the point
     is that the angels wanted God all to themselves, so they
     diverted the attention of the prophets to the world.

41. Miracle. In explaining that a miracle (*mu'jiza*) "disables" (*i'jaz*)
     the intellect, Shams is looking at the etymological sense of the
     word.

     Seventy-two creeds. Reference to the hadith, "My com-
     munity will split into seventy-two sects."

42. Ten intellects. This was the position taken, for example, by
     al-Farabi, Avicenna, and Suhrawardi.

     Permitted and forbidden. The typical discussion of jurists.

43.   Necessary in existence by His Essence. Shaykh Muhammad is represented as criticizing this expression, which is probably cited because it is typical of the language used by Shihab (see 1.36). It is worth noting that Ibn Arabi often uses this expression in his writings, without any hint that he disapproves of it.

45.   He does not know the particulars. This is a philosophical position that was harshly criticized by both theologians and Sufis. Compare the similar argument in 2.198.

47.   He's reading his own page. See the note on 1.37.

    Those people destroy the souls. For some of Rumi's remarks on false teachers, see SPL 145-47.

    True companionship kills. That is, being a disciple of a true shaykh results in the death of the lower soul (annihilation) and life in God (subsistence). See SPL 183-86.

    Studied knowledge (*'ilm-i ta'allumi*). As for Ibn Arabi, he certainly did not hold that "studied knowledge" is better than unveiling and witnessing. Much like Shams, he was overcome by the presence of God at an early age (SPK xiii–xiv). His position was that studied knowledge is a veil that prevents ultimate disclosure of the truth; see, for example, his critique of Ghazali in SPK 237.

    Shihab Maqtul. This is the philosopher Shihab ad-Din Suhrawardi, founder of the school of Illumination. As far as I know, Ibn Arabi never refers to him in his writings; nor does he criticize Fakhr-i Razi, though he did write a letter to him pointing out the inadequacies of the merely rational approach to knowledge.

49.   David (chain of justice fleeing to heaven). According to the version of this story found in Kisa'i (286-88), God commanded David to hang a bell from a chain to settle disputes between litigants. Those who spoke the truth would be able to ring the bell, but liars would not be able to reach the chain. A man stole some jewels from someone, and then by hiding the jewels in his staff and having his opponent hold the staff, he was able to grasp the chain and deceive David for a time. After this case, the chain rose up and never returned.

52. "He was nothing but following itself." This would be a likely response to Shams's critique if this is in fact the famous Ibn Arabi, given the great stress that Ibn Arabi placed upon following the Prophet in his writings.

53. Children (*farzandân*). That is, the circle of Rumi's disciples.

54. Ungodly and fortunate. In other words, Awhad would be "ungodly" (*fâsiq*) for breaking the Law, but "fortunate" because he was now the companion of Shams. As for Shams, it is less clear what he means by "ungodly and unfortunate." Perhaps he is saying that he would be ungodly for sitting with a shaykh who is drinking, and unfortunate because he now had the additional burden of guiding this shaykh on the path. On the burden of guidance, see his remarks in 3.169.

PART 2.

2. Intellect takes you to the threshold. See SPL 220-26.
Intellect is a veil. Compare these lines of Rumi (D vss. 11590-1):

> Intellect is the traveler's chain, my child,
>   break your bonds—the road is clear.
> Intellect a bond, the heart a trap, the spirit a veil—
>   the road is hidden from all three, my son.

"Secret heart." I read *sirr*, though the editor vocalizes the word as *sar*, "head."

6. *Tanbih.* This is probably *at-Tanbih fi furu' ash-shafi'iyya* by Abu Ishaq Shirazi (d. 1083), one of the first teachers in the Nizamiyya madrasah in Baghdad. It was considered one of the five most important books in Shafi'i jurisprudence.

12. O you who died. Attar, *Mukhtar-nama*, p. 74.

13. Our spirits are in dread. From a qasida by Fakhr-i Razi (more verses are cited in Maq 933). Rumi alludes to the qasida and ascribes it to a "philosopher" in M IV 3353-56.

14. Let the days be blessed from you. Passages 3.207 and 208 make clear that Shams is referring here to the idea that holidays bring blessings for people. In fact, he says, people should make the holidays blessed.

The Night of Qadr. Reference to Koran 97:1: "Surely We sent it [the Koran] down in the night of Qadr." The word Qadr is interpreted in a variety of ways by the Koran commentators, such as power, destiny, and decree. This night is said to occur on one of the last odd days of the month of Ramadan, and it is considered to be one of the most blessed days of the year. Perhaps Shams is saying that the real Night of Qadr is found in the human soul.

The knower of speech. Given the reference to the Night of Qadr, Shams may be saying that the Koran as embodied in the saint is the real Koran, as opposed to the Koran written on paper. Ali is reported to have said about the Koran, "I am the speaking Book of God, and that is the silent Book of God" (Sufism 84).

Speaking-companion. A standard epithet given to Moses, to whom God spoke through the Burning Bush. In the Koranic verses to which Shams is referring here (and also in passages 2.145, 229, and 249), Moses says to God, "Show me, that I may behold Thee!" God replies to him, "You will not see Me. . . ." Then God discloses himself to the mountain, which crumbles to dust, and Moses is knocked unconscious. The passage is important for theological discussions of the "vision" (ru'ya) of God. It is also the source of the term "self-disclosure" (tajalli), which plays a major role in Sufi discussions of the nature of the divine signs (ayat) displayed in the universe, the human soul, and scripture.

17. The verse is not found in Sana'i's Diwan.

18. O servant of the body. The editor thinks that the poem is not in fact by al-Ma'arri and cites a later source (Maq 526-27).

The Sage. I.e., Sana'i. The line, however, is not found in his Diwan.

19. Commanding to evil. See Glossary under "soul."

23. God's work has no causes. In other words, human deeds are not the cause of reward and punishment, because newly arrived things can have no effect on the Eternal. This is a common position taken by the Muslim theologians. For some of Rumi's relevant teachings, see SPL 113-18.

If you had debated about the road to Damascus and Aleppo. This sentence shows that the addressee is Rumi's son Sultan Walad, who went to Aleppo looking for Shams (compare 3.223).

Aksaray. The first city after Konya on the road to Aleppo. Shams uses it to symbolize the goal of the Sufi path.

Iblistan. This does not seem to be the name of a known place. Perhaps it is jocular, since it can be understood to mean "camel land" and could refer to the trackless desert.

28. Rumi provides an elaborate version of this story in M VI 2376–509, using it to illustrate the empty claims of those who do not draw from the source of true knowledge. He ends his version with the lines, "O you whose proof is like a cane in your hand proving your blindness, your harrumphing and putting on airs mean, 'I can't see, I'm sorry.'"

The fourth heaven. In his *mi'raj*, the Prophet met one of the prophets in each of the seven heavens, and many accounts say that Jesus was in the second. In Persian poetry, however, he is commonly associated with the fourth heaven, the sphere of the sun (for examples from Rumi, see SPL 73).

29. The fire of love. On these verses, see the note on 2.211.

Lessons have not been digested. Compare Rumi's discussion of how people memorize the Koran but gain no profit because they do not digest the words. In contrast, the Prophet's Companions memorized only a few verses but gained a great deal of benefit (Fih 81–82; Arb 94). In M III 1386 ff., he says something similar, summing up with the verse, "In short, when a man falls into union, the go-between is cold in his eyes."

30. The interpretation of narratives. The Koranic verse is typically taken as a reference to Joseph's ability to interpret dreams. What Shams says in 3.74 suggests that he understands the expression as a reference to prophetic and saintly insight.

31. The first paragraph seems to be Shams's account of a meeting with a shaykh; possibly, it is a conversation with Rumi. In the second paragraph, "He said" seems to refer to the words of Shams, who is criticizing the shaykh for quoting the words of

others and having nothing to say on his own. From this passage to 2.41, Shams is referring to two sorts of knowledge. These are often called "imitation" (*taqlid*) and "verification" or "realization" (*tahqiq*), though Shams employs both terms only in 2.40. Imitation is knowing things by hearsay, and verification is knowing things face-to-face—by direct experience, or by unveiling. For a few of the passages in which Rumi contrasts the two, see SPL 125-35.

What use to me are. . . . See the note on 2.211.

36.   Sometimes a cloak will speak. Compare 3.140.

Samaritan's calf. In the Koranic version of the story of the golden calf (7:148, 20:88), it is "the Samaritan," not Aaron, who makes the calf (cf. Exodus 32), and the calf emits a mooing sound.

Abu Yazid and seeing God. Ibn Arabi tells the same story on a number of occasions. See SDG 403-4.

Moses and Abu Yazid. Compare the famous account of Shams's original meeting with Mawlana, of which Shams gives his own version in 3.62.

37.   In seeking the Friend. Ruba'iyyat # 1119.

41.   Rumi tells a version of this story in M I 3360-95 (SPL 132-33).

42.   Declaring God's similarity (*tashbih*) and declaring his incomparability (*tanzih*) are roughly equivalent to asserting God's immanence and declaring his transcendence. Ibn Arabi may be the first to have paired these two expressions (each of which has a long history in theological texts) to describe the complementary attributes of God that are implicit in *tawhid*. On the combination of *tanzih* and *tashbih* to reach a proper understanding of *tawhid*, see Murata, *Vision* 70 ff.

43.   He has become the companion of someone like this. Apparently Shams is addressing Rumi's circle. If so, "he" refers to Rumi and "someone like this" means Shams himself. In the next paragraph, Shams tells the disciples that they are not worthy of being Rumi's disciples, much less his.

44.   The "Sunnis" are normally contrasted with "Shi'ites," but here Shams probably has in mind the Ash'arites, who represent mainstream theology, as opposed to the rival Mu'tazilite school.

45. Possessors of the kernels. Shams provides a bit more explanation of this Koranic expression in 2.192. It is often translated as "possessors of minds." Literally, the word *lubb* means "kernel" and implies a "shell." "Intellect" would be a standard interpretation. Shams's understanding is more along the lines of Ibn Arabi's (see SPK 230, 238-39).

46. When the eye turns completely white. This is probably a reference to the Koranic account of Jacob (12:96): When Joseph's shirt was placed on his face, his sight came back.

47. If that person. Persian translation of the hadith, "Were Moses alive, he would find it impossible not to follow me."

49. Ghazali and Khayyam. Another version of this story is told by the thirteenth century historian Qazwini, but in that case Khayyam's student is an unnamed jurist, who would secretly study with him and then criticize him before his flock for being a philosopher (Maq 898). The *Isharat* (*al-Isharat wa't-tanbihat*) is one of Avicenna's best known books.

50. His words swallowed. The editor interprets this to mean that the words of Shihab the philosopher had greater worth than those of Shihab ad-Din Suhrawardi the Sufi.

52. Muhammad the Arab. I.e., the prophet Muhammad.

54. Those who pretend to philosophy (*mufalsif-i falsafi*). Shams perhaps has in mind Shihab Hariwa, whose attitude toward death seems to fit in nicely with this account.
    A bright mirror. Compare Rumi's verses (M III 3439-40):

    Everyone's death, O youth, takes his own color—
          for the enemy an enemy, for the friend, a friend.
    A mirror held before a Turk has a fine color;
          a mirror before a black man shows blackness.

56. If a tailor does blacksmithing. Compare D vss. 21291-2, 98:

    O tailor, blacksmithing is not your work.
          You don't know fire's activity, don't do that!
    First take instruction from blacksmiths—
          otherwise, don't do it without instruction. . . .
    Shams-i Tabrizi dwells in the Presence—
          don't make your station anywhere else.

61. He is the leader. Allusion to the hadith, "We are the last and the foremost." Compare M II 3056, III 1128, IV 3764.

63. Qushayri. The treatise (*risala*) of Qushayri (d. 1072) is a classic handbook of Sufism. If "Qurayshi" is not simply a rhyming word for rhetorical effect, it may refer to the Sufi Abu Sa'id Qurashi of Nishapur (d. 992).

    They don't give. The whole quatrain (Ruba'iyyat # 738) is quoted in 3.85.

67. Awhadian. This seems to be a critical reference to Awhad ad-Din Kirmani, whom we met in passages 1.54 and 55.

    Aksaray. See the note on 2.23.

68. The surah Hud has whitened my hair. Ibn Arabi explains why the commandments laid down in this surah whitened the Prophet's hair in *Futuhat* IV 182 (SPK 300).

    Meaning is God. Shams repeats the statement in 3.17. Nothing in Ibn Arabi's writings suggests that he would have objected to it. Rumi cites it in M I 3338: "'Meaning is God'—so said the shaykh of the religion, the ocean of meanings of the Lord of the worlds." Up until the publication of Shams's *Maqalat*, the identity of "the shaykh of the religion" remained a puzzle. Nicholson, in his note on this verse, agreed with the early commentators on the *Mathnawi* that it was probably Sadr ad-Din Qunawi, Ibn Arabi's most important disciple.

    You may hear about meaning, and also eat. Compare Rumi's words: "My knowledge is substance, not accident. . . . I am a mine of candy, a plantation of sugar cane—it grows up within me and I eat of it myself" (M II 2427-28; SPL 131).

69. He would get no consideration. For a parallel anecdote, see 3.178.

71. Your putting up with a little bit of prescription. Ibn Arabi repeatedly tells us that the acts of worship prescribed by the Law bring about a greater perfection of the soul than voluntary acts of worship. See, for example, SPK 329-31.

72. New arrival (*hadath*). A juridical expression for anything that breaks ritual purity, such as going to the toilet.

    Although Muhammad was there. Not found in Sana'i's *Diwan*. an-Najm: "The Star." Sura 53 of the Koran.

74. He said, "Have they said the prayers?" Rumi retells the anecdote in M II 2771 ff.

77. Abu Sa'id and Avicenna. The biography of Abu Sa'id Abi'l-Khayr (d. 1049), a well-known Sufi shaykh, tells of his meetings with the great philosopher Avicenna, but it does not mention the episode to which Shams is referring. See Ebn-e Monavvar, *Secrets,* pp. 300-2.

79. Noble writers. For more on these two angels, see Ibn Arabi's remarks in SDG 123.

80. This passage recalls Shams's account of his initial words to Rumi (see 3.62).

81. So-and-so (*fulân*). This is clearly a reference to the Prophet (perhaps the note-taker's shorthand in order to avoid the obligatory prayer formula after the Prophet's name). The two sayings, "We have not known You" and "We have not worshiped You," imply "as You should be known" and "as You should be worshiped." Compare Sana'i's line in *Sayr al-ibad* (216), "*We have not worshiped You* is the effort of everyone, *We have not known You* is the belief of everyone."

83. King of the gnostics. A title commonly given to Abu Yazid.

84. O you who died. For the whole quatrain, see passage 2.12.

     The Messenger gained faith. Reference to Koranic verses such as 2:14 and 2:285.

     He has pride in that. Reference to the hadith, "Poverty is my pride." The "fakirs" are the "poor," those with poverty.

87. A shaykh passed a corpse. This seems to be a version of a well-known story about Jesus and the corpse of a dog (Khalidi 122).

     They are predestinarians on their Companion's side. I follow the reading of this sentence given in the footnote. Rumi makes a similar point in the verse, "Whatever your soul desires, you have free will in that; whatever your intellect desires, you claim to be compelled" (M IV 1401). Or again: "The prophets are predestinarians in the work of this world, the unbelievers predestinarians in the work of the next world. The prophets have free will in the work of the afterworld, the ignorant have free will in the work of this world." (M I 638-38).

88. The Sufi tore his clothing. Ibn al-Jawzi tells a longer version of this anecdote in his critique of Sufism, *Talbis Iblis* (203). According to him, "the Sufi" is Shibli and the "someone" is Ibn Mujahid (d. 936), a well known master of Koran recitation. Ibn al-Jawzi explains that it was Shibli's habit to tear any new piece of clothing that he might come to possess (presumably as a mark of poverty). Ibn Mujahid objected that the practice was not sanctioned in the Koran. Shibli responds with a verse whose interpretation is much disputed by the commentators. In the common interpretation that both Shibli and Ibn Mujahid seem to have in mind, Solomon was given a large number of horses and then, having missed the time of prayer because he was busy reviewing them, he began to slaughter them. Those who interpret the verse in this way need to explain how Solomon could have performed such an act, forbidden by God's laws. Shibli seems to be saying to Ibn Mujahid that here we have a forbidden act performed by a prophet, though the prophet is by definition protected from sin. In his comments on the anecdote, Ibn al-Jawzi first doubts the reliability of its source. Then he remarks that if it is true, it demonstrates the ignorance of both Shibli and Ibn Mujahid. The latter must have remained silent because he was ignorant of the Koran commentators' explanations of why Solomon's act was legitimate in the circumstances. Shibli was ignorant because he had no excuse for ruining a good piece of clothing.

He comes toward the servant. Shams is alluding to the precedence of God's grace, perhaps to counteract any suggestion that the servant can reach God by his own free choice. For some of Rumi's discussions of the relationship between divine grace and human effort, see SPL 160-63.

90. The greatest multitude. In the hadith, the expression refers to the majority opinion of the community, but it is also commonly used to designate a large city. The poet Khaqani has a similar interpretation (*Diwan* 8): "This is 'the greatest multitude': gaze upon the station of intelligence! This is 'the greatest struggle' [*jihad-i akbar*]: rend the ranks of caprice!"

95. If you seek for the reality. Compare the prose introduction to M, Book V.

96. This is separation. These are Khizr's words to Moses when Moses objected to his conduct for the third time (see passage 2.133).

To abandon existence. This recalls the famous line of Junayd, "Your existence is a sin to which no other sin can be compared." For some of Rumi's views on abandoning existence, see SPL 175–78.

Whatever is in the whole world. For more on man as microcosm, see 2.194–98.

98. If I can seize. Ruba'iyyat # 821 (also FP 105). The second line of the quatrain reads, "But if I am called to the plain of paradise without You, paradise's plain will be too tight for my heart."

100. Foreteller (pīshgū). One who tells of events before they happen. It is not clear what Shams has in mind.

Seven-colored cloak. See "cloak" in the Glossary. Traditionally, there were seven primary colors, so "seven-colored" means "many colored." On the need to pass beyond colors, see "variegation."

101. Alif. Compare 2.8 ff.

Seven hundred veils. See the note on 1.38.

103. Glorification. The second line of this quatrain is found in Ruba'iyyat # 804.

105. Possessors of Steadfastness (ulu'l-'azm). A title given to the greatest of the prophets on the basis of Koran 46:35.

106. You should hold to the religion of old women. One common explanation is that the Prophet gave this advice to his Companions after he had asked an old woman if she believed in God. She said that of course she did, how could a spinning wheel turn without a hand? Ghazali (3:118) applies the hadith to the situation of disciples on the Sufi path. Sometimes they may have visions that lead them to false imaginings and disregard for the Shariah. They should stick to the religion of old women, which is "acceptance of the root of faith and the apparent meaning of the creed by way of imitation [taqlid] and occupying oneself with good deeds, for there is great danger in turning away from this."

107. The soul is a thing's existence. The Arabic dictionaries give a variety of meanings for *nafs* or "soul," including spirit, body, reality, aspiration, desire, and the thing itself. Shams is saying that a thing's *nafs* is the thing itself, its very existence, embracing all its dimensions, including its body, spirit, and reality.

Thou knowest. These are the words of Jesus, part of his answer to God when God asked him if he had told the people to take him and his mother as gods apart from God.

109. There's not much. Shams takes these verses as typical of the improper language of certain Sufis. This quatrain may have inspired the famous line from the *Gulshan-i raz* ("The Secret Rose-Garden") of Shabistari: "The difference between Ahmad and *Ahad* is one *m*: A world is drowned in that one *m*."

110. Kerman. Taking cumin to Kerman is equivalent to taking coals to Newcastle.

They love Him is the trace of. . . . Compare Rumi's remarks on this verse, SPL 196.

111. What's best. Rumi begins a ghazal (D # 1056) with this line and also incorporates it into a quatrain (Ruba'iyyat # 55).

112. Seek someone lovely. Love is the response to beauty, a point implicit in the well-known hadith, "God is beautiful, and He loves beauty." One of Rumi's basic teachings is that love, "whether from this side or the other side, in the end leads to God" (M I 111). "When the trail reaches its end, the object of love will be the All-Merciful" (D vs. 338). See SPL 205-6.

His Lord arranges. Shams is probably alluding to the hadith, "I am not like one of you. I stay the night with my Lord—He feeds me and gives me to drink."

113. Each person worships something. Compare Rumi's remarks on true and derivative love, SPL 201 ff.

I love not those. Compare M III 1430.

When you have negated yourself. On this sort of "negation" (*nafy*) and "affirmation" (*ithbat*), which refer to the two halves of the first Shahadah ("No god" and "but God"), see SPL 181-83.

118. Breaking the pearl. See the next passage.

119. The vizier said. The well-known story of Mahmud, Ayaz, and the pearl is told by Rumi in M V 4037-119, where the phrasing reflects this version.

My all. The two Arabic sentences derive from an often told anecdote whose Arabic version is found in *Sharh-i ta'arruf* (vol. 2, p. 154) by Abu Ibrahim Bukhari, one of the earliest Persian works on Sufism: "I saw a beautiful woman, and my heart became busy with her. I said to her, 'My all is busy with your all.' She said, 'If your all is busy with my all, then my all is given to your all. But, I have a sister. If you were to see her beauty and loveliness, you would not remember my beauty and loveliness.' I said, 'Where is she?' She said, 'Behind you.' I turned around. She gave me a slap and said, 'You imposter, if your all is busy with my all, why did you turn toward another?'"

121. What is the utmost end of the sought. The mutuality of relationship between seeker and sought (servant and Lord, creature and God) is a key to understanding Shams's allusive remarks about his own special relationship with God. See the note on passage 3.2.

127. Law of divorce. The text has *ila'* and *zihar*, which are two obscure formulae of divorce much discussed in Islamic law. Compare 3.73.

Night of Qadr. See the note on 2.14.

Blind and deaf. Reference to the hadith, "Your love for a things makes you blind and deaf."

129. What use is satisfaction. Compare 3.121.

130. Nonbeing (*nistî*). Compare 2.96.

131. When he falls into the ocean. Rumi sometimes uses this imagery, as in the story of the fish who feigned death (M IV 2266-86). See also M I 2842-43 (SPL 183).

133. Who in the world knows more than I? Shams provides an Arabic text for these words in 2.221.

Khizr. The Koranic story of Moses and Khizr (18:65-82) is often understood in Sufi texts as a warning to the disciple (Moses) not to question the actions of the shaykh (Khizr). Rumi sometimes speaks of Khizr in these terms (e.g., M I 224-26, 236-37, 2969-72; II 436-37). Surprisingly perhaps, he devotes only one short passage in the *Mathnawi* to this story (M III 1962-71).

134. We are two spirits. A famous line of poetry by Hallaj.

137. We offered the trust. For Rumi's explanations of the significance of the trust, see SPL 61-65.

140. The Simurgh. The best known version of the story of the birds' journey is told by Attar in *The Conference of the Birds*. In his version "thirty birds" (*si murgh*) survive the trip across the seven valleys and discover that they are identical with the Simurgh.

141. In a day whose measure is fifty thousand years. The verse begins "To Him the angels and the spirit rise up." Shams may have in mind a hadith that says the day of resurrection will last fifty thousand years (cited by Ibn Arabi in *al-Futuhat al-makkiyya*, I 309-10, 320-21).

From this knee to that knee. "Fathom" and "span" refer to the partially cited hadith (see index), but "knee" refers to the anecdote of the mouse and the camel told in 3.212.

The day of the unveiling. Allusion to Koran 86:9, "On the day the secrets are tried."

145. God's speaking-companion. See the note on 2.14.

150. When you see drops. Compare M III 4707.

152. I'll pay the tribute. Reference to the tax paid by non-Muslims under Muslim rule.

Zimmi (*dhimmi*). A non-Muslim living under a covenant of Muslim protection.

156. Pharaoh was a logician. Shams probably has in mind Pharaoh's question to Moses, "What is the Lord of the worlds?" (26:24). Ibn Arabi takes this as a question about "whatness" (*mâhiyya*), i.e., quiddity or essence, which is just the sort of question that a "logician" would ask (see the chapter on Moses in Ibn Arabi's *Fusus al-hikam*, "Bezels of Wisdom").

Shaykh Abu Bakr. This is Abu Bakr Sallabaf ("the basket-weaver") of Tabriz, who, according to Aflaki, was Shams's first shaykh (RPP 145-46). Nothing is known about him except what Shams mentions. In another passage Shams says, "There were dervishes staying with Shaykh Abu Bakr. When one of the assistants of the vizier or someone else would come to see him, they would show reverence to him a hundred times more than they did before the stranger arrived. They would stand and sit with courtesy far away when anyone came. The shaykh was indifferent to [such visitors], while others used to die for them to come" (Maq 687).

157. When he becomes a serpent-knower. Not only is there a nice play on the words "serpent-knower" (mâr-shinâs) and "Companion-knower" (yâr-shinâs), but this sentence can also be taken as a translation of the famous saying, "He who knows his soul knows his Lord." In the teachings of Shams and Rumi, the soul (nafs) is typically understood negatively, and it is often called a serpent or a dragon.

The Koran-bride. The line is by Sana'i (Diwan 52).

The Prophet had revelation. . . . Ibn Arabi distinguishes between prophets and saints in a similar way (SPK 260–61).

158. At first the fish went toward the water. Compare Rumi's line: "Seek water less and acquire thirst—then water will gush up from above and below" (M III 3212; see SPL 206 ff.).

159. The treatise of Muhammad. One can guess that this conversation was preceded by reference to the treatise of Qushayri (as in 2.63), and Shams is saying, "What good are such treatises? If Muhammad himself had a treatise, it would be useless." The issue is of course verification and realization, which are utterly different from rote learning (see 2.31–41).

160. The high places. This is half a line of a poem by al-Ma'arri (Maq 466).

The soul . . . interprets. In other words, when the egocentric soul begins interpreting, it usually does so with the intention of explaining away rather than explaining. Its goal is to escape the moral or spiritual obligation laid down in the text.

The Garden is surrounded by detestable things. The hadith continues, "and the Fire is surrounded by objects of appetite." For some of Rumi's comments, see M II 1835 ff., IV 1857.

161. Your teacher is love. According to Furuzanfar, this well-known verse is the second line of a quatrain by one Athir ad-Din Akhsikati. The first line reads, "Remove the empty

madness from your head, lessen your disdain [*naz*] and increase your need [*niyaz*]" (Maq 878).

162. The trial of Abraham. Maybudi (1:375-76) tells a longer version of this anecdote in his commentary on Koran 2:131.

164. Whenever he saw that someone was bad. Rumi cites this verse in the heading of M V 1974 ff., and he incorporates part of it into the heading of I 2365 ff., which begins "Explaining that everyone moves from where he is, and everyone looks from the circle of his own existence."

165. Sana'i. The first half of the line reads, "O you whose caprices have stirred up caprice!" (*Diwan* 197).

170. Galen. Rumi tells this anecdote in M III 3960 ff.

171. Blood-letters (*ragzanân*). Apparently, Shams means the section of the bazaar where the blood-letters had their shops, perhaps next to the herbalists.

180. Moses became selfless. Reference to God's disclosing himself to the mountain (Koran 7:143; see note on 2.16).

182. A duck seeking. This is the second half of a line from Sana'i (*Hadiqa* 154). The first half reads, "Even new-born and just-started."

186. That book. I.e., not the famous Persian book by that name (*Kimiya-yi sa'adat*), written by Ghazali.

I and we (*man u ma*). Rumi sometimes uses this expression (e.g., D vss. 33594, 37271, SPL 193, 173) and he even turns it into an abstract noun, "I-and-we-ness" (*man-u-ma'i*, M IV 2763, SPL 183).

187. *Sayr al-ibad*, "The Journey of the Servants." One of several short *mathnawis* written by Sana'i in addition to his long *Hadiqat al-haqiqa*.

That you may see the heart. Sana'i, *Diwan*, 545.

O Sana'i, in this world. Sana'i, *Diwan* 719.

He asked for the sash. A sash (*zunnar*) was the mark of being a Christian. Shams refers to this account again in 2.192, mentioning Sana'i as being similar to Abu Yazid, and he speaks of Abu Yazid's asking for a sash in 2.206. Attar (MMS 123) explains why Abu Yazid did so, and perhaps something similar applies in the case of Sana'i: Abu Yazid entered into nearness with God seventy times, and each time, upon returning, he put on a sash and then broke it. At the time of his death, he bound up the sash, and then prayed to God, telling him that he had never before been a true Muslim, and he was just now entering Islam and cutting the sash for good.

188. If the disbelievers begin saying "No." Compare Rumi's line: "He says, 'He does not exist and I do not believe in Him.' From that 'not,' brother, I am as I am" (D vs. 17682). Cf. SPL 111-13.

I eat, I taste. Compare Rumi's line quoted in the note to 2.68: "I am a mine of candy. . . it grows up within me and I eat of it myself."

189. The gnostic is aware of everyone's state. Compare Ibn Arabi's remarks about the greatest of the gnostics, who pass through all the stations and then stand in "the station of no station," surveying all the stations of the travelers (SPK 375 ff.).

192. All that commotion appeared. Presumably Shams means the various statements attributed to Ali that are taken as allusions to his knowledge of the divine mysteries, such as, "I would not worship a Lord whom I do not see."

Possessors of the kernels. See the note on 2.45.

On the sash and Abu Yazid, see the note on 2.187.

196. Someone said to a Sufi. Rumi retells this anecdote in M IV 1358-72.

197. The macrocosm. As Rumi puts it, "You are the microcosm in form, the macrocosm in meaning" (M IV 521). For more on Rumi's views, see SPL 65-68.

198. Did God ever say, "And We honored." Rumi expands on this discussion (which makes reference to Koran 17:70, "And We honored the children of Adam"), in Fih 14-15/Arb 26-27 (cf. SPL 63-65).

God knows the universals. A position attributed to the philosophers. See 1.45.

199. Cow and Fish. Mythical beasts that support the earth.

I don't want a shop. There is wordplay here: shop (dukân), two mines (daw kân), being (kân), location (makân).

There's a poverty. Compare Rumi's discussion of these two sorts of poverty in M I 2752 ff.

Beloved, cast a glance. Rumi incorporates the last hemistich of this ghazal into the first line of a short ghazal of his own (Diwan # 327):

> In the book of my life, there's only one page left,
>> for His gentle jealousy has left my soul in tumult.
> In that book He's written words sweeter than sugar—
>> embarrassed by those words, the moon is left sweating.
> Everlasting life is shining on the page of the garden:
>> no fear of change or place of disquiet is left.
> Its name is "page," but within it is the everlasting kingdom,
>> the secrets of all the pure are left in its twilight.
> A light from the Lord has wrapped around the page—
>> Shams al-Haqq-i Tabrizi is left with shining eye.

Throw yourself into the water. Presumably Shams means that one should depart from the world of multi-coloredness and immerse oneself in the ocean of God. The nature of the opposites and the danger of being deceived by superficial love, discussed in the rest of the passage, are two of Rumi's frequent themes. See, for example, SPL 200-6.

200. He called John a saint. The reference is to the prayer of Zachariah in Koran 19:5: "So give me, from Thee a *wali*, who shall be my inheritor. . .". The word *wali* has several meanings, including close associate, friend, helper, relative. In Sufi literature, the Koranic expression *awliya' Allah*, "the friends of God," takes on a meaning rather close to English "saint" (see Glossary, under "sanctity"). Here Shams is suggesting that there is something special about John, because he alone among the prophets is explicitly called a *wali*. More literal-minded types might reply that the word has a different meaning here, other than "friend of God." But Sufis, like Kabbalists, are convinced that God intends much more than superficial meanings in his words (compare Ibn Arabi's remarks in SPK 243-44).

201. Whatever has been said. The poem is the last line of a well-known qasida by Sana'i (*Diwan* 57).

202. When you're the confidant. Ruba'iyyat # 1667.
Look at my face. Ruba'iyyat # 980.

203. Abu Yazid and the hajj. Rumi tells this well-known story in M II 2218-51; Attar gives a brief version in MSM 114.

205. Despite a hundred intercessions. This is the first couplet of a quatrain found in Ruba'iyyat (# 1758). The second couplet reads, "Whether You give me water or fire, in any case You're the sultan of sovereignty and Yours is the command."

206. He wanted a sash. See the note on 2.187.

207. After one hundred and fifty years. Rumi tells the story of this prediction and Abu'l-Hasan's hearing about it in M IV 1803-55, 1925-34. He also tells a story about the evil disposition of Abu'l-Hasan's wife that drove him to become a saint (M V 2044-152).

210. Ahmad the Heretic. Shams tells the story more briefly in Maq 71, and Sultan Walad elaborates upon it in *Walad-nama* 272-73. In his version, Junayd's difficulty is solved when he sees Ahmad spin.

211. Umar Ghazali. Other sources make no mention of a third brother.

   Ahmad Ghazali. For more on this anecdote, see 3.176.

   Unlettered. The Koran calls Muhammad the "unlettered prophet" (7:157-58), and the term is given several interpretations by the Koran commentators. Sufis typically understand it to mean that Muhammad's knowledge came directly from God, without human intermediary. Interestingly, in a chapter on "unlettered knowledge," Ibn Arabi cites Muhammad Ghazali as an example of someone who was held back from full perfection because of book-learning (*Futuhat* II 645.12, translated in SPK 237).

   What use to me are *Dhakhira* and *Lubab*? A different version of the quatrain is quoted in 2.29. If Ahmad Ghazali is in fact its author, it is unlikely that Shams' interpretation is accurate, given that his representation of Ahmad as unacquainted with the Islamic sciences has no historical basis. Muhammad Ghazali wrote no book by the name *Dhakhira*, though he did write a *Lubab an-nazar*. Ahmad himself, however, is known to have written *adh-Dhakhira fi ilm al-basira* as well as *Lubab al-ihya* ("The Gist of the *Ihya*," a summary of his brother's *Ihya ulum*

NOTES TO THE PASSAGES 2.212–221 · 331

ad-din). Thus, if the poem is by Ahmad, he is most likely referring to his own books. He wants to say that he himself has no need for such books; he wrote them only for his students.

212. Sangan. A village in eastern Iran, south of Mashhad and near Turbat-i Haydariyya.

Lovely boy. Other sources also say that Ahmad Ghazali used to contemplate God's beauty in young men. Interestingly, Shams criticized Awhad ad-Din Kirmani for engaging in this practice, but he has nothing but praise for Ahmad.

Atabeg. The title of the Turkish rulers of Tabriz.

Saddle-cloth. See Glossary. That Ahmad Ghazali was wealthy—in addition to his scholarly and spiritual rank—is related by other sources. For example, the author of *Tabsirat al-mubtadi*, a Sufi text written in Konya around the year 1260, writes as follows: "Someone remarked to Ahmad Ghazali, 'You spend the whole day blaming this world and encouraging people to cut off their attachments, but you have several tethers of horses, mules, and donkeys. How do you explain that?' He replied, 'I have driven the tethers' pegs into the ground, not into my heart'" (FP 96).

213. Though the mountain be full. The verse is by Sana'i, *Hadiqa* 85. Rumi makes use of the same imagery: "Adam was a mountain. Though he was full of serpents, he was the mine of the antidote, so no harm was done" (M VI 1345).

214. That idol, the beauty. Ruba'iyyat # 158.

219. Surely I love him and I love his voice. Compare M I 1774 ff., a passage that begins with the verse, "I wail because wailing makes Him happy—He wants the two worlds to wail and grieve."

220. Ibn Mas'ud said. Possibly a reference to his saying, "Were you to know of my knowledge, you would dump dirt on my head" (Abu Nu'aym, *Hilya* 1:123).

Ashura. The tenth day of the month of Muharram. The Prophet used to fast for the first ten days of the month.

221. For Shams's retelling of the encounter of Moses and Khizr, see 2.133.

It is revealed to him. The Koran has "It is revealed to me" (18:110; also 41:6).

225. Bishr has sat upon Iraq. This poem by Akhtal is the standard example given by theologians and dictionaries (e.g., Lane's *Arabic-English Lexicon*, under *istiwa'*). Bishr (d. ca. 663) was appointed governor of Iraq by his brother, the Umayyad caliph Abd al-Malik ibn Marwan.

   Without asking how (*bilâ kayf*). The Ash'arite theologians refused to interpret certain scriptural statements, maintaining that these should be accepted on faith without asking how they can be so. Other forms of theology were not nearly as inhibited. Shams is obviously not impressed by al-Ash'ari's position.

   The exegesis of *taha*. These two syllables, which begin chapter 20 of the Koran, have received many explanations, a sampling of which Shams provides. For most of these "outward explanations" and others, see Maybudi 6:96-97, 109-10.

   He stood so long. Persian translation of the hadith, "Until his feet. . . ."

   Faculties of reflection, conception, and imagination. The Persian text has *mufakkira wa musawwira wa mukhayyila*, technical terms drawn from Islamic philosophy. These are three of the internal senses (often, but not always, enumerated as five).

   If not for thee. Reference to the purported hadith qudsi, "If not for thee, I would not have created the spheres."

226. That Throne is the heart of Muhammad. Ibn Arabi among others often discusses the human heart as God's Throne (SPK 107), and a hadith is sometimes cited in support.

227. He places a piece of bread in his sleeve. Compare 1.18, 3.127, 132.

   Oners (*ahadiyyân*). The "Oners" are presumably those like Hallaj who, in Shams's interpretation, left aside following Muhammad by proclaiming their identity with God. His use of the expression "Oners" here is not unlike the later use of the term *wahdat al-wujud* ("the unity of existence"), which was employed to criticize those like Ibn Arabi who were said to proclaim *hama ust*, "All is He."

   Someone wanted to fly above the Kaaba. Ibn Arabi repeatedly tells us that the gnostics and great saints purposefully avoid performing miracles, though they possess the ability to do so (SPK 265, 267, 268, 313; SDG 382-83).

229. You will not see Me. These are God's words to Moses when he asked Him for vision. See the note on 2.14.

230. Everyone is blind and lame. Shams could almost be quoting Ibn Arabi, who writes, "He who is stricken by some blight has no fault, and all the cosmos is stricken by a blight, so it has no fault in the view of him whose insight has been opened by God. This is why we say that the final issue of the cosmos will be at mercy, even if they take up an abode in the Fire and are among its folk. *There is no fault in the blind, and there is no fault in the lame, and there is no fault in the sick* [24:61]. And there is nothing but these. . . . For the cosmos is all blind, lame, and sick" (*Futuhat* IV 434.34; cf. SPK 347).

The narrations tell us that a great man. Perhaps a reference to Abu Yazid, as recounted in 2.207.

234. Houris, etc. The interpretation is reminiscent of that offered by Rumi's father Baha Walad in his *Ma'arif:* "It is proper that the 'houris, palaces, gardens, fountains, and ginger' consist of the states of seeing God. Each time you see, you find a different taste" (Sufism 99).

Salsabil. A fountain of paradise mentioned in Koran 76:18. The word suggests easy flowing or easy to drink.

These people. Shams means the Koran commentators. Maybudi, for example—who is a mainstream Sunni commentator—cites a long report from Ibn Abbas about Ali and Fatima that explains the occasion for the descent of this verse (Maybudi 10:319-21).

244. The angels will praise you all night. This passage seems to be incomplete. Rumi quotes Shams to similar effect in Fih 92 (Arb 103-4), nicely catching the sarcastic tone:

Someone said in the presence of Mawlana Shams ad-Din Tabrizi, "I have established God's existence with an incontrovertible proof!"

The next morning Mawlana Shams ad-Din said, "Last night the angels came and were praying for that man: 'Praise be to God! He has established our God! May God

give him long life, for he has not been lacking in his service to the creatures!'

"Idiot! God is established. His existence needs no proof.
If you want to do something, establish yourself in a level and
a station before Him. Otherwise, He is established without
proof. *There is nothing that does not proclaim His praise* [17:44]."

245. Abu Bakr Siddiq. For a short version of this story from the traditional biographies of the Prophet, see Lings, *Muhammad* 184.

246. The veils of the Koran. Compare Rumi's description of the
Koran as a veiled bride (Fih 229/Arb 236–37; SPL 273).

Messenger and possessor of steadfastness. For a typical explanation of the types of prophet, see Murata, *Vision* 133–34.

Moses gives it a pot. Allusion to the story of God's coming
to Moses' door as told in 3.143.

249. Am I not your Lord (*alastu bi-rabbikum*)? This verse is the
source of the expression "Covenant of Alast." God lined up
Adam and all his children before their entrance into this
world and had them acknowledge His status as their Lord.
He did this so that they would not be able to object, on the
Day of Resurrection, "We were heedless of this" (7:172). For
Rumi's views on Alast, see SPL 68–72 and passim.

Iblis enters into the veins. Reference to the hadith, "Satan
flows in Adam's children. . .".

Tall hat. As becomes clear in 2.251, this was a popular
depiction of Satan, like our red man with horns and tail.

Bagpipe (*nay-anbân*). Rumi mentions the instrument on
occasion (D vs. 16830, SPL 272).

Moses. On his asking for vision, see the note on 2.14.

250. Mercy has taken precedence. Reference to the hadith, "My
mercy takes precedence over My wrath."

251. This is of Satan's doing. The Koranic passage cites these
words of Moses after he had struck and killed an Egyptian
in defense of a fellow Jew.

The son of Jalal Warakani. This should be the Shihab ad-
Din mentioned in 2.175. Although Shams criticizes him
here, he also writes, "That son of Warakani, who was a
judge—the envious did not understand his words. They

criticized him: 'He's a preacher, what does he know?'
Unfairness arises from envy" (Maq 295).

252. Adam and Iblis. Rumi often explains the difference between
the two in terms of these Koranic verses. See SPL 84-85.

By Your exaltedness. These are the word's of Iblis, telling
God that he will lead everyone astray (for the Koranic story,
see Murata, *Vision* 139-42).

254. I was told of it. The Koran puts these words in Muhammad's
mouth as his reply to one of his wives when she asked how
he knew a secret of hers.

Part 3

2. The sought one who has no mark. Shams seems to be referring to himself, though he also seems to be referring to himself as seeker; Rumi is then the seeker who is sought by the
sought one's seeking. As becomes clear at the end of 3.4, he is
intentionally ambiguous. The fact that man is God's "sought
object" (*matlub*) or "intended object" (*maqsud*), discussed in
the next few passages, is a common theme in Sufism and
often mentioned in Rumi's poetry (e.g., SPL 209-11).
According to Shams, realizing the station of being God's
beloved is higher than seeking Him (3.44). Recalling the
phrasing in 3.5, Sultan Walad writes, "Beyond the world of
the saints is another world, and that is the station of the
beloved. This report had not yet come into the world and had
not reached any ear. Mawlana Shams ad-Din appeared to
Mawlana Jalal ad-Din so as to take him from the world of
being a lover and the level of the arrived saints to the world
of being the beloved" (*Walad-nama* 192).

Jesus. Jesus spoke "quickly," because he spoke in the cradle. Muhammad spoke only at forty because that was when
his prophetic mission began. Compare 2.61.

3. Seeker and sought. See the note on the previous passage.

4. This knowledge cannot be gained by struggle. That true
knowledge is inaccessible to unaided human efforts is common theme in Islamic texts, going back to the Koran (e.g.,

"They encompass nothing of His knowledge save such as He wills," 2:255). Nonetheless, without effort nothing can be achieved. See Rumi's remarks, SPL 160-63.

7.   Joseph. Reference to the Koranic story, as told in Surah 12.

     The tongue of your state. That is, it is not sufficient to voice the words. You must show through your very mode of existence and your interaction with others that you are overcome by need for God. On need, see the Glossary.

     Aksaray. See note on 2.27.

11.   Two basins (qullatayn), a technical expression drawn from the Shafi'i school of Law. Two basins is the amount of water (roughly 150 gallons) that is pure by definition, so any impure substance that enters it (such as blood or urine) is thereby purified.

13.   Your soul found your soul. That this a commentary on Koran 93:7 is shown by 2.235.

     God did not consider it feminine. That is, God did not use the feminine pronoun in Koran 93:7. See 2.235.

     Does anyone ask a corpse to pray? Shams is apparently responding to predestinarianism and arguing for the necessity of struggle. Rumi has a number of passages reminiscent of this discussion, such as the verse, "No one says to a stone, 'Come!' No one expects kindliness from a clod of earth" (M V 2969). See SPL 115-16.

     When your holy bird. The verse is referring to the standard Islamic teaching that free will and the resulting obligation to observe the Shariah cease at death.

17.   Meaning is God. See passage 2.68.

23.   Alchemy. Rumi often talks of this sort of spiritual alchemy (see SPL, index, under alchemy).

24.   One color. For Rumi's use of the image in similar contexts, see SPL 58-59, 105, 275.

25.   His father' tradition is once. See the note on 1.24.

33.   The plain of speech is extremely spacious. Notice that in 1.49, Shams objected to Shaykh Muhammad for saying this.

35.   Knowledge is seldom accompanied by practice. This, despite the fact that the Prophet, the shaykhs, and the learned always

held that knowledge demands practice (as in the hadith, "Knowledge without practice is a tree without fruit") and practice must be built on knowledge ("A worshiper without religious learning is like a donkey in a mill").

36. Sun. Throughout the passage, the word for sun is Persian *âftâb*, the equivalent of Arabic *shams*. Compare 3.18, 78.

38. I've never seen any prison. Compare Rumi's lines (M II 3552-53):

> Don't look at me from your own weakness—
>> what for you is night for me is morning.
> For you it's a prison, for me a garden;
>> for me busyness itself has turned into leisure.

39. The heart is greater. On the greatness of the heart, see 2.173 ff.

40. The spirit has found perfection. The second half of this verse reads, "rise up and travel to the higher world!" The editor (Maq 503) says that the author is Sana'i, but the qasida he cites is not found in the edition of the *Diwan* at my disposal.

Either be manly. This line is incorporated into three different quatrains in Ruba'iyyat (# 1444-46).

42. Sun. As in 3.36, the use of the Persian word for sun is suggestive.

Sîsfûr. The word is not found in the dictionaries. Some later manuscripts have "salamander," the mythic beast that thrives in fire.

43. Aren't you ashamed. The first lines are from a qasida by Sana'i (*Diwan* 183), but not the last.

44. The Messenger slept. The text has "did not sleep," but a footnote tells us that the longer version of the same passage has "slept." Either reading makes sense, but the context suggests that Shams has in mind the sound hadith, "My eyes sleep, but my heart does not sleep" (Bukhari, Muslim). Rumi cites the hadith and explains the sense that Shams seems to have in mind here in M II 3547-61.

45. Abu Najib. The name is mentioned twice in the texts and the editor thinks that it is Abu Najib Suhrawardi (d. 1168), Sufi shaykh and uncle of Shihab ad-Din Suhrawardi. However, the second mention of the name, in a disjointed fragment (Maq 368), makes this unlikely, unless we are deal-

ing with two Abu Najibs: "Shaykh Muhammad was a man such that Abu Najib came to offer his services, just throwing himself on his face. Rather, a hundred like Abu Najib pick at his harvest." But Abu Najib Suhrawardi died long before Shaykh Muhammad could have been "a mountain" (Ibn Arabi, who in any case was Shaykh Muhammad's contemporary, was born in 1165).

52. Everyone's insight. Rumi explains the world's diversity in similar terms. See SPL 198-200.

53. Seven inner senses. Reference to the hadith, "The Koran has an outward sense. . . ."

60. The story of the command and the breaking of the pearl. I.e., the story of Mahmud and Ayaz told in 2.119.

62. The first words I spoke. On this first meeting and the various accounts of it, see RPP 159 ff. It is noteworthy that Aflaki's two accounts (87, 619) have "We have not known You as You should be known" instead of "We have not worshiped You as You should be worshiped." The latter form of the saying seems to be found in early sources, though it is not ascribed in the earliest to the Prophet.

73. You are my mother and my sister. Words to this effect were recited in a form of pre-Islamic divorce known as *zihar*, which was forbidden by the Shariah but much discussed by the jurists. They held that if a man recited the formula, he could not have sexual relations with his wife until he paid expiation. "These scholars" probably refers to jurists. Compare 2.127, which begins with a scholar regretting the time he has wasted on "the law of divorce"—the text mentioning *zihar*.

74. My own shaykh. This is probably Shaykh Abu Bakr Sallabaf, or perhaps Shams ad-Din Khunji, whom he mentions as having left in 1.26.

Interpretation of narratives. See the note on 2.30.

79. If a person's fortress. The verse is by Sana'i, *Hadiqa* 74. The reference is to the Prophet's taking refuge in a cave with Abu Bakr, and the spider web that convinced the pursuing Meccans that no one could be inside.

81. The needle-maker. Reference to the anecdote told in the next passage.

85. Gamble your soul. Ruba'iyyat # 738. A slightly different version is quoted in 3.198

88. Footstool Verse. I.e., Koran 2:255: "God, there is no god but He, the Living, the Ever-Standing. . . . His Footstool encompasses the heavens and the earth."

There are people who are the Footstool Verse. Presumably Shams means that there are saints who embody the Koran through their very existence. Something similar is often understood from the Koranic verse, "They are degrees with God" (3:163).

It's the same with trees. Compare 2.216.

90. I read a story. Rumi has the story in mind in M VI 3462-64.

91. *Two spirits.* Part of Hallaj's half-line quoted in 2.134. The text has, "The words of the spirituals is '*We dwell in one body,*'" but this seems to be an error. Nowhere else does Shams use the word "spirituals" (*rûhâniyyân*), and its orthography is close to "two spirits" (*rûhân*).

Seventy veils of light. Reference to a version of the hadith, "God has seven hundred. . .".

That is the day of mutual defrauding. The Koranic verse refers to the day of resurrection, when people will see things clearly and come to understand how they were deceived in this world.

Harun ar-Rashid and Layla. Rumi tells the anecdote in M I 407-8, then comments on it.

94. Let me give you headaches. Shams gives a different version of this line as part of a longer poem in 2.199.

96. Someone said. Rumi tells this anecdote in M III 1376-79 and draws this moral: "This 'picking them out' is questions and answers—the suffering of religion has no head for that." In other words, the lover has no patience for discussion and debate.

98. The stone was even more Indian. Shams's anecdote seems to have inspired this ghazal of Rumi (D # 1159):

> Love is soul, but love for you is more soul.
> > Gentleness heals, but coming from you it heals more.
> The unbelief of your unbelieving tresses
> > has become more faith than faith.

Entrusting the soul to love is easy,
    and to your love it's even easier.
All are guests at the table of your gentleness,
    but this servant's child is more of a guest.
Without you all are disordered,
    but I am even more trackless and disordered.
Love for you is the mine of endless good fortune,
    but union with your beauty is more of a mine.
The Indian blade of separation is sharp,
    but the Indian blade of love is even sharper.
Every heart flies after you with four wings—
    my heart has a hundred wings and is more of a flier.
Seeing you would be cheap for a hundred souls—
    in exchange for my half-soul, it's even cheaper.
Though this celestial wheel turns quickly,
    the wheel of love's spheres turns even quicker.
All are afraid of the sphere of love,
    but that sphere is more afraid of your heartache.
Shams of Tabriz! Give me an aspiration
    so that in you I may be even more knowing of wonders.

Moses was more Pharaoh than Pharaoh. Compare these verses of Rumi (M III 964-65):

The deception of obstinate Pharaoh was a dragon
    that devoured the deception of the world's kings.
But someone more Pharaoh than he appeared
    and gobbled down him and his deception.

102-103. Ibrahim Adham. For Rumi's version of the story of his abandoning his kingdom, see M IV 726 ff., 829 ff.
105. The fellow who was beating the dawn drum. Rumi tells a much expanded version of this anecdote in M VI 846 ff.
113. To call a scholar's shoes [*kafsh*] "booties" [*kafshak*]. The expression is not found in the classical dictionaries, but something like it is mentioned as a modern colloquialism. When a person unexpectedly becomes upset at your words, you say, "What happened? Did I call your shoes 'booties'?"

114. Abu Yazid Taqawi. So says the text. Taqawi may be a misreading for Bastami. The editor makes no reference to Taqawi in the notes or index, but the index does include this passage among those that mention Abu Yazid Bastami. Nonetheless, this is not typical of Abu Yazid anecdotes.

117. Noah's son. Reference to a story that goes back to Genesis 9:22-24. According to Kisa'i's version (105), upon seeing their father naked, Ham laughed, but Shem jumped up and covered him.

118. Moses. Reference to the story of the Burning Bush in Koran 20:10, 27:7.

121. *Marul.* This may be a variety of cherry, or some other fruit, like a plum. The word is not in the dictionaries. The editor thinks it may mean "lettuce," but that fits neither the context nor the growing season.

122. The Indian slave who spoke. Rumi elaborates on this anecdote in M II 3027 ff.

123. I take it. Second line of a quatrain found in Ruba'iyyat (# 360). The first line reads: "As long as any of your existence remains with you, don't sit secure, for idol-worship remains."

127. The saying of the Sufi, i.e., directed at the piece of bread in his sleeve. See 2.227.

128. Seeing the ruler. Shams is probably referring to the hadith, "The worst of scholars are those who visit rulers, and the best of rulers are those who visit scholars." Rumi devotes the beginning of Fih (1-2/Arb 13-14) to an explanation of its meaning.

131. On the hearts is a seal. Persian translation of part of Koran 2:7.

   Though I sit and laugh. A version of this quatrain is found in Ruba'iyyat # 1052.

   Come back. The quatrain is also found in Razi, *Mirsad al-ibad* 92.

135. Hashish. The word used is *sabzak*, "the green stuff." Compare 3.143.

139. Every one of your sins. Ghazali (4:485) tells us that this line was recited by a voice from the unseen world to Ibrahim Adham.

140. Soul at peace. See "soul" in the Glossary.

143. Baha ad-Din. Rumi's son Sultan Walad.

   Two-month road. Reference to the fact that it was Sultan Walad who went to Aleppo to bring Shams back to Konya. Compare 3.223.

   Weed. A parallel account in Aflaki (633) makes it clear that by "weed" (*giyah*—"plant" or "vegetable"), Shams means hashish: "When Mawlana made Walad the disciple of Mawlana Shams ad-Din Tabrizi, the latter said, 'My Baha ad-Din, do not eat hashish and never engage in sodomy [*lauwâta*], because both of these acts are immensely unpraiseworthy and blameworthy in the eyes of the Generous God.'"

   Abraham killed those four birds. Reference to Koran 2:260. The Koran commentators generally say that the four birds are the peacock, the crow, the rooster, and the vulture. They often interpret the birds as references to blameworthy character traits (Maybudi 1:718 says that the peacock is prideful display, the crow avarice, the rooster appetite, and the vulture wishful thinking). Sana'i (*Hadiqa* 724) makes them the four natures (hot, cold, wet, and dry) and tells us that they must be transmuted into faith, intellect, truthfulness, and guidance. Rumi devotes a quarter of Book V of the *Mathnawi* (31 ff.) to interpreting the Koranic verse. He says that the four birds are the duck (avarice), the crow (wishful thinking), the peacock (reputation), and the rooster (appetite).

   The four birds have been killed and come to life. This of course is a reference to annihilation and subsistence. See SPL 179-81.

144. Oh, all the world's sated. Ruba'iyyat # 1422.

   Cheese is the food of a leopard. Compare Rumi's verse: "I eat nothing but livers and hearts, for I'm a lion's offspring — I'm not a base leopard that I should eat cheese" (D vs. 16894). Leopards were easily domesticated and used in hunting, and perhaps they were rewarded with cheese.

145. If someone throws off a cloak. To take back a cloak discarded during the *sama* was a custom approved by some Sufi shaykhs, such as Shihab ad-Din Suhrawardi (Maq 437-38). Rumi

refers to not taking it back in M V 1008 and VI 4415 ff.

Patience (*sabr*). Concerning its importance on the path to God, see SPL, index.

The mule asked the camel. Rumi tells this anecdote twice (M III 1746-55, IV 3377-3430).

148. The tale-bearer is God. There is probably an allusion here to Koran 66:3 (compare passage 2.254).

149. Companion of the heart. A standard expression for someone who lives in the awareness of God, a true dervish. By "possessor of the soul" Shams clearly means someone who has not gone beyond the lower, egoistic stages of the soul—the soul that commands to evil and the blaming soul. In one text he says, "A Man is never called 'companion of the spirit' or 'companion of the intellect'—only 'companion of the heart'" (Maq 856).

151. God is greater. Compare passages 2.104, 105.

152. Lote Tree of the Far Boundary. A tree growing at the uppermost limit of paradise from which the Prophet had a vision of God during his *mi'raj* (Koran 53:14).

157. Mawlana is detached. Compare 3.165.

Knowing this is perfection. The antecedent of "this" does not seem to have been recorded. Perhaps Shams has in mind the principle put down in an often quoted saying of Abu Bakr: "Incapacity to perceive is perception." In other words, knowing God is perfection, but recognizing that one does not in fact know God and that God is always "greater" is true knowledge. Ibn Arabi frequently cites Abu Bakr's saying (see SPK, SDG, indexes).

160. Eighteen thousand worlds. Texts often mention this expression, meaning all of God's creation. For some of the significance given to the number 18 in the Mevlevi Order, see Schimmel, *Mystery of Numbers*, 222-23.

Donkey. The donkey, as in Rumi's writings, represents the animal soul, or the soul that commands to evil.

Water seeks a thirsty man. Compare M III 4398-99:

The thirsty man laments, "O sweet water!"
　　The water too laments, "Where is the drinker?"

This thirst in our souls is the attraction of that water—
we belong to it and it belongs to us.

The soul has the nature of a woman. Compare Rumi's line: "Consider your soul a woman—worse than a woman, for the woman is a part, and the soul is the whole of evil" (M II 2272). On the soul as woman, see SPL 163-69; Murata, *Tao*, pp. 236 ff.

168. New Year's. *Naw-ruz*, a pre-Islamic festival marking the beginning of the solar new year (the first day of spring); in Iran it is still today the most important festival of the year.

Breath of Jesus. Reference to Koranic words of Jesus quoted later in the passage.

176. Ahmad Ghazali. See 2.211.

178. This is reversed. Shams explains what he means in 2.236.

He killed his mother. Women from Qazvin apparently did not have a good reputation (in contemporary Persian humor, it is the men from Qazvin who are the butt of jokes). Rumi tells a related anecdote, making the mother's sin explicit, in M II 776-80.

He sits in front of me like a son. Compare 3.61.

180. A *sama* in the east. Compare passage 1.9.

When he died he was veiled. A reference to Abu Yazid (see 2.207).

185. Without blemish (*salâmat*). Shams is pointing to the root meaning of the word *muslim*: to be unblemished, intact, safe, secure.

186. Nimrod. The story of Nimrod's throwing Abraham in the fire is alluded to in Koran 21:68-69 and 29:24 (see Kisa'i 128-50). Rumi tells a tale about him in M VI 4797-869.

187. A five-year old child. Compare 1.18.

191. Refresh me with the fresh fragrance. This is part of a supplication that is recited while rinsing the nose during the minor ablution. Rumi tells the anecdote and provides the correct texts to recite in M IV 2213-29.

194. They became drunk from the Speech. Compare Rumi's discussion of the effects of God's speech in Fih 81-82/Arb 93-94.

196. Ala' ad-Din. This must be Rumi's second son, not least because Shams has spoken to him "behind the curtain," that

is, inside the house, where only family members are allowed. The editor thinks that the passage is important because it confirms the reports of Shams's hostility towards Ala' ad-Din. Sipahsalar, one of the earliest biographers, suggests that Ala' ad-Din, who was handsome and well-mannered, was infatuated with Kimiya, Shams's young wife. Shams had been given a room in Mawlana's house and was being treated as a member of the family. According to Sipahsalar, Ala' ad-Din seemed to be taking advantage of the situation to catch glimpses of Kimiya when he came to the house to visit his parents. Shams advised him to come into the house as if he were a guest—not just to walk in, but to let people know from outside that he was coming, so that any women who did not want to be seen by him could go into another room or cover themselves appropriately. He was offended by this advice and told other members of Rumi's circle about it, and they took the opportunity to stir up more enmity toward Shams. See Maq 508-9. On Ala' ad-Din and the suggestion by some later accounts that he was involved in the "murder" of Shams, see RPP 185-87.

197. Brother of a whore (*ghar khwâhar*). According to Aflaki (152), Rumi would use this imprecation when angry. Compare Fih 88: "These people say, 'We saw Shams ad-Din Tabrizi. O sir, we saw him!' Brother of a whore! When did you ever see him? Someone fails to see a camel on a rooftop and says, 'I saw the hole of a needle and inserted the thread!'" Translators of Rumi tend toward prudery when dealing with passages of this sort. Arberry (Arb 100) translates the expression in this passage as "fool" and Thackston (*Signs* 92) as "pack of fools."

198. Beware, they won't put. See the note on 3.85.

199. Siraj ad-Din. He was clearly the type of jurist who wasted his life in the details of the Law (compare 2.127). Presumably, a four-by-four pool would be too close to the minimum purity requirements (see 3.11) for one to be sure that there was always enough water in it.

204. I'll not put you. Ruba'iyyat # 1926.

207. Jesus, Muhammad. Reference to Jesus' speaking in the cradle

and Muhammad's receiving revelation at the age of forty.

The day will no longer have dayness. Shams seems to be referring to the human role as vicegerent of God. In the teachings of Rumi and others, human beings are the means whereby all things return to their Creator: As their inner mystery unfolds and they develop in the direction of God, the inanimate comes to life, the living comes to awareness, the aware comes to self-consciousness, and the self-conscious enters into God-consciousness. See SPL 72–82.

208.   Ramadan. Sinning breaks the fast, just as eating and drinking do, so preachers often talk as if abstaining from sin was peculiar to this month. The month of Sha'ban is also considered especially sacred.

210.   Tie the camel's leg. Reference to the hadith, "Hobble it, and trust." According to Sultan Walad's retelling of the story, the Prophet spoke these words to a bedouin whose camel ran away after he had neglected to hobble it, trusting in God instead (Maq 510). Rumi cites the hadith in M I 913.

212.   A mouse took the reins. Rumi tells the story in M II 3436 ff.

Oh would that I could sit. Persian translation of the hadith, "Oh, the yearning."

213.   There are illnesses that can't be treated. Rumi expands on this point in M III 2909 ff.

Nile's water. Rumi comments on this sign of Moses' prophecy in M IV 3431 ff.

Yasin. Chapter 36 of the Koran, thought to have special blessing.

When you see the lion's fangs. Compare M I 3039–40.

216.   Tel Basher. Name of a citadel on the outskirts of Aleppo.

217.   Congregational mosque. Presumably Shams means the Umayyad Mosque, one of the oldest and most famous mosques in the Islamic world.

Paradise is Damascus. Ibn Jubayr (d. 1217), author of a well-known travelogue, was entranced by the beauty of the city. Having described it, he says, "How right they are, those who have said about her, 'If paradise is on earth, then it is certainly Damascus; and if in heaven, then this city vies with its glory and equals its beauties.'" Rumi devotes a fourteen-verse

ghazal to the city (D # 1493). According to Aflaki, he composed it on the way to Damascus when he went there looking for Shams after his second disappearance. It begins, "I am
in love and dizzy and crazy for Damascus, I've lost my soul
and maddened my heart for Damascus." Another line reads,
"Damascus is the paradise of vision in this world, so I'm waiting for the vision of the beauty of Damascus." The final line
says, "If my master Shams al-Haqq of Tabriz is there, I will be
lord of Damascus—what a lord of Damascus!"

223. When you came to Aleppo. The addressee is presumably
Sultan Walad.

INDEX OF KORANIC VERSES

354 INDEX OF HADITHS AND SAYINGS

INDEX OF HADITHS AND SAYINGS

This list provides minimal documentation for the sources of Arabic sayings quoted by Shams. Many of the hadiths that he cites are not found in the best known sources, by which I mean the nine Sunni collections that are indexed in Wensinck, *Concordance et indices de la tradition musulmane* (These are the collections of al-Bukhari, Muslim, Abu Dawud, at-Tirmidhi, an-Nasa'i, Ibn Maja, ad-Darimi, Malik ibn Anas, and Ahmad ibn Hanbal). When I was not able to find a saying in the *Concordance*, I turned to other well-known sources, specifically *Ihya ulum ad-din* of Ghazali (d. 1111), *al-Jami as-saghir* of the hadith authority as-Suyuti (d. 1515), and the massive encyclopedia of Shi'ite hadith, *Bihar al-anwar*, compiled by Majlisi (d. 1699). I was also able to make good use of Maybudi's Persian commentary on the Koran, *Kashf al-asrar*, a book completed in 1126. In many cases, the sayings are drawn from Sufi authors who employ criteria of authenticity different from those of the hadith specialists.

Unless otherwise noted, the saying is attributed to the Prophet. "Cf." means that the referenced saying does not have the exact same wording. A hadith qudsi is a saying of the Prophet that quotes words of God not found in the Koran.

Ablution upon ablution is light upon light. 2.120, 184. Ghazali 1:203.

Adam and everyone beneath him. . . . 3.140. Cf. Suyuti 3:42.

Affairs are in pawn to their times. 3.1. Proverb.

Alms fall into the hand of the All-Merciful. . . . 3.166. Cf. Ghazali 1:323.

Alms in secret extinguish the wrath of the Lord. 2.205. Ghazali 1:335.

And he arrived. *See* Two strides.

Assume the character traits of God! 3.175. Some texts (Maybudi 2:186, Bihar 61:129) ascribe it to the Prophet, but Ghazali (4:444) cites it without attribution.

Backbiting is worse than fornication. 3.23. Ghazali 3:208; Bihar 75:222.

The believer . . . does not lie. 3.143. Cf. Bihar 72:263.

The believer is an examiner. 2.189. Not traced.

The believer is the mirror of the believer. 1.30. Abu Dawud (Adab 49), Tirmidhi (Birr 18).

The believer sees with the light of God. 2.114, 124. Tirmidhi (Tafsir 15:6).

The believers are like one soul. 2.94, 214. Rumi translates it in M IV 408 and 418. Muslim (Birr 67) has "The believers are like one man." Ghazali (2:476) has "The Muslims are like one soul." *See* The knowers are like.

The believers do not die. Rather they are transferred from one abode to another. 1.31, 2.54. A hadith, not considered authentic by the specialists, has this text: "O folk of everlastingness, O folk of subsistence! You were not created for annihilation. You will only be transferred from one abode to another abode, just as you were transferred from the loins to the wombs" (FAM 104).

The best of people. . . . 3.149. Cf. Suyuti 3:481.

The best of speech. . . . 2.241. Proverb.

Blessing is with your great ones. 2.29. Bihar 75:137.

The companion, then the path. 2.194. A proverb that is sometimes cited as a hadith.

Conceal your going [*dhahâb*], your gold [*dhahab*], and your school [*madhhab*]. A proverb sometimes taken as a hadith; Rumi paraphrases it in M I 1047.

Congregation is a mercy. 1.49. Ahmad 4:278, 375.

Consult with them, then oppose them. 3.84, 160. Although Shams ascribes this to the Prophet, the specialists doubt its authenticity (FAM 30-31). Rumi interprets "them" to refer to souls that command to evil (M I 2954-57; II 2271-75; SPL 163-69).

Cross over, O believer, for your light extinguishes my fire. 2.230, 3.90. Suyuti 3:265.

Crowing belongs to the rooster. . . . 3.156. Proverb.

The days are there between us. 2.14. Not traced.

Do not prefer me over Jonah. . . . 2.239. Cf. Bukhari (Anbiya 34).

Eat from the effort of your hand. . . . 2.246. Not traced.

Everyone returns to his root. 2.24. Proverb.

The fire, without shame. 1.35. Not traced.

First put up the house, then paint. 2.43. Proverb.

The folk of the Koran. . . . 2.217, 218. Part of the hadith, "God has folk among the people: the folk of the Koran, who are the folk of God and His elect." Ahmad 3:128, 242.

The food of one is sufficient for two. 2.60. Bukhari (At'imma 11).

From heart to heart there is a window. 1.18. Proverb.

The Garden is surrounded by detestable things. 2.160. Muslim (Janna 1), Abu Dawud (Sunna 22).

Generosity should not be rejected. 1.18. Not traced.

Glory be to me. . . . 1.50, 2.80, 82, 85, 221, 3.64. Abû Yazîd.

Glory be to You! We have not worshiped You. . . . 2.80, 81, 3.62. The earliest source for this saying seems to be *as-Sahîfat as-sajjâdiyya* of the Prophet's great-grandson, Ali ibn al-Husayn, who puts it in the mouth of angels gazing upon the suffering of people in hell. I have not been able to trace the form "We have not known You" earlier than Sana'i (see the note on 2.81).

God created Adam in His form. 2.42. Bukhari (Isti'dhan 1), Muslim (Birr 115).

God created the spirits before the bodies. 2.72. Hujwiri 337, Maybudi 8:511, Bihar 5:266.

God has seven hundred veils of light. . . .1.38 n., 2.184, 3.91 n. As given by Muslim (Iman 293), the first sentence reads, "God's veil is light." Less authoritative versions mention numbers such as seventy or seventy-seven, often "of light and darkness" (FAM 50-51).

God is beautiful, and He loves beauty. 2.112 n. Muslim, Iman 147.

God is greater. 2.78, 104, 105, 3.151. A formula of invocation that is recited to mark every movement of the *salat*.

God willing. 2.183, 213, 3.13, 77, 84. A Koranic formula recited in reference to future activity.

The good deeds of the pious are the ugly deeds of the proximate. 2.245. Sufi saying (FP 250).

Gratitude to the Blessing-giver is incumbent. 3.53. Not traced.

Guide my people. 2.198, 3.60, 140. Ibn Arabi cites the hadith in this form (SDG 221). The version that comes in the standard sources is "Forgive my people, for they do not know" (Conc 4:318.47).

I am the most eloquent. . . . 3.140. Bihar 17:158.

I am the Real (*ana'l-haqq*). 2.36, 49, 93, 221, 231, 250, 3.64, 175. Hallaj. In contrast to Shams, Rumi interprets this saying in a positive light (SPL 191-93).

I am with those whose hearts are broken for Me. 2.176, 177, 3.205. Maybudi tells us that these are God's words to "one of the prophets" (1:135) and elsewhere suggests that the prophet is Moses (6:171).

I have a moment with God. . . . 1.51, 2.66, 240-42, 3.53. Hujwiri 365.

I know better the affairs of your religion, and you know better the affairs of this world of yours. The second clause is found in Muslim (Fada'il 143) and Ibn Maja (Ruhun 15).

I saw my Lord in a red robe. 2.42. More commonly, this hadith reads, "I saw my Lord in the form of beardless youth" or "in the most beautiful form." It is not considered sound by the specialists (SPK 396 n. 3; FP 187).

I see that the length of the era is forgotten. 3.193. Not traced.

If I approach another inch. . . . 2.75, 230. In Abu Nu'aym Isfahani, *Hilyat al-awliya* (5:55), these are Gabriel's words in response to a question put by the Prophet.

If not for thee, I would not have created the spheres. 2.225. It is difficult to trace any version of this hadith qudsi earlier than the eleventh century (FAM 173). Rumi often cites it (e.g., SPL 63-64, 66, 197, 198, 292, 293, 334).

If someone wants to look at a dead man walking on earth, let him look at Abu Bakr. 2.131. Cited by the Sufi Ayn al-Qudat Hamadani (FP 225).

In the days of your era. . . . 2.186. Ghazali 1:278, 3:16, 4:114. Rumi quotes the Arabic text and comments on it in M I 1951 ff.

Increase me in bewilderment. 3.69. Sufi texts attribute this saying to Abu Bakr, Shibli, Abu Yazid, and the Prophet.

Intentions are through works. 3.11 Shams has reversed the sound hadith, "Works are [judged] through intentions" (Conc 7:55).

Islam began as a stranger. 3.154. Muslim (Iman 232), Tirmidhi (Iman 13). See Rumi, M V 925 ff.

The knowers are like one soul. 1.48. Rumi cites this saying in the heading of M IV 406. *See* The believers are like.

The Koran has an outward sense and an inward sense up to seven inward senses. 2.192, 217, 3.53 n. Often cited in Sufi texts, a more common version talks of two senses in addition to the outward and inward (Ghazali 1:432; SPK 363).

Leave Me and My servant, for I am not less merciful than you. . . . 2.219. Hadith qudsi found in *Nawadir al-usul* by the ninth century author Tirmidi (Fih 265). Rumi translates it into Persian in Fih 37 (Arb. 49).

A little indicates much. 2.162, 237. Proverb.

Love in God and hate in God. Cf. the hadith, "He who loves in God and hates in God. . . has perfected his faith" (Abu Dawud, Sunna 15; Tirmidhi, Qiyama 60).

Love of the homeland is part of faith. 3.154. Not found in the earliest sources (FAM 97-98). For Rumi's interpretation, see M III 3806-11; IV 2210-11.

Love your friend with some easiness. . . . 3.180. Ali. Bihar 74:177.

Make me one of the community of Muhammad. 2.5, 43, 145, 212. Maybudi (7:336) provides a long hadith about Moses' conversation with God that includes this sentence.

A man is concealed by holding his tongue. 1.38, 39. Rumi quotes the saying in this form and attributes it to the Prophet (M I 1270), but Shams is attributing it here to Ali. Furuzanfar cites a saying of Ali as the source (FAM 51). See also M III 1538.

A man is with him whom he loves. 2.14. A sound hadith (Conc 1:406).

Meaning is God. 2.68, 3.17. See the note on 2.68.

The metaphor is the bridge to the reality. 3.84. Proverb.

Most of the folk of the Garden. . . . 2.160. Cf. Suyuti 3:522.

The Muslim is he from whose hand. . . . 3.68. A sound hadith (Conc 2:507.4).

My all is busy with your all. 2.119, 232. See the note on 2.119.

My community will split into seventy-two sects. 1.41 n. Maybudi 6:305; Raghib 132.

My heart spoke to me of my Lord. 2.247. According to Ibn Arabi, the saying is by Abu Yazid (SDG 106).

My mercy takes precedence over My wrath. 2.250 n., 3.7 n., 186. A sound hadith qudsi (Conc 2:239).

My heaven does not embrace Me. *See* Neither My heaven.

The spirits are ranked troops. 1.1, 2.249. The hadith continues, "Those acquainted with one another become familiar, and those not acquainted keep apart." Bukhari (Anbiya 2), Muslim (Birr 159).

The spirits of the martyrs. . . . 3.184. The first clause is found in Muslim (Imara 22).

The Sufi is the son of the moment. 3.98, 142. Sufi saying.

The surah Hud has whitened my hair. 2.68, 69. Cf. Tirmidhi (Tafsir 56:6).

Sweeter than the age of youth. 2.6. Not traced.

There is many a reciter of the Koran that the Koran curses. 2.217. Ghazali (1:410) attributes this saying to Malik ibn Anas, the eponym of the Maliki school of law.

There is no god but God. 2.98, 3.90. Found in many Koranic verses and hadiths.

"There is no god but God" is My fortress. . . . 2.100. Ghazali 1:251–52.

There is no monasticism in Islam. 3.53, 54. Furuzanfar traces the hadith to a work by Ibn Qutayba (Fih 283). For a related hadith, see the note on 1.17.

There is no power and no strength but in God. 2.214, 3.215. A formula of invocation found in many hadiths.

There is no *salat* without recitation. 2.73, 75. Tirmidhi (Mawaqit 116), Ibn Maja (Iqama 11).

There is no *salat* without the presence (of the heart). 2.73, 75. Rumi cites this as a hadith in M I 381. Cf. Ghazali 1:228.

They see with the light. *See* The believer sees with the light.

This world is a bridge. 3.84. Bihar (14:319) ascribes the saying to Jesus.

This world is forbidden to the folk of the afterworld. . . . 2.155. Not traced.

This world is the prison of the believer. 1.31, 2.141, 3.37, 38. Muslim (Zuhd 1), Tirmidhi (Zuhd 16).

Through opposites things become clear. 3.11. A proverb that goes back to the poet al-Mutanabbi (Fih 291); Rumi frequently quotes it (SPL 49–53).

Transferred from one abode. *See* The believers do not die.

Two strides, and he arrived. 2.19, 81, 141, 146, 3.212. The saying goes back to Shibli (Maq 397).

The ulama of my community. . . . 2.84. Cited by Ibn Arabi in this form (SPK 377). In Bukhari (Ilm 10) and other standard sources, the closest text is, "The ulama of my community are the inheritors of the prophets."

Until his feet became swollen. 2.78, (225). The hadith reads, "The Prophet stood [in prayer] until his feet became swollen. Then it was said to him, 'God has forgiven thee thy former and thy later sins.' He said, 'Shall I not be a grateful servant?'" (Bukhari, Tafsir 48:2).

Visit at intervals. 2.244, 245. The full text reads, "O Abu Hurayra, visit at intervals. That will increase you in love." Suyuti 4:62. Rumi comments in M II 2671 ff.

We are satisfied with God's decree and destiny. 3.120. Not traced.

We are the last and the foremost. 2.61 n. Bukhari, Muslim, etc. (Conc 1:31).

We have not known You. *See* Glory be to You.

Were Moses alive, he would find it impossible not to follow me. 2.47 n. Maybudi 7:286; SPK 240.

Were the covering removed. . . . 1.39. Ibn Arabi (SPK 277) and others, like Shams, attribute the saying to Ali. Maybudi (1:58), Qushayri, and others ascribe it to the second generation Muslim Amir ibn Abd al-Qays.

Were the dead man to reveal. . . . 3.133. Not traced.

Were the faith of Abu Bakr. . . . 2.84. Sana'i, *Hadiqa* 226; cf. Ghazali 3:235.

What differences there are between him who lives. . . . 3.143. Maybudi (4:73) cites a parallel saying from the Sufi Bishr al-Hafi.

What does dust have to do with the Lord of lords? 2.110. Proverb.

What no eye has seen and what no ear has heard. . . . 2.192, 193. This sound hadith begins with the words, "I have prepared for My worthy servant" (Bukhari, Bad' al-khalq 8; Muslim, Iman 312).

When poverty is complete, he is God. 2.184. Sufi saying.

When someone comes toward Me by a fathom. 2.141. Cf. the hadith qudsi, "When someone approaches Me by a span, I approach him by a cubit; when he approaches Me by a cubit, I approach him by a fathom; and when he comes to Me walking, I come to him running" (Conc 3:58.26).

When someone devotes himself purely to God for forty days, the

INDEX AND GLOSSARY OF NAMES AND TERMS

Aaron, 2.36 n.

ablution (*wudû'*), 2.72, 120, 149, 184, 189. Ritual washing in preparation for the salat.

Abraham, 1.24, 2.113, 162, 178, 195, 3.56, 143, 186, 21.1

absent (*ghâ'ib*), 3.121. *See* presence.

abstinence (*parhîz*), 1.27, 2.166, 3.87, 121

Abû Bakr (as-Siddîq), 2.84, 131, 221, 229, 244, 245, 253, 3.46, 67, 69, 79 n., 157 n. Companion of the Prophet and the first caliph of Islam.

Abû Bakr, Shaykh, 2.156, 3.74 n., 216. See the note on 2.156.

Abû Bakr Rubâbî ("the rebeck-player"), 3.203. A proverbial trickster and scoundrel. Rumi pairs him with Juhi as a thief in the line, "O trial of every spirit, O cutpurse of every Juhi—you've stolen the rebeck from the hand of Abu Bakr Rubabi" (D 925). But Rumi also alludes to accounts of him as a saint who did not speak for seven years (M II 1573, 1916; D vs. 23283).

Abû Hâmid Ghazâlî. *See* Ghazali.

Abû Hanîfa (d. 767), 2.189, 3.151. The eponym of the Hanafi school of jurisprudence.

Abû Hurayra, 2.245. Companion of the Prophet.

Abû Lahab, 3.213. An uncle of the Prophet and one of his most virulent enemies (immortalized in Sura 111 of the Koran, which speaks of his ill outcome).

Abu'l-Hasan Kharaqânî (d. 1033), 2.207. Sufi shaykh.

Abû Najîb, 3.45. See the note on the passage.

Abû Sa`îd, 2.77. This is probably Abu Sa'id Abi'l-Khayr (d. 1049).

Abû Yazîd Bastâmî (d. 874 or 877), 1.37, 50, 2.23, 36, 55, 80, 82-85, 134, 184, 187 n., 192, 203-8, 230 n., 3.13, 24, 62, 69, 91, 118, 180, 194, 199. A Sufi shaykh, especially well known for his ecstatic exclamation "Glory be to me!" MSS 100-23.

Abû Yazîd Taqawî, 3.114. See the note on the passage.

Adam, 1.23, 2.115, 195, 211, 212, 252, 3.54, 140, 200, 211, 212; slip of, 1.24, 3.25, (26); child of Adam (*âdamî*). *See* human being.

affirmation (*ithbât*), 2.113, 188, 244

Antioch, 2.133

apparition (*wâqi'a*), 1.4, 2.210, 3.45, 60, 69, 85, 185, 193. A true vision, usually one that occurs in wakefulness. The literal meaning of the word is occurrence, event, happening. The technical use derives from the Koranic passage, "When the happening happens, none will deny it" (56:1-2). Typically, the verse is said to refer to the Last Day or to death, when veils will be rent and people will see things as they truly are.

appetite (*shahwa*), 1.17, 2.151, 185, 212, 213, 231, 3.52, 54, 90, 91. The desires of the animal soul, especially sexual desire. In Islamic psychology, the term is paired with "wrath" or "irascibility" (*ghadab*). Ghazali calls appetite and wrath the pig and dog of the soul. They have their proper roles to play, but they must be kept in check by the intellect. Many authors use "appetite" interchangeably with "caprice," but Shams distinguishes between the two (e.g., 3.91).

Arabic, 1.45, 2.20, 21, 3.136, 140

Armenian, 2.242, 3.101

Arshad, 3.57, 62. A Sufi teacher in Konya. The editor of the text thinks that this is probably the same as Rashid ad-Din (Maq 917).

Asad, 2.50, 224. A contemporary whom Shams did not hold in high esteem. According to Aflaki, he lived in Sivas (RPP 148).

ascetic discipline. *See* discipline.

asceticism (*zuhd*), 1.17, 27, 2.33, 103, 241, 3.54, 180. More literally, "renunciation." Turning one's gaze away from this world and focusing on the afterlife. Rumi and other Sufis often contrast the "ascetics," who tend to immerse themselves in the strict disciplines of self-denial, with "lovers," who are so immersed in the Beloved that they have no thoughts of self.

Ash'arî, Abu'l-Hasan (d. 935), 2.225. The eponym of the Ash'arites (2.44 n.), who represent mainstream Sunni theology.

Âsiya, 2.195. The wife of Pharaoh. Along with Mary she is considered the most pious of pre-Islamic women. She is referred to in Koran 66:11.

aspiration (*himmat*), 2.4, 69, 3.20, 72, 145, 189. The power of the soul to concentrate on the goal of the path. As Rumi puts it, "A bird flies with its wings, but the believer flies with his aspiration" (Fih 77/Arb 89; SPL 212).

Badr Zarîr, 2.175. Mentioned only in this passage.

Baghdad, 2.15, 127, 210, 218, 3.6, 94, 168, 190

Bahâ', Judge, 3.172. Unknown; mentioned only this once.

Bahâ' ad-Dîn. *See* Sultan Walad.

Bahâ' Walad, 2.234 n.

Basra, 2.203

beauty (*jamâl*), 2.15, 20, 93, 159, 172, 223, 246, 3.13, 22, 30, 52

being. *See* existence.

belief (*i`tiqâd*), 1.25, 43, 44, 2.37, 39, 42, 62, 78, 192, 209, 212, 214, 248, 3.5, 36, 56, 60, 72, 90, 93, 136, 137, 139, 159, 161, 163, 168, 187, 200, 202, 213. Conviction; the creed in which one has faith. Shams typically uses the word to refer to a disciple's devotion to and "belief in" his shaykh.

believer (*mu'min*), 1.9, 30, 2.54, 79, 115, 152, 188, 230, 245, 3.37, 46, 185. A person with faith; a true Muslim. *See* faith.

beloved (*mahbûb, ma`shûq*), 1.31, 2.118, 119, 127, 160, 3.12, 91, 200; God as, 2.194, 199, 2.7, 88, 101, 102, 140, 3.154, 194; God's, 2.249, 3.44, 207

Bishr, 2.225

body (A. *jism, badan*; P. *tan*). *See* spirit.

Book of God (*kitâb Allâh*), 2.88, 127. The Koran.

Bû Latîf, 3.189. Unknown.

Buhlûl (d. 816), 2.238. A wise fool during the time of Harun ar-Rashid. Rumi tells an anecdote about him in M II 1884 ff.

Bukhârî, Abû Ibrâhîm Mustamlî (d. 1042), 2.119 n.

burning (*sûkhtan*), 1.9, 2.5, 29, 56, 62, 64, 118, 133, 192, 213, 244, 3.19, 42, 53, 87, 90, 121, 138, 164, 186, 191

caliph, caliphate, 2.15, 70, 127, 238, 253, 3.91

calligrapher (*khattât*), 2.84, 223

caprice (*hawâ*), 2.94 n., 100, 124, 127, 151-54, 156, 157, 159-62, 231, 244, 3.15, 91, 101, 114, 136, 148, 181. The whims of the soul, the internal wind that blows the self this way and that; contrasted with intellect. The Koran criticizes "following caprice" and makes it equivalent to the worst of all sins, *shirk*, i.e., associating another god with God (25:43, 28:50). Intellect is able to harness and control caprice and direct it toward the good (e.g., 3.148). Shams takes the usual meaning of caprice for granted, but he also speaks of another sort of caprice that can be a dangerous obstruction to those already well advanced on the path to God (e.g., 2.156, 3.91).

cat (*gurba*), 1.6, 22, 2.155, 3.26, 129, 188

catamite (*amrad*), 2.214; (*mukhannath*), 3.223

causes, secondary (*asbâb*), 2.74, 3.77, 213. The things, events, and phenomena of the world. Secondary causes manifest the wisdom of the First Cause, which is God. See SPL 21-22.

certainty (*yaqîn*), 2.122, 3.56, 185. Realized knowledge of the truth. *See* realization.

character (trait) (*khulq*), 1.49, 2.174, 184, 3.91, 101, 143 n., 145, 175. The good and bad qualities of the human soul; virtues and vices. Shams would probably not disagree with Ibn Arabi when he says that the essence of the Sufi path is "assuming the character traits of God" (SPK 283), that is, becoming qualified by God's own names and attributes, made possible because God created human beings in his own image.

charismatic act (*karâmat*), 2.43, 68, 186, 3.64, 168, 180. A miraculous deed performed by a saint; contrasted with *mu'jiza*, a "miracle" performed by a prophet.

chastisement (*'adhâb*), 2.54, 67, 89, 100. The infliction of suffering, especially after death.

chivalry (*futuwwat*), 1.24

choice, (free) (*ikhtiyâr*), 1.35, 2.68, 88. *See* predestination.

Christian (*nasrânî, tarsâ*), 2.28, 37, 58, 59, 135, 142, 173, 184, 3.104, 140, 191, 212

church (*kalîsâ*), 3.47, 119

clemency (*hilm*), 2.223, 253, 3.7, 8, 55, 195. Gentleness, kindness, and mercy.

cloak (*khirqa*), 2.66, 100, 3.21, 23, 44, 101, 104, 216; speech of, 2.36, 3.140. A robe that was bestowed upon disciples as a sign of initiation, successorship, or permission to initiate others. The literal meaning of the word is rag or patch, because the cloak was traditionally sewn together from old pieces of cloth as a sign of poverty.

cold, coldness (*sard, sardî*), 1.22, 47, 2.126, 174, 225, 234, 3.56, (64), 70, 77, 87, 91, 161, 194, 199; and hot, 2.37, 95, 98, 100, 101, 133, 160, 3.85, 114, 159

darkness (*târîkî*), 2.54, 56, 59, 68, 101, 129, 131, 159, 160, 171, 184, 188, 211, 213, 3.59, 90, 136, 194, 201, 207, 212, 213

David, 1.49, 2.176, 3.213

death (P. *marg*, A. *mawt*), 1.31, 32, 36, 47, 2.54, 126, 141, 174, 206, 3.140; of soul (self), 2.129, 131, 132, 184

debate (*bahth*), 1.20, 29, 36, 2.23, 68, 71, 92, 228, 3.97, 98. The Arabic word means both investigation and discussion. It is typically used for the group study and interpretation of texts that go on in madrasahs.

deception (*makr*), 1.28, 2.27, 50, 96, 3.140. On God's deception, see the note on 1.28.

deceptively, to speak (*mughâlata*), 1.38, 2.244, 3.8, 74, 77, 141. The word suggests throwing someone into error. In philosophy, it has the technical significance of "sophistry." Shams uses it to refer to statements that are false, though they may be instructive for the uninformed. Compare his use of the word "hypocrisy."

decree (*qadâ'*), 2.121, 129, 3.121. God's ordainment for his creation.

defect (*naqs, nuqsân*), 1.1, 41, 45, 2.29, 73, 77, 84, 90, 249, 3.157, 181, 189, 207. Contrasted with perfection.

deliverance (*khalâs*), 1.30, 2.67, 70, 154, 187, 3.20, 21, 23, 29, 44, 90, 119, 123, 212. Salvation.

denial (*inkâr*), 1.36, 39, 47, 52, 2.37, 42, 43, 46, 62, 109, 162, 188, 212-14, 223, 249, 252, 3.146, 163, 167, 168, 177, 194

dervish (*darvîsh*), 1.18, 27, 2.5, 32, 42, 66, 74, 75, 90, 111, 207, 246, 249, 3.19, 21, 26, 31, 54, 59, 84, 98, 101, 102, 113, 114, 132, 143, 163, 173, 180, 203. Literally, "poor," the Persian equivalent of Arabic *faqîr* (fakir). The word can mean a poor person or a beggar, but technically it means one who has entered on the Sufi path with the intention of achieving poverty (*faqr*), the spiritual station of Muhammad. The Koranic source for this notion of poverty is the verse, "O people, you are the poor toward God, and God—He is the rich, the praiseworthy" (35:15). To be a dervish is to recognize one's poverty and nothingness before God. For Shams and Rumi, the perfect dervish has been annihilated in God, and God speaks through him (2.249; SPL 186-91). Shams sometimes refers to himself in the third person as dervish.

desired, object of desire (*murâd*), 2.192, 3.127, 159

Finally they achieve "sobriety after intoxication," in which they see everything in its proper place. Shams offers other analyses. See 2.154-56. For Rumi's views, see SPL 318-23.

duck (*batt*), 1.4, 10, 2.181, 182, 3.42

ecstasy (*wajd*), 3.193

effusion (*fayd*), 1.47, 2.68, 3.56

egoism (P. *manî*, A. *anâ'iyya*), 2.221, 227, 3.63, 73. Literally "I-ness." Living in caprice, or being overcome by the soul that commands to evil.

Egypt, Egyptian, 2.251, 3.213, 223

elect (*khâss, khawâss*), 2.23, 77, 186, 215, 217, (225), 3.90, 181, 185, 202. God's special friends; contrasted with common people (`*awâmm*). See the hadith, "the folk of the Koran. . .".

Elias, 2.195

encounter (*liqâ'*), 2.239, 3.180. Meeting God; derived from the Koran, the term is generally applied to meeting God after death. Sufis also use it to mean finding God in this world and living in His presence.

envy (*hasad*), 1.32, 2.50, 68, 162, 167, 213, 251 n., 3.99, 136, 149

Erzerum, 1.14, 17

Erzincan, 1.18

essence (*dhât*), 2.235, 249, 3.168; of God, 1.35, 36, 2.142, 157, 184, 224, 250. The thing in itself; contrasted with attribute.

eternal (*qadîm*), 2.241, 3.149. *See* newly arrived.

Eve, 2.195

excellence (*hunar*), 2.87, 115, 124, 156, 199, 3.61, 109. Virtue, talent, learning.

exegesis (*tafsîr*), 2.54, 219, 222-25, 230, 3.140, 218. Explanation of the meaning of the Koran; often contrasted with *ta'wîl*, "interpretation," which is the attempt to delve more deeply into the text.

existence, being (P. *hastî*, A. *wujûd*), 1.1, 2, 49, 2.79, 86, 100, 107, 130, 150, 196, 226, 229, 235, 244, 3.15, 23, 52, 75, 87, 109, 151, 195, 200; of God, 2.99, 106, 244; negation of, 2.96, 97, 130, 183, 199, 3.180, 181, 195. Strictly, existence belongs only to God. Loosely, existence designates God and everything other than God. The illusion of existing independently of God is the root ignorance of the human situation and the ultimate source of suffering. The cure is found in the annihilation of false existence and the subsistence of true existence.

expression (`ibâra), 2.20, 142, 3.33, 151. Speech, language.

faith (îmân), 2.33, 42, 84, 103, 127, 152, 157, 187, 192, 3.68, 100, 121, 132, 154, 189, 197, 201, 213. The attribute of the believer. Technically, faith is defined as acknowledging the truth in the heart, voicing it with the tongue, and putting it into practice with the limbs. The truth—that is, the object of faith—encompasses the knowledge of God, his angels, his scriptures, his prophets, the Last Day, and "predestination." See Murata, *Vision* 35 ff.

Fakhr ad-Dîn, 3.73. Unknown.

Fakhr-i Râzî (d. 1209), 1.36, 47, 2.13 n., 23, 34, 51-53, 108. A famous theologian and philosopher, to whom later generations gave the title *imam al-mushakkikin* ("the leader of the doubters"). Shams's account (2.51) of how Fakhr presented his learning to Khwarazmshah suggests something of his reputation. See RPP 57-60.

fakir (*faqîr*), 2.29, 66, 75, 84, 3.140, 163, 219. *See* dervish.

fasting (*rûza*), 2.67, 70, 221, 3.13, 118

Fâtiha, 3.137. The first chapter of the Koran, recited in every cycle of prayer.

Fâtima, 2.33, 234 n., 3.161. The daughter of the Prophet and wife of Ali.

fatwa (*fatwâ*), 1.33, 2.36. A legal ruling; the pronouncement of a jurist on a point of law.

fault (`ayb), 1.6, 2.87, 91, 114, 115, 3.34, 123, 205

felicity (*sa`âdat*), 2.186, 233, 3.2, 4, 203. Happiness, specifically that of paradise; contrasted with wretchedness, the misery of hell.

fire (*âtish*), 2.42, 48, 59, 135, 157, 164, 166, 178, 199, 3.42, 77, 84, 90, 118, 120, 133, 138, 140, 180, 186, 200

following (*mutâba`at*), 1.52, 53, 2.43, 50, 67, 68, 73, 74, 80, 83, 85, 91, 94, 133, 145, 227, 246, 3.57, 60, 62, 90, 140, 164, 210. Taking the prophet Muhammad as one's guide on the path to God. Words from the same root are often used in the Koran. The concept is expressed most clearly in the verse, "Say [O Muhammad!]: 'If you love God, follow me, and God will love you'" (3:31). The notion of the "Sunnah" or the custom and wont of the Prophet is precisely that of following Muhammad. For Shams, following is the key characteristic that the seeker must acquire, but the prophetic Sunnah that he has in mind is not limited to physical and moral acts, since it embraces states and stations as well (e.g., 2.74).

Footstool (*kursî*), 2.42, 100, 104, 194, 195, 199, 3.52; Footstool Verse, 3.88. *See* Throne.

forbidden (*harâm*), 2.138, 155, 3.119, 135, 139, 180. Declared unlawful by the Shariah; contrasted with permitted (*halâl*), 1.42, 3.11, 185; and with allowable (*mubâh*), 3.180.

forgetfulness (*nisyân*), 2.155, 252

form (*sûrat*), 1.49, 2.73, 3.10; of God, 2.42. The outward aspect of something, contrasted with meaning (q.v.). The "folk of form" (*ahl-i sûrat*), also called "the folk of the outward sense," are scholars who see only superficialities and do not enter into the spiritual dimension of things; 2.246.

fornication (*zinâ'*), 1.27, 2.253, 3.23

Franks (*farang*), 1.19. Crusader troops.

friend (*dûst*), friendship (*dûstî*), 1.18, 2.28, 33, 62, 167, 214, 229, 3.2, 12, 67, 72, 80, 84, 99, 115-19, 143, 157, 173, 174, 175, 181, 186, 190, 202, 203, 207, 223; with God, 2.116; God as, 2.37. Friend is used as an equivalent of companion, saint, and beloved.

Gabriel, 1.40, 45, 2.75, 76, 109, 157, 162, 167, 230, 3.178

Galen, 2.170

Garden (*jannat*), 2.100, 115, 3.40. Paradise.

gaze (*nazar*), 2.15, 63, 87, 105, 137, 196, 199, 244, 246, 3.2, 45, 52, 91, 103, 132, 133, 136, 153, 190, 200, 209; perfect, 2.47, 3.145

gentleness (*lutf*), 3.127; and severity, 1.18, 2.79, 89, 157, 232, 253, 3.3, 53, 88, 175, 179-81, 204, 212. Gentleness is mercy, kindness, and concern. The divine attributes are often divided into two basic categories: those of gentleness and severity, or mercy and wrath, or beauty and majesty. This division is fundamental to the outlook of both Shams and Rumi. A whole series of qualities and images are associated with the two sides. Gentleness, for example, correlates with angel, intellect, paradise, light, Adam, saint, union, religion, meaning, hope, laughter, intoxication, joy, kindliness, sugar, spring, day, and rose. Severity is associated with their opposites (devil, ego, hell, darkness, Satan, unbeliever, separation, irreligion, form, fear, tears, sobriety, sadness, cruelty, vinegar, autumn, night, and thorn). See SPL 45-58, 88-93.

Ghazâlî, Abû Hâmid Muhammad (d. 1111), 2.49, 106 n., 186 n., 211, (3.176). Famous theologian and Sufi. The best known of his many books is *Ihya ulum ad-din*, "Giving life to religious knowledge." He rewrote this book in Persian, in a much more popular and accessible style, under the title *Kimiya-yi sa'adat*, "The Alchemy of Felicity."

Ghazâlî, Ahmad (d. 1123?), 2.29 n., 211-14, 3.176. The younger brother of Abu Hamid Ghazali. Ahmad wrote books in both Arabic and Persian, the most famous of which is the Persian *Sawanih*, a classic exposition of love for God. He is known to have taught for a time in place of his brother at the Nizamiyya Madrasah in Baghdad. Shams's depiction of him as illiterate is so much at odds with other accounts that the editor suggests that this is another Ahmad Ghazali (ST 17).

Ghazâlî, `Umar, 2.211. A third Ghazali brother, not known from any other source.

gnosis (*ma`rifat*), gnostic (`*ârif*), 1.52, 2.14, 32, 33, 68, 83, 88, 89, 90, 96, 189, 194, 210, 228, 230, 3.6, 57, 91, 163, 210. Gnosis is often simply a synonym for knowledge. Technically, it is used to mean true, direct knowledge of God, without the intermediary of learning; it is roughly equivalent to unveiling. The gnostic is the knower of God, the Sufi shaykh.

God (*khudâ*), 2.65, 102, 3.102, 174, 180; aroma of, 2.59, 219; becoming God, 2.175, 184; seeing God, 2.36, 84, 86, 122, 184, 188; unchangingness of, 1.31; world of, 2.187, 234, 3.4. *See* Real.

God-given (*min ladunî*), 2.192, 3.29

Gog, 1.2., 2.160. The Koran tells us that Dhu'l-Qarnayn (sometimes said to be Alexander the Great) built a wall to hold back the tribes of Gog and Magog (18:94) and that they will be released at the end of time (21:96). For a few details, see Kisa'i, passim.

grapes (*angûr*), 2.157, 158, 3.10, 150, 199, 210

gratitude (*shukr*), 2.42, 3.51, 53, 131, 149, 169

great ones (P. *buzurgân*, A. *akâbir*), 1.42, 47, 2.5, 29, 35, 68, 69, 88, 92, 108, 3.70, 91, 107, 130, 160, 176, 194, 202. The shaykhs, the saints.

Greeks (*yûnâniyân*), 2.47

Herat, 1.38

heresy (*zindiqa*), 3.7. *See* disbelief.

hidden. *See* servant.

Hindi, 1.45

Hippocrates, 2.47

homosexuality, 2.214, 3.143 n., 223

Homs, 1.22

houris (*hûr*), 2.234, 3.91. The black-eyed maidens of paradise mentioned in the Koran.

Household (*khânadân*), 1.31, 32. The family of the Prophet (specifically his daughter Fatima, her husband Ali, and their children Hasan and Husayn).

Humâm, 2.219. From a few mentions, it is clear that both he and his father were members of Rumi's circle.

human beings (*insân, âdamî*), 2.194-98; goal of, 2.13; as microcosms, 2.96, 175, 194-98, 3.52, 141

humility (*tawâdu`*), 1.18, 2.23, 202, 3.13, 54, 55, 63, 170, 199. Modesty, unpretentiousness; acting with recognition of one's own shortcomings.

hypocrisy (*nifâq*), 1.17, 30, 50, 2.71, 163, 248, 3.22, 65-67, 69-71, 73, 78, 91, 123, 149, 151, 167, 194, 201, 212, 213, 220. The word is contrasted with sincerity and typically understood to mean outward adherence to Islam accompanied by hidden rejection. It is considered the worst moral failing, and the Koran places the hypocrites in the deepest pit of hell. More generally, it means "to make manifest something other than what is in your heart" (3.67). Shams often speaks of hypocrisy in the usual negative sense (e.g. 1.30), but he also gives the word a positive twist, saying that the prophets and saints need to be hypocritical in order to lead people on the straight path (3.67, 69). In this understanding, the term begins to sound like the Buddhist concept of *upaya*.

Iblis, 2.87, 167, 211, 249, 250, 252, 3.89, 136. The personal name of Satan.

Iblistan, 2.23

Ibn `Abbâs, 2.79, 208, 234 n. A Companion of the Prophet from whom many hadiths are transmitted.

Ibn al-Jawzî, 2.88 n.

Ibn 'Arabî, Muhyî ad-Dîn Muhammad ibn 'Alî, 1.17 n., 43 n., 47 n., 52, 2.42 n., 68 n., 71 n., 156 n., 189 n., 211 n., 227 n., 230 n., 3.45 n. The greatest master of theoretical Sufism. Born in Murcia in Andalus, he lived in Damascus from 1223 until his death in 1240. According to one early but unreliable account, Rumi met him in his youth (RPP 112). He may or may not be the same as Shaykh Muhammad (see introduction).

Ibn Jubayr, 3.217 n.

Ibn Mas`ûd, 2.220. A well-known Companion of the Prophet.

Ibn Mujâhid, 2.88 n.

Ibrâhîm, Shaykh, 2.188, 3.115, 127. A participant in the discussions with Shams, he had known Shams before coming to Konya (3.115). Rumi says about him, "Shaykh Ibrahim is a fine dervish. When I see him, I remember the friends. Mawlana Shams ad-Din had a tremendous affection for him. He always used to say, 'My shaykh Ibrahim,' ascribing him to himself" (Fih 176; Signs 183). He may be the same as Qutb ad-Din Ibrahim, a disciple of Rumi's father who later became close to Shams (Aflaki 632).

Ibrâhîm Adham (d. 776 or 790), 3.102, 103, 139 n. A famous Sufi who is said to have abandoned the throne of Balkh to enter the path. MSM 62-79.

idol (but), 2.20, 3.116, 123, 151, 207

Idris, 2.167. The Koranic name of the prophet Enoch, usually considered the same as Hermes.

Ikhwân as-Safâ', 2.47. An early philosophical school with strong leanings toward Neoplatonism and Pythagoreanism.

`Imâd, 1.1, 2.156, 192, 3.62, 91, 197, 198. A Sufi teacher in Konya and a disciple of Awhad ad-Din Kirmani (Maq 408). Shams did not have a good opinion of him. There may, however, be others by the same name in the text (e.g., 3.198)

`Imâd ad-Dîn, 3.35. Probably the same as Imad.

imagination, imagining, image (khayâl), 2.15, 67, 94, 100, 105, 113, 159, 225, 3.39, 53, 54, 101, 102, 134, 135, 164. Shams typically takes the term in a negative sense; occasionally, as in 2.113, he acknowledges its positive role (concerning which, in Rumi's teachings, see SPL 248 ff.).

imam, 1.22, 2.133, 167. Leader. The person who leads the prayer.

imitation (taqlîd), 2.31, 36-40, 67, 86, 87, 106 n., 3.47, (140).

Following the beliefs of others without knowing the truth for oneself; contrasted with realization. See the note on 2.31.

immersion (*istighrâq*), 1.25, 2.70, 93, 157, 185, 205, 249, 3.46, 49, 60

inanimate (*jamâd*), 1.39, 2.175, 249, 3.175, 207

incarnationism (*hulûl*), 3.91. The idea, always criticized in Islamic thought, that God can descend into a human soul.

incomparability (*tanzîh*), 2.42. *See* similarity.

Indian (*hindû*), 1.23, 45, 3.98, 122

infidel (*gabr*), 1.27, 2.78, 142, 3.106, 140, 143, 193

infinite (*bî-nihâyat*), 1.38, 2.190, 237, 3.52, 135

innovation (*bid'at*), 2.212, 3.24. A teaching or practice represented as Islamic but not based on the Koran or the Sunnah.

inspiration (*ilhâm*), 2.19, 205, 208, 212, 3.29, 168. Knowledge from the spiritual world, or from God. Generally, but not always, inspiration is distinguished from revelation, the latter being received only by prophets.

intellect (*'aql*), 1.33, 38, 41, 42, 47, 2.1-3, 8, 14, 22, 43, 72, 107, 109, 187, 3.41, 62, 88, 102, 120, 148, 180; lordly, 2.45; this-worldly, 2.3, 27; intellectual truth (*ma'qûl*), 1.36, 2.27, 45, 54; intelligent (*'âqil*), 1.41, 2.59, 119, 3.73, 93, 102. The intellect is the characteristic of the human soul that sets it apart from the animal soul. The term is usually employed in a positive sense, denoting the power of intelligence that differentiates truth from falsehood, right from wrong. It is often contrasted with caprice (q.v.). In Islamic philosophy, the intellect is the radiance of the divine light. In contrast, the soul is a potential intellect that needs to be actualized. For both Shams and Rumi, the word has a positive sense, but it can also mean dry rationality, devoid of love for God and empty of insight into the nature of things (e.g., 2.45). The "universal intellect" (1.47) is the first creation of God, through which He then creates the universe. It is typically identified with the Pen, which writes the destinies of all creatures on the Tablet. See SPL 33-37, 220-26.

intention (*niyyat*), 2.79, 100, 138, 3.11, 105

interest, best (*maslahat*), 1.36, 2.68, 160, 3.46, 126, 163, 220. The means to achieve *salâh*, that is, the well-being, wholesomeness, and worthiness of the human soul in this world and the next. *See* worthiness.

interpretation (*ta'wîl*), 2.37, 42, 59, 90, 117, 160, 186, 210, 228, 250,

Jesus, 1.22, 2.28, 58, 59, 61, 79, 87 n., 107 n., 173, 184, 195, 3.2, 67, 168, 207
Jew (*juhûd*), 1.27, 2.7, 2.28, 37, 58, 68, 121, 127, 142, 248, 3.44, 56, 212
Job, 3.121
John, 2.200
Jonah, 2.239
Joseph, 2.30, 46 n., 210, 3.7, 74
Joshua, 2.133
Jûhî (A. Juhâ), 2.68, 3.203. A proverbial joker and scoundrel. Rumi tells stories about him in M II 3116-28, V 3327 ff., and VI 4449 ff. *See* Abu Bakr Rubabi.
Junayd (d. 910), 2.23, 96 n., 209, 210, 3.5, 6, 13, 180, 199. One of the greatest of the early Sufi masters. MSS 199-213.
jurisprudence (*fiqh*), 2.43, 3.52, 61, 73, 163; jurist (*faqîh*), 1.27, 29, 2.5-7, 15, 96, 3.137, 148, 163. Jurisprudence is a science concerned with applying the teachings of the Koran and the Sunnah to the practical situations of life, i.e., the science of the Law (q.v.). It is commonly characterized as the knowledge of the outward teachings of Islam, in contrast with Sufism, which is knowledge of the inward teachings of Islam. Thus "jurists" and "dervishes" represent two rather different approaches to putting the Koran and Sunnah into practice, though the two approaches may be combined in one person. In Sunni Islam, there are four schools of jurisprudence, all considered equally valid.
Kaaba, 1.27, 2.84, 227, 3.58, 119, 220. The House of God at Mecca.
Kalandar (*qalandar*), 2.187. A type of wandering Sufi. Sana'i, Rumi, and others use the term for a great shaykh who gives no thought to the conventions of the world. See SPL 187-90; RPP 35.
Kerman, 2.110
khanaqah (*khânaqâh*), 1.20, 2.133, 148, 211, 3.35, 105, 176, 219. A Sufi center.
Khâqânî, 2.90 n., 3.144. Persian poet who died toward the end of the twelfth century.
Kharaqân, 2.207
Khayyâm, 'Umar (d. between 1112 and 1136), 2.49, 188. Philosopher and mathematician, made famous in the West by

Laylâ, 3.54, 91. The beloved of Majnun. Their love affair is celebrated in both Arabic and Persian poetry.

learning (*fadl*), 2.15, 19, 224, 3.59, 131

light (*nûr*), 1.11, 38, 41, 2.54, 83, 101, 104, 141, 159, 161, 171, 213,
3.2, 18, 56, 69, 149, 164, 219; of God, 2.64, 114, 124, 157, 176,
184, 3.52, 91, 181, 201; of Muhammad, 2.86, 145, 3.62; vs. fire,
2.157, 164, 3.90

limpidness (*safâ'*), 1.45, 49, 2.40, 54, 94, 148, 3.12, 19, 149, 184.
Purity of mind and heart.

lion (*shîr*), 1.19, 22, 131, 3.36, 144, 213

location (*makân*), 2.42, 199, 239; (*hayyiz*), 3.93

logic (*mantiq*), logician (*mantiqî*), 1.21, 33, 2.156, 3.61. Logic was a
science studied mainly by philosophers and theologians.

lordly (*rabbânî*), 2.45, 93, 105. Pertaining to the Lord, divine.

Lote Tree (*sidra*), 3.152

love (*'ishq, mahabbat*), 1.9, 31, 41, 2.5, 10, 14, 22, 48, 71, 78, 79, 101,
103, 110, 112-15, 129, 135, 160, 199, 219, 3.36, 44, 52, 76, 79, 91,
140, 147, 157, 173, 185, 192, 205; for God, 2.29, 71, 110, 155, 225,
3.90, 102; for position, 1.41, 3.152, 198; for the world, 2.3, 127,
3.76, 152; love-letter (*'ishq-nâma*), 2.222; lover (*'âshiq*), 1.5, 2.68, 74,
112, 3.44, 101, 103. As a divine attribute. love is that which drives
the universe, bringing about both creation and the return to God,
both multiplicity and subsequent reunification. God created
human beings out of love for them ("I was a Hidden Treasure, and
I loved to be known"), and human beings return to God out of
love for Him. As Sufis often note, the Koran declares a mutuality
and equivalence between God and human beings only in respect
of love: "He loves them, and they love him" (5:54). For Rumi's
views on the utter centrality of love for the divine/human relationship, see SPL, especially pp. 194-231.

Ma'arrî, Abu'l-'Alâ' al- (d. 1057), 2.18, 160 n. Famous Arab poet.

macrocosm (*'âlam-i kubrâ*), 2.96 n., 175, 197. The universe as a
whole; contrasted with the microcosm (*'âlam-i sughrâ*), i.e., the
human being (q.v.).

mad (*dîwâna*), 1.4, 7, 10, 21, 2.15, 247, 3.13, 54, 101, 103, 206

madrasah (*madrasa*), 1.20, 27, 46, 2.26, 126, 133, 247, 3.70, 98, 101. A
school for the study of the religious sciences, especially jurispru-

dence and theology. Sometimes contrasted with khanaqah.

Mahmûd (r. 997-1030), 2.69, 119, 3.178, 215. The third and most powerful king of the Ghaznavid dynasty.

majesty (*jalâl*), 2.176, 180, 190, 3.23, 26. A divine attribute; contrasted with beauty.

Majnûn, 3.54, 91, 140. *See* Layla.

Malatya, 2.23, 3.217

Malik `Âdil (r. 1146-74), 3.137. "The Just King," title of Mahmûd ibn Zangî, the atabeg of Syria, who ruled in Damascus.

man (*insân*). *See* human being; Man (P. *mard*, A. *rajul*), 2.74, 86, 98, 114, 147, 209, 3.19, 24, 26, 40, 54, 82, 106, 149 n., 159, 189, 223; of God (the Real), 3.20, 75, 90, 147, 180. The saint, the true shaykh. Manliness (P. *mardî*, A. *muruwwat*), 2.145, 181, 212, 213, 3.59, 117, 121, 143

Mansûr Hafada (d. 1175), 3.64. Abu Mansur Muhammad ibn Asad Nishaburi, a Shafi'i jurist. In Sufism, he was a disciple of Najm ad-Din Kubra (Maq 553).

Mawlânâ (Rumi), 1.27, 38, 2.23, 29, 35, 37, 77, 211, 229, 3.7, 102, 149, 157, 165; criticism of, 1.47 (?), 2.34 (?), 3.24 (?), 73, 101 (?), 105 (?), 120 (?), 136, 140 (?), 153 (?), 174, 175, 194 (?), 219; his disciples, 3.60, 63, 73, 91; his discipleship, 3.52, 59, 60, 67; his dreams, 3.185 (?); his gentleness, 3.127, 133, 180, 181; his jealousy, 3.178; his learning, 3.83; and money, 3.88, 94; his preaching, 3.21, 35, 64, 75, 213; his state, 1.53, 2.155, 167, 192, 3.22, 55-64, 67, (89), 91, 152, 216, 223; his words, 2.186, 187, 3.29, 31, 34, 59, 109

meaning (*ma'nâ*), 1.26, 38, 45, 49, 50, 2.17, 20, 54, 56, 68, 80, 83, 150, 189, 192, 226, 3.17, 23, 33-35, 109, 120, 143; and form, 2.190, 192, 226, 249, 250, 3.10, 157; outward, 2.157; world of, 2.92, 101. The inner reality of something, contrasted both with form and with speech or word. The pair "form/meaning" is often used synonymously with body/spirit or outward/inward. Rarely does "meaning" designate simply the "sense" or "significance" of a thing or of words. Rather, it designates the inner, spiritual reality that is linked ontologically to the outward object or word and that gives rise to its external existence. See SPL 19 ff.

Mecca, 2.202, 3.154

meditation (*tafakkur*), 2.75

mercy (*rahmat*), 1.49, 2.42, 118, 127, 250, 253, 3.53, 170, 186. *See* gentleness.

messenger (*rasûl*), 2.57, 73, 88, 246, 3.57, 141, 194. A prophet who has brought a scripture. Every messenger is a prophet, but not every prophet is a messenger.

Michael, 2.109

miracle (*mu`jiza*), 1.41, 2.39, 186, 202, 3.136, 140. An act performed by a prophet that breaks the laws of nature. *See* charismatic act.

mi`râj, 2.28 n., 74, 239, 3.152 n. Ascent to God. According to the traditional accounts, Gabriel took Muhammad from Mecca to Jerusalem, and from there up through the seven heavens to the Lote Tree at the far boundary of paradise. From that point he ascended alone. This journey recapitulates the descent of the Koran from God on the hand of Gabriel and serves as the basic model for the spiritual path.

mirror (*âyina*), 1.41, 2.54, 3.7, 91, 204, 205

misguidance (*dalâlat*), 2.37, 67, 3.124, 200. *See* guidance.

moment (*waqt*), 1.18, 51, 2.66, 226, 240-42, 245, 3.53, 98, 142, 176. As a technical term, it is roughly synonymous with state, specifically the state being undergone at the present time.

monasticism (*rahbâniyya*), monk (*râhib*), 1.17 n., 2.156, 3.53, 54

Moses, 2.5, 14, 28, 36, 58, 79, 133, 141, 145, 178, 180, 221, 246, 251, 3.26, 56, 67, 93, 140, 143, 156, 212

mosque (*masjid*), 1.27, 2.34, 149, 3.45, 90, 118

Mosul, 3.94

mufti (*muftî*), 3.83. A scholar who gives fatwas.

Muhammad, the Prophet, 1.27n., 41, 52, 2.28, 47, 50, 52, 56-70, 72-74, 78, 83, 84, 137, 159, 192, 202, 214, 225, 247, 253, 3.34, 44, 62, 69, 121, 140, 160, 178, 207, 210; imitation of, 2.40; his voicing the secrets, 2.69, 192, 193, 220. *See* following.

Muhammad, Shaykh, 1.43, 46-53 bis, 2.68, 3.33 n., 45 n., 84. Possibly the same as Ibn Arabi (see the introduction, and the note on 3.45).

Muhammad Ghazali. *See* Ghazali.

Muhammad Gûyânî, 1.33, 2.33. Unknown. Shams must have known him both in Damascus and in Konya.

Muhammadan, 1.9, 2.75, 137, 145, 227, 3.88; stride, 2.141, 3.212. Related to Muhammad; a true follower of the prophet

Nishapur, 1.38, 43, 2.166

Nizâmî (d. 1217), 3.144. Persian poet, famous for his epic romances.

Noah, 2.126, 3.117, 140, 211, 212

obedience (*tâ`at*), 2.42, 70, 71, 74, 77, 103, 105, 139, 202, 3.103. Observing the rulings of the Shariah; contrasted with disobedience (*ma`siyat*).

obliteration (*mahw*), 2.249, 3.52. Annihilation, selflessness.

occasion (*sabab*), 2.220, 221, 234, 237, 3.135. The circumstances surrounding the revelation of a given verse of the Koran. This is one of many factors taken into account in exegesis and interpretation of the Koran.

ocean (*daryâ*), 1.4, 39, 45, 2.12, 131, 132, 140, 181, 3.51, 62, 128, 154, 189

Og son of Anak (`Âj ibn `Anaq), 3.212. Og, king of Bashan, whose gigantic (but still human) stature is noted in the Bible. For the legends to which Shams refers, see Kisa'i 251-53. Rumi mentions Og in M II 2305.

oneness (*yakî, yagânagî*), 2.100, 134, 3.119. Unity, whether as an attribute of God or of created things.

opening (*gushâd, gushâyish*), 1.8, 2.94, 144, 3.76, 77, 102, 103, 106, 121, 123, 143, 148, 161, 198. Unveiling, inspiration, direct awareness from God. The Arabic equivalents of this term are *futuh* (as in the title of Ibn Arabi's *al-Futuhat al-makkiyya*, "The Meccan Openings") and *fath* (as in Koran 48:1).

opposition (*mukhâlafat*), 2.152, 161, 3.7, 45, 84, 148, 160, 171. Going against the commands of God, the Prophet, or the shaykh. Contrasted with conformity.

other (*ghayr*), 2.187, 199, 3.53, 131. Anything that is not God. Given that God is "with you wherever you are" (Koran 57:4) and present with all things, the status of the others is ambiguous. *See* jealousy.

outward(ness) (*zâhir*), 2.29, 73, 127, 3.5, 20, 124. *See* inward. "The folk of the outward sense" (*ahl-i zâhir*) are the literalists, those who are unable to see beneath the surface of scripture; 2.133, 225, 246

page (*waraq*), reading one's own, 1.37, 47, 2.69, 187, 3.164, 207. *See* state.

paradise (*bihisht*), 2.28, 79, 104, 120, 141, 160, 167, 3.23, 41, 67, 77, 119, 165, 180, 185, 212

Râbi`a (d. 801), 2.92. A famous woman saint.

Ramadan, 1.21, 22, 3.208. The ninth month of the lunar year, during which fasting is obligatory.

Rashîd, 1.27. Unknown. Possibly the same as Rashid ad-Din.

Rashîd ad-Dîn, 2.73. Apparently a member of Rumi's circle.

raw (khâm), 1.9, 2.29, 3.19. See cooked.

Real (haqq), 2.115, 133, 142, 190, 239, 3.43; man of, 2.39, 154, 3.20, 75, 147, 202; world of, 2.68, 115, 128, 192, 3.27, 67. This Koranic name of God also means truth, rightness, and worthiness.

reality (haqîqat), 2.80, 94–96, 106, 133, 154, 175, 236, 249, 3.211. Generally, a thing's essence, the thing in itself, or the thing as it is known to God. The word may also designate God himself, the goal of the Shariah and the Path (2.95).

realization (tahqîq). See verification.

religion (dîn), 2.3, 37, 42, 69, 74, 84, 98, 103, 135, 136, 212, 214, 251, 3.40, 43, 87, 140, 189; highwaymen of, 2.55, 101, 3.127, 128; of Muhammad, 2.55, 212, 3.24, 129; of old women, 2.106, 108, 109. Generally, a path to God brought by a prophet and followed by a community. More specifically, the roots and branches of Islam. The most basic elements of a religion are tawhid and worship. The Prophet defined Islam as a "religion" in terms of three basic dimensions: submission to God through right activity (islam), faith in God through sound understanding (iman), and love for God through choosing the beautiful over the ugly (ihsan). See Murata, Vision.

remembrance (yâd), 2.208. As a technical term, this Persian word is equivalent to Arabic dhikr, translated here as "invocation."

repentance (tawba), 1.24, 2.3, 52, 91, 205, 3.26, 212, 219

resurrection (qiyâmat, hashr), 1.27, 36, 37, 2.23, 33, 110, 120, 141, 179, 233, 3.114, 165, 212

revelation (wahy), 2.72, 157, 220, 221, 225, 3.8, 133. God's speech addressed to a prophet.

rogue (rind), 2.183. Someone who is indifferent to social conventions but conforms inwardly to the prophetic model. Rumi writes, "If you are an utter rogue, then flee from fools! Open the eye of your heart to the eternal Light" (D vs. 32975; cf. SPL 316–17).

Rostam, 2.4. The great mythic warrior of Firdawsi's Shahnama, "Book of Kings."

Russian (rûs), 3.73

saddle-cloth (*ghâshiya*), 1.37, 2.212-14. A mark of high rank that was placed over a person's saddle when he dismounted. It was the duty of one member of his entourage to carry it.

sage (*hakîm*), 1.36, 39, 2.38, 43. A philosopher, a wise man, a physician. "The Sage" is Sana'i, who received the title because of the depth of his learning.

Sa`îd ibn al-Musayyib (d. 703), 2.15. A well-known scholar and ascetic who lived in Medina (not Baghdad, as Shams would have it, nor Damascus, which was the seat of the caliphate during his time).

saint (*walî*), 2.68, 125, 159, 207, 241, 3.1, 59, 64, 93, 98, 136, 138, 140, 143, 169, 185, (200); and prophets, 1.32, 2.36, 94, 139, 141, 157, 192, 198, 200, 201, 252, 3.56, 62, 91, 202. *See* sanctity.

saki (*sâqî*), 2.133, 3.49. The cup-bearer, the one who pours the divine wine, the shaykh, the beloved.

Salâh ad-Dîn, Mawlana, 2.73. Salah ad-Din Zarkub (d. 1258), one of Rumi's closest companions (RPP 205-15). Rumi and Shams are reported to have met together in his house for several months after Shams's first arrival in Konya (RPP 176).

salat (*salât*), 2.73, 75. The obligatory, five-times-a-day, ritual prayer. *See* prayer.

salvation (*najât*), 2.33, 120. Deliverance from hell.

sama (samâ`), 1.9, 54, 55, 2.146-51, 212, 245, 3.13, 21, 121, 145, 180, 185. Literally "listening." The word designates sessions of music and recitation of poetry, often accompanied by dancing, with the aim of heightening the participants' awareness of the divine presence. *Sama* grew out of the importance of reciting the Koran and the divine names, practices that were often carried out with great attention to beauty and musicality. *Sama* has always had an ambiguous legal status (see Shams's remarks in 3.180). It takes many forms, few of them as elaborate as the "dance of the whirling dervishes" codified by Sultan Walad and performed by the Mevlevi Order (and nowadays by the Turkish Ministry of Culture). The *sama* mentioned by Shams may or may not be similar to the codified version.

Samaritan, 2.36

Sanâ'î (d. 1131), 2.17, 18, 72, 81 n., 142, 157, 165, 182 n., 187, 192, 201, 213 n., 3.40 n., 43 n., 79 n., 101, 143 n., 144. The greatest

seclusion for forty days (A. *arba'în*, P. *chilla*) as an innovation or, at best, a practice that belongs properly to the community of Moses (2.145, 212, 3.140). The goal in most of Sufism, in any case, is to achieve *khalwat dar anjuman* (*al-khalwa fi'l-jalwa*), that is, seclusion with God while living in the midst of society.

secret, secret heart (*sirr*), 1.18, 49, 54, 2.2, 11, 14, 59, 69, 79, 141, 159, 160, 162, 174, 192, 193, 207, 220, 241, 244, 3.13, 34, 52, 53, 62, 74, 75, 107, 115, 119, 143, 149, 189, 194. A teaching kept from the unworthy; insight into the divine mysteries; the inmost heart.

seeking (*talab, justan*), 1.47, 2.13, 24, 71, 101, 104, 105, 121, 124, 133, 217, 3.2-5, 34, 60, 77, 85, 101-3, 106, 113, 114, 219. Searching for God (or for a shaykh, who is the guide to God). By the fact of their seeking, seekers demonstrate that the sought object (*matlûb*) is seeking them. As in love, where God's love for man precedes and gives rise to man's love for God (2.110), so also, man's desire for God is explicable only because God desires man (2.121). See the note on 3.2.

self (*khwud*), selfhood (*khwudî*), 3.101, 107, 207; negation of, 2.113. On selfhood and selflessness in Rumi, see SPL, especially pp. 173-75.

self-worship (*khwud-parastî*), 2.98

selflessness (*bî-khwudî*), 2.82, 180, 192, 3.46

senses (*hiss, hawâss*), 2.13, 27; sensory (*mahsûs*), 2.27, 59, 166

separation (*firâq*), 2.12, 185, 3.7, 85, 140, 144, 213, 220, 223. Being apart from one's beloved; contrasted with union. The word is used both for the typical human situation vis-à-vis God and for human relationships. For the central role that separation and union play in Rumi's teachings, see SPL 232 ff.

Seraphiel, 3.133. The angel who will blow the Trumpet on the Last Day.

sermon (*wa'z*). *See* preaching.

servant (P. *banda*, A. *'abd*), 1.17, 30, 32, 35, 2.39, 43, 52, 55, 70, 72, 88, 102, 112, 126, 127, 131, 133, 154, 164, 175, 186, 189, 191, 192, 210, 219, 224, 231, 3.8, 29, 37, 50, 74, 90, 91, 114, 128, 129, 132, 140, 147, 151, 166, 175, 204, 212; hidden, 1.54, 2.127, 192, 209, 3.5, (20), 64, (138, 156, 181); servanthood (*bandagî, 'ubûdiyyat*), 2.70, 77, 78, 188, 3.4. Generally, a servant is a human being vis-à-vis the Lord. Like Ibn Arabi and others, Shams uses the term to refer to

soul" (75:2), which is the soul aware of its own shortcomings, and "the soul at peace" (89:27), which is the soul of the saint, reintegrated into the spirit and at rest in God. See the note on 2.107.

sour (*tursh*), 1.21, 35, 2.78, 181, 3.7, 79, 126, 150, 157, 199, 210

speaking-companion (*kalîm*), 2.14, 36, 133, 145, 249. A standard epithet for Moses.

speech (A. *kalâm*, P. *sukhan*), 1.3, 2.14, 17, 25, 27, 30, 33, 36, 37, 74, 114, 185, 241, 249, 3.18, 26, 52, 149, 157; of God, 1.45, 2.9, 35, 72, 102, 157, 175, 186, 192, 208, 215, 216, 230, 232, 3.53, 175, 194; plain of, 1.49, 50, 3.33; knower of (*sukhandân*), 2.37, 114. As a divine attribute, speech is God's self-expression and self-revelation by means of both scripture and creation. The Koran is frequently called simply "the speech of God."

sphere (celestial) (*falak*), 1.36, 2.96, 113, 115, 189, 212, 3.39, 59

spirit (*rûh*), spiritual (*rûhânî*), 1.1, 45, 2.69, 107, 183, 236, 3.40, 53, 56, 57, 91, 114, 133, 145, 185, 218; animal, 2.194; and body, 1.37, 2.13, 54, 72, 97, 110, 212, 240, 249; drunkenness of, 2.154, 156; food of, 2.246; holy, 2.194, 210; perfection of, 2.54; vision of, 2.47, 93, 154; world of, 2.93, 113, 154. Contrasted with body, spirit is the inner, aware dimension of existence and is associated with God's breath, as in the Koranic verse, "I blew into [Adam] of My spirit" (15:29). Spirit is always clearly differentiated from God Himself (as in 2.93, 98, 110). In Rumi and Shams, spirit is usually considered a higher level of being than soul (e.g., 2.139). See SPL 27 ff.

state (*hâl*), 1.4, 5, 9, 22, 26, 31, 39, 51, 2.32, 39, 54, 56, 69, 73, 89, 108, 139, 164, 188, 189, 192, 214, 240, 3.12, 13, 21, 25, 52, 53, 60, 63, 67, 72, 77, 79, 84, 114, 120, 126, 176, 186, 193, 200, 218; folk of, 3.180; going into, 1.48, 2.92, 140, 151, 3.5, 69, 105, 211; speaking on basis of, 2.35, 69, 188, 232 (*see* page). The situation or condition of the moment. As a technical term, it means a passing spiritual gift from God and is contrasted with "station," which is a permanent acquisition of the soul, a deeply rooted virtue, the result of struggle on the path. State may also designate an ecstasy or illumination that overcomes a person during *sama* or some other form of practice. State and station are both used loosely, in which case they can be interchangeable (e.g., 1.48). The common expression "tongue of the state" (*zabân-i hâl*, from Arabic *lisân al-*

hâl) means the acts and reactions that express the situation of a person or a thing at any given time, the mute language of things themselves; 2.31, 87, 3.7, 131, 205, 208, 212.

station (*maqâm*), 1.48, 2.79, 137, 189, 213, 240, 3.19, 56, 72, 79, 91, 122, 185, 216. Literally, "residing place" or "standing place." *See* state.

steadfastness (`azm*), 2.69, 105, 246, 3.80, 193. The "possessors of steadfastness" are the highest ranking prophets.

stride (*khutwa*), 2.19, 141, 146, 3.212

struggle (*mujâhada*), 2.54, 94, 142, 236, 245, 3.4, 7, 55, 210. Exerting effort on the path of God. The word *jihâd*, from the same root, is grammatically equivalent, but it is more often used for the outward, military struggle in defense of the community.

study (*ta`allum, tahsîl*), 1.47, 2.15, 16, 23, 26

submission (*taslîm*), 2.29, 68, 3.31, 61, 104, 122

subsistence (*baqâ'*), 1.18, 2.124, 132, 3.143 n. Everlastingness; union with God. In technical language, it is contrasted with "annihilation," following the Koranic verse, "Everything [on the earth] comes to be annihilated, and there subsists the face of your Lord" (55:26). The goal of the Sufi path is to experience the annihilation of human limitations and the subsistence of the divine attributes that are latent in the original human disposition, created in the image of God.

suffering (*ranj*), 1.2, 2.29, 42, 118, 166, 225, 226, 3.85, 86, 121, 123, 149, 159, 164, 195

Sufi (*sûfî*), 1.18, 2.24, 88, 96, 135, 136, 148, 162, 196, 245, 3.57, 91, 98, 142, 154, 221; the bread in his sleeve, 1.18, 2.227, 3.127, 132. A follower of the Path; a dervish.

Sulaymân Tirmidî, 2.55. Unknown; mentioned only once.

Sultân Walad, 2.23 n., 210 n., 3.2 n., 143, 210 n., 223 n. Rumi's son Baha ad-Din. He succeeded his father as shaykh and wrote a good deal of poetry. RPP 230–41.

sun (P. *âftâb*, A. *shams*), 1.41, 44, 2.86, 171, 188, 189, 254, 3.18, 36, 42, 78, 131

Sunnah (*sunna*), 3.60, 142. The teachings and practices of the Prophet (as contrasted with the Koran, the speech of God). *See* following.

Sunni, 2.42, 44. A follower of mainstream Islam (as contrasted with Shi'ite Islam).

supplication (*du`â'*), 1.16, 38, 2.54, 66, 69, 78, 87, 174, 219, 249, 3.60, 149, 153, 191, 219. Petitional prayer.

surah (*sûra*), 1.16, 47, 2.68, 127. A chapter of the Koran.

Surmârî, 2.167. The editor thinks that this is Yusuf from Surmari (a region between Tiflis and Ahlat), who was a companion of Awhad ad-Din Kirmani.

Syria, 3.220

Tablet (*lawh*), 1.45, 2.8, 225. A pre-temporal record of creation kept by God; or the spiritual realm in which the realities of creatures are written out by the Supreme Pen (the First Intellect) before they become embodied in the world.

Tabriz, 2.212, 240, 3.85, 94, 140, 154, 155

Tariqah. *See* Path.

taste, tasting (*dhawq*), 1.49, 2.31, 63, 64, 93, 129, 135, 160, 183, 204, 215, 3.12, 54, 64, 123, 135, 145, 201, 211, 213. Unveiling, state, pleasure.

Tatars (*tatâr*), 1.1, 31, 2.182, 198. The Mongols.

tavern (*kharâbât, maykada*), 1.1, 9, 2.103, 3.23, 47, 49, 119. A place where wine is drunk. For the symbolic usage of the term, see SPL 315-16.

tawhîd, 2.134, 174, 214, 3.75. The assertion of God's unity; the statement "There is no god but God."

teaching (*ta`lîm, âmûkhtan*), 1.14, 15, 26, 2.4, 56, 78, 84, 113, 133, 249, 3.7, 13, 101, 109, 119

Tel Basher, 3.216

test (*imtihân*), 2.162, 213, 3.7, 121, 186, 200-2. The trials to which a shaykh subjects his disciples to establish their sincerity.

theology (*kalâm, usûl*), 2.43, 3.52, 61, 73; theologian (*mutakallim, usûlî*), 2.29, 115, 142, 224. Theology is a science concerned with the rational defense of Koranic teachings about God. Ash'arism and Mu'tazilism are its two most famous schools.

thirsty (*tashna*), 2.229, 3.4, 60, 87, 160

Throne (*`arsh*), 2.100, 104, 194, 195, 197, 199, 225-27, 3.52. The seat of God as All-merciful. The Throne encompasses the entirety of creation, and God lets down His "two feet" upon the Footstool, which "encompasses the heavens and the earth" (Koran 2:255). The Throne is sometimes associated with the starless sphere, and the Footstool with the sphere of the fixed stars. According to a hadith current in Sufi circles, the human heart is God's Throne in the microcosm.

togetherness (*jam`, jam`iyyat*), 1.1, 1.48, 2.66, 101, 159, 3.129. Being together; one-pointed concentration on God; finding God in the heart. Contrasted with dispersion.

tongue of the state. *See* state.

Torah, 2.14, 47, 3.143

transmission (*naql*), 2.31, 70, 71, 154, 212, 3.24

tree (*dirakht*), 1.38, 2.29, 216, 3.88, 153

tribe (*tâ'ifa, qawm*), 2.190, 3.101, 148. The Sufis; Junayd is called, "the shaykh of the Tribe."

trust (*amânu*), 2.137, 228. The burden of responsibility toward God that mankind accepted at their creation. See Murata, *Vision* 134–37; SPL passim.

trust in God (*tawakkul*), 2.137, 3.210. A virtue that is highly praised in the Koran and considered an advanced station on the Path.

truth(fulness) (*râstî*), 3.35, 46, 69, 71, 73, 149, 212

Turk, 2.212, 214, 3.52, 215

Turkoman, 2.251

Tûsî, 2.222. This may be the Shi'ite scholar Abu Ja`far Muhammad ibn Hasan (d. 1068), author of the well-known Koran commentary *al-Tibyan*.

ulama (`*ulamâ'*), 2.84, 192, 3.56, 151. The scholars, the learned, the experts in the Law.

`Umar, 2.47, 69, 202, 253, 254, 3.90, 116, 144. Companion and second caliph, after Abu Bakr.

unbelief (*kufr*), unbeliever (*kâfir*), 1.30, 43, 44, 45, 2.42, 52, 79, 103, 121, 146, 152, 173, 174, 184, 198, 214, 220, 242, 249, 3.5, 6, 38, 46, 104, 107, 116, 118, 119, 130, 131, 140, 167, 180, 185, 189, 204, 209; Muslim unbeliever, 3.121. An "unbeliever" is a non-Muslim. The word is contrasted with *mu'min*, "believer," a person who has faith (*iman*). Shams often interprets the word in a positive sense by contrasting the unbelievers with so-called believers, that as, insincere Muslims or people caught up with the outward trappings of religion (e.g., 1.43). Thus the "Muslim" is busy with the externals of the Shariah and the Path, but the "unbeliever" is busy verifying the inner truths of Islam and striving for union with the Real. Such an "unbeliever" transcends the opposition between faith and unbelief and includes both within himself (2.121; cf. 3.204).

unification (*ittihâd*), 2.185, 3.209. Oneness with God, union.

Human perfection is typically pictured as a combination of the receptivity of servanthood (submission to God) and the activity of vicegerency (acting on God's behalf). In other terms, the servant is "annihilated" before God and the vicegerent "subsists" through God.

a servant of God. In a broader sense, the word designates the proper human response to the reality of God, a reality that is summed up in the formula of *tawhid*. The Koran makes this point by declaring *tawhid* and worship to be the essential message of every prophet (21:25). The "acts of worship" (*`ibâdât*) are the ritual activities specified by the Shariah and the Tariqah; 3.20.

worthiness (*salâh*), 1.16, 2.37, 3.23, 191, 202, 220. Moral integrity and spiritual wholeness; an important Koranic term (often translated as "righteousness"). Contrasted with corruption.

wrath (*ghadab*), 1.38, 2.133, 250, 3.7. The divine attribute of anger; the correlative of mercy (see *gentleness*). As a human attribute, wrath is often paired with appetite (q.v.).

wretchedness (*shiqâ'*), 3.2. *See* felicity.

Zachariah, 2.200 n.

Zâhid Tabrizi, 2.84. This is probably Mu'in ad-Din Muhammad ibn Ramadan (d. 1196), better known as Faqih Tabrizi (a name by which he is mentioned in Maq 359).

Zâhir, King (r. 1186-1216), 2.50. Ayyubid ruler of Aleppo.

Zahrâ, 3.218. One of the women of Rumi's household. She is mentioned in one other passage, also in connection with food (Maq 844).

Zayn Sadaqa, 3.62, 196. A disciple of Awhad ad-Din Kirmani, apparently his most important successor. He taught in Konya and had many female disciples (Maq 408).

Table of Sources

Maqalat	Me & Rumi				
69	2.110	99–100	3.92	138	3.198
69–71	3.205	100–1	3.157	138–39	3.34
72	2.35	101–3	3.143	139	3.71
73–74	3.180	103–5	3.91	139–40	3.86
74	3.22	105–6	3.108	140	2.73
74–75	3.135	106	3.24	140–41	1.20
75	2.58	106–7	2.138	141–42	2.33
75–76	2.19	107	3.8	142	3.16
76	3.110	107–8	2.166	142–43	2.121
76–77	2.22	108–9	3.145	143–44	3.106
77	1.4	109	3.9	144	1.53 bis
77–78	3.185	109–10	3.186	144–46	2.160
78–79	2.155	110	3.6	146	3.77
79–80	3.165	110–11	1.39	146–47	2.157
80	2.150	113–15	3.7	147–48	2.242
81–82	3.136	115	3.78	148	2.131
82	3.14	115–16	3.27	148–49	3.23
82	1.33	116–17	3.148	150	3.99
82–83	3.197	117–18	2.207	150–51	3.123
83	2.200	118–19	1.38	151–53	3.213
83	3.97	119	1.5	153–54	2.135
83–84	2.47	119–21	2.68	155–56	3.203
84–85	3.103	121–22	3.70	156–57	3.211
85–86	2.89	122	2.163	157–58	3.42
86–87	2.54	123–24	2.210	158–60	2.245
87–89	2.119	124–25	3.105	160	1.103
89–90	3.102	125–26	2.142	160–61	2.114
90	2.181	126–27	3.149	161–62	2.37
90	2.201	127	3.5	162–63	2.94
90–91	2.87	127–28	2.23	163	2.139
91–92	3.101	128–29	2.168	163–64	2.220
92–93	2.164	129	2.162	164–65	2.115
93	3.204	129–30	3.55	166–67	1.24
93–94	3.93	130	2.238	167–68	2.237
94–95	3.194	130–31	2.141	168	1.50
96–97	1.49	131	2.25	168–69	3.217
97	2.124	131–32	2.120	169–71	3.140
97–98	3.33	132–33	3.147	172–73	2.216
98–99	3.207	133–34	3.44	173–75	2.249
99	2.101	134	2.7	175	2.102
		134–36	3.212	175–76	3.98
		136–38	2.29	176–78	2.42

178	2.26	209–10	1.13	240	3.68
179	3.45	210	2.132	241	1.25
180	2.148	210–11	2.91	241	2.12
180	2.2	211–12	3.184	241–42	3.120
180–81	3.96	212–13	2.195	242–43	3.175
181–82	3.153	213	2.140	243–45	3.168
182	2.230	213–14	2.39	245–46	2.88
182–83	2.189	214	2.146	248	3.26
183–84	3.189	214–15	2.251	249	2.5
184	2.215	215	3.156	249–50	2.108
185	2.191	216–17	2.205	252–53	3.190
185	2.21	217	2.67	253	2.218
185–86	2.231	217–18	1.55	257–58	2.227
186	3.32	218	3.42	258–59	2.100
187	3.174	218–19	2.97	259–61	2.199
187–88	2.143	219	2.254	262	2.106
188	3.139	219	3.187	263	3.172
188	2.11	219–20	3.81	263–64	2.247
188–89	3.80	220–21	2.96	264	2.203
189	2.239	221	1.26	265	2.209
189	3.40	221–22	3.74	265–66	2.183
190–91	2.24	222	1.19	266	3.141
191–92	3.132	222–23	3.57	267	2.153
192–93	1.41	223	2.171	267	2.173
194	2.208	224–25	3.30	267	3.134
195–96	2.98	225–26	1.45	268	2.57
196	1.7	226	3.107	268	1.11
196–97	2.61	226–27	3.104	268–69	3.195
197–98	2.246	227	2.18	269	2.182
198	3.196	227	2.180	270–71	2.159
199–200	3.210	227–28	2.81	271–72	1.40
200	3.166	229–30	2.204	272	2.223
200	2.194	230	2.137	272	3.146
202	1.16	231	2.117	272–73	2.136
202–3	3.130	231	2.48	273	3.66
203	2.198	231–33	3.90	273	3.111
204–5	1.31	233–34	3.131	273	3.183
205	2.90	234	3.76	274	3.171
205	2.177	234–35	3.188	275	1.44
206	2.123	235	2.125	275	3.199
206–7	2.219	235–36	3.48	276–78	2.202
207	2.122	236	1.8	278–79	1.18
207–8	2.38	236–37	2.116	279–80	3.209
208–9	2.75	237	2.170	280	2.93
209	3.116	238–39	2.236	280	2.99
209	2.63	239–40	1.48	280–81	2.64

281	2.66	317	3.177	625–26	1.6
281–82	2.232	317–18	3.38	626–27	1.21
282–83	2.72	318–19	2.248	627–28	3.46
283	1.23	319	3.167	628	3.15
283–84	2.176	319–20	2.225	628–29	3.118
284	2.145	320–21	2.211	629	3.125
284–85	3.64	321–23	3.52	629–30	2.149
285–86	2.213	323–25	2.212	630–33	2.215
286–87	1.32	325–26	3.176	634–35	2.222
287	3.160	326–27	3.163	635–36	1.35
288	2.52	338	1.47	636	2.14
288–89	3.113	340	3.218	638	2.76
290	3.11	340	1.15	638–39	3.75
290–91	3.201	343	1.14	639–40	2.252
291–94	1.16	347–48	3.35	640	2.56
294	1.54	349	2.34	640–41	3.159
294–95	2.224	353	3.94	641	3.155
295	2.251 n.	368	3.45 n.	641	1.34
295–96	3.82	607	2.152	641	2.53
296–97	2.50	607–8	1.30	641–42	2.109
298–99	3.119	608	1.29	642	2.196
299	1.52	608	2.27	642	2.60
299–300	2.86	608–9	2.161	643	2.92
300–1	3.79	609–10	3.117	644	2.158
301–2	2.188	610	3.173	645	2.74
302	3.47	610	3.39	646	3.88
302	3.150	610–11	3.37	646–47	2.45
302	3.50	611–12	3.137	647	3.58
303	3.126	612–13	2.70	647	2.206
303	3.158	613	3.129	647–48	2.105
303	2.65	613	2.178	648	2.9
303–4	3.151	614	3.138	648–49	3.59
304–5	1.53	615	1.12	649	2.49
305	3.122	615–16	3.181	649–50	2.151
306–7	3.200	616–17	2.253	650	2.193
307	2.8	617–18	2.214	650–51	3.84
308–9	2.113	618–19	3.12	651	2.112
309	3.191	621	3.214	651–52	2.233
309–10	2.107	621–22	2.221	652	2.28
310–11	2.4	622	3.192	653–54	2.84
312–13	2.169	622	3.124	655	2.104
313	2.1	622–23	3.19	655	3.144
313–14	2.3	623	2.147	657	2.226
314–15	2.167	623	3.44	657	2.82
315–16	3.169	624	2.128	657	2.190
316–17	2.127	624	2.118	657–58	1.36

658–59	2.51	697	3.100	744–45	2.31
659	2.10	697–98	1.46	745	2.129
659–60	3.170	698–99	2.217	745–46	3.49
660	3.18	700	2.154	749–50	3.56
660–61	3.178	700–1	2.156	750–51	2.186
662–63	3.121	701	2.165	751	3.63
663–64	2.79	701	2.240	752–53	3.13
664	2.243	701–2	3.114	753	2.46
665	3.17	702	1.3	753–55	1.27
666	3.51	702–3	3.128	755–56	3.161
666–67	2.41	703–4	1.1	756	3.216
667	2.234	704	3.4	756–57	3.85
667–68	2.220	706	3.89	758–59	2.133
668	2.17	706	2.144	759	3.202
668	3.162	710	3.152	759–60	3.1
668–69	2.111	710–11	3.109	760	3.95
669–70	2.15	711–12	2.43	760	3.221
674–75	2.40	712–13	3.60	760–61	3.83
676	2.6	713	3.41	761–62	2.36
676	2.20	713–14	2.174	762	2.229
676–77	2.175	716	2.126	762–63	2.250
677–78	1.9	716	2.55	763	3.2
678	2.13	718	2.197	763–64	3.206
678–79	3.222	721–22	3.54	764	3.3
679	3.182	727–29	2.192	764–65	2.69
679–80	2.71	729	3.115	766	3.219
681	3.28	730	3.61	766–67	3.25
684	2.30	731–32	3.164	767	3.29
684–85	3.62	732	2.179	768	3.87
685–86	2.134	732	3.31	768–69	3.208
687	2.156 n.	732–33	2.184	769–70	3.127
687	2.32	734–35	2.59	770–71	2.185
688–89	2.244	736–37	3.154	772–73	3.223
690	2.85	737–38	2.187	773–74	3.21
690	3.10	738–39	2.83	774–75	3.133
690–91	2.172	739	2.130	775–76	3.69
691	2.62	739	3.20	776	1.17
691–92	3.53	739–40	2.44	777	1.51
692–93	3.193	740	3.179	777–78	3.67
693	3.36	740–41	1.10	778–79	3.73
693–94	2.241	741	2.80	779	3.65
694–95	2.235	741–42	2.95	831	1.28
695–96	3.72	742	1.2	856	3.149 n.
696–97	2.78	742–43	2.77		
697	1.37	743	3.112		
697	1.43	744	1.22		

Sculpture on the portal of the Yakutiye Medrese in Erzurum (1308) representing two confronted lions on either side of a palm tree. The palm represents the Tree of Life and the Fountain of Immortality at the center of Paradise. The lions symbolize the cherubim guarding the way and stand for the duality which must be overcome in order that one enter therein.

Publisher